FREDERICK DOUGLASS

FREDERICK DOUGLASS

Frederick Douglass

By BENJAMIN QUARLES

Introduction by
James M. McPherson

DA CAPO PRESS • NEW YORK

Library of Congress Cataloging-in-Publication Data

Quarles, Benjamin.
    Frederick Douglass / by Benjamin Quarles: introduction by
James M. McPherson.—1st Da Capo Press ed.
        p.   cm.
    Originally published: Washington, D.C.: Associated Publishers,
1948.
    "An unabridged republication of the edition first published in
Washington, D.C. in 1948, with the addition of a 1968 introduction by James M. McPherson that has been slightly revised for
this reprint"—Verso t.p.
    Includes bibliographical references (p.) and index.
    ISBN 0-306-80790-4 (alk. paper)
    1. Douglass, Frederick, 1817?–1895. 2. Abolitionists—United
States—Biography. 3. Afro-American abolitionists—Biography.
4. Antislavery movements—United States. I. Title.
E449.D75Q37 1997
973.8′092—dc21
[B]   97-15046
                                                              CIP

First Da Capo Press edition 1997

This Da Capo Press paperback edition of *Frederick Douglass*
is an unabridged republication of the edition first published
in Washington, D.C. in 1948, with the addition of a 1968
introduction by James M. McPherson that has been
slightly revised for this reprint.

Published by Da Capo Press, Inc.
A Subsidiary of Plenum Publishing Corporation
233 Spring Street, New York, N.Y. 10013

CONTENTS

INTRODUCTION
BY
JAMES M. MCPHERSON

Frederick Douglass was one of the most eminent Americans of the nineteenth century. The story of his life could almost have been written by a black Horatio Alger. Born a slave on Maryland's Eastern Shore, Douglass knew privation as a child. One of his most vivid recollections of slavery was a constantly gnawing stomach: he was often "so pinched for hunger as to dispute with old 'Nep,' the dog, for the crumbs which fell from the kitchen table." His only clothing was a knee-length sackcloth shirt, and in the winter he had to crawl into a feed-bag and sleep in a closet to keep warm. For one year in his youth he was farmed out to a "slave breaker" who was widely known for his skill in beating obstreperous Negroes into cringing submissiveness. From such inauspicious beginnings Douglass rose to the heights of fame and power. He became a leading abolitionist, a militant spokesman for Negro rights, a friend of Abraham Lincoln and other Presidents, the holder of three major government offices, and the recipient of homage and honors from his fellow Americans. Without a day of formal schooling, he developed into a writer of vigorous prose and an orator whose sense of timing, mimicry, wit and pathos was unexcelled even in that age of oratorical giants. Starting as a penniless day laborer and calker, Douglass amassed a fortune of more than $100,000 from lecture fees, book royalties, and shrewd

vii

investments.

One of Douglass' most popular lectures was titled "Self-Made Men," whom he described as "men who, without the ordinary helps of favoring circumstances, have attained knowledge, usefulness, power, position, and fame in the world. They are the men who owe nothing to birth, relationship, friendly surroundings, wealth inherited, or to early and approved means of education." Never inordinately modest, Douglass was in effect describing himself. With an unknown father and a mother whom he rarely saw, he benefited little from the "favoring circumstances" or "friendly surroundings" of a family upbringing. Denied "early and approved means of education," he taught himself to read and write with only limited assistance from sympathetic whites. Owing nothing to birth, relationship, or inherited wealth, he nevertheless achieved knowledge, usefulness, position, and fame. Douglass was a prime example of an "inner-directed" personality; he grew up subject to all the power of a "peculiar institution" that crushed the spark and ambition of most of its victims, yet somehow he found the inner resources to overcome the disadvantages of slavery. Early in life he conceived a desire for freedom which burned and grew inside him until, after the failure of one bold plan for escape, he finally struck out for the North and freedom at the age of twenty-one. Douglass found the North no paradise; the cruelties of race prejudice and Jim Crow placed countless obstacles in his path, but these too he surmounted.

Even self-made men cannot go far without some help, however, and Douglass received aid from members of both races. A white woman taught him the alphabet and awakened the desires and opportunities born of literacy. When he escaped from slavery in Baltimore to freedom in New Bedford, Massachusetts, his path northward was smoothed by the aid of friendly blacks. In New Bedford a white abolitionist shipbuilder offered Douglass a job as a calker, but when the white calkers threatened to strike if Douglass was hired the escaped slave had to accept more menial employment. His first regular job was in a whale-oil refinery owned by a Quaker abolitionist. In 1841 Douglass, who had been reading the *Liberator* for two years, made his first speech before whites at an antislavery rally. Impressed by his simple but eloquent recital of the wrongs of slavery personally experienced, the Massachusetts Anti-Slavery Society launched Douglass' career by signing him on as a paid lecturer. In later years, when asked where he got his education, Douglass replied: "From Massachusetts Abolition University, Mr. Garrison, president."

But Douglass soon chafed under the restraints of the limited curriculum offered by this university. As he grew in mental stature he began to discuss the slavery issue in more depth. Abolitionists who believed that Douglass' chief value to the cause was as a direct, living representative of slavery feared that the growing intellectual content of his speeches would impair his credibility as a former slave. They advised him to stick to the simple facts "and we will take care of the philosophy." Their fears were well founded. Audiences began to doubt that this articulate, well-read young black man who spoke with little trace of a southern accent had ever been a slave. To avoid the danger of recapture, Douglass refused in his lectures to give details of names and places connected with his slave background, and this refusal increased the skepticism of audiences. To put an end to all doubts Douglass wrote a detailed autobiography in 1845 and published it under the title *Narrative of Frederick Douglass.* Soon after the book appeared Douglass sailed for England to escape the very real possibility or recapture if he remained in the United States.

Douglass had become famous on both sides of the Atlantic, and while in England he was feted by the elite of antislavery society. English and American friends raised the money to purchase his freedom. Douglass returned to America in 1847 a legally free man. British abolitionists had also contributed toward a fund to enable Douglass to start his own newspaper. Garrison and other American abolitionists discouraged this project, but after some delay Douglass went ahead and established a weekly paper, *The North Star*. For the next sixteen years he spoke out for freedom and equal rights as an editor as well as orator.

Douglass' disregard of Garrison's advice against founding a newspaper led to a growing coolness between these two friends and coadjutors. When in 1851 Douglass renounced Garrisonian disunionism and announced his conversion to the Liberty party, the split between Garrison and Douglass became complete. There ensued an unedifying exchange of accusations and recriminations that soon degenerated to name-calling. Garrison and Douglass never spoke to each other again. This episode was but one more example of the numerous schisms and internecine controversies that marred the history of the antislavery movement. Time softened Douglass' bitterness over this incident, and in 1881 he wrote of the Garrisonians under whom he served his antislavery apprenticeship: "To these friends, earnest, courageous, inflexible, ready to own me as a man and brother against all the scorn, contempt, and derision of a slavery-polluted atmosphere, I owe my success in life."

Douglass became an active participant in the antislavery politics of the 1850's. He was by turns a leader in the Liberty party, a Free Soiler, and a Republican.

When war came in 1861, he bent every effort to make it an abolition war, and once this was achieved he helped to recruit black soldiers to fight for Union and freedom. When the war was over, Douglass' mission as an abolitionist was not ended. Along with other abolitionists and Radical Republicans he outspokenly advocated civil and political rights for the freedmen, for "I see little advantage in emancipation without this." The Republican party's Reconstruction policy, culminating in the Fourteenth and Fifteenth Amendments, made the Negro theoretically equal before the law. But practice fell short of theory, and Douglass spent much of the rest of his life unsuccessfully urging the government to make good on its commitment to equality. Despite his sometimes sharp criticism of Republican leaders for their failure to protect Negro rights, Douglass remained a staunch Republican the rest of his life, campaigning for every presidential candidate from Lincoln to Benjamin Harrison and using his influence among black voters to keep them faithful to the Grand Old Party. Before his death in 1895 he was rewarded for his services by appointments as Marshal of the District of Columbia in 1877, as Recorder of Deeds for the District in 1881, and as Minister to Haiti in 1889.

Douglass never failed to protest vehemently against segregation, and often resisted attempts by railroad conductors, hotel clerks, and the like to deny him equal facilities. (He once held on to the seats in a railroad coach so tightly that it took several trainmen to eject him from the car, and the seats were torn loose along with Douglass.) When his children were denied admission to the white public schools in Rochester, Douglass led a movement that brought about desegregation of the schools. In 1895, according to a story that may be apocryphal but nevertheless contains the essence of truth, a black student asked Douglass, then in the twilight of his career, what advice he had for a young man just starting out. Douglass replied without hesitation: "Agitate! Agitate! Agitate!"

Frederick Douglass' career is relevant to our own age. Douglass' insistence on "Freedom Now" found its parallel in the civil rights movement of the 1960's. More than a century ago Douglass asserted that agitation of the race problem would go on "until the public schools shall cease to be caste schools," "until the colored man's pathway to the ballot-box . . . shall be as smooth and as safe as the same is for the white citizen," "until the courts of the country shall grant the colored man a fair trial and a just verdict," "until color shall cease to be a bar to equal participation in the offices and honors of the country," "until the trades-unions, and the workshops of the country shall cease to proscribe the colored man," "until the American people shall make character, and not color, the criterion of respectability."

Douglass' life offers also a key to understanding the disillusionment with non-violence that occurred in the civil rights movement after 1965. In his autobiography Douglass described the year he spent as a slave under Edward Covey, the famed "Negro breaker," as the low point of his life. Covey whipped him frequently in an effort to break Douglass' spirit, until one day the seventeen-year-old slave decided he had had enough. He turned on Covey and fought with him desperately for two hours, drawing blood from his oppressor and finally vanquishing him. After this encounter Covey was afraid of Douglass and never whipped him again. The whole experience was one of exhilaration and enlightenment for Douglass, "the turning-point in my life as a slave. It rekindled in my breast the smouldering embers of liberty . . .

and received a sense of my own manhood." Douglass had "reached the point at which I was *not afraid to die. This spirit made me a freeman in fact*, though I still remained a slave in *form.*" He concluded that "the doctrine that submission to violence is the best cure for violence did not hold good as between slaves and overseers. He was whipped oftener who was whipped easiest." This psychological insight helps to explain the peculiar sense of exhilaration and release exhibited by urban black rioters from the 1960's to the 1990's. For them as for Douglass, retaliatory violence against the white man had a cleansing and lifting effect on the spirit, and seemed to bring about a psychological, if not physical, emancipation from the intolerable tensions of submission.

In addition to three autobiographies (the second and third were revisions and expansions of the first, with different titles) there have been nearly a dozen biographies of Douglass. Although several of those that have been published since the initial appearance of Quarles' book in 1948 have offered important insights or provocative interpretations, none has surpassed Quarles' study in fairness and readability.

Since the autobiographies are the best account of Douglass' life as a slave, Quarles has wisely refrained from going over the same ground and has introduced his story of Douglass' adult career with an interpretive chapter on the formative influences of the years in slavery. Avoiding the temptation to portray Douglass as an unsullied hero, Quarles has brought to his task the insight and balance of a trained historian and the skill to portray his subject as a human being with faults as well as virtues. Especially good are the sections on Douglass' personal and family life and on his relations with the two white women (Julia Griffiths and Helen Pitts, who became his second wife) who played important roles in his life. Quarles has also done a fine job of placing Douglass' career in the context of the important events of which he was a part: the antislavery movement, the Civil War, Reconstruction, and the history of the Republican party during its first forty years. Only in its discussion of the Radical Republicans has this book been superseded by research done since 1948; in other respects the research and interpretations have stood up remarkably well for half a century. Quarles' writing style flows smoothly and is imbued with a quiet sense of humor and irony. The reader of this biography will be rewarded with a well-rounded understanding of Frederick Douglass and of the age in which he lived.

FOREWORD

No study of the Garrison school of reformers, Liberty party abolitionism, the technique of anti-slavery agitation or the rôle of the Negro in the Civil War and Reconstruction is complete without constant reference to the career of Frederick Douglass. The most prominent American Negro of the nineteenth century, he was identified with most of the reformist movements of his day.

In accordance with the best American tradition, his life history reads like a romance. His youth and early manhood were spent in slavery. His flight from bondage brought him to New Bedford, Massachusetts, where for three years he lived a hand-to-mouth existence. After the accidental discovery of a talent for platform speaking in 1841, he joined the Garrison abolitionists and quickly became the prize exhibit of the Massachusetts Anti-Slavery Society.

His career in the crowded years that followed touched on the major political and economic controversies then current. In 1847 he became editor of an anti-slavery weekly which he published for sixteen years — a longevity unusual in abolitionist journalism. In 1848 he took a prominent part in the proceedings of the Seneca Falls Convention in New York which formally inaugurated the woman's rights movement in the United States. His other varied activities as a reformer included participation in the temperance agitation, the underground railroad and the colored convention movement.

In the early 'fifties, after moving to western New York, he abandoned sole dependence on moral suasion as a means of combatting slavery, and announced himself a member of the voting school of abolitionists. For a decade he advocated the overthrow of slavery by political action. A confidant of John Brown, he fled the United States within three days after the abortive raid at Harpers Ferry. His anti-slavery addresses in the British Isles during his two trips abroad were a factor in the pronounced anti-Confederate attitude of the English masses during the Civil War. His vigorous support of that war, which he regarded solely as a struggle to free the slaves, was surpassed only by his zeal for a Reconstruction policy which would guarantee political equality to the Negro. After 1876 the Republican party, to which he helped deliver the Negro vote quadrennially, rewarded his loyalty with appointment to lucrative positions. Until his death in 1895, at the age of seventy-eight, the Negro people regarded him as their chief spokesman.

It is not easy to arrive at a composite, balanced judgment of Douglass. His detractors were numerous in both races. His denunciations of many of the practices of existing institutions, secular and religious, alienated middle-of-the-roaders. Well-tailored men "of property and standing," whose consciences had been lulled into tranquillity, instinctively distrusting the perfervid oratory of the agitator, regarded him as a demagogue in black. People of conservative temperament viewed as presumptuous, if not impudent, his manner of disturbing the *status quo* by an insistence on what he called his "civil rights."

In contrast is the attitude of many contemporaries, and particularly of the majority of Negroes of a later generation to whom Douglass has become a legend. To Northerners like Charles Sumner he was a shining example of the perfectibility of the Negro. To his admirers, white and black, he stood a well-rounded character, high-principled, rich in ability — a giant of unparalleled resourcefulness whose early hardships and subsequent setbacks resulted neither in the loss of the courageous spirit nor the acquisition of a persecution complex.

Douglass' career is silhouetted against an historical background that is undergoing redefinition. While making no claim to being revisionist, the present study strives to portray Douglass in the light of recent historical scholarship and the newer interpretations of the abolition movement and the Reconstruction period. Douglass was broad rather than deep. He participated in so many activities that a balanced treatment of his public life necessitates a crowded canvas. Without sacrificing any vital detail in Douglass' life, this biography attempts, nevertheless, to cover his career against a backdrop of incident sufficient for purposes of readability.

The opening chapter differs from the others; it is interpretive primarily. There is a reason. Douglass is the exclusive authority for the story of the early years of his life. Therefore, I have attempted to make the first chapter an essay in interpretation instead of a re-hash of Douglass' autobiographies. Although analytical and interpretive, rather than descriptive, the opening chapter presents all of the factual material necessary to an understanding of Douglass' life in slavery.

The writer is happy to express his gratitude to those who have been of assistance in one way or another. Library employees have been uniformly helpful; they are pleasant people — occupationally conditioned, no doubt. In company with hundreds of others I am indebted to the trustees of the Frederick Douglass Memorial and Historical Association who have preserved Douglass' home as a historic shrine. An especial acknowledgment is due to Mrs. William H. Davis, former caretaker of the home, who never tired of placing at the writer's disposal the Douglass papers and her own knowledge of the man. Mrs. Dorothy Porter, in charge of the Moorland Foundation collection at Howard University, encouraged the widest use of that

excellent source. The late Mr. Arthur Schomburg, curator
of the collection that goes by his name, gave several hours
of his time in discussion of bibliographical data. Mrs.
Joseph H. Douglass, widow of a grandson, and Mr.
Arthur Spingarn made available the Douglass letters they
possess. At Syracuse University Dr. W. Freeman Galpin
gave the writer free access to the valuable Gerrit Smith
papers, and also showed him the diary of Samuel J. May.
Travel to the points where these documents are kept and
the stipended leisure necessary to their examination were
made possible by grants from the Julius Rosenwald Fund
and the Social Science Research Council. To these
foundations I express sincere thanks.

My indebtedness to a great teacher, Dr. William B.
Hesseltine of the University of Wisconsin, merits a word
of deepest appreciation. This study of Douglass was
originally written as a doctoral dissertation under Dr.
Hesseltine's supervision. At every point in the writing of
the dissertation he gave stimulating criticism. Other
acknowledgments the writer gladly makes are due
Messrs. George W. Morton and Marcus B. Christian,
colleagues at Dillard University, who read the manuscript, blue-pencilling many of the writer's more glaring
literary lapses.

LIST OF ILLUSTRATIONS

CHAPTER I

Douglass' Mind in the Making

> The reader must not expect me to say much of my family. Genealogical trees do not flourish among slaves.
>
> DOUGLASS

From some month in the year 1817 — the circumstances of his birth are not known — until his escape twenty years later, Frederick Douglass was a part of the institution that he was to denounce for a quarter of a century. That he had been held in bondage became the cardinal fact in his life. His slave background was his springboard into public notice; it gave an authenticity to his invective, it furnished his ram's horn with a fathomless arsenal to sound against the Southern "lords of the lash," and, finally, as his great abilities unfolded, it enabled him to stand forth in dramatic condemnation of an institution that would enthrall a man of his capacity.

Douglass' fame rests largely upon his impassioned outbursts of rhetoric by which he gave vent to an uncompromising hostility to the slave system. The sources of this militant abolitionism are varied. After he had grown to manhood, his ten-year association with the Garrison school of reformers and his labors as a professional agitator obviously entered into the fabric of his thinking. What portion of his hatred of slavery may be traced to the experiences of his days in bondage is difficult to determine.

The man himself is the exclusive authority on the early period of his life.[1] The story, shorn of certain dramatic

---

[1] Douglass' autobiographies are: *Narrative of the Life of Frederick Douglass* (Boston, 1845); *My Bondage and My Freedom* (New York,

1

incidents, is soon told. Of typically obscure parentage, Douglass was born in Talbot County on the eastern shore of Maryland. His knowledge of his mother was "very scanty."[2] Her duties as a slave required her presence at a point twelve miles distant from her young son. Douglass saw her only a few times before she died when he was eight or nine. His father remains anonymous.[3]

The absence of parental care was filled in part by a shrewd, warm-hearted grandmother[4] around whose slave cabin the child's world centered. During these years Douglass led the life of a normal youngster — fishing, roaming the fields, and playing with his numerous cousins. When he was seven he was taken some twelve miles from his birthplace to the residence of his master, Captain Aaron Anthony, on the banks of the river Wye.[5] Captain Anthony, a slave-owner in his own right, was also general overseer for Colonel Edward Lloyd, "the greatest and most successful wheat grower and cattle raiser in Maryland," and the fifth Edward of a historic Maryland family, the Lloyds of Wye.[6]

On the Lloyd plantation Douglass ran errands and did other simple chores. Here he witnessed the harsher aspects of slavery, growing familiar with cold and hunger —

1855); *Life and Times of Frederick Douglass* (Hartford, 1884). There are three book-length studies: Charles W. Chesnutt, *Frederick Douglass* (Boston, 1899); Frederic May Holland, *Frederick Douglass* (New York, 1891); Booker T. Washington, *Frederick Douglass* (Philadelphia, 1906).

[2] *Bondage and Freedom*, 52.

[3] That Douglass' father was a white man is inferential from such inconclusive evidence as a contrast of the "deep black" complexion of the mother with the brown hue of her son.

[4] "She was to me a mother and a father." *Anti-Slavery Bugle* (Salem, O.), Sept. 29, 1848.

[5] For a sketch map of the rivers of Maryland's eastern shore see Hulbert Footner, *Rivers of the Eastern Shore* (New York, 1944), 2, 3.

[6] See the chapter, "The Lloyds of Wye," in Footner, *op. cit.*, 269–293.

privations unsoftened by the attitude of "Aunt Katy," an unsympathetic cook, into whose charge he had been placed.

A turning point occurred during the summer of 1825 when the eight-year-old slave was overjoyed at the decision to send him to Baltimore [7] to a distant relative of Captain Anthony. Here for seven years he served Hugh Auld, as a houseboy minding Auld's son, and then as an unskilled laborer in his ship-yard. This Baltimore period was doubly idyllic compared to the years that immediately followed. The change of ownership as a consequence of the death of Captain Anthony placed Douglass in the possession of Thomas Auld, Anthony's son-in-law, who resided at St. Michaels, some forty miles from Baltimore.

Inevitably Douglass proved refractory in the new environment. The spirit of insubordination was stimulated by the notions of freedom which had entered his head, and by the more rigorous regimen of the plantation system following the freer city life. Early in 1834 Douglass was hired out to Edward Covey, a small farmer and professional slave-breaker who, as Douglass' master expected, would provide the proper conditioning. For six months Douglass was flogged every week. One day, steeled by desperation, the goaded youth soundly thrashed Covey, who thereupon abandoned the whip for the four remaining months of hire.

During the two years that followed this experience Douglass' master hired him out to a nearby plantation owner whose technique of handling slaves contrasted sharply with Covey's. But Douglass had now reached the stage of aspiration that only freedom could satisfy. A

---

[7] After 1820 it was common in Maryland to send slaves to towns. Slave labor in agriculture had been paying such diminishing returns that by 1836 it ceased to be generally profitable in the state. E. A. Andrews, *Slavery and the Slave Trade in the United States* (Boston, 1836), 42.

kind master, an abundance of food, a moderate work assignment, the thrill of conducting an undercover Sunday school — these things were not enough. Furthermore, from Talbot County the runaway journey would be a short one.

To reach free soil Douglass conceived a plan to paddle down the Chesapeake to its head and then strike northward on foot. However, one of the half dozen conspirators prematurely disclosed the plan. As originator of the scheme Douglass was put in chains. But his daring brought unexpected results; for his attempted escape he was not sold to the lower South as was customary. His master, not bad at heart, and troubled about slavery, hoped to induce a more tractable spirit in Douglass by sending him back to Baltimore with a promise of freedom when he reached twenty-five.

For the next two years the young slave worked in the ship-yards, first as an apprentice, then as an expert calker. At first, every penny of his earnings belonged to his master, but finally he persuaded Auld to permit him to bargain for his own employment in return for a weekly payment of three dollars.[8]

A quarrel with Auld in the summer of 1838 hastened Douglass' determination to go north. He chose a familiar stratagem to effect his departure. From a sea-faring friend he borrowed (to be returned by mail) a sailor's "protection," a paper enumerating the physical characteristics of its rightful owner who ostensibly was a free American sailor. To avoid scrutiny Douglass waited until the train, running from Baltimore to Philadelphia, was in motion. To carry off the impersonation he relied on the nautical knowledge he had acquired at the ship-yards.

---

[8] "Not a few slaves in Maryland, particularly in the cities, were allowed by their masters to live and act as freemen, and also to buy their own freedom by their extra earnings." Jeffrey R. Brackett, *The Negro in Maryland* (Baltimore, 1889), 107.

The train conductor, deferring to a man in naval service, was satisfied with the "protection" in the absence of the "free papers" which Maryland law required that all free Negroes carry and produce on demand.[9] Fortunately too the conductor did not compare Douglass' features with those described by the "protection."[10] On September 4 Douglass rode into New York City with his heart beating high.

* * *

Douglass defined slavery as "perpetual unpaid toil; no marriage, no husband, no wife, no parent, no child; ignorance, brutality, licentiousness; whips, scourges, chains, auctions, jails and separations; an embodiment of all the woes the imagination can conceive."[11] Obviously, however, the great hatred he came to bear against the slave system was not traceable in full to Douglass' personal experiences. Many bondmen would have been contented with his lot. Slavery in Maryland was more "enlightened" than in the lower South; town slaves were better fed and less likely to feel the whip than their plantation brothers. Nor, after his young boyhood, did Douglass experience the most heart-rending of slave sufferings — the separation from a beloved family member. He never saw his half-brother or his three half-sisters until he was seven. His acquaintance with them extended over less than half a year before he was sent away. The brief, sporadic visits of his mother under cover of night, and his ignorance of his paternity left in Douglass an absence of sentimental ties whose severance might have resulted in a long-remembered emotional upset.

---

[9] A free Negro who lent his "free papers" to a slave was subject to be fined, or sold into service if unable to pay the fine. *Ibid.*, 77.

[10] Douglass, "My Escape from Slavery," *The Century Magazine*, I, 124–131 (Nov. 1881).

[11] *Bugle*, Aug. 11, 1849.

Douglass' attitude toward his slave status was perhaps grounded less in external circumstance than in psychological make-up. Here was a youth, sensitive, intelligent and ambitious. The slave whippings and deprivations, although neither uncommon nor unusual to a hereditary bondman, left a lasting impression on his plastic mind. The memory of a slave being flogged would make his nights sleepless. He was profoundly moved by the piteous cries and heavy footsteps of the chained gangs in Baltimore, on their way from the slave pen to the general depot. Few human beings, he concluded early in life, could be trusted to exercise absolute power over their fellows with moderation.

He meditated on the coarseness and meagreness of the slave diet as contrasted with the groaning table at the "big house." He meditated on the raiment of his master and his mistress as contrasted with the semi-nudity of the slave whose yearly wardrobe of two shirts and two pairs of trousers was scarcely equal to the vagaries of the thermometer. With little of the traditional light-heartedness ascribed to his race, he held back from the singing and dancing and year-end celebrations. Such festivities he regarded as escapist. To him the slave sang because he was relieved by song "as an aching heart is relieved by tears." [12] Others might spend themselves in emotional outbursts; he would earn his bitter bread in moody silence. Others might don cap and bells to cloak themselves against spiritual bruise; he would see it through unsupported by any avoidance-of-pain mechanism.

Combined with his sensitiveness was an alert intelligence. An aptitude for reflection led him to conduct imaginary conversations. No satisfactory answers were forthcoming to the questions he was always asking himself: "Why am I a slave? Why are some people slaves,

---

[12] *Narrative*, 15.

and others masters? Was there ever a time when this was not so? How did the relation commence?" [13] In response to his importunities, his religiously-minded Baltimore mistress taught him to read in order that he might come to know the Bible.[14] When his master arrested this instruction, on the ground that "learning" would spoil a slave, the enterprising youth learned how to spell by various ingenious methods.[15] The first pennies he could call his own went for a popular book of declamation, the *Columbian Orator.*[16]

Douglass was ambitious. He had no capacity for finding happiness in a humble sphere under adverse circumstances. Slavery had always been an enemy to his self-expression. It thwarted him at every turn. If he attempted to gain knowledge, slavery grew suspicious; if he attempted to teach his fellows, slavery cracked the whip; if he attempted to run away, slavery dragged him back to his chains.

The Baltimore environment, with its weak master-slave relationship, gave a stimulus to Douglass' ambition for complete freedom. As a boy on the streets he measured his mind with the minds of his white playmates; as a young man he learned the lessons of self-control and self-discipline. Free and equal in his own mind, he, nevertheless, had little control over his wages and less over his locomotion. About him lived a large free Negro population,[17] possessing, in 1835, ten churches and more than

---

[13] *Bondage and Freedom*, 89.

[14] "The education of free negroes and slaves was not forbidden by law in Maryland, but the black man was indebted for what he got to the interest of individuals." Brackett, *op. cit.*, 196.

[15] For these methods see *Narrative*, 38, 43.

[16] The copy purchased by Douglass may still be seen at the Douglass home at Anacostia Heights, Washington, D. C.

[17] For tables showing the increase of the free colored population in contrast with the steady decline in the number of slaves in Maryland from 1790 to 1840 see John L. Carey, *Slavery in Maryland* (Baltimore, 1845), appendix.

thirty-five benevolent societies.[18] From membership in the latter Douglass, as a slave, found himself excluded. The East Baltimore Improvement Society alone — as a special concession — permitted him to become a member. Through this society he met Anna Murray, and fuel was added to his burning desire to change his status. Escape and freedom would enable him to marry as a man![19]

The very privileges he had enjoyed made him freedom-conscious. Give a man a bad master, he wrote, and he aspired to a good master; give him a good master and he aspired to be his own master.[20] By 1838 Douglass was psychologically ready to become his own master. His subsequent fulminations against slavery were not, therefore, based exclusively on the experiences he underwent, nor, as he pointed out, did he use the public platform to dramatize his personal grievance.[21] Rather, he preferred to base his opposition to slavery on the sufferings and hardships of three million slaves whose rights were violated. Yet his own memories must inevitably have entered in. Who, tracing backward the savor of his personality, can say with certainty:

> This portion of the river of my mind
> Came from yon fountain?

*   *   *

The exultant joy that came over Douglass upon his arrival in New York soon gave way to loneliness and fear.

---

[18] John Fortie, William Levington and Nathaniel Peak, "A Reply to a note from 'White Citizen,'" *Niles' Register*, XLIX, 72 (Oct. 3, 1835).

[19] A Maryland slave might marry with his master's consent but the master might at any time dissolve the marriage. James M. Wright, *The Free Negro in Maryland, 1634–1860* (New York, 1921), 243.

[20] *Bondage and Freedom*, 262.

[21] *Letter to Douglass from H. C. Wright with His Reply* (pamphlet, Manchester, Dec. 22, 1846), 3.

He knew no one in the city and his money was low. The shadows of the slave-catchers still fell dark upon the free states. In desperation, Douglass confided in a passing sailor who put him in touch with David Ruggles, secretary of the New York Vigilance Committee.[22] Ruggles spent much of his time in assisting runaways and in preventing the seizure of free Negroes under the pretext of their being slaves. At the time Douglass sought his aid, Ruggles had just published the first issue of an anti-slavery quarterly, *The Mirror of Liberty*, the first magazine edited by a Negro.[23]

While sheltered in Ruggles' editorial rooms, Douglass was joined by Anna to whom he had disclosed his refuge. Twelve days after Douglass' escape the couple were married by Reverend James W. C. Pennington, a self-educated former blacksmith who, some ten years previously, had also fled from a Maryland master.[24] A day or two after the ceremony, the Douglasses were on their way to New Bedford, Massachusetts, with a five-dollar bill which Ruggles had pressed upon the bridegroom.

Ruggles' kindnesses were equalled by those of the family to whom he sent the newlyweds. Mr. and Mrs. Nathan Johnson provided board and lodging and made the welfare of their guests a matter of personal concern. Under Johnson's roof and with his encouragement Douglass began his career as a freeman. His name was of

---

[22] For the origin and object of this group see *The First Annual Report of the New York Committee of Vigilance for the Year 1837* (New York, 1837), preface. Ruggles subsequently stated that during his five year affiliation with the committee he aided some 600 slaves in making good their escapes. *The North Star* (Rochester, N. Y.), Apr. 14, 1848.

[23] For an account of Ruggles' anti-slavery activities see Dorothy B. Porter, "David Ruggles, an Apostle of Human Rights," *The Journal of Negro History*, XXVIII, 23–50 (Jan. 1943).

[24] There is an autobiographical treatment of Pennington's early life, *The Fugitive Blacksmith* (London, 1849).

Johnson's choosing. His mother had named him Frederick Augustus Washington Bailey. On reaching New York he had dropped the two middle names and had changed the surname to Johnson. The multiplicity of New Bedford Negroes also with that name, led his benefactor, who had been reading *The Lady of the Lake*, to give Douglass the name by which he is known to history.

His first job was loading oil on a sloop bound for New York. Unable to get work as a calker — he was discovering that color prejudice was not sectional — he turned his hand to whatever unskilled or menial work came his way: blowing bellows, sweeping chimneys, sawing wood, driving a coach or waiting on table. His earnings averaged one dollar a day.[25]

His early struggles were eased by the co-operative spirit of his wife. Anna Murray was born free, date unknown, in a Maryland county, Caroline, adjoining her husband's birthplace.[26] While in her late 'teens she became housekeeper for a well-to-do family in Baltimore. Here she met Douglass, became engaged to him and aided him financially in escaping. She followed him to New York, bringing a few household furnishings. In New Bedford she created a homelike atmosphere in the two rooms occupied by the family. Thrifty and industrious, to add to their income she sought employment as a domestic whenever time could be spared from attending her own children, Rosetta, who was born in June 1839, and Lewis, who came sixteen months later.

These early days as a freeman were days of hardship for Douglass. But they were also days of development.

---

[25] *Address at the Annual Meeting of the American Missionary Association, in Lowell, Mass., 1894* (New York, undated pamphlet), 2.

[26] Her daughter is the only source for the few fragments of information on Mrs. Douglass' early life. Rosetta Douglass Sprague, *Anna Murray Douglass: My Mother as I Recall Her* (pamphlet, Wash., D. C., 1900).

He found it stimulating to bargain for his labor, to earn money that he could call his own, and to assume the responsibilities of a husband and father. The colored people in New Bedford had a higher standard of living and a higher level of education than in Baltimore. He was impressed by the platform ease and parliamentary ability exhibited at their gatherings.[27] As in Baltimore where he had been a class leader and choir singer in the Sharp Street Methodist Church,[28] his own powers of self-expression sought scope along religious lines. When he found that he could attend white Methodist churches only on humiliating conditions he joined a small sect of his own race, the Zion Methodists, and soon became a leading member.[29]

The church did not occupy his attention exclusively; he became aware of the abolitionist movement. Despite his poverty, within six months after reaching New Bedford he became a subscriber to Garrison's paper. The editor's invective found in Douglass a hearty response and the abolitionist cause gained a disciple. Douglass mastered

---

[27] One of these organizations was the Young Men's Wilberforce Debating Society. *The Liberator* (Boston), Aug. 26, 1839. New Bedford Negroes held a "social meeting" every two weeks to discuss anti-slavery principles and events. *The Anti-Slavery Standard* (New York) Aug. 26, 1841.

[28] Douglass was a member of this church from 1836 to 1838. Richard T. Greener, "Reminiscences of Frederick Douglass," *The Champion Magazine*, I, 291 (Chicago, Feb. 1917). According to his own statement Douglass joined the Centennial African Methodist Church in 1831. (Baltimore *Sun*, Sept. 7, 1891.) He was then a boy of thirteen or fourteen.

[29] The Reverend Thomas James of Rochester, New York, related the story that while preaching in New Bedford in 1841 he became impressed by Douglass and licensed him to preach. *Wonderful Eventful Life of Thomas James, By Himself* (Rochester, 1887), 6. However, Douglass' name is not included on the official list of all ministers and preachers attached to the several conferences of the African Methodist Episcopal Church in 1842. *African Methodist Episcopal Church Magazine*, I, 89 (Phila., Dec. 1842).

its principles and its philosophy through the columns of the *Liberator*. He began to attend the abolition meetings held by colored people.[30]

At one of these gatherings, held at the Christian Church on March 12, 1839, he was among those who sustained resolutions condemning slavery and African colonization and commending Garrison "as deserving of our support and confidence."[31] Gradually he rose to leadership among his fellows. On June 30, 1841, he was chairman at a meeting censuring the Maryland Colonization Society for threatening to remove colored people from that state by coercive means. The New Bedford group entreated the Maryland Negroes to resist intimidation. The meeting also passed a resolution "discountenancing" an assault on David Ruggles who had been roughly handled for resisting segregation while on a steamboat plying between New Bedford and Nantucket.[32]

Six weeks later, on August 9, Douglass attended the annual meeting of the Bristol Anti-Slavery Society, held in New Bedford. William Lloyd Garrison was there. Douglass entered into the discussion and made a favorable impression on the great abolitionist.[33] Douglass in turn was impressed. He was awed by the grave, sonorous voice and by the iron strength of Garrison's face. There

---

[30] In 1836 New Bedford Negroes donated $61 to the American Anti-Slavery Society. H. B. Stanton to L. Tappan, Aug. 15, 1836. Gilbert Barnes and Dwight L. Dumond, eds., *Weld-Grimke Letters* (2 vols., New York, 1934), I, 330. For references to abolitionist meetings of New Bedford Negroes see *Liberator*, May 29, Aug. 26, Oct. 18, Nov. 1, 1839 and June 5, 1840. Perhaps additional meetings were held, but not reported in the *Liberator* whose coverage of abolitionist conventions, though broad, was unequal to the volume of notices sent in by local secretaries, particularly when heated controversial points at issue required several columns of airing.

[31] *Liberator*, March 29, 1839. This is undoubtedly the first printed reference to Douglass.

[32] *Ibid.*, July 9, 1841.   [33] *Ibid.*, Aug. 20, 1841.

stood the spearhead of the movement, the man who gave no quarter, the ultra-abolitionist in person. There stood the figure who had so identified himself with the cause of the slave that many people thought that he was a Negro. In abolitionist circles it was common knowledge that he had been associated with Benjamin Lundy, the abolitionist pioneer; that he had spent seven days in a Baltimore jail for accusing a shipowner of transporting slaves; that he had set up the type for the *Liberator* with his own hands; that in 1832 he had founded the New England Anti-Slavery Society and that a year later at the formation of the American Anti-Slavery Society he had drafted the unequivocal Declaration of Sentiments; that for his abolitionist convictions he had been dragged half naked through the Boston streets with a rope around his body, and that he was so detested in the South that the Georgia legislature had offered a reward of $5,000 to whosoever should arrest him, bring him to trial and win a conviction.

The first sight of Garrison was a remembered experience to Douglass. His impressions of the militant leader were sharpened by the events of the two succeeding days. On the day after the New Bedford meeting, Douglass, taking his first holiday since he became free, was overjoyed in joining Garrison and forty of his followers, convention-bound for Nantucket. The Garrisonians enlivened the sixty-mile sail by holding an impromptu meeting on deck to protest against segregation on the steamboat.[34]

The next day at the morning session at Athenaeum Hall, Douglass was unexpectedly called upon to speak. William Coffin, a New Bedford abolitionist, presented him to the group, with local pride. Uncomfortable and ill at ease, Douglass spoke haltingly, yet with deep feeling, of his recollections of slavery. Garrison followed with a stirring address, using Douglass' remarks as a text.[35]

---

[34] *Anti-Slavery Standard*, Aug. 26, 1841. [35] *Ibid.*

Before the meeting adjourned, John A. Collins, general agent of the Massachusetts Anti-Slavery Society, urged Douglass to become a lecturer.[36] Douglass was hesitant — it was one of the few times he under-rated himself — but finally he was induced to agree to work for the Society for three months. When, at an abolitionist meeting at Millbury a week later, he took part in the discussions along with Garrison and Wendell Phillips,[37] it was the launching of a career.

Asked later in life if, prior to joining the abolitionists, he had been aware of his latent oratorical powers, Douglass entered a complete denial.[38] Yet the urge to speak had been upon him from his first purchase of a book on elocution. Fascinated by those with the gift of tongue, he had sought out debating societies and had gained experience in self-expression among church groups. Had the abolitionist movement not offered an opportunity — had quiet times prevailed — Douglass' abilities would doubtless have led him into the pulpit. His logical mind, his air of sternness and rectitude, his imposing physique and the rolling thunder of his voice had fitted him for the public platform.

---

[36] Garrison's sons assert that it was their father who first advised the employment of Douglass. W. P. Garrison and F. Garrison, *Life and Times of William Lloyd Garrison* (4 vols., New York, 1885–89), III, 292. However, Edmund Quincy believed that it was he who first "suggested to him becoming an anti-slavery lecturer." Quincy to R. D. Webb, Dec. 13, 1845. *Anti-Slavery Letters to William Lloyd Garrison and Others* (Boston Public Library), XV. Forty years after the event, another reformer remembered sharing the distinction of bringing Douglass into the society. "Mr. Garrison and myself thought it would be a good thing if a man who had endured some of the penalties of slavery could go out and tell his story. And so he was engaged." James N. Buffum, *Commemoration of the Fiftieth Anniversary of the American Anti-Slavery Society* (Phila., 1884), 42.

[37] *Liberator*, Aug. 27, 1841.

[38] S. H. Taft, in *In Memoriam: Frederick Douglass* (Phila., 1897), 247.

CHAPTER II

Prize Exhibit

> Those who profess to favor freedom and yet depreciate agitation are those who want crops without plowing up the ground — they want rain without thunder and lightning.
>
> DOUGLASS

"I have often been asked," said Douglass as he approached seventy winters, "where I got my education. I have answered, from Massachusetts Abolition University: Mr. Garrison, president."[1] This was an obvious truth. For the youthful Douglass was naturally predisposed to adopt the beliefs and doctrines of the kind-hearted men and women who befriended him. These newly found associates of Douglass' were a motley group of earnest reformers whose work consisted less in guiding public opinion than in exciting it. As one of their most gifted writers phrased it, "a good test for deciding the soundness of any moral stand which a man has taken is the amount of opposition it excites."[2]

Among the reformers with whom Douglass now found himself was the inevitable lunatic fringe; neurotics who sought in fancied Utopias an escape from the present, crackpots who were possessed of a congenital facility for being displeased, and exhibitionists who attached themselves to unpopular causes to secure attention and court a vicarious martyrdom.[3] However, the minds of the leaders of the

---

[1] Holland, *Frederick Douglass*, 363.

[2] James Russell Lowell, Pennsylvania *Freeman*, Jan. 16, 1845.

[3] For the behavior of some of the Garrisonians see Thomas Wentworth Higginson's chapter on "Eccentricities of Reformers," in his

15

abolitionists were lucid and penetrating, if somewhat narrow. Although charged with ignoring the compulsions of economic law and the complexity of social relationships, such men as Garrison, Phillips and Samuel J. May were seldom attacked on the fundamental soundness of their propositions or on the closely-knit and lengthy expositions that inevitably accompanied a presentation of their disturbing views.

Almost without exception, the Massachusetts reformers were abolitionists. Highly individualistic as they were, they could always unite on their hatred of slaveholding which they had come to regard as the most heinous offense in the catalogue of crime. Whenever possible they avoided the purchase and consumption of commodities produced by slave labor.[4] To them slavery was simply a question of ethics. Hence, with little regard for the sociological implications of freeing the bondmen, and with complete indifference to the economics of slavery, they announced immediate and uncompensated emancipation as their program.

On one other matter were the Massachusetts reformers agreed. Though they might not subscribe to every one of Garrison's enthusiasms, by 1840 they had come to look upon him as their leader. After that year he was the perennial president of the American Anti-Slavery Society. Despite the powerful opposition of the New York aboli-

---

Contemporaries (Boston, 1899); and Emerson's well-known essay, "The New England Reformers."

[4] Garrison's advocacy of the boycott of slave produce came as a result of his early association with Lundy. Ruth Ketring Nuermberger, *The Free Produce Movement* (Durham, N. C., 1942), 21. The boycotting of slave labor goods found its greatest strength among the Quakers. None of the Garrisonians were as zealous in this respect as Lucretia Mott who carried a little bag of free sugar in order that she might sweeten her tea undisturbed by the thought that she was swelling the coffers of the slaveowners. William Wells Brown, *The Rising Son* (Boston, 1874), 406.

tionists — Gerrit Smith, William Goodell and Arthur and Lewis Tappan — Garrison had seized control of the Society. The cause of the breach had centered around the employment of women in the anti-slavery movement, and the efficacy and wisdom of the doctrines of non-resistance and moral suasion.[5] Vexed with Garrison for his insistence on presenting the troublesome "Woman Question" and distrusting some of his other enthusiasms, the New York school withdrew from the parent society in 1840 and formed a rival group, the American and Foreign Anti-Slavery Society, styled "the new organization" by abolitionists.

Abolitionism did not exhaust Garrison's reformist zeal; his sheet proclaimed that his country was the world; his countrymen, mankind.[6] The church was one of the institutions, in the opinion of the Garrisonians, standing in the need of correction. Because many prominent clergymen stood aloof from the humanitarian causes of the day, the Massachusetts reformers persisted in regarding the church as little better than a sectarian corporation created by conservative interests to become an apologist for reaction. The true Garrisonian, therefore, had separated himself from an unregenerate church. His leader's position was even more extreme. Garrison repudiated the divine inspiration of the Scriptures. It was harmful, he protested, to refer to the Bible as the

---

[5] The columns of the *Liberator* for 1840 are filled with discussions of the breach. See also "The True History of the Late Division in the American Anti-Slavery Society," *Second Ann. Rep. of the Mass. Abolition Soc.*, part II; and Bayard Tuckerman, *William Jay* (New York, 1893), 107 and *passim*.

[6] Indeed the charge was made against Garrison that he deliberately used the anti-slavery platform as a sounding board for his other enthusiasms which were even more unpopular and which standing alone could not have gotten a hearing. See "Garrison's Infidelity Exposed in Two Letters from the Rev. John Guthrie," *Sec. Ann. Rep. of Mass. A. S. S.*, 15–30.

Holy Book inasmuch as it was written nobody knew when by nobody knew whom, that it settled nothing in theology or ethics and affirmed conflicting doctrines. An anti-Sabbatarian, he shocked a deeply religious America by regarding as superstition the setting aside of the first day of the week for religious worship. He attributed Sunday observance to the selfishly-motivated machinations of the "priestcraft." [7]

The Garrisonians comprised the membership of the New England Non-Resistance Society, formed in 1838.[8] This organization held that the way to overcome evil was to resist it with good. The taking of life was contrary to God's laws. Because the state used force and its officers were sworn to use coercive measures if necessary, the non-resisters denounced human government. This hostile attitude of the Garrisonians toward participation in politics was strengthened by their interpretation of the Constitution which they regarded as a pro-slavery document. Inasmuch as an oath to support the Constitution was a requirement for holding office (and by implication, for voting), the true Garrisonian eschewed the ballot and became in politics, as in religion, a "come-outer," holding that all sects and parties were corrupted by slavery. Garrison clearly distinguished between the principles motivating abolitionist societies and the policies guiding political parties. The objective of abolitionist societies was "the promulgation of righteous principles by righteous means; while theirs [political parties] is the advancement of men by any means." [9] The woman's rights question

---

[7] For a lucid explanation of Garrison's many points of view, by an associate, see Oliver Johnson, *William Lloyd Garrison and His Times* (Boston, 1855).

[8] For a detailed account of this organization see W. Freeman Galpin, *Pioneers for Peace* (Rochester, 1933), 124–151.

[9] Garrison to David Lee Child, May 14, 1843. *MS.* in New York Historical Society.

had not gained momentum by 1840, but once it had been launched Garrisonian tied it in with abolitionism, anti-clericalism, anti-Sabbatarianism, pacifism and no-human-governmentism.

Appropriately enough in an age of societies and convention-holdings, nearly every one of these reforms had its distinct organization. But the same handful were key figures in various groups; together they formed an interlocking directorate in the vanguard of those ardent spirits bound for Millenia.

Through the columns of the *Liberator* Douglass had become familiar with these reforms. Now he began to hear them espoused from the platform. In his first public addresses he did not discuss them; he was hired to tell the story of his slave experiences. The Massachusetts Anti-Slavery Society, capitalizing upon the rarity of a fugitive who could vividly describe the hardships of those in bondage, sent him out to dramatize the cause. "The very look and bearing of Douglass," wrote James Russell Lowell, "are an irresistible logic against the oppression of his race." [10] With an eye to receipts the Society expected him to solicit donations and receive subscriptions to the *Liberator* and the *Anti-Slavery Standard*, the latter the official organ of the American Anti-Slavery Society.

During his first three months as a lecturer Douglass travelled with Collins, the general agent of the Massachusetts Society. Douglass' companion was well qualified to initiate him into the movement. A graduate of Andover Theological Seminary, Collins had organized the Garrison faction which had captured control of the parent society in 1840. Later in that year he had gone abroad, seeking British financial support for the abolition crusade.

Douglass and Collins needed no assistance in covering the small towns. As was customary they would be joined

---

[10] Pennsylvania *Freeman*, Feb. 13, 1845.

by other abolitionists at the county-wide gatherings.[11]
But the presence of others on the rostrum did not detract
from the attention invariably attaching to the recent
recruit. At Abington Douglass' public appearances "gave
a fresh impulse to anti-slavery." [12] At Georgetown in
mid-September a crowded audience listened attentively.[13]
At a convention of the Worcester North Division Society
a resolution was passed welcoming him and extending
"the right hand of fellowship." [14] At a November meeting
of the Plymouth Society the editor of the Hingham
Patriot, on observing Douglass, was reminded of Spar-
tacus.[15] To an editor who heard him at Providence,
Douglass had "wit, argument, sarcasm, pathos," and his
voice was "highly melodious and rich." His head "would
strike a phrenologist." [16]

After his early appearances Douglass widened his range
of subject matter. He continued to narrate his experience
while in Maryland and to give a graphic imitation of the
style of preaching to slaves, but he added to his repertoire.
He began to offer prayer at the openings of meetings.
Within two months after his hiring he was discussing the

---

[11] Wright and Foster were with them at the Middlesex County
A. S. S. convention on Aug. 31. *Liberator*, Sept. 17, 1841. Garrison
was with them at the quarterly meeting of the Norfolk County Soc.
on Oct. 20. *Liberator*, Oct. 29. Garrison also attended the quarterly
meeting of the Plymouth Soc. on Nov. 4. *Liberator*, Nov. 12.
N. P. Rogers, Parker Pillsbury, S. S. Foster and Abby Kelley were
with them at Providence on Nov. 12 through 14. *Liberator*, Nov. 19.
Foster and Miss Kelley were with them Nov. 23 at the Bristol
County Soc. convention. *Liberator*, Dec. 14. Pillsbury, Kelley and
Foster were with them at Providence on Dec. 27. *Liberator*, Jan. 14,
1852.
[12] *Liberator*, Sept. 24, 1841.
[13] *Ibid.*, Oct. 15, 1841.
[14] *Ibid.*, Oct. 29, 1841.
[15] *Ibid.*, Dec. 3, 1841.
[16] *Herald of Freedom* (Concord, N. H.), Dec. 3, 1841.

"progress of the cause." [17] Early in November he was pressing the case of Lunsford Lane,[18] an industrious former slave from North Carolina who had purchased his freedom and was then engaged in raising money to buy his wife and children.[19]

As the year drew to a close Douglass in company with five other abolitionists, spent two weeks in Rhode Island in an effort to defeat the adoption of a state constitution that restricted the suffrage to white persons. The people of Rhode Island, still governed under a charter issued by Charles II in 1663, sought a new constitution which would abolish the property qualification for voting. A so-called "People's Convention" had met in October 1841 and had drafted a constitution which abolished the property qualification and extended the suffrage to every white male, but denied it to the Negro. The abolitionists, viewing the struggle through colored glasses, bent their energies to defeating the proposed constitution. Douglass and his associates were denounced as an entourage of outsiders by the urban labor groups but were welcomed by the propertied conservatives to whom white male suffrage was a fearful portent. With the aid of their strange bedfellows, the abolitionists held a series of enthusiastic gatherings at which nearly $1,000 was raised to fight the "People's Constitution." [20] Some violence was inevitable. At Woonsocket Falls and North Scituate the meetings called by Douglass, Foster and Miss Kelley were broken up by mobs opposed to "nigger voting." [21] The annual December meeting of the Rhode Island Anti-Slavery Society appointed Douglass on a

---

[17] *Liberator*, Nov. 12, 1841.

[18] *Ibid.*, Nov. 19, 1841.

[19] For an account of Lane's experiences see *The Narrative of Lunsford Lane, Published by Himself* (Boston, 1842).

[20] *Liberator*, Nov. 19, 1841.

[21] *Standard*, Dec. 23, 1841.

committee to go before the suffrage convention when it re-assembled in January to canvass the ballots. The committee was instructed to protest against the insertion of the word "white" into the new constitution.[22]

From Rhode Island Douglass returned to Boston. Here, in company with the cream of seaboard abolitionism, he attended the three-day proceedings of the Massachusetts Society. These annual meetings, held late in January, gave the Society "opportunity to pass on the conduct of the executive committee and recommend new lines of action, to publicize the achievements of the cause . . ., to rejoice over past progress and pledge new and larger contributions of time and money for the future." [23]

At this first state-wide meeting he attended, Douglass proved that he had already passed his novitiate. At one of the sessions he delivered an address. He also entered into the general discussions on the various resolutions; eloquently he upheld the proposed declaration affirming "that the sectarian churches are combinations of thieves, adulterers and pirates . . . and should be treated as brothels and banditti by all who would exculpate themselves from the guilt of slaveholding."

Such a resolution, characteristic of the Garrisonians, was bound to have its effect on Douglass. Their denunciatory language clearly indicated that the abolitionists had no appreciation of the literary effect of understatement. As a result of his exposure to the speeches of reformers to whom the English language was inadequate in invective, Douglass developed no sense of the precise shadings of

---

[22] *Standard*, Dec. 23, 1841. The constitution that was finally adopted (1843) had no color qualification. All male citizens were enfranchised who paid a yearly tax of not less than one dollar. For an account of the suffrage struggle in Rhode Island see John Bach McMaster, *A History of the People of the United States* (8 vols., New York, 1883–1913), VII, 165–178.

[23] Janet Wilson, "The Early Anti-Slavery Propaganda," *More Books* (Bulletin of the Boston Public Library), IX, 346 (Nov. 1944).

the nouns and adjectives he used in reprobating his opponents. The severe criticism he heard levelled by the Garrisonians against the church weaned him away from his religious bent and led him to go through life examining religious institutions from the outside.

Immediately following the sessions of the Massachusetts Society the reformers held a one-night meeting to agitate for the immediate abolition of slavery in the District of Columbia. Faneuil Hall, the place of assembly, presented a shabby appearance; its lower story was occupied by stores, its third floor was reserved for military drill, and the second story, where public meetings were held, had a barn-like appearance relieved only by portraits of George Washington and Peter Faneuil.[24] However, the hall had historic associations with liberty; moreover, as a municipally-owned property its use was free when properly requested by tax-payers. An audience of 4,000 heard Douglass and Garrison, each at his best. Douglass' slaveholder's sermon was never preached to a more appreciative audience: with appropriate gesture and voice inflection he mimicked the manner in which a clergyman preached to a congregation composed of both slaves and masters.[25]

Any lingering doubt as to Douglass' effectiveness on the platform was dispelled by Collins' annual report to the Massachusetts Society. The general agent affirmed that Douglass, who had travelled with him to "upwards of sixty towns and villages," was a prize to be cherished. His style of speaking, reported Collins, was free and forcible, his enunciation clear and distinct, his manner energetic, his description of slavery graphic, and his discourse spiced with humor and satire.[26]

The Society needed no further convincing. To their

---

[24] Lady Emmeline Stuart Wortley, *Travels in the United States During 1849 and 1850* (New York, 1851), 46.

[25] For a note on Douglass' slaveholder's sermon see appendix.

[26] *Tenth Ann. Rep.*, 105–106.

invitation to continue as a lecturing agent, Douglass responded with alacrity. The Society had paid him $170.34 for his three months services.[27] This was as much as he had earned at common day-labor in New Bedford, and the future promised more. He could risk throwing his lot in with the abolitionists, safe in the knowledge that however low would be his income in the months ahead, the kind Boston ladies who conducted the anti-slavery bazaars would see to it that Anna and the children would not go ill-clothed and unfed.

* * *

The abolitionist conventions that were to be a part of Douglass' life for the following twenty years were exciting affairs. The major business of the meetings consisted of passing resolutions, framing addresses, circulating petitions and raising money to support the cause. At their meetings the abolitionists, in order to set an example to the "timid" clergy, "corrupt" government and "venal" press, encouraged freedom of expression. An atmosphere of informality, therefore, pervaded the gatherings. One of the reformers, N. P. Rogers, was such a no-government man that he opposed having any presiding officer at the meetings. Since freedom of debate was stressed, abolitionist conventions were characterized by the presence of persons of widely varying opinions on matters of policy. Individualism ran unchecked. In attendance were the one-idea men (rare among Garrisonians) such as the zealot who held that slavery could be abolished by means of habeas corpus and never missed an opportunity to express that conviction.[28] Sometimes the discussion would be enlivened by the participation of a rash young minister who came to protest against the regular pummelling meted

---

[27] *Tenth Ann. Rep.*, 106.
[28] William Lloyd Garrison, *Boston Anti-Slavery Days* (Boston, 1905), 97.

to the clergy; sometimes a fledgling lawyer would come to try out his oratorical wings.

Speakers at abolitionist meetings had to be hardy. Prankish boys delighted in disturbing the proceedings. In the audience were also sober-minded citizens who sometimes found it impossible to listen in silence to what they regarded as the incendiary aberrations of professional troublemakers. Because they incited an urge to combativeness, the abolitionists found it difficult to secure meeting places, especially since they were unwilling to agree to make good any loss resulting from a destruction of property.

Douglass throve on the give-and-take of these meetings. The early months of 1842 found him again stumping through eastern and central Massachusetts in company with various members of the Society.[29] Among his habitual lecture companions were Garrison, Samuel J. May, Charles Lenox Remond and the Hutchinsons. May, whom Bronson Alcott called "the Lord's chore boy," was a Unitarian minister with an active conscience.[30] His candor was so extreme as to impel him to refuse to preach at a funeral unless he were left entirely free to dwell upon the awful warning suggested by the sad close of a mis-spent life. Another of Douglass' associates was Remond — spare, thin-faced, dark-skinned, the first colored man to take the field as a lecturer against slavery. Proud that he was a free-born Negro, he nevertheless "bore about him, like a ceaseless neuralgic pain, the consciousness that he was the object of a hateful race prejudice."[31] In 1840 he

---

[29] The abolitionist press published the itineraries of lecturers and agents. See, for example, the *Liberator*, April 1, 1842 for Douglass' scheduled itinerary for April 1842.

[30] May has an uneven book, *Some Recollections of Our Anti-Slavery Conflict* (Boston, 1869).

[31] Lillie Buffum Chace Wyman and Arthur Crawford Wyman, *Elizabeth Buffum Chace and Her Environment* (2 vols., Boston, 1919), I, 139.

had visited England as a delegate to the first World's Anti-Slavery Convention. British reformers had made his two-year sojourn a pleasant experience. The Hutchinsons, "the minnesingers of American freedom," were a musically self-trained family who put fire in the meetings with their vigorous rendition of anti-slavery songs, many of their own composition.[32] One of their original songs was dedicated to Douglass.

Occasionally Douglass occupied the rostrum with the stalwart Garrisonian, Parker Pillsbury, a former Congregational pastor who left the church "for the divine ministry of freedom, humanity and holiness."[33] Douglass also had ample opportunity to observe Wendell Phillips in action. Phillips was the most effective orator in the abolitionist ranks. A passion for human liberty had led him, a Harvard graduate, to sacrifice social standing, a lucrative law practice and a career in politics in order to work for the slave.

In his various appearances Douglass continued to develop his power over audiences. Among other things worth bringing to its readers, the *Herald of Freedom*, reporting the annual May meeting of the New England Anti-Slavery Society, after describing the hand-clapping reception to Lunsford Lane's announcement of his family's recent release from slavery, went on to name those illustrious convention worthies who "brought fear to freedom's foes." Particularly did the reporter single out Douglass whose "heroic figure was dilating in anti-slavery debate," and who had "made color not only honorable but enviable."[34] Two days later, on May 26, another journalist heard Douglass speak at the Chardon Street Chapel in

[32] For this family see John Wallace Hutchinson, *Story of the Hutchinsons* (2 vols., Boston, 1896). The "Introduction" is by Douglass.

[33] Parker Pillsbury, *Acts of the Anti-Slavery Apostles* (Concord, 1883), 87.

[34] *Herald of Freedom*, June 3, 1842. The reporter was undoubtedly the editor, N. P. Rogers.

Boston and came away with marked respect for "his talent, his good sense, his zeal." [35] A *Liberator* subscriber who heard him a week later at Northbridge wrote that he had seldom listened to a speaker who had moved him so deeply.[36] At Nantucket, where Douglass informed his audience that he was a reformed slave who had taken the pledge never to be a slave again, a Nantucket Islander who confessed his coolness toward abolitionism and his previous doubts concerning Douglass' abilities, experienced the change common to those hearing Douglass for the first time. This man, wrote the correspondent, was "chaste in language, brilliant in thought, truly eloquent in delivery." [37]

From the middle of August until the end of October, Douglass was in the employ of the American Society. His itinerary, arranged by Collins,[38] took him to western New York.[39] His most vivid memory of that short and unreported tour was the cordial reception he received at the home of Isaac and Amy Post, two locally prominent Rochester abolitionists whom he was to know much better in later years.

During the month of November Douglass' attention was occupied by the Latimer case. As was to be expected, the abolitionists seized upon any circumstance that would serve as ammunition for the cause. Such an event took place in October 1842. George Latimer had been arrested and locked up in a Boston prison solely on a written order to the jailer of Suffolk County from James B. Gray of Norfolk, Virginia, who claimed Latimer as his runaway slave. Abolitionist opinion, aroused by the arrest, was further agitated by the refusal of Chief Justice Shaw of

---

[35] Boston *Courier* in *Herald of Freedom*, June 3, 1842.

[36] *Liberator*, June 17, 1842.

[37] *Ibid.*, July 8, 1842.

[38] *Herald of Freedom*, Aug. 19, 1842.

[39] *Eleventh Ann. Rep. of Mass. A. S. S.* (Boston, 1843), 23.

the Massachusetts courts to grant a writ of habeas corpus releasing Latimer from jail. Alarmed at "this daring assault upon the palladium of their liberty," the abolitionists held "Latimer meetings" throughout the state.[40] Moved by Latimer's plight and ever eager to sound freedom's harp, the poet Whittier sent word to Virginia that Massachusetts had registered a vow in heaven that she would suffer

> No slave-hunt in our borders, — no pirate on our strand!
> No fetters in the Bay State, — no slave upon our land.

The swelling chorus of dissent was echoed by Douglass, as he informed Garrison in the first public letter he ever wrote. In New Bedford during the first week in November he and Remond had spoken day and night in behalf of "our outraged brother" who had been "hunted down like a wild beast and ferociously dragged through the streets of Boston." The meetings had been characterized by "deep and solemn feeling." [41]

When Latimer obtained his freedom in mid-November — Gray sold him for $400 — he joined forces with the abolitionists. A Salem audience, assembled to express sympathy for the suffering he had undergone, observed a light-skinned young man with none of the physical characteristics of a Negro. Embarrassed, he had little to say after mumbling his thanks. But his lack of platform aplomb was more than balanced by Douglass who "moved the audience at will," in "the most wonderful performance of the evening." [42] Five days later Douglass and Latimer were joined by Lane and Pillsbury at the quarterly meeting of the Essex County abolitionists. Latimer recited the story of his escape.[43]

Latimer was never to amount to anything — he was

---

[40] May, *op. cit.*, 306–310.
[41] *Liberator*, Nov. 18, 1842.
[42] *Ibid.*, Dec. 9, 1842.
[43] *Herald of Freedom*, Dec. 16, 1842.

arrested in Boston in 1854, charged with picking pockets [44] — however, the abolitionists used the Latimer episode to send a petition, signed by 65,000, to the Massachusetts legislature. The result was the enactment of a law forbidding state officers to aid in the capture of fugitive slaves, and denying the use of state jails for their detention.

Following the Latimer agitation, Douglass spent three months in Rhode Island. The state anti-slavery society employed him to lecture, collect funds and give a series of Sunday discourses at various points in the state. Heavily in debt and with declining revenues, the society hoped that Douglass' drawing power would fill an empty treasury. The expectations were vain. Pledges were few, money came in slowly.

Douglass' chief work during the remainder of 1843 was his participation in the "Hundred Conventions." In New York City at the tenth annual meeting of the American Society, at which Douglass served on the Business Committee, a proposal to hold a series of one hundred conventions in the western states was considered. The meeting adjourned before definite action was taken. The Executive Committee of the New England Society placed the proposal prominently on the agenda for its annual meeting. By the end of May, when the Society gathered, the "Hundred Conventions" had been the subject of much favorable discussion. Douglass, appointed to the Business Committee here also, was one of several who urged the experiment. A vote of affirmation resulted.[45]

Shortly after adjournment the Society issued circulars soliciting financial support. They announced that the speakers selected to invade the West were Douglass, Collins, Remond, Jacob Ferris and George Bradburn. The latter, unusual among Garrisonians, was a Unitarian minister and had served four years in the Massachusetts

---

[44] *Frederick Douglass' Paper* (Rochester, N. Y.), Feb. 24, 1854.
[45] *Twelfth Ann. Rep. of the Mass. A. S. S.* (Boston, 1844), 34, 35.

legislature.[46] William White of Watertown and Sidney Gay, editor of the *Anti-Slavery Standard*, volunteered their services. It was the plan of the Hundred Conventions to divide the agents into two groups, hold meetings at various places and occasionally re-unite and re-group. The agents were to go singly or in pairs to the various towns in a county. When a county had been combed, the lecturers were to unite temporarily for a monster meeting. The tour was scheduled for six months.

In the middle of July Douglass and Remond set out for the West. Passing through Vermont they met with disheartening response. At one of the few meetings in the state, prankish college students posted placards in the Middlebury public square describing Douglass as a convict and a jailbreaker. Their tour to New York state led them to Syracuse, not yet a flourishing center of abolitionism, where they held their first meeting in a park to an audience of some five hundred. Here they were joined by Collins whose discipleship to Fourier had come to outstrip his other interests. The general agent tried to turn the tenor of the meetings from abolitionism to no-propertyism. His procedure was to organize an abolitionist meeting, speak briefly against slavery, and then conclude with an announcement that a socialist meeting was to be held immediately after.[47] Douglass and Remond objected to the attempt to preach communism to a gathering that had assembled to hear a different gospel.[48]

---

[46] As a legislator Bradburn had promoted measures advancing the rights of the Negro. See *A Memorial of George Bradburn (1806-1880). By His Wife* (Boston, 1883).

[47] John Humphrey Noyes, *History of American Socialism* (Phila., 1870) 163.

[48] Later in the year Collins deserted the anti-slavery cause to devote his energies to an experiment in community living at Skaneateles, N. Y. Twenty-six years later he wrote Douglass, reminiscing over the Syracuse episode. Collins to Douglass, Apr. 12, 1869. *Douglass MSS.* (Anacostia Heights, Washington, D. C.).

At the meeting of the Western New York Anti-Slavery Society in Rochester the Negro abolitionists were joined by Ferris and Bradburn. Douglass sang an abolition solo at a session held in the public square.[49] At Rochester Douglass left Remond and went westward to Buffalo with Bradburn. Upon discovery that the local committee had provided wretched accommodations, Bradburn left the city. He collapsed in Cincinnati, unable to stand the hardships of a travelling lecturer.

Undeterred by Bradburn's departure from Buffalo, Douglass single-handedly proclaimed abolitionism at an abandoned post-office site to an audience of curiosity-seekers. Three or four days later he was joined by Remond who promptly attributed the public indifference to the clergy.[50]

For Douglass and Remond the highlight of the tour was their participation in the National Convention of Colored Men.[51] Here Douglass became better acquainted with William Wells Brown and Henry Highland Garnet, both of them escaped slaves who were becoming prominent in Negro circles. Brown, born in Lexington, Kentucky, had as a freeman served as a cook and a barber before becoming a lecturing agent for the Western New York Anti-Slavery Society.[52] Maryland-born Garnet, before becoming a Presbyterian minister, had attended Oneida Institute, a manual labor school at Whitesboro, New York.[53]

Douglass and Remond went from Buffalo to Clinton County, Ohio, where they held a meeting in company

---

[49] *Liberator*, Aug. 25, 1843.

[50] Remond to Rogers, Aug. 13, 1843. *Herald of Freedom*, Sept. 8, 1843.

[51] For the colored convention movement see below, Chapter VII.

[52] For Brown's early life see *Narrative of William Wells Brown, Written by Himself* (Boston, 1847); also Brown's *Clotel: A Narrative of Slave Life* (London, 1853).

[53] For a sketch of Garnet see the pamphlet publication, *A Memorial Discourse by Henry Highland Garnet with an Introduction by James McCune Smith* (Phila., 1865).

with White and Gay. Douglass and White then proceeded to Indiana — not without misgivings, for that state counted many inhabitants from Virginia and North Carolina who were congenitally unsympathetic to abolitionism. As a professional agitator and a Negro who actively protested against segregation in public places and on common carriers, Douglass had been roughly handled many times.[54] But for him a new high in assault and battery occurred at Pendleton.

On the afternoon of September 15 Douglass and White could sense trouble brewing. The hospitality shown to Douglass by a prominent physician, Dr. Russell, who made the ex-slave a house guest, was resented by many. The meeting the following day had scarcely begun when a group of thirty rowdies, armed with eggs and stones, inaugurated a scene of disorder that soon gave way to howling, screeching and brickbat-throwing. Douglass, not standing on the order of his departure, was on the point of hurrying away when he was informed that White had been knocked down. Abandoning the precepts of non-resistance, Douglass seized a club and ran to the platform. The weapon was wrested from his hand and when he attempted to escape he was overtaken and severely beaten amid shouts of "Kill the nigger." [55] Douglass and White

---

[54] For accounts of instances of rough bodily treatment of Douglass or the outbreak of violence at meetings in which he participated see *Liberator*, Oct. 1, Oct. 8, Oct. 15, 1841; Aug. 19, Aug. 26, Sept. 2, 1842; May 26, 1843.

[55] For accounts of this episode (in the order of their probable reliability) see White to Garrison, Sept. 22, 1843 in *Liberator*, Oct. 13, 1843; Bradburn to *Standard*, Sept. 18, 1843 in *Standard*, Oct. 19, 1843; Mary Howitt, "Memoir of Frederick Douglass," *People's Journal* (London), Nov. 28, 1846; Indiana *State Journal*, Nov. 14, 1843, in Paxton Hibben, *Henry Ward Beecher: An American Portrait* (New York, 1927), 111; R. C. Smedley, *History of the Underground Railroad in Chester and the Neighboring Counties of Pennsylvania* (Lancaster, Pa., 1883), 187–188.

recovered rapidly — abolitionists led a charmed life —
but the Negro did not forget the experience. It "haunted
his dreams" [56] and taught him that it was easier to be an
abolitionist in some places than in others.

The return eastward was routine. At Lisbon, Ohio,
Douglass and his companions were "well received." The
Executive Committee of the Ohio Society tried to persuade Douglass to accept a one-year appointment as
lecturer.[57] Wherever the lecturing group went "the people
wanted to hear Douglass." [58] The journey on horseback
through Pennsylvania with Gay and Remond led Douglass
to a convention at New Brighton where he "preached the
old anti-slavery of Massachusetts," [59] nothing daunted by
the memory of Pendleton. The trio of abolitionists went
to Philadelphia during the first week in December to join
in the celebration of the tenth anniversary of the formation
of the American Anti-Slavery Society. In the absence of
Garrison, the perennial president, the sessions were conducted by Robert Purvis. Light-skinned and Edinburgh-
educated, Purvis resided in comfort at Byberry, Pennsylvania, the only Negro abolitionist with money.

Upon the return of Douglass and his co-lecturers the
Massachusetts Society proclaimed the Hundred Conventions as "a magnificent movement." The seed had been
flung abroad and undoubtedly it would bring forth an
abundant harvest.[60] The more material results were less
consoling: the total amount collected by lecturers was
$450 beyond their customarily cut-to-the-bone expenses.

Not to be discouraged by poor financial returns the
Society at its annual meeting in January 1844 decided
to make the experiment on a smaller scale. A series of one

---

[56] Douglass to White, July 30, 1846. Carbon copy, *Douglass MSS.*
[57] *Liberator*, Nov. 7, 1843.
[58] Bradburn to Collins, Nov. 22, 1843. *A. S. Let.*, XIII.
[59] *Liberator*, Nov. 28, 1843.
[60] *Twelfth Ann. Rep. of the Mass. A. S. S.* (Boston, 1844), 34.

hundred conventions was scheduled within Massachusetts. Douglass, White and Pillsbury travelled through the central counties of the state during the late months of winter.[61] The trio held a few meetings in New Hampshire. At Concord, at a meeting at which "no man ever closed a speech with more dignity and respect" than did Douglass, a correspondent reported to his paper that "the house was crowded with the best of people — no clergy." [62] The results of the one hundred conventions were encouraging; generally the meetings were well attended.[63]

Returning to the seaboard in April, Douglass presided over a Lynn gathering addressed by Garrison, Foster, Remond and Buffum. The meeting was devoted largely to the drafting of several resolutions expressing indignation at the treatment of John L. Brown of Maine who had been publicly whipped in South Carolina for attempting to aid a slave in her dash for freedom.[64] Three weeks later, at the meeting of the New England Society in May, the most important issue was the familiar "No Union with Slaveholders." Thinking Garrison's thoughts, Douglass supported the resolution calling for the dissolution of the Federal government.

The lecture platform saw little of Douglass during the winter months of 1844–45; he was busily engaged in writing an account of his slave experiences. His *Narrative of the Life of Frederick Douglass* was a slim volume of 125 pages, prefaced by letters from Garrison and Phillips. The book appeared in May 1845 and immediately became a fast seller in reformist circles. Unlike many similar tales of the heroic fugitive, Douglass' story was the product of his own pen; he needed no abolitionist hack to "edit"

---

[61] The *Liberator* for March 15, 1843, has a letter from Douglass, sketching his itinerary for the previous five weeks.

[62] *Herald of Freedom*, Feb. 16, 1844.

[63] *Thirteenth Ann. Rep. of the Mass. A. S. S.* (Boston, 1845), 26.

[64] *Liberator*, May 10, 1844.

his writings.[65] The *Narrative* was a worthy addition to the campaign literature of abolitionism. It revealed a readable prose style, simple and direct, with a feeling for words. It was absorbing in its sensitive descriptions of persons and places — even an unsympathetic reader would be stirred by its vividness if unmoved by its passion. No reader, whatever his temperament, got from the *Narrative* the impression that the slaves were reasonably contented, if not happy.

The publication of his book strengthened the determination to go abroad that had been germinating in Douglass' mind for months. A trip across the ocean would be a welcome diversion after the strain of getting out his book: as Phillips had written Elizabeth Pease, "Douglass who is now writing out his story thinks of relaxing by arranging a voyage." [66] Moreover, Douglass' friends now feared for his safety in the United States because his *Narrative*, in giving names, had revealed his master's identity and divulged his own. Such outspokenness was risky — his former owner would now know his whereabouts. This disturbed Douglass; ever since his escape, the fear of seizure had preyed upon him. In 1844, when the Executive Committee of the Massachusetts Society had assigned him to Pennsylvania, he demurred, not thinking it safe.[67] Now that the publication of his *Narrative* made him a marked man for any slave-catchers his master might send, Douglass thought it best to be out of the country for the time.

There were additional reasons for making the trip. His visit to "the land of my paternal ancestors" (Douglass

---

[65] For a treatment of the authorship and content of the narratives of escaped slaves see John Herbert Nelson, *The Negro Character in American Literature* (Lawrence, Kansas, 1926), 60–68.

[66] Phillips to Pease, Feb. 24, 1845. *A. S. Let.*, XV.

[67] Phillips to J. Miller McKim, Oct. 31, 1844. Oscar Sherwin, *Prophet of Liberty: A Biography of Wendell Phillips* (Ph.D. dissertation, New York University, 1940), 525.

assumed that his father was white) would increase his knowledge and give him opportunities for self-improvement. Furthermore, America's reluctance to have her sins described to a British audience would tend to shame her out of them.[68] Douglass also realized that by going abroad he could promote in person the sale of his book. He had already made arrangements whereby the proceeds from sales in the United States, where the book was selling for 50¢, would go to Anna and thus substitute for his earnings on the lecture platform.[69] His family, now embracing two additional youngsters, Frederick junior and Charles Remond,[70] had moved, late in 1842, to Lynn, then a town of 8,000. His reluctance to leave his family was overcome by a knowledge of Anna's self-reliance, tested by his many and prolonged absences.

Removing as many difficulties as possible, Douglass' well-wishers raised for his travelling expenses a purse of $250 [71] and wrote laudatory letters to sympathizers abroad. "It is quite unnecessary," ran one of the letters "to introduce Douglass. When you know him as intimately as we you will esteem him highly." [72] The prince of

[68] *Narrative of the Life of Frederick Douglass* (third English edition, Wortley, 1846), v–vi.

[69] For 1842 Douglass received $300.36 from the Massachusetts Society. *Eleventh Ann. Rep.*, App., 85. For 1843 no disbursement to Douglass is listed; possibly Collins paid him out of the monies allotted to the general agent. For 1844 Douglass received $142 from the Massachusetts Society. *Thirteenth Ann. Rep.*, App., 6.

[70] Frederick was born in New Bedford, early in 1842. There is no official record of his birth. Charles Remond was born on October 21, 1844. *Vital Records of Lynn, Mass., to 1850* (Salem, Mass., 1905), I, 131.

[71] Hutchinson, *op. cit.*, I, 70.

[72] Ann and Wendell Phillips to Elizabeth Pease, July 5, 1845. *Norcross Collection* (Massachusetts Historical Society). Two other letters were: Phillips to James Haughton, Richard Allen and Richard D. Webb severally, Aug. 13, 1845. *A. S. Let.*, XV. Maria W. Chapman to Webb, Aug. 16, 1845. *Ibid.*

orators gave him a professional hint: "Be yourself," advised Phillips, "and you will succeed." Thus fortified, Douglass prepared to sail. Already he was the leading Negro among the American abolitionists; he did not doubt that his visit to the British Isles would give him an international reputation.

CHAPTER III

Tour of the British Isles

His skin may be black, his skin may be white,
We care na' a fig, if his bosom be white.

Old Scotch Song

Late in August, in company with the four Hutchinsons
— Judson, John, Asa and Abby — and James Buffum,
Douglass took passage on the British ship, *Cambria*. As he
boarded the vessel, he was in the pleasant afterglow of a
farewell reception from his Lynn townsfellows. Lyceum
Hall had been crowded — "hundreds being obliged to
stand all evening" — as Douglass and Buffum listened to
a resolution expressive of "heartiest good wishes for a
successful issue of their journey." [1]

Buffum, an enterprising but slow-thinking carpenter
whose means permitted him to indulge a taste for abolitionism, had attained a vice-presidency in the Massachusetts Society largely because of his financial support of
the movement. Buffum's efforts to get Douglass cabin
passage had been unsuccessful; the Negro travelled steer-
age. During the mornings of the eleven-day trip, his five
white co-workers joined him on the promenade deck and
circulated his book.

With Douglass on board ship, it was too much to expect
a trip without an incident. On the last night before docking
his ship at Liverpool, Captain Judkins, at the request of
many passengers, invited Douglass to the quarterdeck to
lecture. Perhaps a few of the passengers had over-indulged
in champagne in customary celebration the night before

---

[1] *Narrative* (third English edition, 1846), v.

reaching port; at any rate, Douglass' strictures against slavery needed no catalytic agent in causing temperatures to rise. Douglass' attempt to deliver an abolitionist harangue was interrupted by catcalls and by angry yells that he was lying. The captain, unable by verbal means to quell the ensuing clamor, knocked down one man who brandished a fist in his face; other trouble-makers he threatened with the irons.[2]

On August 28, the day after the contretemps, the small group of abolitionists disembarked and took lodgings at a Liverpool hotel. Three days later Douglass and Buffum reluctantly separated from the Hutchinsons and took ship for Dublin. Here they were received cordially in the home of Richard D. Webb, the local agent of the *Standard*, and "the very impersonation of old-fashioned, thorough-going anti-slavery." Douglass remained in Dublin for five happy weeks. He sold over 100 copies of his *Narrative;* the complete lack of color prejudice was pleasingly novel, and his Irish audiences were large and sympathetic.[3]

Anti-slavery was his constant theme, but true to his reformist proclivities he was attracted by domestic questions. His new acquaintances were persevering workers for the repeal of the Act of Union which forty-five years previously had abolished the independent Irish Parliament. Douglass' interest centered less on the repeal controversy than on the temperance movement (perhaps because the latter appeared to have more moral significance) which had been stimulated throughout Ireland in the late 'thirties by Father Theobald Mathew. The day after his arrival

[2] Douglass to Garrison, Sept. 1, 1845. *Liberator*, Sept. 26, 1845. Edward N. Wright to a friend, Aug. 27, 1845. The *Pioneer* (Lynn, Mass.), Oct. 1, 1845. Douglass, speech at Cork, Oct. 20, 1845. *British and Foreign Anti-Slavery Reporter* (London), I, 212 (Nov. 12, 1845). Douglass to Thurlow Weed, Dec. 1, 1845. *Liberator*, Jan. 16, 1846. *Fourteenth Ann. Rep. of the Mass. A. S. S.* (1846), 44–46.

[3] Douglass to Garrison, Sept. 16, 1845. *Liberator*, Oct. 10, 1845. Douglass to Garrison, Sept. 29, 1845. *Ibid.*, Oct. 24, 1845.

in Dublin, Douglass spoke at a temperance gathering of 5,000; [4] thereafter he gave several temperance addresses in the metropolis. He witnessed Father Mathew's administering the pledge to an assembly of 5,000 enthusiasts. [5]

Three weeks later Douglass attended a crowded Repeal meeting at Conciliation Hall where he sat thrilled by the oratory of Daniel O'Connell, aged but still eloquent. Perhaps Douglass' opinion was influenced by the high regard which Negroes held for O'Connell whose interest in the downtrodden embraced the American slave; [6] at any rate, Douglass concluded that the Irish patriot was the most able speaker he had yet heard. Following O'Connell's address, Douglass was gratified by a request to speak. [7] Another of Douglass' remembered experiences was a temperance address he delivered in the Dublin prison in which O'Connell had been held for three months. [8]

With a final rousing meeting on October 3, Douglass and Buffum left the city and travelled southwestward along the coast. Four days later, after a series of meetings en route, they arrived at Cork. A welcoming committee celebrated their appearance with a public breakfast. The fervor of local abolitionist sentiment impressed the American reformers; Douglass noted with pleasure that the Cork Society had resolved never to disband while slavery existed in any corner of the earth. The local abolitionists plied Douglass with questions concerning Remond, affectionately remembering his visit five years earlier. [9]

---

[4] Buffum to Henry Clapp, Jr., Sept. 1, 1845. *Pioneer*, Sept. 25, 1845.

[5] Douglass to Garrison, Sept. 29, 1845. *Liberator*, Oct. 24, 1845.

[6] At a public meeting in 1833, New York Negroes passed six resolutions praising O'Connell for his anti-slavery efforts. *The Abolitionist* (Boston), I, 28 (Feb. 1833). See also William Lloyd Garrison, comp., *Daniel O'Connell upon American Slavery* (New York, 1860).

[7] *Liberator*, Oct. 24, 1845.

[8] *Ibid.*

[9] *Ibid.*, Oct. 10, 1845.

As in Dublin, Douglass, to the annoyance of the distillers, devoted much of his attention to temperance. Father Mathew reciprocated with a "soiree" for the visitors, followed the next morning by a private breakfast at his residence. Charmed by his host's friendliness, Douglass took the temperance pledge, observing that he was "the fifth of the last five of Father Mathew's 5,487,495 temperance children." [10] On the temperance issue Douglass was unequivocal. Ignoring the potato famine which then gripped the country, he attributed all of Ireland's woes to the dram shop. By pointing out that most beggars drank whiskey, he proved to his own satisfaction that intemperance was the main cause of Irish beggary. He excoriated the clergy, Catholic and Protestant, for lack of interest in the temperance movement.

Late in October Buffum left Cork to attend an anti-corn law bazaar at Manchester. A week later, as Douglass prepared to leave, a group of admirers held a soiree in his honor. A local poet, Daniel Casey, called upon to express a fitting sentiment, wrote as follows:

> Stranger from a distant nation,
> We welcome thee with acclamation,
> And, as a brother warmly greet thee —
> Rejoiced in Erin's Isle to meet thee.[11]

Early in November Douglass left Cork, and striking to the north, spent the next weeks in travelling alone through the heart of rural Ireland. He reached Belfast early in December.[12] He believed that his stay of ten days in that city was productive of good results, small thanks to unfriendly Cork and Dublin clergymen who had forwarded adverse reports of his character and activities. He wrote to Webb asking for fifty additional copies of the

---

[10] *Liberator*, Nov. 28, 1845.

[11] *Douglass MSS.*

[12] Douglass to Webb, Dec. 5, 1845. *A. S. Let.*, XV.

Narrative, remarking incidentally that what struck him most forcefully about Belfast people was that they "drink wine and pray." [13]

Leaving Belfast in mid-December, Douglass crossed the Irish Sea for a visit to Birmingham. En route he joyfully spent several hours with the Hutchinsons in Liverpool.[14] The day following, at the annual meeting of the Birmingham Temperance Society, he spoke briefly to the audience of 7,000 at the Town Hall. Here he added the philanthropist Joseph Sturge to his acquaintance list of sterling reformers. Sturge had founded the British and Foreign Anti-Slavery Society and was its driving force at the time of Douglass' visit. Of Quaker persuasion, Sturge promoted that group's enthusiasm for the production of cotton by free labor. Douglass' brief trip to Birmingham was made more agreeable by a dinner at Sturge's home.[15]

Douglass returned to Belfast a week before Christmas, warmed on his arrival by the news that his family was well.[16] Buffum joined him toward the close of the month. Douglass' persuasiveness prompted a group of women to form an anti-slavery society, and in general the two abolitionists found Belfast receptive. A member of Parliament presided over a public breakfast for Douglass. "It is only distinguished persons," wrote a British reformer, "who are thus complimented here." [17]

Douglass and Buffum remained in Belfast through the first weeks in January 1846, after which they crossed the North Channel, reaching Glasgow late in the month. After a few days in Glasgow they went north to Perth, where they were greeted by Henry C. Wright, an indefatigable and

---

[13] *Liberator,* Dec. 7, 1845.

[14] *Ibid.,* Dec. 14, 1845.

[15] Douglass to Webb, Dec. 20, 1845. *A. S. Let.,* XV.

[16] *Ibid.,* Dec. 22, 1845.

[17] J. B. Estlin to Samuel May, Jr., Jan. 29, 1846. *May MSS.* (Boston Public Library).

eccentric abolitionist. Founder in 1838 of the New England
Non-Resistance Society, and the only person who dared
address Garrison as "William," [18] Wright had espoused
the various reforms of the Massachusetts zealots before
Douglass joined the ranks.

At Dundee where they stayed for two weeks, Douglass
and Buffum, with all-embracing zeal, entered into the send-
back-the-money excitement. The Free Church of Scotland, a Presbyterian offshoot, owed its origin to a belief in
the right of congregations to control the appointment of
their own ministers. Seeking aid from those who sympa-
thized with that principle, the Free Church had sent a
money-raising deputation to the United States. The deputation brought back a considerable sum, to which the slave-
holding churches of Charleston had largely contributed. To
the widespread sentiment that money from such a source
was tainted, Douglass and Buffum added their loud laments.
Already stung by domestic censure, aroused Dundee conservatives were especially angered by criticism from a source
they regarded as gratuitous. Douglass and Buffum were
denounced as "strangers unknown to respectable people in
the country." [19] A British acquaintance wrote to Gerrit
Smith that Douglass and Buffum were guilty of "the
most flagrant violations of truth in their representations"
against the Free Church. "Indeed," added the correspondent, "the *character* of the agitation is something new in this
country." [20] A New Orleans sheet, characteristic of pro-
slavery journalism, suggested that perhaps Douglass had
been "coldly received" by the members of the Free Church
because "their organ of smell was too sensitive for a warm
reception." [21]

For three months the abolitionists remained in Scotland

---

[18] Wyman and Wyman, *op. cit.*, I, 140–141.
[19] Douglass to Webb, Feb. 10, 1846. *A. S. Let.*, XV.
[20] William Arnot to Gerrit Smith, June 16, 1846. *Smith MSS.*
[21] *Daily Delta*, May 13, 1846.

which, according to Douglass, was in "a blaze of anti-slavery legislation." [22] After four weeks in Glasgow, the trip was highlighted late in May by their attendance, in Edinburgh, at the annual meeting of the British and Foreign Anti-Slavery Society. Sturge presided. Douglass was asked to speak; as usual he accepted without demur. He played on the strings of anti-slavery and send-back-the-money. While in Edinburgh, Douglass lodged at the home of George Thompson, an old line abolitionist. A self-educated man, Thompson had been a lecturing agent for the London Anti-Slavery Society prior to the Emancipation Act of 1833. Due to Garrison's influence, Thompson came to the United States in 1834 to further the abolition agitation. The Boston mob which dragged Garrison through the streets, a rope around his neck, had really gathered to chastize Thompson, unpopular because of his outspokenness and foreign origin.

One of the reformers at Edinburgh invited Douglass to be the speaker at a mammoth public meeting to be arranged in London. Upon his arrival late in May, he learned that a crowded schedule had been mapped out for him. On successive days he appeared before an anti-slavery meeting, a peace meeting, a "complete suffrage" meeting, a temperance meeting,[23] and finally a public meeting at Finsbury Chapel in his honor. Here, "with the edifice crowded to suffocation," he spoke for three hours on the evils of slavery, bolstering his case by quoting at length from the abolitionist tracts of Weld and Birney. Why, he asked rhetorically, was he addressing the English public on this question? Because, he replied, slavery was not a crime against the slave alone; it was a crime against humanity. Furthermore, as a brother the Negro deserved universal sympathy; and finally, slavery was so monstrous

---

[22] Douglass to Garrison, April 16, 1846. Carbon copy in *Douglass MSS.*

[23] Thompson to Wright, May 23, 1846. *A. S. Let.*, XV.

a sin that no single nation was equal to removing it unaided.[24]

Taking advantage of the audience response, Thompson arose and referred to a recent conversation in which Douglass, with longing in his voice, had spoken of his wife and children. Thompson proposed a subscription to bring Douglass' family to England. A word of appeal was enough to a semi-religious reformist gathering, to whom giving was a moral exercise. Douglass left the meeting with $400.[25] He did not, however, propose to send for his family. He had not authorized Thompson to raise money for that purpose; Thompson had proceeded on the hope that the presence of Douglass' family would induce him to remain indefinitely in the British Isles.

Buffum and the Hutchinsons returned to the United States late in June — Douglass saw them off from Liverpool. Unaccompanied, he spent the month of July travelling through Scotland. He had an eye for the natural beauty of the countryside but his most marked impression was negative. As in the case of Ireland, he counted "the use of wine and spirits as a beverage" the country's greatest curse. In travel he was disturbed to note that heavy drinking accompanied every change of coach horses.[26]

As August drew near Douglass looked forward to the coming of Garrison. That worthy was scheduled to cross the Atlantic late in July, in response to an invitation from the Glasgow Emancipation Society. The Society hoped that a blast of the Garrisonian thunder would constrain the Free Church to refuse the donation from the Charleston clergy.

The night before he sailed Garrison attended a farewell

---

[24] *Report of a Public Meeting held at Finsbury Chapel, to receive Frederick Douglass, the American Slave* (London, 1846), *passim*.

[25] Thompson to Wright, May 23, 1846. *A. S. Let.*, XV.

[26] Douglass to Eliza Nicholson, Aug. 1, 1846. Carbon copy, *Douglass MSS.*

reception given in his honor by the "Colored Population of Boston." "Come as the waves come!" ran the invitation to be present at the Baptist Church in Belknap Street on Wednesday, July 15. The response was gratifying. A goodly crowd, white and colored, heard Garrison pledge himself to "expose the iniquity of the Free Church," and then return to America and renew his fight against slavery.[27] After his address Garrison bowed graciously as William C. Nell read a laudatory resolution offering him "the grateful homage of our hearts." After the benediction "the meeting separated, in the solemn yet joyful exaltedness of spirit which is the best preparation for coming duties." [28]

Garrison sailed the day after the reception. Two weeks later — on the last day of July — he arrived at Liverpool, and met by Wright and Thompson, proceeded to London. Douglass, leaving Newcastle on the first day of August, also went Londonward. The two greeted each other effusively. Garrison brought Douglass news of his family and good wishes from the colored people of Boston.

On the fourth of the month Douglass and Garrison attended the opening session of the World Temperance Convention. Neither was an accredited delegate; however, the habit of speaking at public gatherings was strong on each. Garrison simmered when Mr. E. N. Kirk, a clergyman from his native Boston, found fault with anti-Sabbatarianism. When Mr. Kirk went on to express the opinion "that some Christian slaveholders retained their slaves through charitable motives," [29] Garrison's low boiling point lifted him to his feet. He demanded a hearing. According to the official report of the convention, Gar-

---

[27] Proceedings of a Crowded Meeting of the Colored Population of Boston, Assembled the 15th July, 1846 for the Purpose of Bidding Farewell to William Lloyd Garrison (Dublin, 1846), 10.

[28] Ibid.,15.

[29] Proceedings of the World Temperance Convention (London, 1846), 21.

rison's discussion "was irrelevant and inadmissable because it was calculated to destroy the harmony of the meeting." [30]

Before the convention adjourned Douglass added another irrelevancy. The official American temperance movement, so ran his jarring note, did not include the Negro in its membership nor in the scope of its operations. When a temperance society composed solely of Negroes had attempted to hold a public parade in Philadelphia, a ruthless mob assailed them. [31] The chairman, aware that Douglass' remarks were arousing mixed and heated emotions, whispered that his fifteen minutes speaking time had expired. Mr. Kirk, obtaining the floor, retorted that Douglass had given a false picture of the temperance societies in the United States. Another defender of the temperance groups, the Reverend Samuel H. Cox, an apostate abolitionist, in a long, angry letter to the New York *Evangelist*, charged that Douglass was "supposed to have been well paid for his abomination." [32]

Within a week after his unhappy experience at the Temperance Convention, Garrison, unable to resist his enthusiasm for organization, formed an "Anti-Slavery League for all England." Calmly did Garrison ignore the existence of the British and Foreign Anti-Slavery Society. The new organization was expected to co-operate with the American Society. At the League's first public meeting, held on August 17, at the Crown and Anchor Tavern, Wright opened with a speech that was a "scorcher." [33] Douglass came next, "making one of his very best efforts." [34] He was followed by Garrison. The five-and-a-half-hour meeting adjourned with a speech by Henry Vincent, a Chartist leader and an orator of great skill. Vincent was one of the

---

[30] *Proceedings of the World Temperance Convention*, 21.

[31] Douglass to Cox, Oct. 30, 1846. *Liberator*, Nov. 27, 1846.

[32] *Liberator*, Nov. 27, 1846.

[33] Garrison to his wife, Aug. 18, 1846. *Garrison MSS*.

[34] Garrison to Webb, Aug. 19, 1846. *Ibid.*

very few Chartists in the anti-slavery movement. Although aiming to make possible a social revolution by extending the suffrage and thereby overthrowing the British political oligarchy, the Chartists were unconcerned about the plight of the laboring man in other countries. Reciprocally, Douglass was untouched by the Chartist agitation, and thus missed the broadening political education of observing and understanding a working-class movement in action.

Late in August, Garrison and Douglass went to Bristol. Here they were welcomed by Dr. J. B. Estlin, a physician and a Unitarian clergyman in one. Estlin was a close friend of Samuel May, Jr., from whom Douglass bore a letter of introduction. On the morning of their arrival Douglass visited a blind asylum, where sixty men, women and children who had heard his *Narrative* read, crowded around him, questioning him and running their fingers over him.[35] At the public meeting, the following evening, Garrison noted with elation that, although there was an admission fee, the hall was filled to overflowing.[36] The presence of the mayor of the city as chairman gave the proceedings a formal tone which took some of the starch out of Garrison and caused Douglass to "labor under embarrassment." [37] Douglass called upon Elihu Burritt, an American reformer seated in the audience, to "testify how a Negro was treated in democratic America and monarchial England." [38] Among Douglass' multitude of handshakers at the meeting's close was Mary Carpenter, one of the many socially-conscious women with whom Douglass was to conduct a sporadic correspondence extending over decades. To this admirer there was nothing wrong about Douglass' address; she had never heard "such a union of powerful reasoning, facts

[35] Estlin to May, Sept. 1, 1846. *May MSS.*
[36] Garrison to Clapp, Aug. 27, 1846. *Garrison MSS.*
[37] Garrison to Wright, Aug. 26, 1846. *Ibid.*
[38] Estlin to May, Sept. 3, 1846. *May MSS.*

impressively brought out, touching appeals, keen sarcasm and graphic description." [39]

From Bristol the reformers went to Exeter and then back to London where they defied Mrs. Grundy and got in a blow for anti-Sabbatarianism by spending a September Sunday afternoon "rolling balls on the greensward," in company with a Unitarian divine.[40]

Late in September the visiting agitators found another target for their fire. A year earlier, a group composed largely of Methodists and Free Churchers had formed an "International Evangelical Alliance" whose aim was to unite evangelical churches throughout the world. In August 1846, at its first annual meeting, the Alliance was forced to consider the troublesome question as to whether slaveholders should be excluded from membership. Headed by the Reverend Mr. Cox, a committee to consider the issue brought in a report which excluded only those slaveholders "who retain their fellow men in slavery out of regard for their own selfish interests." [41] The conference accepted this evasive report with marked relief.

Not so the London abolitionists. Professing to regard the Alliance proceedings as a virtual approval of slavery, they arranged to hold a public demonstration of protest. At the meeting on September 14, Douglass, Garrison and Thompson were the speakers. The sixty or more American delegates to the Evangelical Conference were absent, but many Alliance sympathizers were in the audience. Garrison, who led off, was hissed and heckled. Such a reception was an old story; its only effect was to make his speech "less consecutive than it otherwise would have been." [42]

---

[39] Mary Carpenter to Garrison, Sept. 3, 1846. *Garrison MSS.*

[40] Garrison to Webb, Sept. 5, 1846. *Ibid.*

[41] *Protest and Remonstrance to the Christian Abolitionists of Great Britain and Ireland who met at Freemasons' Hall, London, August 19, 1846, to form an Evangelical Alliance* (New York, 1847), 5.

[42] Garrison to his wife, Sept. 17, 1846. *Garrison MSS.*

Thompson proposed a series of condemnatory resolutions. Douglass' address brought the hectic meeting to a close.

In their controversy with the Alliance, the American abolitionists felt that their position was unassailable. Their chief contention was that the American slaveholders were using a familiar pressure tactic: Southern clergymen, by letting it be known that they would not join any union save on condition of no interference with slavery, would thereby compel non-slaveholders to fall in line. Until the middle 'forties such intransigence had proved effective in preventing the various denominations from taking an unequivocal stand against slavery. Douglass and Garrison felt encouraged by the general response to their agitations against the Alliance, but the lesson was not lost on them that even to many sincerely reformist clergymen, humanitarianism must play second fiddle to denominational unity.

After the anti-Alliance demonstration Douglass left for northern England and Scotland. Late in September he spoke at Sunderland in Durham County with the mayor in the chair.[43] As an agent of the Scottish Anti-Slavery Society, he journeyed to Glasgow, Paisley, Edinburgh and Dundee. He came to Liverpool on October 10 to greet Garrison on his return from a seven-day visit to Belfast and Dublin. Together they re-worked Scotland. Douglass was on hand when the abolitionist ladies of Edinburgh presented Garrison with an elaborate silver tea service.[44] Early in November Garrison boarded ship at Liverpool. As the steamer pulled away Douglass proposed three cheers. Garrison was touched by the farewell scene: Thompson, Webb, and Douglass waving and cheering from the receding dock.[45]

---

[43] *Liberator*, Nov. 13, 1846.
[44] London *Inquirer* in *Bugle*, Jan. 1, 1847.
[45] The *Liberator* for Dec. 25, 1846 carries a lengthy account of this sentimental occasion.

Garrison's departure for America tended to accentuate Douglass' homesickness. Having decided, sometime in the summer of 1846, against bringing his family to England, he had for some months been thinking of re-crossing the Atlantic. In July he had written his old friend White asking whether in his opinion it would be safe to return: "Would Master Hugh stand much chance in Massachusetts?" [46] Douglass had planned to sail in November — indeed had written his wife to expect him on November 20 — but Thompson and Garrison had urged him to stay abroad for six months longer.[47]

Douglass' eagerness to return to America was heightened in December 1846 by a change in status. In that month he became legally emancipated. His British friends, headed by Ellen and Anna Richardson of Newcastle, had raised $700 to purchase his freedom. Ownership of Douglass had been transferred from Thomas Auld to his brother Hugh. The latter issued the bill of sale to the Richardsons who then placed it in Douglass' hands.

Many of the American abolitionists criticized the transaction as a tacit recognition of "the right to traffic in human beings." [48] Garrison was one of the few who tried to justify the purchase.[49] He was practically driven to a defense on the grounds of expediency — premises which he found strange and uncomfortable. The logic of the issue rested perhaps with those who censured the purchase. Despite Garrison's wish to drop the subject, the *Liberator*, over a three months' period, was compelled to devote many columns to the controversy. "I am not surprised," wrote

[46] Douglass to White, July 30, 1846. Carbon copy, *Douglass MSS*.
[47] Douglass to Isabel Jennings, Sept. 22, 1846. *Ibid*.
[48] Lucretia Mott to Webb, Feb. 21, 1847. *A. S. Let.*, XVII. A. Brooke to Garrison, Jan. 28, 1847. *Ibid*.
[49] For Garrison's point of view see his letter to Elizabeth Pease, April 1, 1847. *Garrison MSS*. See also editorial in the *Liberator*, March 19, 1847.

an Anglophobe, "that the English should purchase Douglass. They are accustomed to buying slaves." [50]

The spearhead of the opposition, the fiery extremist Wright, addressed a long, rambling letter to Douglass,[51] whose reply was convincing from the standpoint of the end to be accomplished rather than the principle to be sacrificed. Douglass realized that the bill of sale would have a certain dramatic value when waved in front of an emotionally keyed audience. He knew also that it would be hazardous to return to the United States without his legal freedom. His former master, smarting under the bitter platform denunciations hurled against him for nearly ten years by his runaway slave, would certainly have caused Douglass much trouble.

The gift of his freedom was more than a personal tribute to Douglass from the English abolitionists. One uncharitable critic of the British reformers suggested that "Douglass is a good card for the ambulatory gentry, affording them a safety valve for their pent-up pseudo-philanthropy and pugnacity." [52] But Douglass' warm reception in the British Isles resulted from many factors. At the time of his visit, English sentiment still reflected the afterglow of the Romantic movement, with its emphasis on freedom. Disciples of Rousseau beheld in Douglass a personification of the noble savage, unspoiled by the corruptions of civilization. The agitations of the Quakers had created a horror of slavery.[53] The period following 1830 was one of reform in England. Still prevalent, at the time of Douglass' tour, was the religious, humanitarian spirit which had resulted in 1833 in the act to stamp out slavery in the Empire,

[50] J. M. McMillan to *Bugle*, Mar. 5, 1847.

[51] *Liberator*, Jan. 29, 1847.

[52] London correspondent of the New York *Journal of Commerce* in *Liberator*, Dec. 25, 1846.

[53] Eva B. Dykes, *The Negro in English Romantic Thought* (Washington, 1942), 2.

followed five years later by legislation abolishing Negro apprenticeship in the West Indies.[54] The formation in 1839 of the British and Foreign Anti-Slavery Society, whose platform was the universal extinction of slavery and the slave trade, had been a continuing manifestation of this zeal for improving the lot of the black man.[55]

The English reformers, with an equalitarian philosophy and a sweeping breadth of outlook, regarded Douglass simply as a brother whose skin happened to be richly pigmented. To them he was a living symbol of man's struggle and rise. Much of the welcome accorded Douglass sprang from a deep-seated humanitarianism that unfailingly extended to every Negro agitator and runaway who followed Remond and Douglass to the British Isles. "It is good," jeered the New York *Herald*, "to be dyed black if you come up to London, for Negro love is filling all ranks, from Prince Albert and the Queen, down to her poorest subjects." [56]

Douglass' last months abroad were a repetition of his former successes. During the first two weeks in January 1847, he travelled with Wright, whose illness after the middle of the month left the Negro without a companion. Douglass himself began to show the wear and tear from constant getting about. In March he spoke every night, including Sundays. His addresses invariably ran about two and a half hours. After the meetings, people came up to greet the speaker. At Bristol in late March, an audience of 1,000 tried to shake hands.[57] Little wonder that to an

[54] For this neglected aspect of British reform see Charles H. Wesley, "Abolition of Negro Apprenticeship in the British Empire," *Journal of Negro History*, XXIII, 155–199 (Apr. 1938).

[55] For a documentation of the relationship between American Negro slavery and British humanitarianism see "Introduction," Anne H. Abel and Frank J. Klingberg, eds., *A Sidelight on Anglo-American Relations, 1839–1858* (Washington, 1927).

[56] New York *Herald*, July 20, 1840.

[57] Estlin to May, Apr. 2, 1847. *May MSS.*

observer at Warrington, he appeared "to be suffering from great debility." [58]

As the month closed, Douglass prepared for his departure in April. In London, on March 30, his numerous friends and acquaintances gave him a public farewell. Thompson was chairman. Douglass Jerrold, the playwright and humorist, was among the group of "400 persons of great respectability." [59] In a regretful tone, the honored guest spoke of leaving the country in which he had been treated "with utmost kindness and most assiduous attention." Wherever else he was a stranger, in England he was at home. He proposed, so he said, to tell his oppressed colored brethren how England felt about slavery. This "sea of up-turned faces" would be "daguerrotyped upon my heart." [60] Two or three days later Douglass left for Liverpool.

The circumstances of his departure from England were such as to re-orient him to the way of life in his native land. In London, on March 4, he had purchased a ticket for passage on the *Cambria*. On reaching Liverpool a month later, he was informed that he could not go aboard unless he agreed to take his meals alone, and abstain from mixing with saloon company. The Cunard agent, Charles McIver, explained that these measures were purely precautionary. Douglass had caused a serious disturbance on his previous passage, and the company could not permit the repetition of such a commotion. [61] Douglass stormed, but anxious to sail, gave in with a bad grace.

British public opinion was sharply critical of McIver's action. [62] There were innumerable expressions of sympathy

---

[58] *Liberator*, Apr. 30, 1847.

[59] *London Morning Advertiser*, Mar. 31, 1847, in *Liberator*, April 30, 1847.

[60] *Liberator*, Apr. 30, 1847.

[61] For McIver's explanation see his letter to the London *Times*, in *British and Foreign Anti-Slavery Reporter*, May 1, 1847.

[62] The *Liberator* for May 14, 1847 ran eleven columns of quotations unanimously censuring McIver.

for Douglass. One indignant Manchesterian wrote a protest poem of great length.[63] So vigorous was the condemnation of the steamboat company that S. Cunard, in a public letter to the editor of the London *Times*, promised that nothing of the kind would take place again.[64]

Douglass made the sixteen-day trip in enforced privacy. Another type of discomfiture was added by trade winds and a heavy sea. However, these adverse conditions could not wipe out the memory of the past twenty months. Truly, as he might have reflected, he could look with satisfaction on his recent tour. Throughout the Isles he had hurled his ringing words against the sin of man-stealing. The Evangelical Alliance was petering out, and although the Free Church had not sent back the money, it faced internal trouble as a result.

Personally too he had fared well. His social relationships had been unbelievably pleasant. His travels on stagecoach, omnibus and steamboat had not been marred by a single instance of segregation. Tavern-keepers and proprietors of other public establishments had shown a complete color-blindness. Mayors had presided over assemblies gathered to hear him. He had made some warm friends and created a host of admirers. His acquaintance with Sturge and Thompson had been more than casual. He had dined with the great abolitionist, Thomas Clarkson, a month before his death. The night before he sailed he had spent hours in conversation with John Bright and his sister.

Moreover, his trip had not been without financial reward. The *Narrative* had done well; between May and September 1845 over 4,500 copies had been sold.[65] Bristol sympa-

---

[63] *Poem on the Embarkation at Liverpool of Mr. Frederick Douglass upon his return to America*, by F. N. D. (Manchester, 1847).

[64] Cunard's letter to the *Times*, was reprinted in the *Liberator*, May 14, 1847.

[65] *Narrative* (third English edition, 1846), iii.

thizers alone had purchased more than 150.[66] The *Narrative* had also been translated into French, a circumstance likely to yield revenue. His British friends were raising a testimonial fund. Most substantial of all had been the boon of legal emancipation. He had left America a slave; he was returning a free man.

He was on his way back to a country which could scarcely expect of him an overwhelming devotion. But he felt that he owed a service to his native land. The conscience of America needed his irritation and he was prepared "to blister it all over from center to circumference."

---

[66] Estlin to May, Oct. 17, 1847. *May MSS.*

CHAPTER IV

In Journeyings Often

and he was no soft-tongued apologist;
He spoke straightforward, fearlessly, uncowed.

PAUL LAURENCE DUNBAR on *Douglass*

Douglass landed at Boston on April 20. His return was an occasion for several welcome-home toasts (with a soft drink beverage, of course). He could not "attend half the meetings and parties that people are anxious to get up for me."[1] Late in April, at his home town of Lynn, he listened to words of congratulation on the success of his "philanthropic mission." He responded with a graphic sketch of his trip.[2] Ten days later, on May 3, white and colored citizens of Boston held a reception with William C. Nell, a Negro worker in the postal service, in the chair. Garrison and Phillips escorted the guest of honor to the platform. Douglass again related the high spots of his visit. Henry Bibb, an escaped fugitive, expressed joy at Douglass' success. In similar vein ran the burden of a short address by William G. Allen,[3] editor of the *National Watchman*, a Negro weekly published at Troy, New York. The American Anti-Slavery Society, meeting in New York during the second week in May, officially welcomed their returned co-worker.[4]

Now that his homecoming had been duly celebrated, Douglass looked forward to putting into effect the plan

---

[1] *British Friend* in *The Non-Slaveholder*, II, 192 (Aug. 1847).

[2] *Lynn Pioneer and Herald of Freedom*, Apr. 25, 1847.

[3] *Liberator*, May 21, 1847; *Sixteenth Ann. Rep. of Mass. A. S. S.*, (Boston, 1848), 41.

[4] *Ibid.*, May 21, 1847.

that had taken seed in his mind: to publish an abolitionist weekly. The money was available. Earlier in the year, his friends in England had begun to raise a testimonial fund that in May exceeded $2,000. Shortly after his return, Douglass broached his plans to his Massachusetts associates. He was dismayed to learn of their disapproval. Phillips believed that a press would bring Douglass to financial ruin within three years.[5] Garrison protested that there were in existence numerous journals published and edited by Negroes — hence no surprise attached to the appearance of a periodical ably handled by a colored man. Furthermore, ran Garrison's persuasive argument, the prospect of a lengthy subscription list was doubtful. An abolition paper sincere and frank, one that denounced and reprobated political parties, church and state and all other agencies that turned their faces against the morning, could expect very little support. Upon what financial sources could the proposed weekly depend? The high rates of postage precluded English backing; patronage from the free Negro presupposed a unity in political affiliation and attitude toward religion, plus a singlehearted devotion to one of the several abolition sheets. Many were the difficulties, continued Garrison, besetting him who would launch a newspaper. "The land is full of the wrecks of such experiments." That Douglass would make a first-rate editor was possible, but unproved. Finally, his great power and influence as a lecturer would be jeopardized by an attempted career in journalism.[6]

Douglass may have reflected that the editor of the *Liberator* was apparently equal to the dual tasks of lecturing and journalism. However, Douglass realized that to take this step, contrary to the advice of Garrison and Phillips, would be to expose himself to the charge of being ungrateful in

---

[5] Phillips to Elizabeth Pease, Aug. 29, 1847. *A. S. Let.*, XVII.
[6] *Liberator*, July 23, 1847.

view of his debt to them, and presumptuous in view of the limitations of his formal school training. To dissuade Douglass, the American Society offered him the use of two columns weekly in the *Standard*, for which he would be paid $150 a year.[7] Douglass gave in. Garrison urged the English subscribers of the memorial to recommend a different use of the $2,000.

Swallowing his disappointment and resuming his work on the lecture platform, Douglass prepared to accompany Garrison on a western tour. Early in the year, the Western Anti-Slavery Society had invited Garrison to address their annual convention, at New Lyme, Ohio. When he announced his intention of accepting,[8] various societies in New York and Pennsylvania asked that he pay them a visit on the way to or from New Lyme.[9] Garrison proposed to take a southerly route to his destination, and to return by way of western New York. Douglass was scheduled to join him early on the tour.

Garrison's other companion, he announced, would be Stephen S. Foster. A Dartmouth College graduate, Foster was an uncompromising former preacher whose denunciatory language often provoked audiences to assault him physically. Pillsbury once complained that on a stumping tour of New Hampshire "pretty much of his time was consumed in getting Foster out of jail for intervening in religious meetings in his peculiar style." [10] Even Foster's friends felt that he often overstated his case. His *Brotherhood of Thieves* (he had reference to the clergy) was one of the most widely circulated anti-slavery tracts. In 1845 he married Abigail Kelley, a kindred spirit. Foster, ran Garrison's announcement, would join his co-workers at

---

[7] May to Estlin, Oct. 31, 1847. *May MSS.*

[8] In *Liberator*, Mar. 19, 1847.

[9] For a typical invitation see that of "the citizens of Harrisburg, Penn." *Liberator*, July 20, 1847.

[10] Henry B. Stanton, *Random Recollections* (New York, 1886), 76.

Pittsburgh. He had consented to make the trip "though with much inconvenience to his domestic arrangements." [11]

Garrison's first convention appearance was on August 4, at the tenth annual meeting of the Eastern Pennsylvania Anti-Slavery Society. Douglass, fresh from one of the annual August 1 celebrations of West India Emancipation,[12] arrived at Norristown a day after Garrison. The well-attended sessions gave the trip an encouraging start. Although Garrison, Sydney Gay, Robert Purvis and Lucretia Mott were among the participants, Douglass was "the lion of the occasion." [13]

The response at Norristown was characteristic of an audience come to hear Douglass. "A Negro lecturer," he wrote, "is an excellent thermometer of the state of public opinion on the subject of slavery." [14] However, an audience response to Douglass was less a reflection of the prevailing climate of opinion than the evidence of a personal tribute. People simply liked to see him on the platform. There was a dramatic presence about his very appearance — his superb physique, his thick, black hair, and his well-formed nose that seemed to inhale sensitively, critically, as if admitting the possibility that color prejudice extended to the world of nature and that the air itself, if vigilance were relaxed, would offer to black nostrils an inferior oxygen content.

His voice was created for public address in a pre-microphone America. In speaking he sounded every degree of light and shade. His powerful tones hinted at a readiness to defy faulty acoustics. His rich baritone gave an emotional vitality to every sentence. With cascading vehemence he could emit invective and denunciation in the best tradition of the Garrisonian school. Added to his earnestness was an impetuous and stirring eloquence. "In listening to him, your whole soul is fired — every nerve strung

---

[11] *Liberator*, July 20, 1847.   [12] *Standard*, July 15, 1847.
[13] *Liberator*, Sept. 10, 1847.   [14] *Douglass' Monthly*, Apr. 1859.

— every passion inflated — every faculty you possess ready to perform at a moment's bidding." [15]

A sparing user of gesture (except when delivering the slaveholder's sermon), he had all the other gifts requisite to an orator. In his ability to mimic he was unsurpassed. He was apt at repartee and had the power to hit close. During these early years of his speaking career he eschewed a manuscript or any written notes, preferring to rely upon his memory or trust to the inspiration of the moment. Withal, his choice of words was flawless. His imagery was vivid — often gaudy. Even when ideas failed, so asserted a contemporary analyst of Douglass' oratory, "words came and arranged themselves so completely that they not only captivate, but often deceive us for ideas." [16] But for the audience at Norristown, and elsewhere, it was sufficient to them that they had been stirred — they were unconcerned as to how Douglass' speech might have fared under analysis in a seminar on semantics.

At the close of the Norristown convention the colored people of Philadelphia, taking advantage of the proximity of their champions, gave a public meeting for Douglass and Garrison. Purvis presided at the reception. Douglass spoke for two hours to the enthusiastic audience; Garrison followed with fatherly words of counsel on the value of industry and virtue. [17]

At Harrisburg, their next stop, the visitors did not enjoy an orderly meeting. Their audience, finding the experience of being addressed by a Negro less novel than distasteful, exploded fire-crackers, threw stones and pelted the two reformers with garbage, unmindful of Garrison's admonition that "a rotten egg cannot hit the truth." [18]

---

[15] William J. Wilson, "A Leaf from My Scrap Book," *Autographs*, II, 167.

[16] Wilson, *op. cit.*, 167.   [17] *Liberator*, Sept. 3, 1847.

[18] *Liberator*, Aug. 20, 1847. See also Douglass to Sydney Gay, Aug. 7, 1847. *Standard*, Aug. 19, 1847.

The travellers found a different reception at Pittsburgh. Here a group of Negroes met them at the station with " a band of music." [19] Douglass and Garrison, now joined by Foster, held five crowded and spirited meetings in two days. Garrison informed his wife that "he had seen nothing like it on this side of the Atlantic." [20] At the next stop in their itinerary they suffered a let-down. The New Brighton town officials would not permit a meeting in the public square and, on inquiry, they found that no church was available. At rope's end, they hired an upper room in a flour store. Participating in the two poorly-attended meetings was Martin B. Delany, a dark-skinned Negro, then editor of the *Mystery*, a reformist weekly. Leaving New Brighton, their last scheduled stop in Pennsylvania, the trio — Garrison, Douglass and Foster — took the canal boat for Youngstown. By easy stages they reached New Lyme where the three-day convention opened on the eighteenth of August.

The Western Anti-Slavery Society, sponsors of the convention, was an outgrowth of the Ohio Anti-Slavery Society.[21] The Western Society represented a projection of Garrison's influence outside the Eastern circles of abolitionism. Although this was Garrison's first trip beyond the Alleghenies, and although many of the Western abolitionists repudiated his leadership and followed after the Weld-Tappan group — still the influence of Garrison was strong in the West.

The work of organizing the West had been carried on by Theodore Weld, disciple of Charles G. Finney of Lane Seminary and Oberlin. Weld had never known spiritual kinship with Garrison, and had cooperated with the Tappan brothers in the effort to take the control of the parent

---

[19] Garrison to Helen Garrison, Aug. 12, 1847. *Garrison MSS.*

[20] *Ibid.*

[21] *Minute Book of the Western Anti-Slavery Society* (Library of Congress).

organization from the Massachusetts abolitionists, headed by Garrison. Yet even in the region which Weld organized, and among the faithful whom he enrolled in the crusade, Garrisonianism was rife. Significant also is the fact that in the South Garrison was regarded as the personification of abolitionism. In that section, which knew Garrison only to hate him, the name of Weld was practically unknown.

Weld had retired from active agitation in 1844. By that time the spirit of the great revival which he embodied had subsided. Behind him he left a tradition of successful political action (as in the petition controversy) but as the voting abolitionists were to discover, few Northern politicians and voters cared anything for the slave; they were anti-South rather than anti-slavery or else they were anti-slavery because they were anti-South.

Garrison's influence in the West was manifested in many ways. Launched in 1845, the powerful *Anti-Slavery Bugle* of Salem, Ohio, although located in a region where the Weld-Tappan school of abolitionism was strong, took its cue from the *Liberator* and the *Standard*, and was strictly Garrisonian in tone. The masthead of the *Bugle* proclaimed the Garrisonian sentiment: "No Union with Slaveholders." Moreover, such abolitionist leaders as Benjamin S. Jones and Daniel H. Hise were avowed followers of the Massachusetts agitator.[22] Marius Robinson, Lane Seminary product and editor of the *Bugle*, was born in Massachusetts. The Western Reserve, hotbed of trans-Allegheny abolitionism, had been settled by Connecticut people and was in 1840 "still a little New England."[23] "The Western Reserve," wrote the Cleveland *Plaindealer* in 1847, "seems

---

[22] Lewis E. Atherton, "Daniel Howell Hise, Abolitionist and Reformer," *Mississippi Valley Historical Review*, XXVI, 343–358 (Dec. 1939).

[23] Albert Bushnell Hart, *Slavery and Abolition* (28 vols., *American Nation Series*, 1904–18), XVI, 196.

to be the stumping ground of the fanatical disunionists of the East." [24] Joshua R. Giddings, Congressman from the Western Reserve, represented a district where ties of blood and business combined to produce a stout link with the New England seacoast.[25] Garrison, therefore, in coming into Ohio, did not stand amid alien corn.

At New Lyme the sponsors of the convention had made seating arrangements in a huge tent for an audience of 4,000. People came from surrounding and distant communities; to be present "one man (colored) rode three hundred miles on horseback." [26] The motives for attending were various. Some came from curiosity and gregariousness and others came to trade and auctioneer. Many were attracted chiefly by the bazaar booths, where bustling females were busy selling food, ice cream, articles of clothing, "anti-slavery handkerchiefs," and gewgaws inscribed with crusading sentiments. This merchandise the managers of the fair obtained from a variety of sources. The most reliable of these were the sewing circle societies. Most of these met weekly. One of the group would read from the Bible or some other book on religion, while the others sewed. Juvenile anti-slavery societies made their contributions. The six-to-fifteen-year-old misses who comprised the juvenile anti-slavery group of Elyria, Ohio, met

---

[24] *Standard*, Sept. 9, 1847.

[25] For an opposing view, denying the influence of Garrison in the West, see Gilbert H. Barnes, *The Anti-Slavery Impulse, 1830–1844* (New York, 1933); Dwight L. Dumond, *Anti-Slavery Origins of the Civil War* (Ann Arbor, 1939), 99–100; Dwight L. Dumond, ed., *Letters of James Gillespie Birney, 1831–1857* (2 vols., New York, 1938), I, v–xxiii; Barnes and Dumond, eds., *Letters of Theodore Dwight Weld, Angelina Grimké Weld and Sarah Grimké, 1822–1844* (2 vols., New York, 1934), I, v–xxvii. Barnes and Dumond, while presenting valuable new materials on Western abolitionism, have, in the writer's opinion, over-emphasized Weld's influence, and have correspondingly underestimated that of Garrison.

[26] Garrison to his wife, Aug. 25, 1847. *Liberator*, Sept. 10, 1847.

weekly to sew for the slave.[27] The policy of the fair managers was to buy as little as possible; for their few purchases they insisted on wholesale prices. They solicited contributions in kind: the Salem women took pains to inform each of the common occupational groups — saddlers, tailors, shoe dealers, coopers, cutlers, brushmakers, tinners, hatters, milliners, foundrymen, etc., — as to the precise articles each could furnish.[28]

Those who came to attend the meetings witnessed a familiar pattern of proceedings. As soon as Benjamin S. Jones, the chairman, had organized the opening meeting, the choir sang a poetical welcome to the guests. One of the stanzas to Douglass is typical:

> And our hearts are made glad by the presence of one
> Who was chattelized, beaten and sold in our land.
> Who is guilty of naught, save that Afric's sun
> Pressed his ancestors' brow with too heavy a hand.[29]

In addition to their standard denunciations of the clergy and the slaveholders, the visiting abolitionists entered into an exposition of their theory of disunionism. Their chief antagonist was Giddings,with whom they, as fellow reformers, had much in common. Elected to the House of Representatives in 1838, Giddings had gained national prominence as a result of his unwearied struggle on all fronts against slavery. Giddings defended his position as an officeholder. He pointed out that had he been a disunionist, he could not have been elected to go to Washington and carry the good fight into the halls of Congress. Such an argument Garrison found "very specious," even though

---

[27] E. C. Reilly, *The Early Slavery Controversy in the Western Reserve* (unpublished Ph.D. thesis, Western Reserve University, 1939), 179.

[28] *Bugle*, July 20, 1850.

[29] *Minute Book of the Western Anti-Slavery Society*. See also *Standard*, Sept. 9, 1847.

Giddings "alluded to me in very handsome terms, as also to Douglass." [30]

The abolitionists were greatly heartened by the New Lyme meetings which were all well attended. "Enthusiasm . . . is unequalled. Opposition to our holy cause seems stunned," wrote Garrison to Gay. This convention exceeded any which he had ever attended.[31] When the final session was adjourned, "their host of friends" kept "them busily engaged for some time in shaking hands and bidding farewell." [32]

Six days after leaving New Lyme, the trio arrived at Oberlin. En route they held meetings at Painesville, Munson (where Douglass "brooded 'like the black storm-cloud over the capes' upon the future"), Twinsburg and Richfield. On August 26, the travelling abolitionists attended the graduating exercises of Oberlin's class in theology. Two of the departing seniors spoke disparagingly of come-outerism, for which they were publicly rebuked by the eccentric evangelist, Charles G. Finney, then on the faculty.

On the following day the abolitionists began their series of meetings at Oberlin. The proceedings were enlivened by the participation of Asa Mahan. Some twelve years previous, Mahan had brought eighty of the Lane Seminary students to the Oberlin Collegiate Institute, of which he became president upon the express condition that Negroes be admitted to the school. At one of the sessions Mahan a political abolitionist, voiced the familiar contention that the Constitution was an anti-slavery document. Garrison and Douglass spoke in opposition to this viewpoint. One of the eminent faculty members, John Morgan, described Douglass' address as "full of wit . . . and pathos and sometimes mighty in invective." In a letter to Mark Hopkins

---

[30] Garrison to his wife, Aug. 20, 1847. *Garrison MSS.*

[31] *Standard*, Sept. 9, 1847.

[32] *Liberator*, Sept. 10, 1847.

he characterized Douglass as "one of the greatest phenomena of the age."[33]

The abolitionists were sure that they had the best of the controversy. Typically uncharitable toward his opponents, Garrison had little respect for Mahan's mental ability: "As a disputant he is adroit and plausible, but neither vigorous nor profound."[34] If Mahan gave the abolitionists no food for thought, he made partial amends by having them to dinner. Living up to Oberlin's tradition of hospitality, the treasurer of the college also entertained the group.[35] Before leaving town they met the graduating Lucy Stone [36] who was already thinking in terms of women's rights and men's wrongs.

After the Oberlin experiences, Garrison and Douglass, now minus Foster, made a triumphal procession through Richfield, Medina, Massillon and Leesburg to Salem. At their four Salem meetings they were greeted by about 5,000 enthusiasts, "the largest anti-slavery gathering ever convened in the county."[37] At one of the meetings a natural thunderstorm was powerless to disperse an audience that had assembled in expectation of hearing the air rent by verbal peals against the man-stealing Southerners. James and Lucretia Mott were present; unorthodox even among Quakers, "they carried no certificate from their own Meeting as the Meeting was not then 'in unity' with them."[38] Lucretia spoke twice.[39]

A week later at Cleveland, Douglass and Garrison con-

---

[33] John Morgan to Mark Hopkins, Dec. 15, 1847. *Morgan-Hopkins MSS.* in Robert Samuel Fletcher, *A History of Oberlin College* (2 vols., Oberlin, 1943), I, 270.

[34] Garrison to his wife, Aug. 28, 1847. *Garrison MSS.*

[35] *Ibid.*

[36] *Ibid.*

[37] *Bugle*, Sept. 10, 1847.

[38] Anna Davis Hallowell, ed., *James and Lucretia Mott: Life and Letters* (Boston, 1884), 289.

[39] *Standard*, Sept. 23, 1847.

ducted the last series of meetings that they ever held as friends. For two days they held forth, pleased by the response. Complimenting his audience, Garrison reported that neither he nor Douglass had met any violence since coming within the confines of Ohio. Douglass found "nothing mean, narrow, or churlish about a true Buckeye."

Before the Cleveland visit ended, Garrison had a physical breakdown. The trip had been full of the hardships of travel in a semi-pioneer country. Private hospitality had been generous and unfailing, but the agent of the Western Society, Samuel Brooke, had arranged appointments for every day, generally at towns from thirty to forty miles apart. As a rule, Garrison and Douglass had travelled in horse drawn vehicles — usually a wagon. They had spoken in damp groves, in tents and in drafty halls. Douglass, troubled by tonsillitis, had been forced to cancel two or three of his scheduled addresses.

To cap it all, Garrison spoke in Cleveland at an open air meeting in a drizzling rain. Exhausted and feverish, he went to his lodgings where he was immediately placed under a doctor's care. Douglass proposed to remain at the sick bed, but Garrison urged him to go on to fulfill their scheduled engagements.[40]

Douglass, considerably depressed, set out for Buffalo alone. Retarded by the "pro-slavery" winds of the lake seas, he was a day late in reaching his destination. Pending his arrival, Remond had attempted to hold the small group which assembled. Douglass' presence made no difference — few persons showed up, a circumstance which Douglass attributed to a series of meetings being held by the American Board of Commissioners for Foreign Missions. The sympathies of Buffalo people, he wrote Gay with some bitterness, were engaged more in the interests of "the heathen of the South Sea Islands" than in "the

---

[40] Douglass to Gay, Sept. 26, 1847. *Standard*, Oct. 7, 1847.

heathen of our own Southern States."[41] The meetings at Rochester were "interesting and spirit-stirring," he reported. The local newspapers, however, had expressed much regret "that so many respectable persons attended."[42] At Syracuse, the zealous Samuel J. May had arranged two meetings at the Town Hall. At the sight of a large audience, Douglass expressed "unmitigated pleasure" that so many had come out "to consider the subject of American Slavery."[43] Many in the audience winced at Douglass' ridicule of "the current religion of our country,"[44] but the response was a welcome contrast to the Buffalo reception. Mirroring local sentiment, Syracuse's leading newspaper found "something fascinating in the oratorical efforts of an earnest, talented, eloquent man, who feels deeply, and speaks out fearlessly and boldly what he feels."[45] The only audience disappointment was the absence of Garrison.

The latter, in Cleveland, had been seriously ill. Douglass was much upset when he learned, a week after his departure from Cleveland, that Garrison's condition was critical. He reproached himself "for leaving him at all."[46] But he did not return to Cleveland.

Garrison recuperated slowly. Writing to his wife five weeks after Douglass' departure, the convalescent abolitionist expressed wonder that his recent co-worker had not written to him or inquired about his health.[47] Doubtless Garrison's fevered condition led him to charge Douglass with an indifference of which he was obviously guiltless. Evidently Garrison had forgotten a letter from Samuel J. May, describing Douglass' sorrow and suspense over

[41] Douglass to Gay, Sept. 26, 1847. *Standard*, Oct. 7, 1847.
[42] *Ibid.*
[43] Syracuse *Daily Star*, Sept. 27, 1847.
[44] *Standard*, Oct. 14, 1847.
[45] Syracuse *Daily Star*, Sept. 27, 1847.
[46] Douglass to Gay, Sept. 26, 1847. *Standard*, Oct. 7, 1847.
[47] Garrison to his wife, Oct. 20, 1847. *Garrison MSS.*

the news of Garrison's illness.[48] Furthermore, late in September, Douglass wrote to Thomas McClintock that he had received the intelligence that Garrison was better and "thought to be out of danger." [49] Regardless, however, of the validity of Garrison's charge of neglect by Douglass, a breach had come between the two.

*   *   *

Douglass' apparent lack of solicitude was not the sole reason for Garrison's impatience. Late in September the Negro abolitionist announced his intention of going through with his original plan to publish an anti-slavery weekly. Two especial considerations prompted this decision. Garrison to the contrary notwithstanding, the example of a journal excellently managed and edited by a Negro "would be a powerful evidence that the Negro was too much of a man to be held a chattel." [50] Furthermore, Douglass had resolved that the time had come to cut loose from the leading strings of the Massachusetts groups and rely exclusively upon his own abilities, proved and potential.

Garrison was vexed that Douglass had disregarded his advice. On their tour of the West the subject had never been mentioned.[51] Garrison wrote to his wife that Douglass' conduct about the paper "has been impulsive, inconsiderate and highly inconsistent with his decision in Boston." [52]

Undeterred by Garrison's hostile attitude, Douglass left Lynn on November 1, 1847, and moved his family to Rochester in western New York. The completion of the Erie Canal in 1825, joining Lake Erie and the Hudson River, had brought to a close the pioneer era in up-state

---

[48] May to Garrison, Oct. 8, 1847. *A. S. Let.*, XVII.
[49] McClintock to an unknown correspondent, Oct. 1847. *Ibid.*
[50] *Life and Times*, 317.
[51] May to Estlin, Oct. 31, 1847. *May MSS.*
[52] Oct. 20, 1847. *Garrison MSS.*

New York. Rochester in the late 'forties was no longer a village but a flourishing town of 30,000, with distinct possibilities as a location for an abolitionist weekly. It was an important station in the underground railroad. A Rochesterian, Myron Holley, had been one of the founders of the Liberty party, and Liberty party sentiment was still strong in western New York. Furthermore, Douglass' choice of a situs was influenced by a desire to select a locality removed from competition with the *Liberator* and the *Standard*.

During the first three years after the launching of his periodical Douglass kept in contact with the Massachusetts abolitionists. He and Garrison met at the annual meetings of the American Anti-Slavery Society; their platform references to each other were courteous, if sparing. But the old amity was missing, and after May 1851, its recapture became impossible. At that time Douglass publicly announced a fundamental change in his political tenets.

The occasion of Douglass' defection was in open convention. At the eighteenth annual meeting of the parent society, held at Syracuse in May, a proposition was introduced that no paper that did not assume the Constitution to be a pro-slavery document should receive support from the Society's membership. Douglass, his assured manner strangely absent,[53] announced that he had come to the conclusion that the Constitution "might be consistent in its details with the noble purposes avowed in its preamble." As a corollary, it became his duty to use political action as well as moral power for the overthrow of slavery.[54]

Douglass' public avowal of his changed viewpoint may have been "manly and candid," [55] but it came as a painful

---

[53] S. J. May spoke of "the hesitating and embarrassed manner" in which Douglass gave public notice of his changed viewpoint. *Liberator*, May 16, 1851.
[54] Editorial in *North Star*, reprinted in *Liberator*, May 23, 1851.
[55] Worcester *Spy*, May 21, 1851.

surprise to the assembled abolitionists. Garrison, in the chair, was thunderstruck and immediately exclaimed that "there was roguery somewhere." [56] Familiar with the practice of intemperate denunciation, Douglass, nonetheless, was deeply wounded by Garrison's charge. It was the only accusation he ever harbored long, carrying it with him to the grave.

Douglass could find many reasons in support of his about-face. Although anathema to the Garrisonians, Douglass' new beliefs were held by the majority of abolitionists. Moreover, the voting wing of abolitionists had developed a school of polemical writers, headed by Lysander Spooner and William Goodell, whose arguments, though tortured, gave intellectual respectability to the movement.[57] In line with Spooner and Goodell, Douglass now held that the great phrases in the preamble to the Constitution, announcing the purposes for establishing the United States (to form a more perfect Union, promote the general welfare, secure the blessings of liberty) govern the meaning of the document in all its details. Hence, the Constitution was anti-slavery by its declared purposes. It followed then that slavery was not legal, it could never become legal and that it was the duty of the national government to bring about its effacement. Such ratiocination brought Douglass to the conclusions (1) that there was no necessity for the dissolution of the Union in order to abolish slavery, and (2) that the ballot was an effective instrument for the overthrow of the hated slave system.[58]

---

[56] Frederic May Holland, "Frederick Douglass," *Open Court*, IX, 4415 (Mar. 7, 1895).

[57] For a recent re-statement and a summary of the argument for the anti-slavery interpretation of the Constitution see Dumond, *Anti-Slavery Origins of the Civil War*, 70–76.

[58] For an elaboration of Douglass' point of view see two of his addresses: *The Anti-Slavery Movement* (Rochester, 1855), and another pamphlet, *The Constitution of the United States: Is It Pro-Slavery or Anti-Slavery?* (Halifax, Nova Scotia, n. d. [1860?])

Added to this persuasive argument in political abstractions, Douglass could find practical reasons for a change in views. In Rochester he was removed from close contact with the Garrisonians. As a non-voting abolitionist in a region where political action was considered paramount, he had found himself isolated. Furthermore, in central New York he was exposed to the beliefs of the pioneer members of the Liberty party, particularly those of white-bearded Gerrit Smith. A Peterboro landowner of substantial wealth, Smith's "tide of benefaction was perpetually flowing," [59] and as he stated himself, people concluded that he had "a sort of pecuniary plethora that requires constant bleeding to assure health and vigor." [60] His generosity extended to a number of diversified reforms, including any movement designed to benefit the Negro. Smith became Douglass' patron shortly after the *North Star* made its first appearance. His influence on Douglass' political thinking increased with every exchange of opinion on abolitionist strategy. In 1851, after three years of friendly discussion, Smith had won Douglass over to the viewpoint held by all abolitionists outside the Garrisonian fold. "I am impressed," wrote Douglass, "by your reasoning . . . I come to my present position after months of thought and investigation." [61]

Although well aware that he would be accused of permitting considerations of expediency to influence his judgment, Douglass knew that by modifying his political beliefs he could obtain badly needed financial support for his struggling weekly. Early in 1851, Smith, financial backer of the *Liberty Party Paper*, becoming critical of its editor's shortcomings, merged the feeble sheet with the *North*

---

[59] Octavius B. Frothingham, *Gerrit Smith: A Biography* (New York, 1878), 98.

[60] John W. Chadwick, ed., *Sallie Holley: A Life for Liberty* (New York, 1899), 83.

[61] Douglass to Smith, May 1, 1851. *Smith MSS.*

Star.[62] The result of this step was the appearance of a new journal, *Frederick Douglass' Weekly,* with Douglass as editor. While it would be gratuitous to charge Douglass with changing his tenets to suit his patrons, it is obvious that if he began by questioning his political opinions, he ended by accepting pecuniary aid from the New York abolitionists.

Within a year after Douglass' defection, the breach between the Garrisonians and their former prize exhibit had become irrevocable. In December 1852 Phillips informed a friend in England that Douglass "is entirely estranged from us."[63] "With Douglass," wrote Garrison to May some months later, "the die seems to be cast."[64]

Dissension in abolitionists ranks was not uncommon. "If there is anybody who does not like quarreling, I would advise him to join the conservatives," wrote Phillips, "for he will find reformers always in a tempest." However, the rupture between Garrison and Douglass over the nature of the Constitution and the arguments advanced by each was more than another exhibition of the contentiousness of professional reformers. The rupture between the two reveals a fundamental difference in psychological makeup.

There was a moral heroism about Garrison that was lacking in many of his associates. He "revolted at halfness," to use the phrase by which Douglass characterized his actions. In a world of erring mortals, Garrison posited a social order based on pure logic. His own decrees he followed with a fidelity that gave evidence that the cause for which he fought would not falter because its leader became discouraged. However, his righteousness led him to assume that because his own motives were honest, those of his opponents were the reverse. His position of undeviating

---

[62] Ralph V. Harlow, *Gerrit Smith* (New York, 1939), 51.
[63] Phillips to Elizabeth Pease, Dec. 1, 1852. *A. S. Let.,* XXI.
[64] Garrison to May, Sept. 23, 1853. *Garrison MSS.*

denunciation and negation lacked a lasting appeal to a resilient nature such as Douglass'.

Douglass' position, in contradistinction to that of Garrison, was one of reform, rather than of revolution. As a consequence he was a compromiser; he believed that human institutions were based on opportunisms. He had a practical sense of what the exigencies of a situation demanded. It seemed to him that the attitudes sometimes taken by Garrison indicated that the latter would rather retain a grievance than to get what he wanted. To Douglass, however, the theory upon which a course of action rested moved him less than the means by which it could be reached. Few considerations restrained his tongue, but a shrewd common sense guided his conduct. "It is gallant," he once wrote, "to go forth single-handed, but is it wise?" [65]

It is not easy to decide which side started the barrage of vituperative charges between Douglass and his former associates. In May 1852, Douglass charged that the Garrisonians had attacked him on four grounds: that he had changed his opinion about the nature of the Constitution, that he had joined an anti-slavery organization not affiliated with the American Society, that his weekly was a political party organ rather than an abolitionist weekly, and that he had referred to George Thompson as a drunkard. [66]

A year later Douglass wrote to Charles Sumner, airing his grievance. The Massachusetts group hated him because, among other things, he had started his weekly against their advice, and had refused to make it an organ of their Society. Garrison, so continued the letter to Sumner, had written to Douglass' friends in England coun-

---

[65] Douglass to E. Keckley. Elizabeth Keckley, *Behind the Scenes or Thirty Years a Slave and Four Years in the White House* (New York, 1868), 319.
[66] Douglass to Smith, May 15, 1852. *Smith MSS.*

selling them to withdraw their support from *Frederick Douglass' Paper* since it served no need — the *Liberator* and the *Standard* being sufficient.[67]

Inevitably Douglass directed some of his ammunition at the leader of the moral abolitionists. According to Douglass, a history of the anti-slavery movement would disclose that Garrison had not begun the movement. To him "we owe the revival of the anti-slavery movement but he neither discovered its principles, originated its ideas, nor framed its arguments." Garrison, continued Douglass, had brought only one new idea to abolitionism — the doctrine of immediate rather than gradual emancipation.[68]

It was but a short step from a criticism of tenets to an approach less impersonal. When Garrison stated that he wished Douglass' journal had a title (at the time it was called *Frederick Douglass' Paper*), the Negro editor replied that he " may have caught a little of the spirit of our friend Garrison, whom he once heard announce himself to be 'a Garrisonian abolitionist.'" Douglass asserted that he saw no more incongruity in naming his paper after himself than "we do in calling a certain book, which we value very highly, *Garrison's Thoughts on Colonization.*" [69] Once, during the course of an address, Douglass related that "Garrison had been dragged through the streets of Boston with a rope around his person; that he was only rescued by being placed in a common jail; yet he had lived long enough to become quite a respectable gentleman, surrounded by influential friends." [70]

Douglass did not spare Garrison's associates. Becoming

---

[67] Douglass to Sumner, Sept. 2, 1852. *Sumner Letterbooks*, XXII.

[68] *The Anti-Slavery Movement, passim.*

[69] *Liberator*, Nov. 14, 1851.

[70] *Ibid.*, Feb. 3, 1855. *Frederick Douglass' Paper*, Feb. 23, 1855. Under the caption, "Groans from the Wounded," Douglass' weekly reprinted excerpts from hostile periodicals.

more orthodox in proportion to his distance from Massachusetts, breeding place of "isms," Douglass charged Wright, Pillsbury and Foster with religious infidelity.[71] Especially did Douglass become bitter against the Negro followers of Garrison. He referred to Purvis' inherited wealth as "blood-stained riches." [72] Stung by Nell's charge that he was "unkind, ungenerous and ungrateful" toward his former benefactors,[73] he called his former editorial associate "a contemptible tool," and "an enemy of the colored people." [74] Douglass came to regard Remond, after whom he had named his youngest son, as an implacable foe. In turn, Remond, who had long resented Douglass' overshadowing prominence, now added animosity to jealousy. Another Negro Garrisonian, William Wells Brown, on his return from a tour of the British Isles, charged Douglass with having written a letter to an outstanding English abolitionist with intent to destroy his (Brown's) influence abroad.[75]

Finally, as if to silence all opposition with one great salvo, Douglass, in his weekly of December 9, 1853, reprinted several articles condemnatory of him from the columns of the Garrisonian sheets — the *Liberator*, the *Standard*, the *Bugle* and the Pennsylvania *Freeman*. He then proceeded to devote twelve full columns to a detailed rejoinder — a prodigious performance, but one which Oliver Johnson, voicing the opinion of his fellow-Garrisonians, described as "an exhibition of moral perversity, blindness and malice." [76]

Garrison, as if repentant for his outburst at the convention in 1851, sought at first to avoid the appearance of

---

[71] *Standard*, Sept. 24, 1853.
[72] Purvis to Garrison, Sept. 12, 1853. *A. S. Let.*, XXIII.
[73] Nell to Garrison, Aug. 19, 1853. *Liberator*, Sept. 2, 1853.
[74] *Ibid.*
[75] *Standard*, Mar. 10, 1855.
[76] Johnson to Garrison, Dec. 10, 1853. *A. S. Let.*, XXIII.

controversy, making no direct reference to Douglass until nearly six months after the coming of the rift. But Garrison had no genius for biting his tongue; he could not long hold his peace. Characteristic of his later estimate of his former friend was his assertion that "Mr. Douglass was in such a state of mind as unfitted him to represent the views which he (Mr. Garrison) held on any subject."[77] He referred to Douglass, in a letter to Samuel May, as "one of the malignant enemies of mine."[78] Early in 1860 Garrison was invited to go to England. Douglass was there at the time. Garrison decided to remain in America because "it might look as though he had followed Frederick Douglass instead of ignoring him."[79] Later in the same year Samuel May asked Garrison to attend the annual celebration of the rescue of the slave Jerry McHenry, whom Syracuse abolitionists had seized in 1851 from a United States marshal. Garrison's poor health made him decline the invitation. But, added he, in his letter to May, even if he were "in speaking order," the fact that Douglass was scheduled to be present "would powerfully repel me from attending." Douglass, continued Garrison with mounting loss of temper, "is destitute of every principle of honor, ungrateful to the last degree and malevolent in spirit."[80]

It is unlikely that the two ever spoke to each other after the convention of 1851. Certainly they had drifted far apart by 1857 when Garrison, in a letter to his wife, Helen, wrote that "Douglass was present at the anti-slavery meeting at Syracuse. I did not and would not speak to him."[81] Until Garrison's withdrawal in 1865, they both attended the annual meetings of the American Anti-Slavery Society.

[77] *Proceedings of the Twenty-third Annual Meeting of the Massachusetts Anti-Slavery Society, Boston, 1855* (Boston, 1856), 35.
[78] Garrison to May, Sept. 5, 1857. *Garrison MSS.*
[79] S. May, Jr., to Richard Webb, May 6, 1860. *May MSS.*
[80] Garrison to May, Sept. 28, 1860. *Garrison MSS.*
[81] Garrison to Helen Garrison, Feb. 17, 1857. *Ibid.*

When, within a month after the end of the Civil War, Garrison proposed the dissolution of the Society on the grounds that its chief aim had been realized, Douglass was one of those whose vote defeated the motion.

Harriet Beecher Stowe, a friend of both, believed that in Douglass' attitude toward Garrison there was "no underlying stratum of bitterness." [82] But Douglass retained a deep resentment. "Frederick, why have I seen nothing of thee in all these years?" asked Elizabeth Buffum Chace, a gentle Quaker abolitionist of former acquaintance. "Because," thundered Douglass, "you sided with Garrison." [83]

---

[82] Stowe to Garrison, Dec. 19, 1853. *A. S. Let.*, XXIII.

[83] Wyman and Wyman, *op. cit.*, I, 266.

CHAPTER V

Trials of an Editor

> I think the course to be pursued by the colored Press
> is to say less about race and claims to race recognition,
> and more about the principles of justice, liberty, and
> patriotism.
>
> DOUGLASS

Negro journalism was an outgrowth of the Negro's desire
for fuller participation in American life. Significantly, the
first of the Negro periodicals was entitled *Freedom's Journal*, published in New York in 1827.[1] Douglass' venture
into the field, therefore, was not a pioneer undertaking;
his periodical was but one of the seventeen newspapers
published by Negroes prior to the outbreak of the Civil
War. In 1847, when Douglass decided to issue a weekly,
there were then in existence four journals edited by
Negroes.[2]

Douglass, it will be remembered, returned from England
with the determination to start an anti-slavery paper. The
English friends to whom he mentioned the plan had raised
a fund of $2,175 as a testimonial of their affection. For a
few months Douglass had heeded the negative advice of
Garrison and Phillips, but toward the close of September
1847, he presented, through the columns of the *Anti-Slavery Bugle*, a prospectus of the new paper. It aimed to become "a terror to evil-doers." Douglass proposed, so ran
the preliminary statement, to publish a weekly that would

---

[1] L. M. Hershaw, "The Negro Press in America," *Charities*, XV, 66
(*New* York, Oct. 7, 1905). Bella Gross, "*Freedom's Journal* and *The
Rights of All*," *Journal of Negro History*, XVII, 242 (July 1932).

[2] *Standard*, Aug. 26, 1847.

"attack slavery in all its forms and aspects — advocate Universal Emancipation — exalt the standard of public morality — promote the moral and intellectual improvement of the Coloured people — and hasten the day of Freedom to the three millions of our enslaved countrymen."[3]

On December 3, ten weeks after the introductory announcement, the first issue of the paper appeared. Published in the basement of the African Methodist Episcopal Church,[4] it was named *The North Star*. A paper by that title had been published in Danville, Vermont, since 1806. While in England, Douglass must have become acquainted with the Chartist sheet, *The Northern Star*. Doubtless Douglass was familiar with the lines of a song attributed to runaway slaves:

> I kept my eye on the bright north star,
> And thought of liberty.

Douglass was well satisfied with the title. "Of all the stars in this 'brave, old, overhanging sky,' *The North Star* is our choice. To thousands now free in the British dominions it has been the *Star of Freedom*. To millions, now in our boasted land of liberty, it is the *Star of Hope*." Prospective readers were informed that the subscription rates were $2 a year, always, optimistically ran the notice, in advance.[5]

The editors were Douglass and Martin R. Delany. The latter brought to the joint editorship a journalistic experience acquired on the Pittsburgh *Mystery*, a Negro paper. It was agreed that Douglass was to remain in Rochester and edit, and Delany was to travel and raise subscriptions.[6] William C. Nell, a self-taught Negro follower of Garrison,

---

[3] *Bugle*, in *Standard*, Sept. 30, 1847.
[4] Howard W. Coles, *The Cradle of Freedom* (Rochester, N. Y., 1941), 129.
[5] *North Star*, Dec. 3, 1847.
[6] Douglass to Julia Griffiths, Apr. 28, 1848. Carbon copy in *Douglass MSS*.

was listed as publisher. The first issue of the periodical reported the proceedings of the National Convention of Colored Americans, held at Troy during the first week of October. The other most lengthy inclusion was a long letter to Henry Clay, ostensibly exposing his folly on the subject of colonization.

Despite their disappointment, the Garrisonians mustered up the good grace to say a word of godspeed. The *Standard* [7] and the *Liberator* greeted the newcomer cordially. The latter, in a puff to Douglass, proclaimed that his facility in adapting himself to his new duties "is another proof of his genius and is worthy of especial praise." [8] The paper itself, ran a somewhat oblique compliment, "surpasses that of any other ever published by a colored man." Other former friends in Massachusetts were verbally happy over the new arrival. At the yearly anti-slavery bazaar in Boston, Mrs. Maria W. Chapman hung a subscription list for the *North Star*. [9]

The reaction of the people of Rochester was mixed. Doubtless a few felt like acting on the suggestion of the New York *Herald* that the editor should be exiled to Canada, and his equipment thrown into the lake. Many felt that an abolitionist sheet edited by a Negro was a community disgrace, to be carried with resignation, as a cross. But local hostility was feeble and of short duration. It was weakened by the attitude of the printers' association which welcomed the paper to Rochester. One month after the publication of the paper, the printers and publishers of the city, with only one dissenting member, invited Douglass and Nell to an anniversary celebration of Franklin's birthday. [10] At the gathering the assembled

---

[7] *Standard*, Jan. 27, 1848.

[8] *Liberator*, Jan. 28, 1848.

[9] *Ibid.*, Jan. 14, 1848.

[10] William C. Nell, *Colored Patriots of the Revolution* (Boston, 1855), 363.

FREDERICK DOUGLASS IN 1845

Frederick Douglass Printing Press in Rochester, New York

newspapermen greeted the Negroes warmly. In response to a toast of cordial welcome, Douglass adverted to the uniformly kind treatment he had received from the local press and citizenry.[11]

Doubtless the favorable reaction of the printers was an instance of economic motivation. Douglass was expected to attract money to the city, and he did. In his sixteen years in the newspaper business at Rochester, Douglass, according to his own estimate, "paid out to white men in the city little less than $100,000." [12]

Douglass was proud of his printing establishment, which was the first ever owned by a Negro in the United States.[13] His press, types and other printing materials cost between nine and ten hundred dollars,[14] and were, boasted their possessor, "the best that can be obtained in this country." [15] The office, however, was a modest single room. Cases of type occupied the entire wall space, except for Douglass' desk. Douglass' children and a white apprentice set the type and locked the forms.[16] After the edition was printed the young workers folded, single-wrapped and mailed the copies to subscribers and exchanges.

The anti-slavery paper which issued from Rochester from 1847 to 1863 was to an unusual degree the product of one man's thinking. Aside from its fitful flirtation with the Liberty party, Douglass' publication was his personal organ. The early issues of the *North Star* were published under a joint editorship, but Delany, a man of diverse and multiple interests, spent no time at Rochester. His failure

[11] Nell to Garrison, Jan. 23, 1848. *Liberator*, Feb. 11, 1848.

[12] *The Revolution* (New York), Aug. 19, 1869.

[13] *North Star*, Jan. 14, 1848.

[14] *Standard*, Jan. 27, 1848.

[15] *Ibid.*

[16] One of the white apprentices hired by Douglass has written a brief account of his experiences in the Douglass shop: Horace McGuire, "Two Episodes of Anti-Slavery Days," *Publications of the Rochester Historical Society*, IV, 219 (1925).

to raise funds for the paper doubtless led to a dissolution of the dual editorship after a six months' trial. After June 1848, the paper was under Douglass' exclusive control.[17] Nell stayed two years longer, but, as a Garrisonian, his position became untenable when Douglass began to espouse the cause of the Liberty party through the columns of the weekly.

The intimate relationship between the editor and his publication is indicated by the name of the journal for the greater part of its existence. In June 1851, the editor changed the name of the weekly to *Frederick Douglass' Paper*. His alleged reason was to distinguish his periodical from others with "stars" in their titles.[18] Doubtless Douglass also believed that sales resistance would weaken to the magic of his name. In 1853 Garrison, then estranged from Douglass, twitted him on the name of his weekly. Perhaps stung by this criticism Douglass considered other titles. He wrote to Gerrit Smith of possible designations. He thought *The Black Man* "good but common"; *The Agitator* was "good but promises too much"; he liked *The Brotherhood*, but "it implied the exclusion of the sisterhood"; *The Jerry Level* he liked best of all.[19] But he never got around to making the change.

Douglass was not a path-maker in journalistic originality. In make-up and typography he modelled his paper after the *Liberator*, the *Bugle*, the Pennsylvania *Freeman* and the *Standard*. Like these abolitionist sheets, the *North Star* and *Frederick Douglass' Paper* consisted of four pages of six columns each. Their content was also standard abolitionist fare. This included presidential messages, which Douglass published because of their intrinsic interest rather than his agreement with their import. Front page

---

[17] Frank A. Rollin, *Life of Martin R. Delany* (Boston, 1868), 68.

[18] Frederick G. Detweiler, *The Negro Press in the United States* (Chicago, 1922), 42. Douglass, *Life and Times*, 325.

[19] Douglass to Smith, June 14, 1853. *Smith MSS.*

position was also given to anti-slavery speeches in Congress; regardless of length Douglass published in full the attacks on slavery by Henry Wilson, Charles Sumner and Gerrit Smith. A voting abolitionist after 1850, Douglass filled hundreds of columns with the endless debates on the nature of the Constitution and the efficacy of political action. Douglass' weekly welcomed sermons by Henry Ward Beecher and Theodore Parker, each of whom could be relied upon to ally Divinity on the proper side of the slavery question.

Douglass carried full accounts of local and state-wide anti-slavery meetings. Reports from abolitionist societies, generally in the form of letters from the corresponding secretaries, consisted of speeches delivered, resolutions adopted and a statement on the size of the audience and its reaction to the anti-slavery message. Many of the correspondents wrote from a consistently hopeful viewpoint in order to bolster the morale of the faithful. These reports, therefore, were wistfully optimistic except those from Douglass himself, whose pen was realistic rather than sanguine and whose powers of self-deception were small.

As was customary in the abolitionist press, Douglass' weekly lifted and reprinted items from other reformist sheets. However, it had its own regular contributors who sent in reports of happenings in their home towns. Among this all-Negro staff of unpaid local correspondents was J. McCune Smith who each week, under the pseudonym "Communipaw," wrote a breezy, informative letter from New York City. Holder of three degrees from the University of Glasgow, Smith found time for civic affairs despite a large medical practice. William J. Wilson, another local reporter, signed "Ethiope" to his clever, running accounts of the Brooklyn scene. Samuel Ringgold Ward, safe in Canada from the operation of the Fugitive Slave Law, sent letters written in a vigorous prose style. Ward, whose complexion was "considerably darker than that of Othello, in the Dusseldorf Gallery," [20] had been a Congregational pastor and a staunch supporter of the Liberty party. Until he clashed with Douglass, William Wells Brown dispatched well-written communications from his travels on the anti-slavery circuit. Another frequent contributor was William G. Allen, whose marriage to one of his white students at Central College created a local uproar at McGrawville, New York.[21] Prior to his teaching appointment at Central College, Allen had edited the *National Watchman*, a reform-ist sheet published at Troy, New York, from 1842 to 1847. Other correspondents to Douglass' weekly included Loguen from Syracuse, George T. Downing and Delany.

Without exception, these Negroes wrote well. Douglass set a high standard — even a typographical error was rarely found in his journal. He would tolerate no gram-matical gaucheries. Contributors polished their sentences for his paper. Perhaps many of the correspondents paraded their learning too ostensibly. Some of the communications were interlarded with Latin phrases and classical allusions, doubtless in a conscious attempt to refute the charges of scanty book-training and mental inferiority.

Outside of political events and other occurrences which lent themselves to the propaganda of agitation, Douglass' publication carried almost no current news. Strictly speak-ing, Douglass' periodical was not a newspaper; but for its large size and weekly appearance, it might have been termed a magazine. *Douglass' Monthly*, issued during the twilight of Douglass' journalistic career, in make-up and size was actually a magazine.

Douglass carried verse. Most of the poems sent in were sentimental or eulogistic. Commonplace in imagery and

---

[20] *Annual Report of the American and Foreign Anti-Slavery Society* (New York, 1849), 16.

[21] For a first-hand account of this affair see William G. Allen, *The American Prejudice Against Color: an Authentic Narrative, Showing How Easily the Nation Got into an Uproar* (London, 1853).

deficient in literary finish, "anti-slavery verse is proof that by indignation alone one cannot storm Parnassus." Aside from the writings of such figures as Whittier and Lowell, abolitionist verse was rhymed prose — verse perhaps, but not poetry. Their composers, of course, did not write for so much a line. Their rewards were a satisfied conscience and a letter from the editor. A typical recipient of such remuneration was Anne P. Adams who "received a beautiful letter yesterday from Frederick thanking her very kindly for her contributions and regretting his inability to render more substantial evidence of his appreciation of her productions." [22]

Occasionally Douglass reprinted portions of *The Bigelow Papers* or some of Whittier's moving anti-slavery verse. Other purely literary material included the serial publication of a standard novel, generally located on page four, as a sort of filler. One subscriber informed the editor that she read everything except *Bleak House* and the advertisements. The latter were pill medicine encomiums and prosaically-worded publication announcements of anti-slavery tracts and tomes. The book reviews ("literary notices") were handled by Julia Griffiths, an Englishwoman, who for many years was Douglass' closest associate and most intimate friend. Miss Griffiths had met Douglass at Newcastle-on-Tyne. In 1848, she had come to Rochester where for a time she resided in the Douglass home. She had a flair for journalism. Douglass' tribute was heartfelt: "Think what editing a paper was to me before Miss Griffiths came!"

Douglass owed much of his literary precision to Miss Griffiths' careful blue-pencilling. She taught him the rules of grammar that he had hitherto observed simply by an inherent sensitiveness to language forms. Editorials from his pen revealed a style that was uniformly virile and sonorous. Douglass had a feeling for words and a gift of vivid

---

[22] J. C. Hathaway to Smith, Aug. 16, 1851. *Smith MSS.*

phrases. He was indebted to Whittier for his anti-slavery vocabulary; [23] his other literary gifts came from a wide and careful reading in the innumerable sets of books his friends sent him.

It was largely due to Miss Griffiths' efforts that Douglass was able to issue a periodical for sixteen years. A reform paper is beset by chronic financial difficulties. Many of the ante-bellum Negro periodicals disappeared after two or three numbers; [24] others struggled along for two or three years before suspending publication.[25] Douglass' paper survived only by heroic measures.

Due to the generosity of his friends abroad, Douglass began his undertaking debt-free, but he had to depend on his own efforts to meet publication expenses. In 1848, these were $55 a week.[26] Before three issues had been published Douglass was complaining about the discouraging number of cash subscriptions. Douglass had been forced to raise money by giving lectures, he wrote his associate, "in order to keep our heads above water." [27] Four months later the situation had become critical. The *North Star* of May 5, 1848, printed an urgent appeal for "pecuniary aid." The editor informed his public that the number of subscribers was so small that he had been compelled to mortgage his house, and as a result was "heavily in debt." [28]

---

[23] Jane Marsh Parker, "Reminiscences of Frederick Douglass," *The Outlook*, II, 552. (Apr. 6, 1895).

[24] Examples: *African Sentinel, Mirror of Liberty, Impartial Citizen, Northern Star and Colored Farmer, The Colored Man's Journal, The Alienated American.* Apparently there is not a single surviving copy of these periodicals.

[25] Examples: *Freedom's Journal, Rights of All, Mystery, Herald of Freedom.*

[26] Douglass to Delany, Jan. 12, 1848. Carbon copy, *Douglass MSS.*
[27] *Ibid.*

[28] The mortgage deed for $500, dated April 28, 1848, may be seen in the Douglass papers in his home at Cedar Hill in Anacostia, Washington, D. C.

A year after this initial appeal the paper was still $200 in debt.[29] Nell took charge at the printing office while Douglass went out lecturing and soliciting subscriptions. The chief difficulty, in Douglass' opinion, was the "very long list of non-paying and the very short list of paying subscribers." Douglass discovered an "amazing disparity between the disposition to read and the disposition to pay."[30] As if to overrun the editor's cup, many of those who paid did not remit in sound currency. Douglass soon learned that out-of-state bills, even when drawn on solvent banks, had to be discounted at a loss of from five to twelve per cent. Douglass warned that he would accept only "New York money," and would "decline to receive" Western and Southern bills.[31]

Douglass found convenient reasons for the paper's limited mailing list. In May 1848, the *North Star* had fewer than thirty subscribers in Massachusetts.[32] To Douglass this was proof that the Garrisonians would not support the paper because its editor would not denounce all abolitionists who were not moral suasionists. On the other hand, the Liberty party people, remembering Douglass' antecedents, regarded the weekly as strongly Garrisonian, and hence withheld their support.[33]

But more grievous to Douglass than the lack of either abolitionist or political support in these early years was the attitude of the colored people. Negroes did not respond as he expected. In May 1848, the *North Star* had five white subscribers to every Negro subscriber, even though many white friends felt that a Negro paper should be supported primarily by Negroes. On the other hand, Negroes,

---

[29] Douglass to Smith, Mar. 1, 1849. *Smith MSS.*

[30] *Frederick Douglass' Paper*, June 16, 1854.

[31] *Ibid.*, Jan. 12, 1855.

[32] *Ledger No. 1, The Property of Douglass and Delany.* (Anacostia Heights.)

[33] Douglass to Smith, Mar. 1, 1849. *Smith MSS.*

so concluded Douglass, thought that a colored man's paper ought to be supported by white people, and that Negroes "ought to have copies out of compliment." [34] This apparently parasitical point of view held by some Negroes, combined with the indifference of others, provoked a display of Douglass' ire. "Tell them," he wrote editorially, "that a well conducted press in the hands of colored men is essential to the progress and elevation of the colored man, and they will regard you as one merely seeking a living at public expense, 'to get along without work.'" [35]

The editor's indignation prevented him from making objective analysis. With the exception of the *Liberator*, Negroes gave little support to any of the abolitionist sheets. The majority of Negroes were too poor to subscribe to any paper. Then, as now, the Negro reading public believed in spending its money for what seems best and cheapest. Furthermore, odd as it might seem to Negro militants, many colored persons prided themselves on their lack of race consciousness and refused to identify themselves with a cause which they regarded as primarily racial. Perhaps less than twenty per cent of the Negroes in the United States were abolitionists.[36] The Negroes in America were not a homogeneous group with common interests. Having no culture peculiar to a black skin, the transplanted Africans had become a congeries of groups with diverse interests that reflected a typically American individualism. Neither Douglass nor any other Negro leader of his day could assume the role of official spokesman for more than a small fraction of a race whose interests and outlooks were as varied and contradictory as the cross-currents of their adopted civilization.

Douglass' journalistic financial strain was eased somewhat by his conversion to the doctrines of political aboli-

---

[34] *Frederick Douglass' Paper*, June 16, 1854.
[35] *North Star*, Apr. 27, 1849.
[36] Lynn *Pioneer*, in *North Star*, Oct. 20, 1848.

tionism. Early in 1851 he and Gerrit Smith decided to unite the *Liberty Party Paper* with the *North Star*. According to their agreement, Douglass was to assume the editorship of the new publication which would then have a subscription list from two sources. Smith promised to take over the debts of the *North Star* and make a monthly donation to the support of the new party organ.[37] The new arrangement satisfied everyone except John Thomas, retiring editor of the *Liberty Party Paper*, who was demoted from the office to the shop.

The union of the two papers went through as planned. The first issue of the new weekly, now named *Frederick Douglass' Paper*, appeared on June 26, 1851. Essentially it was a continuation of the *North Star* with the addition of sporadic news of Liberty party activities. The immediate effect of the merger was favorable. For two years the paper managed to steer clear of financial shoals, due largely to Smith's generosity. In 1852 he contributed $1200.[38] But after 1853 financial difficulties multiplied. The extremely low fortunes of the Liberty party after 1852 led Smith to decrease his donations. By 1856 the sheet was $1500 in debt and Douglass in desperation proposed to unite it with the *Radical Abolitionist*.[39]

More important in the life of the paper than the temporary aid given by the Liberty party was the endless exertion of Miss Griffiths. With a business perception rare in the cloistered woman of the period, she devoted her time exclusively to the interests of the paper for nearly eight years. Without her effective and energetic management the paper would have been another short-lived abolitionist sheet. More interested in the economics of abolitionism than in its propaganda, she took over the control of the finances of the *North Star* in the summer of 1848. She

---

[37] Douglass to Smith, May 1, 1851. *Smith MSS.*

[38] *Frederick Douglass' Paper*, Dec. 17, 1852.

[39] Douglass to Smith, May 23, 1856. *Smith MSS.*

immediately divorced Douglass' personal finances from those of the paper. Within three years Douglass paid the mortgage on his home and, despite the fluctuating fortunes of the weekly, steadily increased his private savings.

Occasionally an out-of-state organization sent a donation. As a result of an anti-slavery bazaar held during Christmas week of 1848, "The Colored Ladies in Philadelphia" raised $100 for the paper.[40] Another fair for the *North Star* was held in the same city six months later.[41] For the most part, however, projects for financial aid had their origin in Miss Griffiths' resourceful mind. Direct appeal was one method. Late in 1853, she proposed to raise $1,000, in $10 gifts, toward a contingent fund for the paper. To friends of the cause she sent soliciting letters. By January 1854, she was able to report a collection of $420. Among the forty-two donors were Gerrit Smith, Charles Sumner, Horace Greeley, William Jay, Henry Ward Beecher, Salmon P. Chase, Horace Mann, Cassius Clay and the Tappan brothers.[42]

Another money-raising device was the holding of an anti-slavery bazaar or fair. Following Boston precedent, Miss Griffiths organized the women. She became permanent secretary of the Rochester Ladies' Anti-Slavery Society. Conducting the annual anti-slavery bazaar was the chief activity of the group. Friends and well-wishers, particularly in the British Isles, were urged to send dolls, dresses, laces, mats, cushions and crochet work. The most distinctive article for sale at the Rochester fair was *Autographs for Freedom*. Miss Griffiths appropriated this idea from the Boston Female Society which, since 1840, had annually issued *The Liberty Bell*, written cooperatively by "The Friends of Freedom."

---

[40] *North Star*, Jan. 26, 1849.

[41] *Bugle*, July 12, 1849.

[42] *Frederick Douglass' Paper*, Jan. 9, 1854.

Autographs for Freedom was a collection of poems, letters, essays, statements and excerpts from anti-slavery speeches. The authors thus thrown together under a single cover were a motley group — Negro reformers such as Charles Reason, George Vashon, J. McCune Smith and John Mercer Langston; political abolitionists such as Joshua Giddings, William H. Seward and William Jay; preaching abolitionists such as Henry Ward Beecher and Theodore Parker, and strong-minded women such as Antoinette Brown, Jane Swisshelm and Harriet Beecher Stowe. Facsimilies of the authors' signatures, appended to their respective contributions, gave the volume its title. Most of the selections were brief, frequently not more than a page in length.

The contents of *Autographs* were uneven. An occasional piece of fine writing crept in between an uninspired poem and a hackneyed anti-slavery diatribe. William Wells Brown's, "Visit of a Fugitive Slave to the Grave of Wilberforce," [43] in theme and literary finish is among the best pieces of abolitionist *belles-lettres*. George Vashon's "Vincent Ogé," [44] is an ambitious narrative poem of a Haitian leader, written with rich imagery. However, *Autographs* was better known for its artistic typography and clear-cut engravings than for its literary merit. The book sold for $1.25 in plain muslin; $1.50 with gilt edges, and $2.00 with "full gilt sides and edges." Two printings appeared; one in 1853 and the other in 1854.

The proceeds from the joint sales of *Autographs* and needle goods at the bazaar netted between $200 and $300. If sales were poor in Rochester, Miss Griffiths went to Toronto and there disposed of the unsold items.[45] Douglass was deeply grateful to this indefatigable woman. Editorially, late in 1854, he appraised her services: "In referring

[43] *Autographs for Freedom* (Rochester, 1854), 71–76.
[44] *Ibid.*, 44–60.
[45] *Douglass' Paper*, June 30, 1854.

to those who have assisted us in keeping up the paper during the year, and for the past three years, we are indebted to none more than to that ever active and zealous friend of the slave, Miss Julia Griffiths."

Miss Griffiths' fertility in expedients, however, was unequal to the dwindling support from political and abolitionist sources. After 1855, the paper was a rapidly declining enterprise. In desperation, Miss Griffiths decided to go abroad with the express purpose of appealing for aid.[46] She returned to her native land, armed with letters recommending the cause. Lewis Tappan's letter praised Douglass "as a man deserving entire confidence. . . . His paper is well conducted, beautifully printed, and is an able auxiliary to the cause of emancipation." William Goodell praised Miss Griffiths and voiced his regret that it was necessary "to tax our English friends for help to emancipate our boasted land of liberty." Gerrit Smith also commended Miss Griffiths and hoped that she would find many sympathizers.[47]

In the British Isles, Miss Griffiths received indorsements from many local abolition societies. One of these printed appeals recommended Douglass' paper "as a standing testimony against the calumny uttered respecting the inferiority of the coloured man." After briefly reviewing the reasons for the paper's financial straits, the pamphlet concluded that Douglass' journal "should have a vested capital, the interest of which would bring in a regular income, that would enable it to stand its ground, otherwise it must go down." [48]

Douglass' friends had high hopes from Miss Griffiths' mission. Many Englishmen remembered Douglass; the

---

[46] *Anti-Slavery Appeal.* Broadside printed in 1856 apparently at Glasgow.

[47] *Ibid.*

[48] *Glasgow New Association for the Abolition of Slavery.* Glasgow, Oct. 1855 (pamphlet publication).

anti-slavery cause had been kept before the British public by a stream of fugitive slaves and Negro abolitionists bent on exploiting the moral and evangelical sentiments of the English reformers. From its beginning, Douglass' paper had many British subscribers. In 1850, the *North Star* had forty-two subscribers in Glasgow, fourteen in Edinburgh, eight in Falkirk, seven in Belfast, eight in Dublin, and a total of eighteen in Derby, Liverpool and London.[49] From time to time English friends and admirers had sent donations.[50]

Miss Griffiths set herself to the task with typical energy.[51] Due to her persuasion, a few anti-slavery societies made annual donations of $25. In June 1858, Douglass, apparently following her advice, brought out an additional publication, *Douglass' Monthly*, planned mainly for circulation in the British Isles. It is impossible to determine how much Miss Griffiths raised.[52] Undoubtedly Douglass' attack on the Garrisonians weakened her in collecting monies. At any rate, the results were not encouraging; all efforts failed to reduce the outstanding debts. In 1859, Douglass was compelled to bring his weekly out in a reduced size; it looked, wrote May to Webb, "like one of our one-cent papers."[53] The end came in July 1860. Delinquent sub-

---

[49] *Ledger No. 1.* Elsewhere in the Queen's dominions in 1850 the *North Star* had subscribers in Canada, and one in Australia and one in the Sandwich Isles.

[50] A typical acknowledgement, from the *North Star* of Nov. 9, 1849, runs as follows:

RECEIVED

For the *North Star* from English friends

E. Pease	$5.00
Eliza Nicolson	4.00
Miss Blake	1.00

[51] E. Pease to G. Smith, Feb. 8, 1856. *Smith MSS.*

[52] Very few copies of *Frederick Douglass' Paper* are in existence for the period 1856 to 1860.

[53] May to Webb, Feb. 8, 1857. *May MSS.*

scribers were to blame. The weekly expenses of the skele-
tonized paper had been $45 to $50: "the receipts were
nearly zero." [54]

The inglorious exit of Douglass' periodicals does not
diminish the importance of their three-fold contribution:
to the editor's personal development, to the promotion of
racial self-exertion and self-reliance, and to the edification
of the white public in the United States and the British
Isles. As to Douglass personally, his editorship expanded
the scope of his abilities. He acquired the sense of authority that goes with the power to hire and discharge. He
grew familiar with the economics of journalism and learned
the mysteries of debit and credit. The making of policy-
forming decisions stimulated cerebration.

Douglass' newspaper career gave him a broadened insight
concerning the peculiar problems of the Negro. For the
more than six years prior to starting his paper, Douglass
had travelled almost exclusively in company with white
abolitionists and had moved in a white milieu. As a Garrisonian his interest in the many-sided Negro problem
extended little beyond the abolitionist movement. With
the launching of the *North Star*, Douglass became a Negro
leader in the totality of his interests and outlooks. His
attention reached out to the question of Negro exclusion
from "white" churches, to the practice of racial segregation
in the public schools, and to an analysis of the whole principle underlying separate accommodations for white and
colored. While anti-slavery rather than Negro protest,
Douglass' weekly mirrored his concern with all problems
growing out of the color line. His outlook after assuming
editorship showed a keen awareness of the problems con-
fronting the rank and file of Negroes whose modest abilities
were insufficient to bestride even the lower hurdles of color
prejudice.

---

[54] Douglass to Smith, July 2, 1860. *Smith MSS.*

A typical example of his interest in the Negro masses was his editorial advice to "learn trades or starve." Douglass pointed out that white men were taking jobs — porters, stevedores, hodcarriers and brick-makers — formerly held exclusively by Negroes. "Formerly blacks were almost the exclusive coachmen in wealthy families; this is so no longer; white men are now employed and, for aught we see, they fill their servile state with an obsequiousness as profound as that of the blacks." [55] On the unskilled level the answer to this competition was the mastery of some mechanical art: "If the alternative were presented to us of learning a trade or of getting an education, we should learn the trade, for the reason that with the trade we could get the education while with the education we could not get a trade." [56] Douglass praised the gospel of physical labor: "The American Colonization Society tells you to go to Liberia. Mr. Bibb tells you to go to Canada. Others tell you to go to school. We tell you to go to work." [57]

Douglass' periodicals contributed to the development of Negroes other than their editor. Race-conscious Negroes could experience a vicarious pride at the sight of a well-edited Negro sheet. Colored poets, essayists and letter-writers could gratify the American love of seeing one's name in print. College-trained Negroes could give public expression to literary urges which otherwise might have totally escaped posterity. Colored leaders used the columns of the weekly to express their views and denounce detractors of the race. Inevitably many of these contributions from Negro writers were characterized by special pleading. To the charges of Negro inferiority these race champions answered with a counter-propaganda that was often as questionable in logic as the allegations they purported to

[55] *Douglass' Paper*, in *African Repository* (Washington, D. C.), XXIX, 137 (May 1853).
[56] *Ibid.*
[57] *Ibid.*

refute. But their sincerity was unquestioned and their sense of the purposiveness of history was sure. They were confident that they were on the side of right — the side that would triumph ultimately whether the universe were governed by God's moral law, the stars in their courses or the intuitions of nature.

A final influence exerted by Douglass' weekly was its effect on white readers. The white public, particularly that section that did not uncritically accept the slaveholder's contention that the Negro was congenitally inferior, could not fail to receive a favorable impression from the *North Star*, *Frederick Douglass' Paper*, and *Douglass' Monthly*. Here was a paper that stood comparison with the best-edited weeklies of the ante-bellum period. Here was a paper free from orthographical mistakes and rhapsodies in bad grammar. Here — and this was the most telling point of all — here was the work of a Negro who had spent twenty years in the prison-house of slavery. To ignore the influence of Douglass' weekly on reformist sentiment in the decade preceding the Civil War is to tell an incomplete story of the abolitionist crusade.

CHAPTER VI

Family Portrait

> I have an industrious and neat companion and four
> dear children. These dear children are ours — not to
> work up into rice, sugar and tobacco, but to train them
> in the paths of wisdom and virtue. Oh! sir, a slave-
> holder never appears to me so completely an agent of
> hell, as when I think of the look upon my dear children.
>
> DOUGLASS *to his former master*

Douglass' family life was a combination of light and
shade with the latter predominant. His social relationships, his dealings with his children and his response to
the appeal of home and fireside were conditioned by the
limited compatibility between the husband and his wife.
For nearly half a century Douglass and Anna Murray lived
together in amity, yet their common denominators decreased with the passing of the years. That their marriage
was not one long falling in love was a consequence of personality differences.

As the wife of his youth, Anna revealed excellent qualities. During the early years of their marriage she worked
shoulder to shoulder with her husband. During the six
New Bedford years she worked in domestic service between
the births of Rosetta, Lewis, and Frederick junior. The
family moved to Lynn in November 1844. After Charles'
birth late in that year, Anna resumed her efforts to swell
the family income. Douglass' twenty-month tour of the
British Isles left the young mother with four children.
Local sympathizers — and Lynn was a hotbed of abolitionism in the 'forties — and the Massachusetts Society lent

some aid,[1] but Anna's job in a shoe-bindery was the mainstay of the family.[2] So well did she manage the household finances that when Douglass returned from abroad she was able to show him a bank account totalling the sums he had sent.

She was a model housekeeper. When Douglass moved his family to Rochester in January 1848, Anna took charge of the nine-room, two-story brick house which, as Douglass exultingly wrote to his former master, was "as comfortable a dwelling as your own." Anna thriftily budgeted the family income and trained the children to avoid wastefulness.[3] Her cooking would arouse the most jaded palate; her "Maryland biscuit" was celebrated.

She was ever anxious to satisfy her husband's wants. She saw to it that he made his public appearances in immaculate linen; on a long tour bundles of laundry met him without fail at specified points. His long absences on lecture series made his presence at home a red-letter occasion. "Father was an honored guest of mother," wrote Rosetta.[4] Anna was an uncomplaining nurse. She watched over his bed in the summer of 1847 when he "had an operation performed on his tonsils." [5] His tonsillotomy, however, failed to prevent the recurrence of the throat disorder. Anna nursed him during the attacks of bronchitis that seem to have occurred thereafter at regular two-year intervals.

Douglass appreciated Anna's housewifely qualities, but after the first years of their marriage he found little mental stimulation in her company. He was not satisfied unless

---

[1] The Society gave Mrs. Douglass $20 in 1847. *Sixteen Ann. Rep.*, App., 1.

[2] Rosetta Douglass Sprague, "My Mother as I Recall Her," *Journal of Negro History*, VIII, 96 (Jan. 1923).

[3] Jane Marsh Parker, "Reminiscences," *loc. cit.*, 552.

[4] R. D. Sprague, *loc. cit.*, 98.

[5] Phillips to E. Pease, Aug. 29, 1847. *A. S. Let.*, XVII.

he was climbing the heights; she was content to remain put in the low grounds. He literally hungered and thirsted after knowledge; she was totally indifferent to the world of ideas. In the summer of 1849 Douglass hired a teacher for her. But the experiment, to which she reluctantly consented, was a failure. Then over thirty, Anna remained illiterate, able only to recognize the two words that spelled the name of her husband.[6]

Anna had little knack for small talk or aptitude for the observance of the "correct" forms and usages followed by the socially aspirant. She would have been ill at ease in a receiving line or sipping tea and chit-chatting at a reception. She had no liking for polite society: in the words of Rosetta, she was "not well versed in the polite etiquette of the drawing-room."[7] Her appearance was undistinguished. Fredrika Bremer found her "dark, stout and plain."[8] Her straight black hair and her inexpressive features gave her face an Indian cast. Invariably she wore a "dark cotton dress and a red bandanna on her head."[9]

Anna was unlike her husband in her reaction to white people. She was never completely relaxed in their presence. Her retiring disposition resulted in part perhaps from the sparseness of the Negro populations in Lynn and Rochester. "Among colored people my wife is in her element," wrote Douglass later.[10] For years out of touch with large numbers of colored people and psychologically unadjusted to any other group, Anna developed no capacity for inter-racial mingling. Her husband was different. He always opposed racial separation. As a means of dispelling prejudice and demonstrating the practice of civil

[6] Parker, *loc. cit.*, 552. [7] Sprague, *loc. cit.*, 99.

[8] Fredrika Bremer, *The Homes of the New World* (translation by Mary Howitt, 2 vols., New York, 1853), I, 585.

[9] Minnie Blackall Bishop to Charles H. Wiltsie, Feb. 25, 1929. *MS.* in Rochester Public Library.

[10] Wyman and Wyman, *op. cit.*, II, 110.

equality, he made it a point to go into hotels, sit down at tables in restaurants and enter public carriers. By constant association he had reached the stage where he felt no uneasiness whatsoever at being among whites: "he rejoiced," so a reporter quoted him, "to be like white folks." [11]

Douglass liked the company of prominent personages. Himself a travelling lecturer who received the hospitality of others, he in turn entertained anti-slavery speakers who came to Rochester. Celebrities visiting the city were sure to call at the Douglass home. Rochesterians had only to watch Douglass' front door to see reformers such as May and Smith, woman's righters such as Elizabeth Cady Stanton, travellers such as Fredrika Bremer, and literary figures such as James Russell Lowell. When such guests came to dinner Anna doubtless acted as she did when the family moved to Washington — put on cook's attire, prepared the meal and then retired to the back porch to rock, leaving her husband to entertain the guests. [12]

Douglass could not escape the sense of frustration that comes from outgrowing one's mate. His unhappiness was sharpened, perhaps, by an unconscious comparison of Anna with many of his female admirers. From the time of his visit to England Douglass had made an emotional appeal to many women. His well-built physique, his prominent, but regular, facial features and his air of high seriousness, all combined to create the sensation that here was a man of overmastering strength. Perhaps women were moved by an erotic tone-quality in his voice. Whatever the cause, Douglass attracted attention. In England, wrote Estlin, "you can hardly conjure how he is noticed." Many of his admirers "exceed the bounds of propriety, or delicacy as far as appearances are concerned." Estlin's

[11] Syracuse *Daily Standard*, May 12, 1851.

[12] Statement to author by Mrs. W. H. Davis, former caretaker of the Douglass home.

misgiving was prescient: "My fear is that after having associated so much with women of education Douglass will feel a void when he returns to his own family." [13]

If some of his admirers exceeded the "bounds of propriety," Douglass never lost his head. His conduct in England was "most guardedly correct, judicious and decorous." [14] However, the temperamental differences between Douglass and Anna were dramatized by the presence under their roof of Miss Griffiths. Educated and accomplished, she had come to America shortly after Douglass' return from England. In May 1847, Douglass and Miss Griffiths had provoked some comment by the scurrilous press because they made a round trip from Albany to New York. [15]

Miss Griffiths returned to England in 1848. In March of the following year she sailed from Liverpool with her sister Eliza. Douglass met them at New York. The sisters cancelled their reservations at the Franklin Hotel upon learning that Negroes were not admitted. [16] Douglass escorted them to numerous meetings. At the first of these the sisters sat in the audience and listened to speeches by Douglass, Remond, Garnet and Thomas Van Rensselaer, formerly editor of the *Ram's Horn*. At the annual meeting of the American Society, Douglass introduced the English-women to Garrison, May and Lucretia Mott. [17] At the meeting of the American and Foreign Anti-Slavery Society, Julia heard Henry Bibb speak on the duty of giving slaves the Bible. In her opinion it was "a poor weak speech." [18] One day's afternoon and evening was spent listening to a

---

[13] Estlin to May, Jan. 12, 1847. *May MSS.*

[14] *Ibid.*

[15] See the *Liberator*, June 11, 1847 for Douglass' long letter on the episode.

[16] *Diary of Julia Griffiths*, May 5, 1849.

[17] May to Estlin, May 21, 1849. *May MSS.*

[18] *Griffiths' Diary*, May 8, 1849.

public debate between Douglass and Ward over the constitutionality of slavery. From 3 o'clock until 5, and from 7:30 until 11, the two controversialists delivered a total of ten speeches.[19] Between sessions of the anti-slavery gatherings, Douglass and the two sisters strolled along Broadway.

On the return trip to Albany the trio entered the dining room of the *Alida*. The steward ordered Douglass to leave. The Negro was uncooperative. The mate was called. The captain was summoned. Douglass was ejected from the table, the women leaving the dining room in protest.[20] For thirteen hours "we took no refreshment (lozenges excepted)," wrote Julia.[21] Equal to the occasion, she drew upon the inner resources of the spirit and feasted on the beautiful scenery.

Arriving at Rochester in mid-May, the sisters unpacked and Douglass and Rosetta took them sightseeing. On numerous occasions the sisters shocked conservative Rochester opinion by appearing on the streets arm-in-arm with their host. On such a stroll along the Battery in New York City, Douglass was assaulted and "roughed up" by a small band of hoodlums. His offense, explained Douglass, was not that he walked in company with white people, but that he walked in company with them "on terms of equality. Had I been with those persons simply as a servant, and not as a friend, I should have been regarded with complacency by the refined, and with respect by the vulgar class of white persons. . . . We have here," ran his letter to the London *Times*, "an aristocracy of skin," which bestows "the high privilege of insulting a colored man with the most perfect impunity." [22]

The two women did not go unscathed. In Boston a coarse wood-cut was circulated, representing the sisters

---

[19] *North Star*, May 18, 1849.

[20] *Ibid.*

[21] *Griffiths' Diary*, May 13, 1849.

[22] London *Times*, in New Orleans *Daily Delta*, Aug. 18, 1850.

as contending for the caresses of "Nigger Douglass." [23]
This type of indecent abuse seems only to have strengthened Julia's interest in the cause for which Douglass
worked. She became secretary of the Rochester Ladies
Anti-Slavery Society. For nearly a decade she was to be
an important figure in Douglass' newspaper office. From
the beginning of their friendship, Douglass placed confidence in her business ability; after 1850 his doctrines were
shaped by her influence.[24]

Her hostility to Garrison was a factor in Douglass'
breach with his former associates. His early schooling in
ideas under the Massachusetts reformers had led Douglass
to believe that the church and the ministry were pro-
slavery — a viewpoint which logically lent itself to latitu-
dinarian tenets tending to weaken the orthodox religious
impulse. Under Miss Griffiths' persuasion Douglass modified his attitude toward organized religion. He began by
tempering his criticisms of the church, and ended, in 1853,
by denouncing the Garrisonians for their opposition to the
ministry and the observance of the Sabbath.

Miss Griffiths' advice may have been a factor in changing Douglass' views on the efficacy of political action in
the fight against slavery. At any rate, the Garrisonians
blamed her for all of Douglass defections.[25] The *Standard*
referred to her as "a Jezebel whose capacity for making
mischief between friends would be difficult to match." [26]
Phillips wrote that the estrangement between Douglass and
"us" was due to her influence,[27] and Garrison asserted that
she made Douglass hate all his former friends.[28] Garrison

---

[23] May to Estlin, June 5, 1849. *May MSS.*
[24] Phillips to E. Pease, Dec. 1, 1852. *A. S. Let.*, XXI.
[25] Douglass to the Secretary of the Edinburgh New Association
Anti-Slavery Society, July 9, 1857. Carbon copy, *Douglass MSS.*
[26] *Standard*, Sept. 24, 1853.
[27] Phillips to E. Pease, Dec. 1, 1852. *A. S. Let.*, XXI.
[28] S. B. Anthony to Garrison, Dec. 13, 1853. *Garrison MSS.*

did not stop at accusing Julia with a lack of sympathy for the leaders of the American Anti-Slavery Society, nor did he confine his criticism to the charge that she was "facile and mischievous," and had "perniciously biassed" Douglass' judgment. He went further. Heedless of probable consequences, Garrison stated bluntly that Douglass had in his printing office "one whose influence has caused much unhappiness in his own household." [29] The fat was in the fire.

By return mail Garrison received a letter purporting to be Mrs. Douglass' answer. "It is not true that the presence of a certain person in the office of Frederick Douglass causes unhappiness in his family. Please insert this in your next paper," ran the letter in Anna's name [30] and supposedly of her dictation. Somewhat lamely, Garrison termed the note "evasive, as our charge has reference to the past and not to the present." [31] Many of Garrison's friends shared Mrs. Stowe's feeling that his allusion to Douglass' family concerns was "unfortunate." [32] Garrison, thinking the matter over, disclaimed that he had intended to imply anything improper, and expressed regret that he had made the remark. [33]

Garrison's assertion was indiscreet, but apparently not untrue. Mrs. Stanton was convinced that the letter from Anna to the *Liberator* had been "concocted by Fred and Julia," and that Anna would never have signed a paper denying that Miss Griffiths had caused domestic trouble in the Douglass family. [34] Garrison had alleged that he "could bring a score of unimpeachable witnesses in Rochester to prove it." [35] That Miss Griffiths had moved out of the Douglass' residence late in 1852 is significant.

---

[29] *Liberator*, Nov. 18, 1853.   [30] *Ibid.*, Dec. 2, 1853.   [31] *Ibid.*
[32] Stowe to Garrison, Dec. 19, 1853. *Garrison MSS.*
[33] *Liberator*, Dec. 16, 1853.
[34] Anthony to Garrison, Dec. 13, 1853. *Garrison MSS.*
[35] *Liberator*, Dec. 16, 1853.

Mrs. Douglass, although composed and uncomplaining, must have resented Julia's close acquaintanceship with her husband. Miss Griffiths had been in the habit of reading to Douglass at night; [36] she had been unusually solicitous about his health, making constant reference to it in her letters to Smith,[37] and she was aware of Douglass' domestic unhappiness. "He has recently had," she wrote Smith, "a considerable increase of those *home* trials about which I spoke to you and dear Mrs. Smith while at Peterboro." [38]

The unpleasantness stirred up by the charges of Garrison had no effect on the relationship between the two friends. Julia remained in Rochester, a right bower to Douglass, until her return to England late in 1855. Four years later she married a clergyman, H. O. Crofts. She never returned to the United States, but as she mentioned in a letter to Douglass in 1888, "for 42 years our correspondence has been uninterrupted." [39] Whatever the degree of sentiment between Douglass and Julia, her presence had imparted a mental stimulation. Douglass profited immeasurably by contact with her well-stocked mind.

If the family circle did not expand Douglass' intellectual horizon, it provided a partially satisfying emotional outlet. Douglass was fond of young people. In Rochester groups of children would congregate in front of his window on summer nights. For their benefit he would sing "Nelly Was a Lady," and "My Old Kentucky Home." [40] He loved to play the violin for them. Among the cherished memories of one of those youngsters was a toy gift from Douglass of two Negro figures that would dance when wound. She

---

[36] Griffiths to Smith, Nov. 24, 1851. *Smith MSS*.
[37] Griffiths to Smith, Aug. 26, 1851; Sept. 24, 1851; Nov. 24, 1851; Dec. 13, 1851; Feb. 22, 1852. *Ibid.*
[38] Griffiths to Smith, Aug. 26, 1851. *Ibid.*
[39] Julia G. Crofts to Douglass, Aug. 3, 1888. *Douglass MSS*.
[40] Parker, "Reminiscences," *loc. cit.*, 553.

never forgot too that he had taught her brother to whistle on his fingers.[41]

For his own children he had a parent's love. He had Rosetta play the piano for visitors. One of them, the eminent Negro clergyman, Daniel Payne, was impressed by her skillful touch. Her father, he observed, was moved by her performance.[42] His last child, Annie, was born in March 1849. Later in the year, in a letter written with restrained pride, he informed a friend in England that his two eldest sons and his daughter were in school.[43]

Rosetta's schooling, however, was not obtained without difficulties. In August 1848, her father arranged for her to attend Seward Seminary, a fashionable school for girls. Rosetta was put in a room and taught separately. Upon Douglass' protest the principal of the school submitted the question of Rosetta's attending to the pupils and then to their parents. One parent objected and Rosetta was asked to withdraw.[44] The only other school open to her in Rochester was a Negro school, poorly equipped and poorly staffed. Her father sent her to school in Albany for two or three years. In 1850 he hired a white governess for her, Phebe Thayer, a Quaker. Fredrika Bremer admired the force of character which enabled Miss Thayer to stand up under the odium "she must have to bear from prejudiced white people."[45] In 1854–55 Rosetta attended the Preparatory Department of Oberlin College.[46] Finally, in 1857, Douglass succeeded in having the Rochester public schools opened to colored children.

---

[41] M. B. Bishop to C. H. Wiltsie, Feb. 25, 1929. *MS.* in Roch. Pub. Lib.

[42] Daniel A. Payne, *Recollections of Seventy Years* (Nashville, 1888), 143.

[43] Douglass to E. Pease, Nov. 8, 1849. *A. S. Let.*, XVIII.

[44] For an account of the episode see Douglass' letter to H. G. Warner in *Liberator*, Oct. 6, 1848.

[45] Bremer, *op. cit.*, I, 586.

[46] Letter from Edith Stanley, Registrar of Oberlin College, to author, Sept. 12, 1944.

Occasionally an expression of Douglass' solicitude over an illness in the family appeared in the columns of his weekly. The lack of editorials in one of the issues of the *North Star*, confided Douglass to his public, was due to the sickness of one of his children. The editor had been constantly at the bedside of his youngest son, who was then slowly recovering from "typhus fever of a very malignant type." [47]

Douglass was profoundly affected by the death of his youngest daughter, "the light and life of my house." He had left Rochester hurriedly in October 1859, fearing arrest as an accessory in the John Brown raid. Annie grieved at his absence; perhaps she was frightened by the talk of her father's punishment if he were seized and found guilty of complicity in Brown's schemes. The ten-year-old girl finally lost the power to speak or to hear; [48] she died in March 1860. The news at once brought Douglass home from England. [49]

Douglass' love for his children outran his influence on them. None of them had his ambition or his devotion to a cause. Possibly his protracted absences and his multiple interests gave him insufficient time to mould his children and transfer his enthusiasms to them. "They are more like their mother as I remember them," remarked one observer. [50] But Anna's influence seemed greater simply because his was so limited. True, Anna was strict and God-fearing — "our custom was to read a chapter in the Bible around the table, each reading a verse until the chapter was completed" [51] — but the children inevitably

---

[47] *North Star*, Mar. 15, 1849.
[48] Rosetta Douglass to Smith, Apr. 11, 1860. *Smith MSS*.
[49] Undated letter from Anna Richardson to Still (probable date of letter July 2, 1860). William Still, *Underground Railroad* (Phila., 1872), 597. See also *Douglass' Monthly*, Dec. 1860.
[50] Un-named writer in May, *Frederick Douglass*, 225.
[51] R. D. Sprague, *loc. cit.*, 98.

developed a patronizing air toward her, an attitude regrettable in its failure to perceive her rugged worth, but a reaction typical of surface-judging youth toward an adult of unprepossessing appearance and no book learning.

Douglass' failure to mould his children did not result from a lack of interest in their welfare. During the Civil War he used his influence to secure furloughs and honorable discharges for his sons. In April 1865, he asked Sumner to aid his son Lewis in securing a clerkship in the newly created Freedmen's Bureau.[52] Charles, who wrote a beautiful hand, was placed in the Bureau. Douglass obtained a post-office job for Rosetta's ne'er-do-well husband, Nathan Sprague, a former fugitive slave. In 1871 Douglass purchased the *New National Era* for $8,000 and gave it to Lewis and Frederick, junior.[53] The paper's lack of support from Negroes drew a sharp criticism from Douglass. The Negro people were "not conscious of an associated existence or a common cause." Negroes seemed to have confidence in white people alone. Colored women powdered their noses and worked on their hair "to make themselves more acceptable or less objectionable to the white race." [54]

Douglass' family interests extended to two of his mother's children. At Baltimore in February 1862, he met Eliza, one of his half-sisters. He had not seen her in thirty years. She had purchased her freedom by her own labor, and had become the mother of nine children.[55] Five years later, in a meeting, "altogether too affecting for words to describe," Douglass greeted his long-lost half-brother Perry who had been a slave for fifty-six years.[56] For three months Douglass' residence housed Perry and his family of six.

---

[52] Douglass to Sumner, Apr. 29, 1865. *Letterbooks.*
[53] Douglass to Smith, Sept. 2, 1871. *Smith MSS.*
[54] *Ibid.*, Sept. 26, 1873.
[55] Douglass to editor of *Independent. Independent,* Mar. 2, 1865.
[56] Douglass to editor of *Independent, Ibid.*, July 25, 1867.

They moved out when the carpenters completed the construction of "a snug little cottage" built on Douglass' grounds and at his expense.[57] Douglass never saw his other half-sisters else his generosity would have embraced them.

Douglass was in a position to do something for the unfortunate. By 1850 he had passed out of the ranks of the poor. When he returned from the British Isles he found that Anna had started a bank account. Her thrift laid the base for his prosperity. His friends in England had provided him with the means to begin a career in journalism. He settled in Rochester at the time when Gerrit Smith was giving away a portion of his vast land holdings to 3,000 Negroes in the state. Late in 1847, when Douglass came to Rochester, Smith sent him and Nell deeds to forty acres apiece. The plot, according to its donor, was smooth and arable; he wished, however, that it "was in a less rigorous clime." [58]

In the early days of the *North Star* Douglass had been forced to mortgage his house. The holder of the mortgage, Eliza Griffiths, turned it over to her sister. After its payment, sometime prior to 1853, Douglass' savings account showed a steady increase. In May 1851, he was able to inform Smith that his house would be paid for in a few months.[59] In 1855 he published a second autobiography, *My Bondage and My Freedom*. This book, which included an account of his trip abroad, was nearly four times as long as the *Narrative*. Like the latter, it sold well and served as an excellent publicity promoter for its author.

A portion of Douglass' income came from public addresses. During the 'fifties Douglass charged $25 for a lecture.[60] His fame as an orator brought him twenty times

---

[57] Douglass to editor of *Independent, Ibid.*, Sept. 12, 1867.

[58] *North Star*, Jan. 8, 1848.

[59] Douglass to Smith, May 1, 1851. *Smith MSS.*

[60] Douglass to Robert Kinnicut, Oct. 9, 1859. *MS.* in Schomburg Collection.

as many speaking engagements as he could accept.[61] Five weeks in New England in the early months of 1856 netted him $500.[62] Later in that year he wrote that he was "well off." He had a good house, some money in the bank, and his autobiography had found a purchasing public.[63] His second trip to the British Isles — a six months' sojourn early in 1860 — brought him $2,500.[64] After the Civil War his lecture fee shot up to $100. Against these gains there was only one important financial loss; in 1872, his home in Rochester burned to the ground. The insurance on the property — $2,500 on the house and $500 on the furniture — did not cover its actual value. Douglass estimated his net loss at between five and six thousand dollars.

Douglass' generosity to his children did not over-strain his means, and as a father he had inescapable obligations. Nevertheless, he must have been depressed by the attitude of his offspring. As they grew older his children thought of him as the source from which all material blessings flowed. Letters from Rosetta and Charles were invariably of a complaining or a begging nature. After Annie's death he became a lonely man. His wife's stodginess and his children's natural preoccupation with their own affairs acted as a bottleneck to his emotional life. In the late eighteen-sixties, almost as evident as the whitening of his hair was the minor key of melancholy in his manner.

---

[61] *Frederick Douglass' Paper*, Jan. 12, 1855.
[62] Douglass to Smith, Feb. 20, 1856. *Smith MSS.*
[63] *Ibid.*, May 23, 1856.
[64] May to Garrison, June 17, 1860. *A. S. Let.*, XXX.

CHAPTER VII

Varied Activities of a Reformer

I know of no right of race superior to the rights of humanity.

DOUGLASS

In common with other agitators to whom reform was a vocation, Douglass was interested in sundry movements designed to promote human betterment. It might seem that the professional reformer, by the multiplicity of his enthusiasms, would spread himself thin. But during the 'forties and the 'fifties the reform movements complemented one another. Douglass' interests were varied but not diverse. Furthermore, on the reform platform the effectiveness of one's plea had little relationship to its factual content or the mastery of a specific body of knowledge. Technique was the touchstone of success. If a speaker were blessed with a booming voice, had mastered the vocabulary of denunciation, and had picked up a few of the gestures of melodrama, he could command applause regardless of which of the nostrums he was prescribing.

As a concomitant of his efforts to destroy the slave system, Douglass took an interest in the operations of the underground railroad. Himself a runaway, he was strongly in sympathy with those who made the dash for freedom. Douglass was in attendance at the New England Anti-Slavery Convention in 1849, in company with Henry Box Brown and William and Ellen Craft. The escape of these fugitives had been much more dramatic than that of Douglass. At the convention Brown related how he had been shipped in a box from Richmond to Philadelphia.

He also sang the anthem with which he had celebrated his first minute of freedom.[1] Douglass then introduced the Crafts. The story they told was romantic. Ellen, a lady's maid, had disguised herself as an invalid young man. Her husband, a slave cabinetmaker who had earned $220 a year by hiring himself out during his spare time, acted the part of a servant to the "invalid." These roles were assumed with complete success during the four-and-one-half-day trip from Georgia.

Brown, the Crafts, and other runaways had a fair chance of getting beyond the reach of their pursuers prior to the middle of the century. The Fugitive Slave Law of 1793 was stringent in phraseology, but weak in implementation. The lack of national enforcement machinery and the refusal of many states to permit their officers to assist in recovering runaways, tended to make the law a dead letter. The South demanded additional legislation. "When one thousand dollars founded in ebony took to its heels and ran away, the slavemasters felt in their pockets a vacuum which like nature they abhorred." In 1850 Congress passed a fugitive slave law with teeth. The clergy in the South were alleged to have declared this law to have been a "second edition of the apostle Paul's letter to Philemon," but because it placed the burden of proof on the defendant (the Negro charged with being a runaway) and because it provided drastic punishment for those who hindered its operation, the law aroused extreme hostility north of the Mason-Dixon line. Even the mild-mannered were in arms. Ralph Waldo Emerson, "the sage of Concord," abandoned his philosophic detachment, and loosed a volley of attacks against the law.

Naturally, Negroes were aroused. Douglass was legally free, but to him and to many others with pigmented skins the first six months after "the whirlwind and the pestilence

---

[1] *Bugle*, June 15, 1849.

set in" were six of the gloomiest months of their existence. Many Negroes — perhaps a total of nine thousand — who had been living in fancied security hastened across the border to Canada. Militant Negroes breathed fire. At a meeting at the Syracuse city hall, with the mayor presiding, Jermain Loguen vowed that, "I don't respect this law — I don't fear it — I won't obey it"![2] Samuel R. Ward warned that "if anyone came to take him he had better perform two acts for the benefit of himself and his family. He should first make his will and then make his peace with his Maker."[3]

While Congress was voting the measure into law, Douglass was at Corinthian Hall in Rochester "hurling out anathema" against it.[4] A few weeks later, on October 14, he attended a monster indignation meeting at Faneuil Hall. On taking the chair Charles Francis Adams expressed the hope " that neither excess nor violence would be resorted to."[5] Ward was present as were the Crafts who were shortly to leave for England. Douglass and Phillips delivered the main addresses. The colored people of Boston, said Douglass, had resolved to suffer death rather than return to bondage. "We must be prepared should the law be put in operation to see the streets of Boston running with blood." In his hour-long speech, which a local reporter termed "a very eloquent affair," Douglass asserted that the annals of no nation exhibited greater acts of individual heroism and courage than were to be found in the history of fugitives.[6] The resolutions adopted declared the law unconstitutional and unchristian.[7] "No

---

[2] Standard, Oct. 7, 1850. *The Rev. J. W. Loguen as a Slave and as a Freeman* (Syracuse, 1859), 393.

[3] *Standard*, Oct. 7, 1850.

[4] Jane Marsh Parker, *Rochester* (Rochester, 1884), 257.

[5] New Orleans *Daily Delta*, Oct. 24, 1850.

[6] Boston *Herald*, Oct. 15, 1850.

[7] Boston *Atlas*, Oct. 15, 1850.

man," according to the official opinion of the meeting, "who once sets his foot on the sacred soil of Massachusetts shall be carried away from here a slave." [8] The following week Douglass was the chief speaker at a Worcester meeting that passed similar resolutions. [9]

The Fugitive Slave Law gave Douglass additional ammunition to hurl against the slave power. His vocabulary, like that of Loguen and Ward, was unbridled. "The only way to make the Fugitive Slave Law a dead letter is to make half a dozen or more dead kidnappers. . . . The man who takes the office of a bloodhound ought to be treated as a bloodhound," he announced to a Pittsburgh audience. [10] Douglass' journal informed the faithful that "The True Remedy for the Fugitive Slave Bill" was a "good revolver, a steady hand, and a determination to shoot down any man attempting to kidnap." [11] To an audience celebrating West India Emancipation, Douglass proclaimed that "Every fugitive who prefers to perish in a river made red by his own blood, to submission to the hell hounds who were hunting and shooting him, should be esteemed as a glorious martyr, worthy to be held in grateful memory by our people." [12]

Douglass, however, did not stop at verbal attack. To assist runaways to "get Canada under their feet" now became a high moral duty. That such a course involved running afoul of legal authorities simply added a stimulan'. To flout duly constituted authority in promoting the cause gave to the act an element of danger emotionally satisfying to the true reformer. Douglass was quite familiar with the methods of assisting fugitives. Four weeks before the passing of the law, Douglass was elected president of an

[8] *Bugle*, Oct. 22, 1850.
[9] Worcester *Spy*, Oct. 22, 1850.
[10] New York *Herald*, Aug. 12, 1852.
[11] *Frederick Douglass' Paper*, June 9, 1854.
[12] *Two Speeches by Frederick Douglass* (Rochester, 1857), 22.

abolitionist convention which met at Cazenovia, New York. Samuel J. May, Gerrit Smith and thirty fugitives were among the two thousand present. The assembly drew up an "Address of Fugitive Slaves to Brethren in the South," which described the advantages of the North.[13] The convention pledged itself to raise money to defray the expenses for the defense of William Chaplin who had been arrested in Maryland for assisting in the escape of two slaves belonging respectively to Robert Toombs and Alexander H. Stephens.[14] A week later Douglass and J. C. Hathaway, at a Syracuse meeting, raised $350 for Chaplin's legal aid.[15]

Douglass continually raised money to assist escaped slaves. The fees from many of his lectures went to funds earmarked for fugitive aid.[16] At anti-slavery conventions he passed the hat. At one of these gatherings, at Syracuse in March 1851, Douglass introduced five fugitives.[17] Though he had not participated in the stirring "Jerry rescue," he invariably took part in the annual celebrations, generally serving as vice-president of the organization sponsoring the observance.

Douglass' services as an agent of the underground railroad were important. Its close proximity to the border made Rochester one of the chief stations of the route which led to the Canadian towns of St. Catharine's and Toronto.[18] In Rochester many of the white abolitionists and the majority of the Negro inhabitants aided the runaways.[19]

---

[13] New York *Tribune*, Aug. 23, 1850.

[14] *Ibid.*

[15] Syracuse *Daily Standard*, Aug. 29, 1850.

[16] For one such occasion see Syracuse *Daily Standard*, Feb. 8, 1856.

[17] *Ibid.*, March 7, 1851.

[18] For a detailed description of the routes of the underground railroad in New York see Philip Gould Auchampaugh, "Politics and Slavery, 1850–1860," *History of the State of New York* (New York, 1934), VII, 65. For a map showing the routes see *ibid.*, 68.

[19] Nell to Garrison, Feb. 19, 1852. *Liberator*, Mar. 5, 1852.

Douglass was superintendent of the Rochester station; his house on Alexander Street was its headquarters. From his office on Buffalo Street a trap door led to a secret stairway.[20] One of Douglass' newspaper employees related that it was not unusual for him, as he came to work early in the morning, to find fugitives sitting on the steps.[21] These runaways had travelled all night; in the daytime their abolitionist friends hid them from prying eyes. Douglass knew where to take them — to a sail loft, to an out-of-the-way barn or to the quiet home of a trusted sympathizer. When darkness fell the fugitives were despatched to Oswego or Lewiston. Some stayed during the night and were put on the morning train. Douglass gave them food and lodging and paid their train fares.[22]

Douglass proved a circumspect official, and public opinion in Rochester was sympathetic to the fleeing slave. After the Jerry rescue — and in part because of it, according to Douglass [23] — slave-catchers gave western New York a wide berth. No United States marshal ever made a seizure in Rochester, nor was the city ever the scene of a disturbance resulting from an effort to apprehend a fugitive.

Douglass was happy in the work although, being a realist, he was discouraged when he thought of the infinitesimal percentage of the total slave population that was thus enabled to escape. Of the approximately 60,000 who ran away between 1830 and 1860, it is difficult to form an estimate of the number that Douglass personally aided. "Fugitives are constantly passing through here, giving no rest to their feet nor slumber to their eyelids," wrote a visitor to Rochester in 1852.[24] Douglass states that in

---

[20] Coles, *The Cradle of Freedom*, 136.

[21] McGuire, "Two Episodes of Anti-Slavery Days," *loc. cit.*, 219.

[22] Douglass to Anna Richardson, July 2, 1860. Still, *op. cit.*, 598.

[23] *Two Speeches by Frederick Douglass*, 22.

[24] Nell to Garrison, Feb. 19, 1852. *Liberator*, Mar. 5, 1852.

1854, over a two weeks' period, he aided over thirty on their way.[25] In June 1857, four "passed through our hands to Queen's dominions," ran an item in Douglass' paper.[26] Ten runaways found "food, shelter, counsel and comfort," under his roof during May 1860.[27] During the following month he had the satisfaction of speeding ten more to St. Catharine's where they were received by the Reverend Hiram Wilson.[28] "I well remember," wrote Wilson's son, "the large number of fugitive slaves who came to father's house with a letter from you." [29] By his own exertions Douglass assisted approximately eight runaways a month. He generally remained in Rochester about five months out of the year. Over a ten year period Douglas had a hand in speeding four hundred runaways out of the country.

Douglass' own efforts did not prevent him from acknowledging the superior work of Harriet Tubman in the underground railroad movement. This colorful character, herself an escaped slave, fearlessly carried her rescues to the cotton field and the cabin door. In a letter to "the Moses of her people," Douglass expressed his appreciation of her services: "Most that I have done — has been in public, and I have received much encouragement. . . . You on the other hand have labored in a private way. I have had the applause of the crowd while the most that you have done has been witnessed by a few trembling, scared, and footsore bondmen. The midnight sky and the silent stars have been the witnesses of your devotion to freedom and of your heroism." [30]

Douglass' reform interests extended from the plight of

[25] *Frederick Douglass' Paper*, May 19, 1854.
[26] *Ibid.*, June 19, 1857.
[27] *Douglass' Monthly*, June 1860.
[28] Still, *op. cit.*, 598.
[29] J. J. Wilson to Douglass, Aug. 8, 1888. *Douglass MSS.*
[30] Sarah H. Bradford, *Scenes in the Life of Harriet Tubman* (Auburn, N. Y., 1869), 233.

the slave seeking freedom to the welfare of the Negro already living as a freeman. As the foremost Negro in public life after his return from the British Isles, Douglass inevitably became one of the chief figures in the colored convention movement. This movement was an expression of protest against the under-privileged status of the Negro in American life. By 1830 Negro leaders had come to the conclusion that concerted action was necessary to improve the status of the Negro people and make clear their attitudes on pertinent issues. The first of the resulting conventions was held in 1830 at Philadelphia, with Richard Allen, organizer and first bishop of the African Methodist Church, as president. The question of emigration was the main topic before the forty delegates. The convention of the following year owed its origin largely to Arthur Tappan's interest in the education of Negro youth. A New York merchant with a broad humanitarian outlook, Tappan wished to establish an industrial school for colored boys. To gain the support of Negro leaders and to give the proposal wide publicity, Tappan urged prominent Negroes to attend a meeting at Philadelphia in June 1831. The convention indorsed Tappan's proposal and continued in session for an address by Garrison, then on the threshold of his career. These two conventions marked the beginning of organized activity among Negro leaders.

Held annually for seven years, the conventions assembled sporadically after 1837. In 1843 the Negroes met in Buffalo. Douglass was in attendance for the first time. With Amos Gerry Beman, a self-made New Haven clergyman, in the president's chair the delegates commended the Liberty party and drafted the customary series of resolutions. Henry Highland Garnet stirred the assembly with a militant speech urging the slaves to rise in arms against their masters. Douglass, then under the influence of the Garrisonian principles of moral suasion and non-violent resistance, objected to Garnet's address and disapproved of the indorsement of the Liberty party. Remond and Brown concurred with Douglass' point of view. Not sharing Douglass' belief in the ineffectiveness of political action, however, the majority of the delegates went on record as favoring the circulation of petitions to Congress expressing hostility to slavery in the territories and to the annexation of Texas.[31]

The next convention was held four years later at Troy, New York. The presiding officer was a familiar convention figure, Nathan Johnson of New Bedford, who ten years previously had assisted Douglass in making the adjustment from slavery to freedom. Garnet, Pennington and J. McCune Smith were among the sixty-seven delegates from nine states. Charles B. Ray, a Congregationalist pastor and former editor of the *Colored American*, proposed a resolution thanking Gerrit Smith "for donating 140,000 acres of land to 3,000 Negroes." [32] After considering the expediency of establishing a Negro college, the delegates deliberated as to the most effective way to strike at the slave system. Douglass, prominent in all the debates, especially urged his colored fellows to come out of the proslavery churches — "his right arm should wither before he would worship at their blood-stained altars." [33]

At Cleveland the following year Douglass was chosen president. In its personnel this convention represented an unusually wide cross-section of Negro occupational interests. The membership of more than sixty comprised "printers, carpenters, blacksmiths, shoemakers, engineers, dentists, gunsmiths, editors, tailors, merchants, wheelwrights, painters, farmers, physicians, plasterers, masons, clergymen, barbers, hairdressers, coopers, livery stable keepers, bath-house keepers and grocers." Far in advance of their day, the delegates affirmed their belief in the equal-

---

[31] *Herald of Freedom*, Sept. 1, 1843.
[32] *Sketch of the Life of Rev. Charles B. Ray* (New York, 1887), 20.
[33] *North Star*, Dec. 3, 1847.

ity of the sexes, and "Hereby invite females hereafter to take part in our deliberations." [34] As at previous gatherings, the body drafted a series of varied resolutions; they condemned slavery, indorsed the Free Soil party, urged support of the *North Star*, reprobated the church, recommended "a change in the conduct of colored barbers who refused to treat colored men on a basis of equality with whites," and appointed committees in various states to organize vigilant groups, "so as to enable them to measure arms with assailants without and invaders within." [35]

The last-mentioned resolution aimed in part at overcoming the most serious weakness of the convention movement. It lacked continuity. The national meetings were called at irregular intervals by sundry persons acting largely on their own initiative. After adjournment the delegates dispersed indefinitely, thereby failing to implement the consensus of opinion by the necessary follow-up work.

To give the movement a permanent organizational structure, Douglass in August 1849, proposed the formation of a national league. The *North Star* carried a tentative outline of a constitution, "The Union of the Oppressed for the Sake of Freedom." [36] The league proposed to fight slavery, secure intra-racial cooperation by surmounting sectional and political differences, and improve the condition of the Negro people.

For six weeks the columns of Douglass' paper described the plan of organization and carried the call for a convention, which the sponsor proposed to hold in Philadelphia late in September. Despite the prominence of Douglass' name, the proposal aroused almost no response. It was doomed by the failure of Negro press and Negro leaders to publicize it. The organization meeting at Philadelphia

---

[34] *Bugle*, Oct. 13, 1848.
[35] *North Star*, Sept. 19, 1848.
[36] *Ibid.*, Aug. 10, 1849.

was so poorly attended that Douglass immediately abandoned the plan, not, however, without severely criticizing the lack of public spirit on the part of representative Negroes in public life.[37]

Following the Cleveland convention of 1848, the movement was dormant for five years. Then came the Rochester Colored National Convention, the most important of all the gatherings from the standpoint of ability of membership and work accomplished. One hundred and forty delegates from eight states answered the call for "the development of means for the amelioration of the condition of the colored people." [38] The scholarly clergyman, J. W. C. Pennington, presided. Douglass was one of the vice-presidents, and chairman of the important "Committee on Declaration of Sentiments." The statement drawn up by this committee, and read by Douglass, left no doubt as to what the Negro wanted: "We ask that in our native land we shall not be treated as strangers." The committee's resolutions expressed appreciation of the anti-slavery labors of Garrison, alluded to *Uncle Tom's Cabin* as a work "plainly marked by the finger of God," and advocated the establishment of a National Council. "No nobler paper," wrote a *Tribune* reporter, "was ever put forth by any body of men." [39]

One of the chief controversial issues before the delegates was the question of Negro emigration. A perennial topic, the colonization debate had been before the free Negro for fifty years. The formation of the American Colonization Society in 1816 had given impetus to the movement to expatriate the black man. Although the Society was sup-

---

[37] *North Star*, Oct. 26, 1849.

[38] For accounts of this convention see New York *Tribune*, July 9, 1853; *Frederick Douglass' Paper* July 22, 1853; *Proceedings of the Colored National Convention held in Rochester, July 6th, 7th and 8th.* Rochester, 1853.

[39] *Tribune*, July 9, 1853.

ported by influential groups and carried many nationally prominent names on its membership rolls, the free Negro class had disliked the scheme from its inception.[40] By 1830 this hostility to colonization was shared by most of the abolitionists, who had arrived at the belief that its promoters wished to get rid of the free Negro in order to make slavery secure.

Douglass was a vigorous critic of colonization. In common with other Negroes born in the United States, he had completely assimilated the pattern of American culture. He had nothing in common with the native African except skin color. To him colonization was the "twin sister of slavery." [41] He held that the United States was the native land of the American Negro. He had a right to the soil of this country; "his attachment to the place of his birth is stronger than iron." [42] American in his emphasis on bustle and activity, Douglass disliked Africa because "the human race becomes indolent in a warm climate." [43] A tropical environment was not suited to the development of power and enterprise, which "give honor to a nation in this age." [44]

At the Rochester convention Pennington, in a long

---

[40] Garrison devoted the second half of his book, *Thoughts on African Colonization* (Boston, 1832), to a documented description of the hostile attitude of the Northern free Negro toward colonization during the period 1817–31. The first half of the book was a cogent statement of the argument against emigration. See also William Watkins, "Evils of Colonization," *Autographs*, II, 198–200. The pros and cons of the case were set forth in *Committee on the Call for a National Emigration Convention*, Detroit, 1854. The case for colonization may be found throughout the forty-six volumes of the official organ of the Society, *The African Repository*, Washington, 1826–1860. See especially I, 1–5 (1826).

[41] *African Repository*, XXVI, 292 (1850).

[42] *The Claims of the Negro Ethnologically Considered* (Rochester, 1854), 35.

[43] *Douglass' Paper*, May 5, 1854.

[44] *Ibid.*

address, reported unfavorably on colonization. "We intend," ran one of his striking sentences, "to plant our trees on American soil and repose in the shade thereof." [45] In support of this viewpoint, Douglass gave a lengthy discourse which made his own position clear but added little to the literature of the controversy. The convention registered an official disapproval of colonization, although the vote was by no means unanimous.

The convention tackled another controversial issue — the proposed manual labor college for colored youth. This idea had first been introduced and approved in 1831. The failure to put it into operation, in view of Arthur Tappan's willingness to underwrite the project, resulted from the hostility of the citizens of New Haven, the proposed site of the school. Thereafter, Negroes had been divided in their thinking on the issue.

At the Troy convention of 1847 Douglass had opposed a purely Negro college. But by 1850 his attitude had undergone a change. In that year an "American League of Colored Laborers" had been formed. Douglass was a vice-president and a member of the executive committee which included Bibb, Nell, Downing, Ray, Smith and Remond. At the organizational meeting the adopted resolutions urged the colored man to go into business for himself, proposed an industrial fair at which colored mechanics, artisans and farmers exhibit their wares, recommended a wide but thorough training of youth in agriculture, the mechanic arts and commerce, and praised "skillful, honorable, profitable labor" as "productive of wealth and indispensable to the development and perfection of body and mind." [46]

Perhaps Douglass' conversion to the belief in a manual labor college as the way out stemmed from a closer observation of the plight of the unskilled Negro laborer. Doubt-

[45] *Proceedings*, 18.
[46] *Bugle*, July 17, 1850.

less, too, like Charles L. Reason, he noted that although the abolitionists liked to speak of the Negro as a man and a brother, they did not open any employment opportunities for the Negro even when, as in the case of the Tappan brothers, they were influential in the business world.[47] The idea of a manual labor school had been on Douglass' mind when, on March 8, 1853, Harriet Beecher Stowe had informed him of her desire to do something for the Negro. Douglass had suggested the establishment of an industrial college, and now, at the Rochester gathering, he was anxious that the delegates approve the plan.

Those who were hostile to the proposal, Remond and George T. Downing among them, believed that the venture would be too costly — the promoters would need at least $30,000 to put the scheme into operation. The mass of colored people would not be interested in the college and the young men would shun it. The principle was faulty, ran the indictment; a policy of segregation tended to perpetuate prejudice against color. These critics were of the opinion that the apprentice system was preferable to an industrial school.

Douglass, supported by J. McCune Smith and Pennington, held the opposite viewpoint. Few Negro young men could become apprentices, they answered, because there were few Negro craftsmen, and white craftsmen were loath to take Negroes in service. An industrial college, argued its proponents, would arouse young men to the importance of the trades and thereby aid in the promotion of racial self-reliance.[48] The presence of an "industrious, enterprising, upright, thrifty and intelligent free black population would be a killing refutation of slavery." The majority concurred with Douglass' point of view.

The major issues aired, the delegates appointed four permanent committees. Douglass was designated chairman

---

[47] Reason, "The Colored People's Industrial College," *Autographs*, II, 13.   [48] *Proceedings*, 22.

of the committee on the manual labor college. Another committee, the committee on protective union, was charged with safe-guarding the civil liberties of the Negro. A business relations committee was empowered to act as an employment agency, seeking also to broaden the field of job opportunities for colored laborers. A committee on publications was expected to "collect all facts, statistics . . . laws and historical records and biographies of the colored people and all books by colored authors." It was this committee's further duty to challenge and answer "any assaults worthy of note, made upon the character or condition of the colored people." [49]

Prior to adjournment the convention adopted a plan for permanent organization in the form of a National Council of twenty-one members composed of representatives from the state societies. The plan provided for an extension of influence down into the grassroots; the state branches were authorized to supervise the activities of community groups whose members would be required to pay dues of one cent a week.

As the convention adjourned, the delegates were strong in the belief that their deliberations would result in tangible gains. There was seeming justification for their hopes. The speakers had carefully prepared their papers, and the general level of discussion had been high — at the meetings "not a word of nonsense was talked." [50] Douglass wrote Gerrit Smith that the convention had improved "the current of feeling toward colored people in Rochester." [51]

The expectations of the delegates, however, were vain. The work of the convention as of its predecessors, was largely on paper — the concrete results were meagre. The

---

[49] John W. Cromwell, *The Negro in American History* (Washington, 1914), 41.

[50] *Tribune*, July 9, 1853.

[51] Douglass to Smith, July 15, 1853. *Smith MSS.*

first meeting of the National Council, scheduled for January 1854, in New York, failed to show a quorum. Six months later the second and last meeting of the Council was held at Cleveland. Although Douglass was one of New York's two delegates, he failed to appear. A bare quorum was present, and when a single member wished "to frustrate business" he simply absented himself. Despite the small size of the gathering — it numbered eleven — the sessions "stood constantly in need of a sergeant-at-arms." A convention called for Philadelphia in 1855 was very sparsely attended. By the middle of the 'fifties the Negro convention movement had run its course.

The failure to follow up the proposals of the conventions was a serious drawback. But the colored convention movement suffered from other fatal weaknesses. Some Negroes refused to attend on the ground that exclusively colored meetings and programs looked like a tacit acceptance of segregation. To these Negroes the paramount question was, in Nell's words, "that of abandoning, as soon as possible, all separate action and becoming part and parcel of the general community." [52] Furthermore, among Negro leaders there were factional disputes and personal animosities. Douglass' quarrel with the Negro Garrisonians was an effective deterrent to their support of any movement with which he was prominently identified. Finally, the colored convention movement lacked white support. White reformers and philanthropists who were interested in the Negro invariably threw their support to abolitionist societies rather than Negro improvement associations.

The colored convention movement, however, was not without significance. From the meetings the participants gained knowledge of the rules of parliamentary procedure, acquired facility in forms of public address, and practiced the techniques of protest and petition. The conventions

[52] William C. Nell, *The Colored Patriots of the American Revolution* (Boston, 1855), 359.

apprised the country of the stand of the majority of Negroes on the question of colonization. The few colored leaders who were pro-emigration, such as Delany and Bibb, found it increasingly difficult to get a hearing. Their efforts to hold a colonization meeting in 1854 were hampered by a jeering crowd which intimidated the handful of delegates. Nevertheless, this convention commissioned Delany to go to Africa, J. M. Whitfield to South America, and James T. Holly to Haiti, to negotiate with the proper authorities to receive Negro emigrants.

When these missions proved fruitless, it was obvious that colonization was a dying venture. But in 1861 James Redpath, a former associate of John Brown, obstinately sought to infuse new spirit into the movement. He succeeded in convincing the Haitian government that colonization would profit their country. Thereupon Redpath assumed the position of general agent of the Haitian Bureau of Emigration. Two months after the outbreak of the Civil War, Redpath offered Douglass a position as agent. Redpath knew of Douglass' expressed hostility to colonization, but he believed that Douglass "can easily be bought." [53] Redpath's assumption was not based on a knowledge of Douglass' character. Failing to enlist a single prominent Negro in his scheme, Redpath's efforts went little beyond the exchange-of-letters stage.

As unproductive as the colonization movement was the proposal to establish a manual labor school. The failure of the movement for the mechanic arts college was more striking in view of its initial advantages: it had the blessings of the colored conventions, and it was close to Douglass' heart. Its failure was not due to Douglass' lack of zeal. As chairman of the Rochester convention committee on the manual labor school, he drew up an elaborate plan.

---

[53] *Letters and Reports of James Redpath, General Agent of Emigration to Hayti, to M. Plesance, Secretary of State of Exterior Relations of the Republic of Hayti,* 91 (Library of Congress).

The proposed school was to be located within 100 miles of Erie, Pennsylvania; the exact site would be selected as soon as $3,000 had been raised; the workshop would be installed as soon as $10,000 had been raised, and the school would open when $15,000 was in the hands of the Board of Trustees.[54] Its official name would be "American Industrial School." Students were to be admitted without reference to sex, race or complexion. The student's time was to be divided evenly between the classroom and the shop or field: half of his time would be spent in a branch of "literature," the other portion would be spent in handicraft or farming. Handicraft articles would be sold for cash.[55]

Douglass' hopes for the establishment of the school were based largely on Harriet Beecher Stowe's expressed interest in the project. Mrs. Stowe's acquaintanceship with Douglass dated back to his association with Garrison. Later, while *Uncle Tom's Cabin* was revolving in her mind, Mrs. Stowe had asked Douglass to put her in touch with any one "in the circle of your acquaintance" who could give her local color material concerning life on a cotton plantation.[56] Two years later, in response to an invitation, Douglass visited Mrs. Stowe at her Andover, Massachusetts home. An admirer of Douglass,[57] and impressed by his enthusiasm for the manual labor college, she requested him to put his views in writing so that she might show the letter to interested persons abroad.[58]

While in England Mrs. Stowe turned cool toward the project. She resented the charges that she was soliciting money for her own private use. Furthermore, upon in-

---

[54] *Frederick Douglass' Paper*, Mar. 24, 1854.

[55] *Ibid.*

[56] Stowe to Douglass, July 9, 1851. Annie Fields, ed., *Life and Letters of Harriet Beecher Stowe* (Boston, 1897), 133.

[57] Charles E. Stowe to Douglass, Sept. 18, 1888. *Douglass MSS.*

[58] For the lengthy letter Douglass wrote see his *Life and Times*, 316–321.

quiry, she concluded that the school could not succeed because all the manual labor colleges she had heard of had been failures. She doubted, too, whether "the coloured population has advanced sufficiently to carry it through." Thus cold-watered, Mrs. Stowe's money-raising efforts realized the meagre sum of $535. This she turned over to Douglass for his personal use because "as a coloured man he has peculiar disabilities, and we thought it no more than right that he should have peculiar encouragements."

Even more pathetic were the results of Douglass' own efforts to raise money for the school. He was appointed to travel and solicit funds, but by June 1855, two years after the Rochester convention, he had not collected a single dollar for the project. Resigned to failure, Douglass quietly abandoned the scheme. But he never abandoned his emphasis on the necessity for training the hand as well as developing the mind. His advocacy of manual training stamps Douglass as an educational theorist in advance of his day.

Douglass was also a pioneer in another movement — the woman's rights agitation. His interest in this reform was inevitable. The beginnings of the struggle for equal rights for women was closely related to the abolitionist agitation. Negro leaders, in their effort to secure allies in the fight against racial discrimination, made common cause with the militant handful of aroused women who sought for their sex the status of complete equality in marriage, equal rights in property and wages, the right to make contracts, to sue and be sued, to testify in court and, above all, to vote.

During his years in Massachusetts Douglass became accustomed to seeing women participate actively in the anti-slavery crusade. Favorable to the employment of women on the abolitionist platform, the Garrisonians, it will be remembered, had split with the New York abolitionists over that issue. Douglass observed Abby Kelley speaking at abolitionist meetings, and he attended anti-slavery bazaars arranged by the Boston women under the direction of Maria Weston Chapman. He knew how ably Lydia Maria Child edited the *Standard*. He knew of the Grimké sisters who had freed their slaves in South Carolina and had come north to speak against human bondage.

On his lecture tours Douglass had often been hospitably received by high-minded women anxious to further the cause. In England he had met many intelligent women of broad social interests. With his respect for mental ability and his zeal for social action, Douglass' admiration of these women reformers dwarfed his esteem for the consciously unsophisticated Victorian stereotype of the genteel lady, insulated from the world. As soon as he established himself at Rochester Douglass identified himself with the budding movement. "Right is of no sex," ran the opening phrase of the first issue of the *North Star*.

A year later the women were ready to launch their crusade. This first convention for equal rights was held in July 1848, at Seneca Falls, New York. The women who issued the call for this historic gathering were Elizabeth Cady Stanton, wife of an outstanding abolitionist and disciple of Mary Wollstonecraft, Lucretia Mott, self-possessed Quaker reformer, and two sister Quakers, Mary McClintock and Martha C. Wright. Upon convening, the chief discussions centered around the adoption of a "Declaration of Sentiments," and a series of resolutions. The first document was a list of eighteen disabilities allegedly inflicted on women solely because of the "defect of sex." "The history of mankind is a history of repeated injuries and usurpations on the part of man toward woman, having in direct object the establishment of an absolute tyranny over her," ran the preamble.[59]

In substance the eleven resolutions declared that woman

[59] Elizabeth Cady Stanton, Susan B. Anthony, Mathilda Joslyn Gage, eds., *History of Woman Suffrage* (New York, 1881), I, 70–71.

was man's equal and that she should therefore participate without discrimination in the fields of education, industry and public affairs. The most controversial resolution was the one which declared that women should have the right to vote. Many of the feminist leaders feared that such a revolutionary proposal would tend to make the whole movement appear ridiculous. Determined to press the suffrage resolution, Mrs. Stanton sought aid from Douglass.

Her sense of selection was unerring. Of the thirty-seven men who ran the risk of being branded "Aunt Nancy Men," and similar epithets, Douglass alone was prominent in the deliberations. He was the only man to support the suffrage resolution. Mrs. Stanton's motion, seconded by Douglass, asserted that "it is the duty of the women of this country to secure to themselves the sacred right of the elective franchise." In an address that changed many wavering minds, Douglass pointed out that political equality was vital to the women's cause. The resolution passed by a small majority. The *North Star* commented favorably on the convention. The proceedings "were characterized by marked ability and dignity." As editor, Douglass bade the movement his humble Godspeed.[60]

The success of the meeting led its sponsors to continue the sessions in Rochester. Two weeks after the Seneca Falls convention, the women and their adherents assembled in the Unitarian church. Mrs. Stanton and Mrs. Mott requested the delegates to choose Douglass as president. The Rochester women, with a better sense of fitness, insisted that Mrs. Abigail Bush, a local reformer, hold that office. Douglass' supporters yielded.

The well-attended meetings varied little in procedure or program from those at Seneca Falls. The women restated their grievances and proposed resolutions. Many men who counted themselves advanced thinkers were

---

[60] *North Star*, July 28, 1848.

skeptical about the resolution calling for the ballot. Again Douglass entered the lists. "In a long, argumentative and eloquent plea," [61] he attempted to quiet all misgivings. The proposal was adopted, and as a follow-up measure the convention resolved to petition the state legislature to grant them the elective franchise and to continue to petition year after year until they obtained it. Douglass' weekly ran a complete report of the proceedings. The editor reiterated "that the only true basis of right was the capacity of the individuals." [62]

Not to be outdone by their New York sisters, a group of Ohio women met at Salem in the spring of 1850 for the purpose of preparing a statement to the convention that had been elected to revise the state constitution. The women enumerated their disabilities and urged members of their sex to slough off the apathy that chained them to tradition. Douglass was present. He was the house guest of the abolitionist Daniel Howell Hise, who wrote in his diary that "The Woman's Convention was a perfect jam all Enthusiasm." [63]

The Salem meetings were followed six months later by the first national woman's right convention. Paulina Wright Davis, a zealous advocate of equal rights, was the chief promoter of this convention which aimed at attracting a much wider geographic representation than the pioneer gathering at Seneca Falls. The convention was scheduled late in October at Worcester, Massachusetts. Douglass, who was in the state denouncing the Fugitive Slave Law, arranged his itinerary so as to be in Worcester during convention time.[64] He was among the more than 250 representatives from nine states who responded to the

[61] Stanton, Anthony and Gage, *History of Woman Suffrage*, I, 86.

[62] *North Star*, Aug. 11, 1848.

[63] Lewis Atherton, "Daniel Howell Hise," *Mississippi Historical Review*, XXVI, 355 (Dec. 1939).

[64] Worcester *Spy*, Oct. 22, 1850.

call to consider "the question of Woman's Rights, Duties and Relations." [65] (The Boston *Herald* peevishly observed that "Every woman ought to know her rights and duties without going to Worcester. As for the relations let them take care of themselves." [66])

As usual, Douglass made one of the major addresses. At the close of the afternoon session he spoke "with great force and eloquence, urging woman to take her rights as far as she can get them." [67]

The convention voted to petition the legislatures of eight states to grant the elective franchise to women. A series of resolutions specified the substance of things hoped for: women ought to enjoy political rights, property laws discriminating against women should be abolished, and all governmental and professional positions should be open to women. These resolutions were to have wide circulation. Their publication in the *Westminster Review* was to mark the beginning of the organized woman's suffrage movement in England.

One of the resolutions expressed concern over the plight of the slave woman. This anti-slavery touch was more than a reflection of the presence of Garrison, Douglass, Phillips and Sojourner Truth, the unschooled, but moving, Negro anti-slavery lecturer. The motto of the convention, "Equality before the law without distinction of sex or color," was evidence that the woman's righters were interested in reform along a broad front. However, there was a practical aspect to their interest in the slave. Rights for women was a much more unpopular movement than abolitionism. Many feminists championed the slave, therefore, in order to get before a reform-conscious abolitionist gathering and present a public airing of woman's grievances.

As their movement gained momentum, the women continued to find in Douglass a valuable co-worker; he attended

---

[65] Worcester *Spy*, Oct. 24, 1850.
[66] Sept. 14, 1850.   [67] Boston *Chronotype*, Oct. 26, 1850.

many of their state and national conventions which became of regular occurrence after the pioneer meetings of 1848 and 1850.[68] Susan B. Anthony notified one of her friends to look in *Frederick Douglass' Paper* for announcements of woman's rights gatherings.[69] Negro conventions in which Douglass took part invariably placed themselves on record as opposing discrimination on account of sex. With Douglass presiding, the convention of 1848 passed a resolution affirming belief in the equality of the sexes and inviting the women present to share in the deliberations.[70] Eight weeks later, at Philadelphia, Douglass was one of the organizers of a convention of colored people at which a similar invitation was extended to women, white as well as Negro. This broad stand impelled Lucretia Mott to attend the sessions.[71] One of the accredited delegates to the Rochester convention of 1853 was a Mrs. Jeffrey of Geneva.[72] The attendance of a woman delegate caused some eye-brow lifting, but "we had the good sense to make no fuss about it," wrote Douglass.[73]

In 1860 the Radical Abolitionist political party invited women to participate in the proceedings at Worcester. Douglass was on the executive committee of this convention which, by its call for woman representation, initiated the first effort ever made "to organize a political party upon a basis of absolute justice and perfect equality." [74]

Douglass and other woman's righters ignored storms of criticism and ridicule. Hostile newspapers commented

---

[68] For woman's rights conventions attended by Douglass in the early 'fifties see *The Lily* (Seneca Falls, N. Y.), May 1852; *The Una* (Providence, R. I.), June 1, 1853, June 18, 1854.

[69] Anthony to Gerrit Smith, Dec. 25, 1855. *Smith MSS.*

[70] *North Star*, Sept. 29, 1848.

[71] Mott to Stanton, Nov. 3, 1848. *Stanton MSS.*

[72] *Proceedings of the Colored National Convention*, 8.

[73] Douglass to Smith, July 15, 1853. *Smith MSS.*

[74] S. S. Foster to Smith, Aug. 25, 1860. *Ibid.* For a report of the meeting see *Douglass' Monthly*, Nov. 1860.

facetiously or insultingly on the conventions — it was easy to aim jibes at so obvious a target. Sometimes the critics expressed alarm: "We saw in broad daylight in a public hall in the city of New York, a gathering of unsexed women. . . . Is the world to be depopulated? Are there to be no more children? Or are we to adopt the French mode which is too well known to need explanation?" [75]

A description of woman's righters was generally written in a spirit of drollery to which was added a touch of malice. Reformers were characterized as "long-haired men, apostles of some inexplicable emotion or sensation; gaunt and hungry looking men, disciples of a bran bread and white turnip diatetic philosophy; advocates of liberty and small beer, professors of free love in the platonic sense . . . infidels, saints, negro-worshippers, sinners and short-haired women. . . . Long geared women in homespun, void of any trademark and worn to spite the tariff, women in Bloomer dress to show their ankles and their independence; women who hate their husbands and hateful women wanting husbands . . . men and women, altogether the most long-necked, grim-visaged, dyspeptic, Puritanical, nasaltwanged agglomeration of isms." [76]

The New York *Mirror* adopted a tone of indignation. "Woman's offices are those of wife, mother, daughter, sister, friend — Good God, can they not be content with these." [77] But the woman movement was too potent an ingredient in the social ferment of the times to be dissolved by cheap ridicule or spurious righteousness.

As a consequence of his interest in woman's rights, Douglass took part in the temperance agitation. His opposition to strong drink was in keeping with the experience of John H. W. Hawkins, a great temperance lecturer,

---

[75] New York *Herald*, Sept. 7, 1853.

[76] *Ibid.*, Nov. 21, 1866.

[77] Bertha Monica Stearns, "Reform Periodicals and Female Reformers," *American Historical Review*, XXXVII, 692 (July 1932).

who avowed that "he had never known a thorough anti-Slavery man who was not also a teetotaler." [78]   While abroad Douglass had been shocked at the prevalence of guzzling; he was therefore sympathetic to temperance reform although, as he once wrote, he could not "promise to say anything new or original about it." [79]

The ardent feminists with whom he associated arrayed themselves against the Demon Rum largely because of the distress of women who were married to drunkards. Negro leaders supported the movement — "every Negro convention elaborated upon the evils of intemperance" [80] — because drunkenness led to poverty and crime, conditions seized upon to support charges that the Negro was inferior. New Haven Negroes had been especially zealous in the temperance movement, forming a society in 1830 in the Temple Street Congregational church. In Connecticut a state society was organized in 1836 which six years later united with state societies in New York, New Jersey and Massachusetts to form the States' Delevan Union Temperance Society of Colored People. [81]

The national temperance movement, organized in 1808, had in its early existence adopted the educational techniques of moral suasion and the pledge of total abstinence. Soon the obviously close relationship between the use of strong drink and the incidence of vice, crime and inefficient labor, gave to the movement a host of supporters who were indifferent to the moral implications of over-indulgence. By 1850 the temperance leaders decided to go into politics and bring pressure on state legislatures. State laws regu-

---

[78] Lewis Tappan to John Scoble, May 15, 1848. Abel and Klingberg, *op. cit.*, 231.

[79] *North Star*, Mar. 10, 1848.

[80] Harriette R. Short, *Negro Conventions Prior to 1860* (unpublished master's thesis, Howard University, 1936), 56.

[81] Robert A. Warner, *New Haven Negroes: A Social History* (New Haven, 1940), 90.

lating the consumption of strong drink followed the pioneer action of Maine in 1851.

In New York the temperance advocates had a bitter struggle on their hands. Douglass attended the organizational meeting of the Woman's State Temperance Convention in 1852 at Rochester. He gave ear to Mrs. Stanton's culinary admonition that no liquor should be used in preparing food, and listened with approval to the demand that women should be permitted to divorce confirmed drunkards.[82] The convention decided to "work on" the state legislature and keep before the public the evils of intoxicants. Mrs. Stanton appointed Susan B. Anthony to organize auxiliaries and collect monies.

The New York State Woman's Temperance Society was an outgrowth of the convention. At its first meeting, in May 1853, Douglass seconded a resolution praising the action of the legislature in curtailing the number of liquor licenses.[83] A week later Douglass informed Smith that he planned to attend the June session of the Society.[84]

The campaign in New York for the Maine law resulted in the election of a prohibition governor in 1854.[85] The following year the legislature passed a bill forbidding the sale of alcoholic beverages. But the victory was illusory; after 1855 the liquor interests pooled their strength and gradually produced an organized "wet" vote.

Douglass' active interest in the movement does not seem to have outlasted the passing of the prohibitory legislation in New York. The women lost control of the state temperance society which, in 1854, changed its name to the People's League. As his friends, Mrs. Stanton and Miss Anthony,

---

[82] *Lily*, May 1852.
[83] *Una*, June 1, 1853.
[84] Douglass to Smith, June 1, 1853. *Smith MSS.*
[85] For the New York campaign see John Marsh, *Temperance Recollections* (New York, 1866), 275–290.

withdrew from the organized temperance movement, and as the temperance societies headed by men were lukewarm, if not downright hostile, to Negro membership, Douglass tended to place the temperance cause lower and lower on the list of his enthusiasms.

CHAPTER VIII

The Terse Rhetoric of the Ballot Box

The best defense of free American institutions is the heart of the American people themselves.

DOUGLASS

Douglass' conclusion that political action was the best way to strike at slavery came at a time when party lines were blurred and shifting. By 1850 the Liberty party, which was to claim Douglass' allegiance for nearly ten years, had fulfilled its historic rôle and was undergoing rapid disintegration. It had run its course in a decade.

The party owed its origin to several factors. By 1840 the semi-religious "Great Revival" spirit of the 'thirties had spent itself, thus causing non-Garrisonian abolitionists to lose faith in the efficacy of moral suasion alone. The organized abolitionist movement had been further weakened by the schism following Garrison's coup in May 1840. Many abolitionists were ready, therefore, to enter the political arena.

Taking stock of the situation they discovered that anti-slavery sentiment was not represented in politics in proportion to its numerical strength. Abolitionists observed that candidates of existing parties, even though put in office with the aid of anti-slavery votes, were unwilling or unable to carry out their pre-election promises. Anti-slavery voters of Whig or Democratic party affiliation generally voted the party ticket, salving their consciences with the belief that the candidates of their party were more anti-slavery than the candidates of the opposing group. This party regularity tended to weaken the political

141

strength of the abolitionists since politicians performed
little for those whose support could be taken for granted.
Since political action was imperative, and since the existing
parties were congenitally incapable of anti-slavery action,
abolitionists west of Massachusetts were ready by 1840
for a new political alignment.

This attempt to use political instruments for abolitionist
purposes resulted in the formation of the Liberty party.
Organized in 1840 as an outgrowth of anti-slavery meetings
held during the previous year,[1] the party nominated James
G. Birney, a former slaveholder of a deeply religious bent,
and Thomas Earle as its candidates for president and vice-
president. With a hastily organized party behind him,
with no political patronage to bestow, and possessing little
of the political acumen of the professional office-seeker,
Birney polled only 7,069 votes. Refusing to become discouraged, the new party entered the lists in 1844, holding
its national convention at Buffalo. The presence of Garnet,
Ward, and Charles B. Ray was precedent-making — it
was the first time in the United States that Negroes were
active in the councils of a political party.[2] In the presidential election of that year the Liberty party, again
headed by Birney, increased its popular vote to 62,263.
This was high tide.

---

[1] For accounts of the Liberty party origins by two pioneers in the
movement see William Goodell, *Slavery and Anti-Slavery* (New
York, 1853), 468–486; and Elizur Wright, *Myron Holley* (Boston,
1882), 226–275. Holley was one of the first to suggest the formation
of a new party. According to Wright, Holley's zeal was strengthened
by his hostile reaction to the speech on abolition petitions delivered
by Henry Clay in the Senate on February 7, 1839 (Wright, 263).
For Clay's speech, significant because it is perhaps the most reasoned
of the pro-slavery addresses, see *Life and Speeches of Henry Clay*
(2 vols., New York, 1843), II, 395–419.

[2] Charles H. Wesley, "The Participation of Negroes in Anti-
Slavery Political Parties," *Journal of Negro History*, XXIX, 45
(Jan. 1944).

After 1844 the Liberty party lost strength because of its preoccupation with a single issue. Voters wanted to know the party's stand on the tariff, the bank, the distribution of public lands and the annexation of Texas. As the presidential election of 1848 approached, a group of some forty Liberty party men who were opposed to the "one idea" policy determined to force the party's hand. This small group met in Wayne County, New York, in June 1847. They took the name of Liberty League, adopted a platform of nineteen planks and nominated Gerrit Smith and Elihu Burritt, "the learned blacksmith," for the highest national offices.[3]

The Liberty Leaguers were destined for disappointment in their hopes to capture control of the party and broaden its platform. Holding its convention in October 1847, at Buffalo again, the Liberty party ignored the existence of the League. The delegates chose John P. Hale of New Hampshire and Leicester King of Ohio as their candidates for national office. Vexed because the party rejected his planks and failed to give him the presidential nomination, Smith issued a call for another convention to be held at Buffalo the following summer.

One hundred and four delegates responded to Smith's call. Prominent among those present at this rump convention were two of Smith's intimate friends, Elizur Wright, Jr., and the Reverend Beriah Green, staunch abolitionists from northern Ohio. In attendance also were Douglass and Garnet. As a tribute to their presence the convention issued an address to the colored people, urging them to exemplify industry and economy and to come out of pro-slavery political parties and churches. The delegates asked Douglass, then attending his first political gathering of any kind,[4] to say a word. Not yet loosed from his Garrisonian leading strings, Douglass, with hardly the

---

[3] Goodell, *op. cit.*, 477.
[4] *North Star*, June 23, 1848.

best of taste, argued the pro-slavery nature of the Constitution.[5] The delegates proceeded to form a new party, the National Liberty party which, like the Liberty League it now superseded, chose Smith as its presidential nominee.

In the campaign of 1848 the Liberty party was not the only group suffering from internal conflict. The Democratic nominee for president was Lewis Cass of Michigan. Cass' indifference to the slavery issue made him unpalatable to those New York Democrats who favored the Wilmot Proviso prohibiting slavery in any territory acquired from the Mexican War. These New York Democrats, derisively called Barnburners, made overtures to Martin Van Buren. Smarting over his failure to receive the nomination at the national convention of the Democratic party, Van Buren was willing.

In the Whig camp there was disaffection also. Party members like Charles Sumner, in conscience unable to support the party nominee, Zachary Taylor, a Louisiana slaveholder, were ready for a new political alignment. They too began to weigh Van Buren in their minds. These two disgruntled political elements — anti-slavery Democrats and anti-slavery Whigs — met in Buffalo in August 1848. Here amid great enthusiasm they proclaimed their stand: "Free Soil, Free Speech, Free Labor and Free Men."

At this organizational meeting of the Free Soil party many Negroes were present — Douglass, Ward, Remond, Garnet, Bibb "and other colored gentlemen."[6] At the opening session Douglass was pleased when cheers followed the mention of his name by one of the speakers.[7] He circulated around the hall, taking in everything. On the second day, following an address by Joshua Giddings, the delegates called him to the platform. In a short statement — he was recovering from throat trouble — Douglass bade Godspeed to "your noble undertaking."[8]

---

[5] *North Star*, June 23, 1848.
[7] *Ibid.*

[6] *Ibid.*, Aug. 11, 1848.
[8] Wesley, *loc. cit.*, 53.

Editorializing a week later, Douglass, although still counting himself a political come-outer, praised the convention as "springing legitimately out of the principles which the American Anti-Slavery Society and the Liberty party have long been proclaiming." [9] The new party was not all he could ask or wish, but it was "a noble step in the right direction." In unequivocal terms he characterized the Whig candidate: "General Taylor is a well known robber and assassin." [10]

During the weeks immediately preceding the Free Soil convention, Douglass' paper had urged voting abolitionists to cast their ballots for Hale and King, the Liberty party nominees. In mid-September, however, the *North Star* shifted its choice and editorially recommended the Free Soil candidates, Van Buren and Charles Francis Adams. Douglass was well aware that the Liberty party's platform was abolitionist, whereas that of the Free-Soilers was simply anti-extension of slavery. But the Liberty party, he wrote, "was advantaged by the Free Soil Party by the superiority of its circumstances." [11]

Douglass was not alone in adopting this half-a-loaf attitude. In one of his periodic letters to the *Standard*, James Russell Lowell took the identical stand: "It should always be remembered that the Free Soil Party is not an abolition party in any sense of the word. Yet perhaps it will be wiser for us to be thankful for what they are than to reproach them for what they are not." [12] Taking comfort from Lowell's words, many of the Liberty party supporters joined the new party, thus following the example of Hale who withdrew his name as Liberty party nominee.

Shortly after his taste of political excitement at the Free Soil convention, Douglass began to waver in his allegiance

---

[9] *North Star*, Aug. 11, 1848.
[10] *Ibid.*
[11] *Ibid.*, Sept. 10, 1848.
[12] *Standard*, Aug. 10, 1848.

to moral suasion as the sole method of fighting slavery. Perhaps, so ran his thoughts, political action was really the open sesame. Four months after the national elections Gerrit Smith, with the proselyting zeal of the true reformer, invited Douglass for a week's visit at Peterboro.[13] Long in the offing, Douglass' conversion was now at hand.

Meanwhile the abolitionist cause was faring poorly in politics. In the election of 1848 the Whigs had won with Taylor. Van Buren had not carried a single state; only five Free-Soilers had been sent to Congress. The election over, the party was having its troubles. Confronted with the hard and expensive work of keeping an out-of-office national party alive between presidential campaigns, the Free Soil leaders decided that instead of keeping together locally and nationally as a compact bloc, it would be wiser to form coalitions and arrange deals, as expediency should dictate, with various groups in the several states.[14]

Douglass was bitter at this substitution of balance-of-power politics for a program of united, independent action against slavery. Six months after the election he ran an editorial with the rhetorical question, "What Has the Free Soil Movement Done?" It had promised much, ran his indictment, but it had performed little. It had "swallowed up the Liberty Party press and weakened its once powerful testimony against slavery." The Free Soil party had proved to be "a dull and indolent concern." Thinking in terms of abolitionist technique, Douglass was critical of the party's failure to maintain a staff of lecturers.[15]

Now that Douglass had become a political abolitionist and was prepared, as he phrased it, to make use of "the terse rhetoric of the ballot box," he lined himself up closely with Smith. After Hale's withdrawal as Liberty party

---

[13] *North Star*, Mar. 16, 1849.

[14] Theodore Clarke Smith, *The Liberty and Free Soil Parties in the Northwest* (Cambridge, Mass., 1897), 160–161.

[15] *North Star*, May 25, 1849.

nominee in 1848, Smith had become the party candidate by default. In the elections Smith received little support — the Liberty party polled only one half of one percent of the New York vote and made an even more dismal showing in the adjoining states.

After election day in November 1848, it was obvious that the Liberty party was dead but its leader characteristically refused to permit its burial. During the two years following the elections, Smith kept up a correspondence with other political abolitionists, seeking their opinions on the advisability of resuscitating the party. Although the responses were far from encouraging, Smith issued a call for a national convention to be held at Buffalo in the fall of 1851. At this convention Douglass was appointed to the national committee and to the committee on nominations. The latter group brought in the names of Smith and Charles Durkee of Wisconsin as the party's candidates.[16] But as neither consented to accept the honor, the party leaders announced that another meeting would be held a year later, in September 1852.[17] Douglass' paper published this second call and expressed the hope that the convention would be well attended.[18]

However, as the campaign of 1852 got under way and the Free Soil party struck "the busy note of preparation," a far-away gleam filled the eyes of the remaining handful of Liberty party die-hards. Forgetful of the course of the Free-Soilers for the past four years, and anxious to attach themselves to an anti-slavery party that had some prospect of success at the polls, this small group of political abolitionists again played with the idea of supporting the Free Soil group. Early in February 1852, Douglass wrote to Smith, asking his opinion as to the feasibility of pursuing such a course. Douglass indicated that he himself con-

[16] *Douglass' Paper*, Sept. 25, 1851.
[17] *Ibid.*, Apr. 29, 1852.
[18] *Ibid.*, May 13, 1852.

sidered it unwise.[19] But he was wavering. Five months later, in a letter to Smith, he suggested the possibility that at the approaching Pittsburgh convention the Free Soil party "could be made to occupy such a position as that the Liberty party may properly vote for its candidates." He expressed a desire to attend.[20]

The Free Soil party met on August 11 with Henry Wilson of Massachusetts in the chair. The afternoon meeting was well in progress when Douglass entered the hall. Immediately there were several loud calls for him, drowning out the voice of the speaker who had the floor. Amid cheers Douglass proceeded down the aisle. He had not expected to face an audience, but he was full of his subject, and speaking from the inspiration of the moment came easily to him.

"The object of this convention is to organize a party identified with eternal principles," ran his address.[21] "I am, of course for circumscribing and damaging slavery in every way. But my motto is extermination." The Constitution, continued he, was against slavery, inasmuch as "human government is for the protection of rights, and not for the destruction of rights." But even if the founding fathers had stipulated in the Constitution that there was a right to the possession of another man's body, such a law would lack the binding quality of plausibility: "Suppose you and I made a deed to give away two or three acres of blue sky," ran his *reductio ad absurdum*, "would the sky fall, and would anybody be able to plough it?"

He closed with a word of advice. "It has been said that we ought to take the position of the greatest number of voters. That is wrong. Numbers should not be looked to so much as right. The man who is right is a majority. If he does not represent what we are he represents what

---

[19] Douglass to Smith, Feb. 13, 1852. *Smith MSS.*

[20] *Ibid.*, July 15, 1852.

[21] Quotations from a stenographic report of Douglass' address in New York *Herald*, Aug. 12, 1852.

we ought to be." The crowd cheered again and again as Douglass concluded in this high strain.

The speeches, candidates and platform aroused enthusiasm among the delegates. "The only class of people that found fault with the Free Democracy Convention were the rum sellers," wrote John B. Vashon to Smith. "Two of our bust hotel keepers told me, that they did not sell at the bar five dollars worth, but if it had been one of the old parties, they would have sold from one to three hundred dollars worth of Rum." [22]

As if in reciprocity for his cordial reception at the Free Soil convention, Douglass informed his subscribers that he was favorably impressed by the party nominees. Hale was "a dreaded foe to slavery . . . and a large-hearted philanthropist." George W. Julian was one of "the truest and most disinterested friends of freedom whom we have ever met." The Liberty party would do well, advised Douglass, to nominate these men. [23]

Three weeks after the Free Soil meetings the Liberty party held its scheduled convention at Canastota, New York. No sooner had the delegates been called to order than a breach developed. One faction favored supporting the Free Soil nominees, Hale and Julian; the other faction wished to select candidates from the party membership exclusively. Douglass opposed the latter point of view. He expressed the opinion that it was unwise for the Liberty party to "array itself against Free Soilery." He felt that he was sacrificing no basic principle by a policy of compromise. "What is morally right is not, at all times, politically possible." [24]

The issue was put to a vote. The faction that favored confining party nominations to party members met defeat in the balloting. Chagrined, they withdrew from the con-

---

[22] Vashon to Smith, Oct. 4, 1852. *Smith MSS.*
[23] *Douglass' Paper*, Aug. 20, 1852.
[24] *Ibid.*, Sept. 10, 1852.

vention on the afternoon of September 2. That evening they selected two New York staters, William Goodell and Charles C. Foote, as their candidates for the two highest offices in the land.

Ignoring the departure of the schismatics, the dominant faction proceeded with the business of the convention. They made no nominations for president and vice-president. Instead they wound up by appointing a committee to make certain inquiries of Hale and Julian. The party's attitude toward these men would hinge on the replies to these questions. Carrying out its function, the committee, in a printed letter to the Free Soil candidates, asked two questions: (1) whether a political party should regard itself as organized for the purpose of securing equal rights to all, and (2) "whether you believe that slavery, so far as capable of legislation, is a naked piracy, around which there can be no legal covering." [25]

Hale and Julian ignored these questions. Whereupon, the Liberty party met in Syracuse on the last day of September. Douglass was chosen one of the vice-presidents of the convention. With the elections but five weeks away, the party nominated Goodell and S. M. Bell of Virginia as president and vice-president respectively.[26] Hewing to the party line, Douglass withdrew his support from the Free Soil candidates.

However understandable, Douglass' failure to identify himself more closely with the Free Soil movement was fatal to his understanding of the rising labor movement in America. Although not indifferent to the plight of the white workingman, professional abolitionists with the exception of Wendell Phillips were very cool toward the organized labor movement.[27] This refusal of the abolition-

---

[25] *Douglass' Paper*, Oct. 15, 1852.   [26] *Ibid.*

[27] See the penetrating article by Joseph G. Rayback, "The American Workingman and the Anti-Slavery Crusade," *Journal of Economic History*, III, 152–163 (Nov. 1943).

ists to recognize labor's peculiar problems made the workingman indifferent to the progress of abolitionism. Labor concentrated on a program of its own: strong trade unions, shorter work days, anti-garnishee legislation, prohibition of child labor and free grants of public land to settlers. Therefore, while the abolitionists were fighting chattel slavery and the workingmen were fighting wage slavery, the two groups never pooled their strength.

The Free Soil party offered a common ground. Interested in free land for the free laborer, the labor union movement actively supported the Free Soil party. Thus there was a golden opportunity for Douglass, via the Free Soil party, to come to understand the broad program of organized labor. But Douglass remained rooted in the abolitionist tradition of coolness toward the organized labor movement. His indifference was strengthened by the attitude of many white workingmen who regarded the Negro as a competitor and hence hated any movement for the upgrading of Negro laborers or an increase in their numbers.

Moreover, Douglass' close relationship to Smith tended to narrow and localize his political thinking. This became evident in 1852. Douglass' interest in the national campaign was secondary to that of the campaign for representative from the twenty-second Congressional district of New York. Smith was a contestant for the seat. Nominated on an independent ticket, Smith could depend on any existing reform sentiment. However, his campaign manager wisely preferred to emphasize Canadian tariff reciprocity, an issue of local importance.

Douglass threw his energies into the campaign although he was doubtful that Smith, being "too far in advance of the people and of the age," would ever go to Congress. But he canvassed assiduously. As election day drew on his hopes arose although from one town he reported to

Smith the dampening news that "if you are elected it will be without the aid of Chittenango." [28]

In the elections of 1852 the Free Soil vote was smaller than that of 1848 and the Liberty party vote was microscopic. But Douglass' disappointment at the lack of national response to anti-slavery was over-shadowed by his elation over Smith's surprising victory. The unbelievable had happened. "The election of Gerrit Smith — What an era!" wrote he. "With men and money we could carry the state for freedom in 1856." [29] Douglass congratulated his co-reformer: "Your election marks an era in the history of the Anti-Slavery struggle." He expressed joy that Smith went to Congress "a free man" and "not by concealment, bargain or compromise." [30] Other Negroes shared Douglass' elation. Pennington made Smith's election the subject of a sermon.[31]

During the period of Smith's eight-months Congressional career the most important measure before Congress was the Kansas-Nebraska bill. This measure would supersede the Missouri Compromise which for nearly a quarter of a century had kept slavery out of the Kansas-Nebraska territory. Although he put nothing past the slaveowners, Douglass' indignation was boundless: " It is true that the slave power is mean, dishonorable, treacherous, perfidious and guilty of any amount of low scoundrelism, in seeking to throw off the obligations of a bargain, after pocketing the consideration which induced them to assume those obligations." [32]

Douglass applauded the opponents of the bill. In Congress in late February 1854, Charles Sumner, ostensibly

[28] Douglass to Smith, Oct. 21, 1852. *Smith MSS.*

[29] Douglass probably to S. J. May, Nov. 10, 1852. Carter G. Woodson, ed., *The Mind of the Negro as Reflected in Letters Written during the Crisis, 1800–1860* (Washington, 1926), 653.

[30] Douglass to Smith, Nov. 6, 1852. *Smith MSS.*

[31] Pennington to Smith, Nov. 7, 1852. *Ibid.*

[32] *Douglass' Paper*, Feb. 24, 1854.

speaking against the measure, delivered "an essay against slavery." Douglass wrote one of the many approving letters that came to this champion of the Negro. After Chase, Wade and Seward had spoken, so ran Douglass' effusive letter, "I could not see what remained for you to say." Douglass expressed unhappiness at the thought that despite the Senator's efforts "the wicked measure will pass. But God dwells in eternity." [33]

Douglass' other model in Congress lent his weight to the attack on the bill. Early in April, Smith, in a long, moralistic speech, rehearsed the objections to the Kansas-Nebraska proposal. Douglass, with his easy use of superlatives, termed Smith's tirade "the mightiest and grandest ever before delivered in the House or Senate of this nation." [34]

Smith's other speeches in Congress drew Douglass' warmest praise. "He shows the enemy no quarter. He spurns compromise." Douglass wished that all Congressmen from the North were like "our Representative." [35] But Smith was not happy in Washington. A first-termer, he had little influence in Congressional affairs. Legislative routine submerged his individualism. He chafed under the rules and procedures of the House; it was evident that he had paid little heed to Douglass' advice to provide himself with a manual on parliamentary procedure.[36] He resigned his seat in early August 1854.[37] Douglass consolingly wrote that his heart and his judgment had gone with Smith in every step of his Congressional career.[38]

There was some talk of having Douglass run for the vacated seat. But nothing came of it. Douglass was not destined to hold an elective political office.

---

[33] Douglass to Sumner, Feb. 27, 1854. *Sumner Letterbooks.*

[34] Douglass to Smith, May 6, 1854. *Smith MSS.*

[35] *Douglass' Paper*, Apr. 14, 1854.

[36] Douglass to Smith, Aug. 18, 1853. *Smith MSS.*

[37] For Smith's *apologia* see his letter in New York *Tribune*, Aug. 19, 1854.

[38] Douglass to Smith, Aug. 22, 1854. *Smith MSS.*

CHAPTER IX

Last Rites of Political Abolitionism

Slavery cannot stand. Its character is like that of
Lord Granby: "it can only pass without censure as it
passes without observation."

DOUGLASS

The Kansas-Nebraska Act aroused a deep, spontaneous
resentment everywhere outside the South. As Horace
Greeley said, the chief sponsors of the measure, Franklin
Pierce and Stephen A. Douglas, made more abolitionists
in a month than Garrison and Phillips had made in a lifetime. Former "Conscience Whigs," anti-slavery Democrats and Free Soilers became convinced of the necessity
of forming a new party. The bloody conflicts that accompanied the opening of Kansas to slavery threw thousands
of restless voters into the arms of the Republican party,
organized in 1854, and rapidly becoming the stronghold of
anti-Southern sentiment.

But there was one political group in the North that
refused to fellowship with the new party. The two or three
hundred Liberty party members still attempted to maintain their separate identity. They had met in 1853. In
convention they had condemned the national government
as "not a civil government, but a piracy which upholds
slavery." They had deplored the division of sects among
Christians as the "greatest object facing righteous government." Douglass had proposed a resolution affirming the
anti-slavery nature of the Constitution. Turning their
attention to matters of less cosmic importance, the delegates had rejoiced in the increased circulation of Douglass'

154

weekly and expressed disapproval of the McGrawville populace for making it hot for William Allen upon his interracial marriage.[1]

The following year witnessed the birth of the Republican party but this Liberty party remnant still went through the motions of existence. Douglass and twenty-nine other last-ditchers convened at Syracuse in September 1854. They nominated Goodell for governor of New York and passed their usual resolution declaring that it was the right and the duty of the national government to abolish slavery.

To anyone outside the party membership the holding of this convention would seem to be an exercise in futility. But not to Douglass. In clinging to this skeleton of a skeleton, he still had hopes that the party could be galvanized into life. Early in 1855, he reaffirmed his faith in the party in a pamphlet publication analysing the anti-slavery movement. After tracing the history of the other anti-slavery organizations and pointedly criticizing each, he praised the program of the Liberty party. The doctrine of the Garrisonians, wrote he, was only negatively anti-slavery because it aimed at dissolving the Union rather than freeing the slave: "It started to free the slave. It ends by leaving the slave to free himself. It started with the purpose to imbue the heart of the nation with sentiments favorable to the abolition of slavery, and ends by seeking to free the North from all responsibility for slavery." The American and Foreign Anti-Slavery Society was wholly ineffectual, and the Free Soil party aimed simply to limit and de-nationalize slavery — it left the slave in his fetters. In contradistinction to the foregoing groups, the Liberty party, "by its position and doctrines, and by its antecedents, is pledged to continue the struggle while a bondman in his chains remains to weep." [2]

Heartened by Douglass' well-thought-out analysis and

---

[1] *Standard*, Mar. 3, 1853.

[2] Douglass, *Anti-Slavery Movement, passim.*

his brave words, the leaders of the Liberty party began to think in terms of the presidential campaign of 1856. In the spring of 1855, Smith, after an exchange of correspondence with Douglass,[3] wrote a strong call. In response, the party met at Utica in September 1855. The convention nominated George Vashon for state attorney-general. An Oberlin graduate, Vashon had passed the bar in New York state and was then teaching at Central College. The delegates nominated Douglass secretary of state for New York. "Fred must be a proud man now," commented a Southern newspaper: "There is but one step more — his nomination for the Presidency, with Box Brown as Vice-President." [4] The convention did not nominate candidates for national offices; it was awaiting the action of a kindred group, the Radical Abolitionists, scheduled to meet at Boston the following month.

The Radical Abolitionist party was the Liberty party by another name. Its chief sponsor was Gerrit Smith who financed its two organs, the *American Jubilee* and the *Radical Abolitionist*.[5] Despite their inherent optimism, the leaders of the Liberty party doubtless realized that with its members down to the vanishing point, its influence confined to a few localities in western New York, and its history a dreary recital of defeat, it would be well to experiment with a new name.

Early in 1855, a call, signed by Goodell, Lewis Tappan, Gerrit Smith, Douglass and J. McCune Smith, was issued for a convention of Radical Abolitionists to be held at Syracuse three months later.[6] The purpose of the new party (identical, of course, with that of the Liberty party)

---

[3] Douglass to Smith, Mar. 27, 1855. *Smith MSS.*

[4] New Orleans *Daily Delta*, Sept. 22, 1855.

[5] The *American Jubilee* was issued in March and April, 1855. The *Radical Abolitionist*, which succeeded it, appeared from August 1855 to December 1858. Both were published at New York City.

[6] *American Jubilee*, Apr. 1855.

was to effect the removal of slavery from the territories and the states by political action. The old parties, ran the call, were unequal to this task. The Whig, Democrat, and Know-Nothing parties all had a slaveholding membership, while the Free Soil party denied the right of the national government to touch slavery in the states.[7]

Upon assembling in June the delegates to the Radical Abolitionist convention took the revolutionary step of selecting a Negro as chairman. J. McCune Smith presided with "ability, urbanity and impartiality." [8] The first act of the convention was to draw up a "Declaration of Sentiments," perhaps in conscious imitation of the action taken at the organizational meeting of the American Anti-Slavery Society at Philadelphia in 1833. "Our panoply is the truth. . . . The moral government of God as illustrated in pages of unwritten history," ran the gaudy phrases, "forbids us to cherish any expectation of securing our own liberties or the liberties of any portion of the nation to which we belong, by any process short of securing the liberties of each and all." [9]

The convention then adopted an "Exposition of the Constitutional Duty of the Federal Government to Abolish Slavery." This statement was a lengthy repetition of the old contention that the Constitution was anti-slavery. In an "Address to the Public," the convention presented the various proposed solutions to the slavery problem. The delegates took a stand against the Garrisonian doctrine of disunion, pointing out that "the non-slaveholding states share in national responsibilities and are involved in the guilt of slavery." [10]

On the last day of the convention John Brown was pres-

---

[7] *American Jubilee*, Apr. 1855.

[8] New York *Tribune*, June 29, 1855.

[9] *Proceedings of the Radical Abolition Convention, June 26, 27, 28, 1855* (New York, 1855), 9.

[10] *Ibid.*, 43.

ent. He appealed for men and means to carry on the struggle to organize Kansas as a free state. His remarks stirred all of the delegates except Lewis Tappan who disclaimed sympathy with Brown's methods.[11] Another interesting visitor was a comely mulatto. Several of the delegates urged her to describe the methods by which she effected her escape from slavery. Douglass took exception, pointing out that it was not wise for runaways to divulge their techniques of escape.[12]

Before adjournment the convention invited subscriptions to the *Radical Abolitionist* and monthly contributions of cash. The chairman issued a call for a national gathering to assemble at Boston four months later.[13] The meeting adjourned on a note of optimism. The Syracuse convention, reported the party organ, "was a noble gathering, harmonious, thorough, deliberative, determined."[14] Douglass informed Smith that in his lecture during the summer he would "try to uphold the principles laid down at the Radical Abolition Convention."[15]

The convention attracted the attention of Horace Greeley, editor of the New York *Tribune*. His reaction was mixed. While he "most earnestly desired the enfranchisement of the Afric-American race, we would gladly wean them from the sterile path of political agitation. They can help win their rights if they will, but not by jawing for them."[16] Although condemning political agitation, Greeley did not suggest any specific methods which Negroes should employ in the battle for their rights. In answer to the editor, Goodell made the point that if Doug-

---

[11] *Proceedings of the Radical Abolition Convention, June 26, 27, 28, 1855* (New York, 1855), 62.

[12] *Tribune*, June 29, 1855.

[13] *Proceedings*, 65.

[14] *Radical Abolitionist*, Aug. 1855.

[15] Douglass to Smith, Aug. 15, 1855. *Smith MSS.*

[16] *Tribune*, Sept. 22, 1855.

lass and Samuel Ringgold Ward had followed such advice
"the New York *Tribune* and its 200,000 readers would
never have heard of them." [17]

Late in October the scheduled meeting was held at
Boston. Called by the Radical Abolitionists, the action
of this gathering was awaited by the Liberty party who,
it will be remembered, had deferred naming its presidential
candidates. At this Boston meeting Gerrit Smith, Beriah
Green and Douglass were present, but there were few others
in the hall. A competing convention — the National Agri-
cultural Fair — and a drenching rain operated to keep
the attendance down.[18] The small, dispirited group passed
no measures and made no nominations.

During the opening months of 1856, while the Liberty
party and its *alter ego*, the Radical Abolitionist party,
marked time, the major parties prepared to draw up their
platforms and select their candidates. The Know-Noth-
ings, in the last throes of dissolution, convened on Washington's birthday. At Philadelphia on the same day the
Republicans held their first national convention. They
decided to wait until June to name their standard-bearers,
but they drew up "An Address to the People of the United
States." This statement drew fire from the political abolitionists. "The Republican Party," fumed Douglass, "said
nothing of slavery in the District of Columbia. . . . Abolitionists can be induced to follow the Republican movement
only under the teachings of a plausible and sinuous political
philosophy, which is the grand corrupter of all reforms."
He added a note of admonition: "Anti-slavery voters must
not allow themselves to be transformed from one political
demagogue to another until all vitality shall have departed
from them." [19]

---

[17] William Goodell, *Scrapbooks Relating to Slavery, 1855–1865*
(Oberlin College Library), 20.

[18] *Radical Abolitionist*, Dec. 1855.

[19] *Douglass' Paper*, Apr. 25, 1856.

Douglass' analysis of the Republican party was shared by his political associates. Hence, because the Republicans "had failed to rise to the level of abolitionism," and obviously nothing could be expected of the Democrats, the Radical Abolitionists called a national nominating convention to meet at Syracuse in May.[20] Doubtless many who heard of the scheduled convention shared Garrison's reaction: "I see that Lewis Tappan, Douglass, McCune Smith, Goodell and Gerrit Smith have called a convention for the purpose of nominating candidates for the Presidency and Vice-Presidency of the United States!! Can anything more ludicrous than this be found inside or outside of the Utica Insane Asylum?"[21]

Ignoring such jeers Douglass cancelled a number of previously scheduled speaking engagements in Ohio, in order to be present at the convention at Syracuse.[22] Here he saw the familiar faces — Tappan, Gerrit Smith, Green and Abram Pryne. These zealous champions of the slave met in an atmosphere of solemnity arising out of two sobering pieces of news. Charles Sumner had been severely caned by a Southern Congressman and his condition was said to be critical. On top of this, word had come from Kansas that a pro-slavery group had raided the free-state headquarters at Lawrence, looting and pillaging.

Every one of the delegates addressed the convention; the length and sameness of the speeches did not weary the faithful. Douglass' turn came during the afternoon of the first day. He confessed that he had felt some temptation to join the Republican party, "but they do not give a full recognition to the humanity of the Negro." That party sought simply to limit slavery, and such limiting applied only to Kansas and Nebraska. As if the name "Kansas" reminded him of the bloody events in that territory, Doug-

[20] *Radical Abolitionist*, Apr. 1856. *Douglass' Paper*, Apr. 25, 1856.
[21] Garrison to S. J. May, Mar. 21, 1856. *Garrison MSS.*
[22] Douglass to Smith, Apr. 16, 1856. *Smith MSS.*

lass asserted, "Liberty must cut the throat of slavery or have its own cut by slavery." [23]

While the Radical Abolitionists were meeting at Syracuse, that city was also host to the state convention of the Republican party. Douglass attended one of their meetings and was called on to speak. "You are called Black Republicans," said he. "What right have you to that name? Among all the candidates you have selected, or talked of, I haven't seen or heard a single black one." [24] Douglass knew that it was the Republican party's enemies who added the adjective, but he welcomed a chance to strike at the party's failure to champion the slave.

Just prior to adjournment the Radical Abolitionists nominated Gerrit Smith for president and Samuel McFarland of Virginia as his running mate. A local paper uncharitably remarked that Smith would get about as many votes as there were members of the convention. [25] Douglass held otherwise. As he advised his subscribers, he looked forward to a fusion of the Radical Abolition party and the Liberty party in September. [26]

As Douglass predicted, these two parties pooled forces. This was hardly surprising since the membership of both was identical. The truly surprising feature of the joint meeting was the absence of Douglass. Douglass had turned somersault. In June he had characterized the Republican party as "a heterogeneous mass of political antagonisms, gathered from defunct Whiggery, disaffected Democracy, and demented, defeated and disappointed Native Americanism." [27] Douglass' audience was prepared for strong denunciations of this sort, but none of his friends was

---

[23] *Radical Abolitionist*, July 1856.
[24] Syracuse *Daily Standard*, May 29, 1856.
[25] *Ibid.*, May 30, 1856.
[26] *Douglass' Paper*, June 10, 1856, quoted from *Liberator*, Sept. 5, 1856.
[27] *Ibid.*

prepared for the shock when Douglass announced a complete change of mind.

In mid-August Douglass withdrew the names of Smith and McFarland from the head of his leading editorial column. Subscribers were informed that the editor proposed "to support with whatever influence we possess, John C. Frémont and William L. Dayton," the Republican candidates. Those who would cry "inconsistency," continued Douglass, were to understand that the "difference between our paper this week and last week is a difference of Policy, not of Principle." That the Republican party did not go as far as he wished on slavery was no reason for withholding his support: "A man was not justified in refusing to assist his fellow-men to accomplish a good thing simply because his fellows refuse to accomplish some other good thing which they deem impossible." [28] To the disappointed Smith he wrote that he was supporting Frémont "as the best thing I can do now." [29] A month after his conversion, Douglass' resilient mind had reached the conclusion that Frémont would "not countenance slaveholding aggression." [30]

"The defection of Douglass was a sad blow to me," wrote the clergyman Pryne.[31] Douglass' other political associates held their tongues. They realized that Douglass' change of party betrayed his anxiety to be affiliated with a group that had a chance of success at the polls. In common with the overwhelming majority of his countrymen, Douglass received little satisfaction in voting for an abstract principle. It must be remembered also that Douglass' change was symptomatic of the spirit of the times; in all United States history political affiliations were never as fluid as

---

[28] *Douglass' Paper*, Aug. 15, 1856, quoted from *Liberator*, Sept. 5, 1856.

[29] Douglass to Smith, Aug. 31, 1856. *Smith MSS.*

[30] *Douglass' Paper*, Sept. 29, 1856.

[31] Pryne to Smith, Sept. 30, 1856. *Smith MSS.*

during the ten years preceding the Civil War. That Douglass affiliated with a party that did not go as far as he wished was a practice common among honest men who realized that a party that hoped to win in national politics could not afford perfectionism.

On the other hand, as Gerrit Smith and his associates could point out, the abolitionists nominated candidates primarily to preserve the cause. The Liberty party and its fitful successor, the Radical Abolitionist party, did not nominate to elect. They nominated candidates as an effective means of spreading knowledge of their doctrines. Liberty party stalwarts were not disturbed by the certainty that they would never elect a single representative to Congress. The purpose of their existence was accomplished, they felt, when their principles were put into operation.

The Radical Abolitionists needed a long-range outlook; there was little enough reward at the polls. The counting of the ballots in the elections of 1856 revealed that the party polled a total of 165 votes in the entire state of New York.[32] Frémont carried the state but the victory nationally of the Democratic nominee, James Buchanan, was galling to Douglass. As if repenting his heresy he announced six weeks after the elections that he was still a Radical Abolitionist.[33] In the spring of the following year, when the unpleasant aspects of the late campaign were receding in his memory, Douglass consoled Smith with the thought that "we have turned Whigs and Democrats into Republicans and we can turn Republicans into Abolitionists." [34]

Republicans might be changed into abolitionists but not into Liberty party members. For that party drew its last breath in the fall of 1857. Douglass assisted at the

[32] *Standard*, Jan. 31, 1857.
[33] Douglass to Smith, Dec. 15, 1856. *Smith MSS.*
[34] *Ibid.*, Apr. 30, 1857.

obsequies in September at Syracuse. The party's last official act was the nomination of J. McCune Smith as secretary of state.[35]

With the Gerrit Smith group it was a simple matter to have a new party rise from the ashes of the old. In June 1858, Pryne persuaded Smith to head a reform ticket in the gubernatorial election. The following month a "People's State Ticket" nominated Smith for governor. Four weeks later the Radical Abolitionists followed suit.

Garnet and Douglass worked for Smith's election but the great majority of the state's 11,000 Negro voters threw their backing to the Republican party, as Garnet had predicted. For despite their respect and affection for Smith, Negro voters could not support him for governor in 1858. At a convention of colored men held at Troy in September the fifty-four delegates agreed that the paramount aim of the Negro was to bring about the "ruin" of the Democrats. In New York this party represented the white workingman who had been told that the Negro was his economic competitor. Negroes therefore had been driven, willy-nilly, into whatever new party appeared likely to effect the defeat of the Democrats. In turn Federalist and then Whig, the New York Negro was Republican in 1858. The convention of colored men appointed William J. Watkins to travel on behalf of the Republican party. Stephen Myers pledged that he would preach Republicanism in his paper, *The Voice of the People*.[36]

While Negroes agreed with Douglass that "no more honest man ever lived than Gerrit Smith," that good man polled an insignificant vote, somewhat to his chagrin. Smith's defeat was simply a manifestation of the low estate to which the fringe parties had fallen in the years immediately preceding the election of 1860. By 1859, the Radical Abolitionists had apparently sunk into a fatal torpor.

---

[35] *Radical Abolitionist*, Oct. 1857.

[36] *Standard*, Oct. 9, 1858.

FREDERICK DOUGLASS IN 1855

Rochester May 25 1860

Dear Mrs Stanton:

I am much obliged by your letter. I have been in a half and half condition about attending that Worcester Convention ever since I got the call signed by Messrs Foster and Pierpont. Of course your letter has taken something from one half and added it to the other. I am now strongly inclined to go. The only cause of hesitation is that the difference between myself and Mr Garrison might render me an unacceptable member to some who may come from that side of the house Mr Foster himself included. I have always believed in Stephen Foster and never lifted my heel against him or against Mr Garrison until compelled to do so in self defense. I may better to see you on my way to Syracuse next week and talk matters over with you. Thank you for your kind invitation. In haste. Yours very truly

Fredk Douglass.

DOUGLASS' HANDWRITING

"Where is its committee, where its paper, its lecturers and patrons?" wailed Douglass. "All gone!" [37]

But the comatose state of the Radical Abolitionists did not betoken a corresponding gain in strength for their chief political enemies, the Democrats. On the contrary, the Dred Scott decision in 1857 and the hanging of John Brown two years later fanned anti-slavery and Republican sentiment to white-hot intensity. When Douglass returned to the United States in May 1860, after an absence of six months, he found political excitement running high. Late in April the Democrats had split into two factions. A third party, the Constitutional Union party, held a national convention in early May. Foregathering at Chicago shortly afterward, the Republicans nominated Abraham Lincoln.

Touched by the fever, the Radical Abolitionists again prepared to enter the political arena. When the party met at Syracuse in late August, Douglass sat on the Business Committee which presented as one of its resolutions an indictment of the Republican party for its "almost infinitesimal amount of anti-slavery profession," which was "inadequate to quiet the agitation on the slave's right to liberty." The delegates again chose Smith and McFarland as the party candidates. Douglass was chosen as one of the presidential electors.[38]

Three weeks after this group adjourned Douglass took a trip to Worcester, Massachusetts, to attend a meeting of the Political Anti-Slavery Convention. Stephen S. Foster was the moving spirit behind this tiny group which had organized at Boston in May 1860, and were now meeting in mid-September to consider the "propriety" of organizing a political party similar to that of the New York abolitionists. Douglass served on the Executive Committee and was the author of a resolution extending "earnest sympathy and heartfelt Godspeed" to the abolitionists

---

[37] *Douglass' Monthly*, Oct. 1860.
[38] *Ibid.*

in New York who were supporting Smith. Many Garrisonians were present; consistently skeptical of political action, they called the convention a farce.

Nationally the campaign left Douglass a bit cold. To him the most important issue before the country was, as he put it, "the rights of man." But the competing political groups did not rise to this level. "We have," wrote he, "five parties and no principles." But since victory must alight in some quarter, Douglass, with an air of resignation, expressed the hope that Lincoln would win: "The slave-holders know the day of their power is over when a Republican President is elected." [39]

Although he hoped for a Lincoln triumph, Douglass did not backslide; he worked for Smith's election as president. But his greatest effort politically centered around a proposed measure to amend the state constitution so as to place colored citizens on a footing of equality with others in the exercise of the right to vote. The first constitution of the state of New York, adopted April 20, 1777, required a property qualification of all male inhabitants. After 1821, under an amended constitution, the property qualification was abolished for white voters; no Negro, however, could go to the polls unless he was worth $250 in real estate. (One of Gerrit Smith's aims in giving land to 3,000 Negroes was to enable them to meet this property qualification.) Furthermore, whites were required to be in residence only one year in order to qualify for the ballot; a Negro had to be a citizen of the state for three years. In 1846 the question of equal suffrage had been submitted to the voters who had rejected it by a three-to-one majority.[40] Thirteen years later the legislature again submitted

[39] *Douglass' Monthly,* Sept. 1860.
[40] See tract *The Suffrage Question in Relation to Colored Voters in the State of New York,* New York, 1860. Also Emil Olbrich, *The Development of Sentiment on Negro Suffrage to 1860* (Madison, Wis., 1912), 30, 38, 77, 126–128.

the issue to the voters, who were to act on it at the time of the presidential election of 1860.

During the twelve weeks prior to election day, Douglass covered the western part of the state. He undertook to distribute 25,000 tracts issued by "The New York City and County Suffrage Committee of Colored Citizens." [41] This civic-minded group had established forty-eight suffrage clubs in New York city and eighteen in Brooklyn. For financial support it assessed its members 10¢ a week.[42] In Rochester on November 6, election day, Douglass stood at the polls for ten hours,[43] button-holing voters. To no avail. The equal suffrage measure was rejected by a decisive majority, 337,984 to 197,503. The insignificant vote Smith received for the presidency is unrecorded.

The results of the presidential election, however, were not without their compensations. Douglass regretted that under Lincoln slavery would still be safe ("he proposes no measure which can bring him in collision with the South"), but he rejoiced that the political power of the slave-owners had suffered a set-back. Moreover, he reasoned that Lincoln's triumph demonstrated the possibility of eventually electing an abolitionist president.[44]

But the immediate results of the election were not encouraging to the foes of slavery. Conservative Northerners strove to convince the South that Lincoln would exercise moderation. The tone of the Northern press grew timid. The cotton-dealing and commercial interests, tied to the South by economic bonds, were fearful of the spectre of financial ruin — repudiated debts and business stagnation — that might follow a sectional rupture. (Douglass often quoted the aphorism: "Beware of a Yankee when he is feeding.") These Northern businessmen with a stake in

[41] J. M. Smith to G. Smith, Sept. 29, 1860. *Smith MSS.*
[42] Myers to Smith, Sept. 21, 1860. *Smith MSS.*
[43] *Douglass' Monthly*, Jan. 1861.
[44] *Ibid.*

the South's economy covertly supported the paid hoodlums who engaged to break up abolitionist meetings. These rowdies now became bolder. Four weeks after the elections, at a meeting in Boston held to commemorate the anniversary of John Brown's execution, hired plug-uglies came to turn out the hall. In the melee that ensued, Douglass "fought like a trained pugilist." But his valor was little more than its own reward; he was eventually thrown "down the staircase to the floor of the hall." [45] Six days later at the Music Hall in the same city, "a handful of very coarse samples of human nature" attempted to keep Douglass from lecturing.[46] A month later the mayor of Boston refused to permit a meeting of the Massachusetts Anti-Slavery Society. In January and February, throughout the free states — Massachusetts, New York, Illinois, Michigan — the story was the same: the mob spirit had taken on new life.[47]

Small wonder then that Douglass despaired as the new year got underway. To him the 'fifties had been a decade of unfulfillments. He had no new plans for hastening the good time coming. His feelings were so caught up in the day-to-day struggle that his perspective was distorted. With his gaze endlessly on the immediate, how could he pierce the veil and divine that in a short time his eyes would see the glory?

---

[45] Boston *Evening Transcript*, Dec. 3, 1860; New York *Tribune*, Dec. 6, 1860; *Douglass' Monthly*, Jan. 1861; Edith Ellen Ware, *Political Opinion in Massachusetts during the Civil War and Reconstruction* (New York, 1917), 86 *et seq.*

[46] *Twenty-Eighth Ann. Rep. of Amer. A. S. S.* (New York, 1861), 180.

[47] For an account of mob violence in various cities throughout these states see *ibid.*, 175–186.

CHAPTER X

Douglass and John Brown

One with God is a majority.

DOUGLASS

Douglass' sweeping denunciations of the slave oligarchy brought him into the orbit of John Brown, the personification of uncompromising and armed resistance to slavery. At the time he became acquainted with Douglass, Brown's hectic course had still eleven years to run before he was sentenced to death by hanging. But by the time he first met Douglass, in 1848, Brown had already had a varied career.

Born in Connecticut, of a line of hardworking, religious forbears, Brown had been taken to Ohio when he was five. Maturity settled early upon the boy; his mother died when he was eight. His formal schooling was meagre in a region where the paramount consideration was taming the wilderness. Brown's first marriage took place in 1820; his children found him a stern parent, but one who inspired love and respect. A typical nineteenth century American in one respect, Brown was a jack-of-all-trades. But he had a poor business head, and his enterprises generally wound up in bankruptcy.

Brown's interest in the Negro dated from the middle 'thirties when he proposed to take a Negro boy, preferably a slave, into his family and "bring him up as one of our own." By the late 'forties, Brown had come to the conclusion that slavery was not to be undone simply by educating individual Negroes. In an essay contributed to the Negro periodical, *The Ram's Horn*, Brown advised his

169

readers that more was to be gained by resisting brutal aggression than by "tamely submitting to every species of indignity contempt and wrong. . . ." [1]

In November 1848, at the time when Brown was a merchant at Springfield, Massachusetts, Douglass received an invitation to visit him. [2] Brown wished to confer with one whom he had come to regard as a kindred spirit. After receiving a cordial welcome, followed by a hearty meal, Douglass had leisure to observe the "looks" of his host. The Brown Douglass saw was "lean, strong and sinewy, built for times of trouble." According to Douglass, he had an impressive bearing. His hair was "coarse, strong, slightly gray, closely trimmed and grew low on his forehead." He had a "square mouth, prominent chin, bluish gray eyes. . . ." [3]

With Douglass as an audience, Brown proceeded to reveal the plan which had been revolving in his mind. This course of action was to establish squads of five armed men in the Allegheny mountains. These bold fighters would aid slaves to escape. Some of the runaways would remain in the mountains to harry their former masters. Such a scheme, Brown argued, would endanger and gradually destroy the money value of slave property. [4]

---

[1] Oswald Garrison Villard, *John Brown* (New York, 1943, fifth printing), 50.

[2] Douglass is the only informant that this meeting took place. In his *Life and Times* (338 *et seq.*) he places 1847 as the year of his short stay at Brown's house. More likely (and more susceptible to proof) the visit occurred late the following year. Douglass lectured in the Town Hall at Springfield on October 29, 1848 (*North Star*, Nov. 17, 1848), and on November 18 of the same year (*North Star*, Nov. 24, 1848). Douglass left Springfield shortly after his November lecture there. Within ten days after his return to Rochester he "alluded prominently to his recent interview with Mr. John Brown of Springfield," during the course of some casual remarks to a group of colored men (*North Star*, Dec. 8, 1848).

[3] Douglass, *Life and Times*, 339.

[4] *Ibid.*

Skeptical, Douglass indicated the difficulties: masters would sell their slaves to the lower South; it would be impossible to supply the squads with food and ammunition, and bloodhounds would track them down. To all of these objections Brown had a ready reply. Finally, as if to silence further questioning, he asserted that even if he were to die in the attempt to free the slaves there could be no better use for his life.[5]

Douglass came away half convinced. Brown might succeed in undermining slavery — "men do not like to buy runaway horses, nor to invest in a species of property likely to take legs and walk off with itself" — and possibly Brown's efforts, even if unsuccessful, would revitalize the conscience of the nation.

As a result of this visit Douglass found it necessary to refashion his thinking. Brown's insistence that there was no possibility of converting the slaveholders weakened Douglass' faith in the Garrisonian principle of non-resistance.

From the time of their first meeting the relations between the two men were cordial. They reciprocated visits whenever fortune took either to Rochester or Springfield. At Syracuse in June 1855, Douglass was present at a meeting of the Radical Abolitionist party when Brown addressed the convention in an appeal for "men and means to defend freedom in Kansas." Brown was then on the eve of his departure for Kansas to aid in the movement to bring that territory under the political control of Northerners. Stirred by his remarks, the delegates gave him $60.[6]

Later in 1855 Mrs. Stanton wrote to a friend that in December she expected to see Brown at Rochester where he would be "on a visit to Frederick Douglass."[7] Brown

---

[5] Douglass, *Life and Times*, 340–341.
[6] *Proceedings of the Convention of Radical Political Abolitionists*, 62.
[7] Elizabeth Cady Stanton to Elizabeth Smith Miller, Nov. 15, 1856. T. Stanton and H. S. Blatch, *Elizabeth Cady Stanton*, II, 69.

and Douglass were in Worcester during the same days in the spring of 1857; [8] it is likely that they saw each other then and exchanged experiences.

But Douglass could see little of Brown as long as Kansas was the scene of a bitter political conflict between the free-soil and pro-slavery groups. When the free-soil settlers of Lawrence were attacked, their appeal for aid was heeded by Brown who led one of the volunteer groups that went to the rescue. Brown's belief that "without the shedding of blood there is no remission of sin" prompted him, in May 1856, to lead a retaliatory party which killed five pro-slavery men at Pottawomie Creek.

As the Kansas troubles temporarily quieted down, Brown cast about for another scene of operation. In the winter of 1857–58, he began to ponder the possibilities of a raid into Virginia. Needing money for the project, he came east. On the first or second day of February 1858, he presented himself at Douglass' suburban home in Rochester.[9] He asked for lodgings; he said that he would not stay long and he insisted on paying for his accommodations. In his room at Douglass' home Brown sat long hours, writing letters to sympathizers on whom he counted to underwrite a venture the nature of which he did not disclose. The recipients of these letters from Nelson Hawkins (the title Brown had informed them he would use) sensed something unusual in the wind.

When he was not writing to obtain funds Brown was drafting and revising a constitution which he proposed to put into operation once he came into power. This singular document, comprising forty-eight articles, provided a

---

[8] Franklin B. Sanborn, *Recollections of Seventy Years* (Boston, 1909), 138.

[9] Brown sent a letter to Theodore Parker addressed from Rochester and dated Feb. 2, 1858. F. B. Sanborn, ed., *The Life and Letters of John Brown* (Boston, 1885), 434. For a chronology of Brown's movements in 1858 see Villard, *op. cit.*, 675–676.

framework of government that gave great power to the military chief.[10] Doubtless Brown thought of himself as a Cromwell purging the country of its unregenerated elements and maintaining a quasi-theocracy through control of the army.

Brown was so full of his plans that he made listeners of the Douglass children after he had tested the patience of their parents. To the delight of the youngsters he demonstrated his plans, illustrating "each detail with a set of blocks." [11] Before these three fruitful weeks in Rochester came to an end Brown became acquainted with a fugitive slave, "Shields Green," who proved to be one of his most devoted followers.[12]

Despite his talkativeness at the Douglass residence, Brown did not divulge the full nature of his matured plot to his host. It was then too early to reveal the scope of his plans except to those who were in a position to finance them, and Brown did not place Douglass in this category. From Rochester Brown went to Peterboro where he could depend upon Gerrit Smith to give him a receptive ear and financial assistance.

Brown had not left Rochester without planning to see Douglass within a fortnight. They planned to meet in Philadelphia on March 5, but Douglass found it necessary to postpone his arrival five days.[13] On March 11, Brown

---

[10] In Colonel Robert E. Lee's report to the Adjutant-General on the disturbances at Harpers Ferry there is included a copy of Brown's "Provisional Constitution and Ordinances for the People of the United States." 36th Cong., 1st sess. (1859–60), *Executive Documents*, II, no. 2 (Report of the Secretary of War, 1st part), 19 *et seq.* Douglass claimed possession of a copy prepared at his home by Brown. *Life and Times*, 387.

[11] Parker, "Reminiscences," *loc. cit.*, 553.

[12] For a brief sketch of Green see the New York *Herald*, Oct. 29, 1859.

[13] Douglass to Brown, Feb. 27, 1858. Sanborn, *Life and Letters of John Brown*, 443.

and his eldest son conferred with Douglass, Garnet, and the Negro underground operator, William Still.[14] Brown made an appeal for men and money, without, however, disclosing plans. Three weeks later on April 3, Brown and his son spent the night at Douglass' home. From Rochester, in company with J. W. Loguen, Brown went across the border to St. Catharine's where he had an appointment with Harriet Tubman. With her unparalleled knowledge of the underground railroad routes, she would be just the person (so speculated Brown) to act as chief guide for the slaves he planned to free.

It had been Brown's intention to stage the raid into Virginia in 1858 instead of 1859. "I expect to need all the help I can get by the first of May," he wrote Douglass in April 1858.[15] A postponement of Brown's plans was necessary because of the unreliability of Hugh Forbes, an English adventurer who had seen military service as a follower of the Italian patriot, Garibaldi. Forbes had been introduced to Brown in March 1855. He had agreed to drill Brown's men, in Kansas and later in Virginia, and to write appeals to army officers inviting them to join the movement for the forcible destruction of slavery.

Late in 1857 Forbes' interest waned. He was receiving little money, and he felt that he was more competent than Brown to lead a group of soldiers. Ever in search of personal funds, Forbes presented himself to Douglass in November 1857. Douglass was unfavorably impressed by the visitor, but for Brown's sake he took the Englishman to a hotel and paid his bill in advance. Forbes related his customary harrowing story of a destitute family across the Atlantic. Douglass gave him "a little money" and, not knowing Forbes' proneness to blackmail, furnished him with a letter of introduction to other friends of the cause.

[14] Douglass to Brown, Feb. 27, 1858. Sanborn, *Life and Letters of John Brown*, 451.

[15] Brown's diary, Apr. 14, 1858. Harlow, *Gerrit Smith*, 399.

Forbes put to good personal use the roster of names Douglass gave him. Friends of the slave received letters informing them that a loan (or a gift) to Hugh Forbes would be a sound investment in the cause of freedom. This appeal brought some scattered monies. When, finally, his begging letters brought no further returns, Forbes began to send denunciatory letters to Brown's supporters, threatening to expose their connection with his conspiracies.[16]

Informed of Forbes' tactics, Douglass relayed the intelligence to Brown. According to Douglass, his warning that Forbes had prematurely disclosed the plans led Brown to postpone for seventeen months his bold attack on Harpers Ferry.[17]

Douglass appears to have exaggerated his influence on the postponement of Brown's plans. In May 1858, Douglass did not know of the real nature of Brown's project. True, Forbes' betrayal caused a delay in putting the plot into operation. But Brown was guided less by Douglass' warning than by the advice of his philanthropist friends. Early in May, Forbes, in general terms, had informed Senators Hale, Wilson and Seward of the proposed foray. In alarm, Wilson wrote to Samuel Gridley Howe, one of Brown's backers, protesting against the move.

Wilson's letter brought results. On May 24, a committee of five of Brown's financial supporters met in secret at the Revere House in Boston. This group — Howe, Gerrit Smith, Theodore Parker, George L. Stearns and Thomas Wentworth Higginson — were united in deciding that Brown should go to Kansas at once and thus ostensibly discredit Forbes' allegations. Brown regretted the

---

[16] For an account of Forbes' devious conduct see "John Brown and His Friends," *Atlantic Monthly*, XXX, 50–61 (July 1872). Very likely the article was written by F. B. Sanborn, a confidant of Brown. The New York *Herald* for Oct. 27, 1859, has a lengthy exposé of Forbes.

[17] Douglass, *Life and Times*, 387.

decision, but bound himself to obey it on the prospect of receiving additional funds from the committee in the spring of the following year.[18]

Brown returned to the Kansas regions in June 1858, where he remained for ten months. Now again in the border territories, he characteristically engaged in running off a number of slaves from Missouri. "Old Brown will have to keep out of sight for a little while. The Governor of Missouri has a reward of $3,000 offered for his capture," wrote Rosetta to her father.[19]

Early in 1859 Brown left the West. En route to Massachusetts, it is likely that he made it a point to converse with Douglass in Rochester. On March 10, 1859, he had written to Douglass, who was then in Detroit.[20] A month later Brown arrived at Smith's house for a four-day visit. On the way to Peterboro he spent a few hours in Rochester.[21] One of the employees in Douglass' printing office related that "a tall white man, with shaggy whiskers," called at the shop one morning "several months prior to October 16, 1859," and asked for Douglass. The visitor had the air of a man who came to fulfill an appointment. Upon Douglass' arrival the two "talked freely," and "in most earnest terms." [22]

In the autumn of 1859 Brown was ready to strike. He had purchased the necessary "Boxes Hardware" and the public had forgotten about Forbes' allegations. But before he struck, Brown decided to reveal his completed plans to Douglass in an attempt to enlist him for service at Harpers Ferry. On August 9, Brown's eldest son came to Rochester

---

[18] Sanborn, *Recollections*, 155, *et seq.* See also "John Brown and His Friends," *loc. cit.*, 55 *et seq.*

[19] Rosetta Douglass to Douglass, Feb. 2, 1859. *Douglass MSS.*

[20] Brown's diary, New York *Herald*, Oct. 25, 1859.

[21] Villard, *op. cit.*, 395.

[22] McGuire, "Two Episodes of Anti-Slavery Days," *loc. cit.*, 219, 220.

where he learned that Douglass had gone to Niagara Falls. On his return the following day Douglass conversed at length with the son of his old friend.[23]

Young Brown returned to Rochester six days later to learn that Douglass had left the city to meet Brown's lieutenant, John Kagi, a versatile young man who had taken part in the Kansas troubles. Douglass was then en route to Chambersburg, Pennsylvania (about twenty miles from Harpers Ferry), to fulfill an invitation from Brown requesting his presence at an old stone quarry.[24] Douglass reached the rendezvous on August 19, escorted by Shields Green and bringing with him a letter to Brown containing $25 and "best wishes for your welfare and prosperity," from Mrs. J. N. Gloucester, a well-to-do colored woman in Brooklyn.[25] Four were present at this secret meeting — Brown was a hunted man — Brown, Kagi, his "Secretary of War," and the two Negroes, Douglass and Green.

The discussion between Douglass and Brown was reminiscent of their first meeting, eleven years previously. Brown asked Douglass' opinion of the feasibility of the plan to seize the government arsenal at Harpers Ferry, and to lay hold of the leading citizens and use them as hostages.[26] Douglass was emphatic in his objections. He was more than willing to run slaves off by the underground railroad, but such an invasion as Brown now presented was an attack on the national government and would, Douglass contended, prove fatal to its perpetrators. Brown was adamant. He believed that evils must be dramatized before legislatures would take action. Brown informed

---

[23] Letter from J. Brown, Jr., to Kagi, Aug. 11, 1849. Sanborn, *Life and Letters of John Brown*, 536.

[24] Douglass, *Life and Times*, 387. Octavius B. Frothingham, *Life of Gerrit Smith* (New York, 1878), 255.

[25] Letter from Mrs. Gloucester to Brown, Aug. 18, 1859. Sanborn, *Life and Letters of John Brown*, 538.

[26] Douglass to Smith, Aug. 9, 1867. Frothingham, *Gerrit Smith*, 255.

Douglass that the proposed seizure would capture the attention of the country and compel people to do something about the sin of slavery.[27]

Douglass made clear his unwillingness to participate in such a venture. As he was preparing to leave Chambersburg, Brown made a final plea: "Come with me, Douglass. I will defend you with my life. I want you for a special purpose. When I strike, the bees will begin to swarm and I shall want you to help me hive them." [28]

Douglass was moved, but discretion had formed his decision. As he was leaving he asked Green if he had come to a decision as to whether he would stay with Brown. Douglass was surprised at the former slave's slow answer, "I b'leve I'll go wid de ole man." [29]

Despite his failure in the three days at Chambersburg, Brown did not give up his hope to win Douglass. With the single-mindedness and undespairing ardor of the zealot, he still hoped to prevail. A few weeks after the meeting with Brown, Douglass received a letter signed by a number of colored men inviting him to represent them at a convention to be held "right away" at Chambersburg. If Douglass would come the writers would agree to pledge themselves to see "your family well provided for during your absence, or until your safe return to them." [30]

Douglass never learned the identity of the individual who prompted the Negroes to get in touch with him. He surmised that it may have been Kagi. At any rate, it is certain that Brown knew of the communication for a copy of it was found among his papers at the Kennedy farm, five miles from the scene of the raid. Twenty-five years after Brown's death his daughter, Anna, called attention to the "missing link" in her father's movements late in

---

[27] Douglass, *Life and Times*, 354–358.

[28] *Ibid.*, 390.

[29] *Ibid.*

[30] Sanborn, *Life and Letters of John Brown*, footnote, 541.

September and early in October 1859. A close associate of Brown, Franklin B. Sanborn, implies that during this period Brown was at Chambersburg at the convention of colored men, waiting for Douglass.[31]

Brown believed that with sufficient urging Douglass would reconsider. But Brown had not judged his man correctly. Douglass failed to attend the convention; doubtless he guessed its nature. Brown made the best of his disappointment.

These two foes of slavery never saw each other again after their conversations at the old stone quarry. On October 17, eight weeks after their meeting, Douglass was in National Hall in Philadelphia, giving his oft-repeated lecture on "Self-Made Men," when he was informed of Brown's arrest. On the preceding day Brown and twenty-one men-at-arms, five of them Negroes, had attempted to seize a government arsenal at Harpers Ferry. Lacking a clear and definite plan of campaign, Brown's raid was doomed. It was staged in a section of Virginia — the northwestern part — where slaves were relatively few, and Brown had given those few no foreknowledge of his plans.[32]

The startling news of Brown's foray alarmed Douglass; he feared that some letters implicating him might be found by Brown's captors. Douglass hurried to New York on the advice of well-wishers who urged him to leave Philadelphia posthaste. Their counsel was timely. John W. Hurn, a telegraph operator, and an admirer of Douglass, suppressed for three hours the delivery of a despatch to the sheriff of Philadelphia instructing him to arrest Douglass.[33]

Douglass felt unsafe in New York. The hue and cry had been taken up and the morning papers screamed that the

---

[31] F. B. Sanborn, *Recollections of Seventy Years* (Boston, 1909), 153.
[32] Herbert Aptheker, *American Negro Slave Revolts* (New York, 1943), 352.
[33] Washington *Evening Star*, Feb. 21, 1895.

government would spare no pains in bringing to justice all those connected with the attempt on Harpers Ferry. Leaving the metropolis and avoiding main-travelled roads, Douglass made his way to his home in Rochester to secure or destroy any papers that could be used to implicate him.

His alarm took panic proportions as the New York *Herald* headlined the information that "Brown has made a full statement, implicating Gerrit Smith, Joshua Giddings and Frederick Douglass." [34] Brown's statement was "enough, it seems," ran the item from the *Herald*, "to justify a requisition from Governor Wise of Virginia, upon Governor Morgan, of New York, for the delivery over to the hands of justice of Gerrit Smith and Fred Douglass, as parties implicated in the crime of murder, and as accessories before the fact." [35]

Friends advised Douglass that the Federal government would surrender him to the state of Virginia on receipt of a proper requisition. Douglass did not believe that his supporters in Rochester would permit pursuers to take him south. He did not doubt, however, that President Buchanan would use the agencies of the national government to aid Governor Wise. After hurried thought Douglass fled to Canada.

Douglass' unceremonious departure, if unheroic, was good common sense. Wise sent communications to Buchanan and the Postmaster General of the United States asking that two agents from Virginia be given legal power to act as detectives for the postoffice department for the purpose of effecting the "delivery up" of Douglass, who was charged with "murder, robbery, and inciting to servile insurrection in the State of Virginia." [36]

Less than a week after Harpers Ferry, the United States district attorney for western New York appeared in

[34] Oct. 20, 1859.
[35] *Herald*, Oct. 21, 1859.
[36] Douglass, *Life and Times*, 379.

Rochester. One of the local papers hinted that he was looking for Douglass.[37] Another local daily, noting the presence of "United States Attorney Ould and other federal officers," supposed that they came for the purpose of seizing Douglass.[38]

If Douglass had been apprehended by federal authorities and summoned to attend court anywhere in the country he would have had no choice other than to appear. Once within the legal confines of a hostile state and subjected to its judicial processes, Douglass might have been accused on specious or flimsy evidence. The country's nerves were on edge; feelings ran high. The presence of a Negro abolitionist in the courts of Virginia in October 1859, would have placed a severe strain on the quality of mercy.

Safe in his retreat in Canada, Douglass realized that his flight might appear ignoble. An opportunity to explain his position came when John E. Cook charged him with cowardice. Cook, one of the men taken at Harpers Ferry, informed his captors that if Brown had followed his (Cook's) advice and retired to the mountains immediately, with his prisoners and whatever arms could be gathered, their venture would have been successful. The sequel to Harpers Ferry was disastrous, according to Cook, solely because of the pusillanimity of Douglass. The latter had been scheduled to bring a large number of men to the schoolhouse on an agreed date. Despite the fact, ran the charges, that Cook conveyed to him the necessary arms and waited for him for several hours, Douglass did not appear.[39]

Douglass answered, in his best epistolary vein, this obviously false accusation. He notices, he wrote in a letter to the editor of the Rochester *Democrat*, that Mr. Cook, "now a prisoner in the hands of the thing which calls itself the Government of Virginia, but which in fact is

---

[37] Rochester *Democrat*, Oct. 26, 1859, in *Herald*, Oct. 28, 1859.
[38] Rochester *Union*, Oct. 25, 1859, in *Herald*, Oct. 28, 1859.
[39] *Liberator*, Nov. 4, 1859.

but an organized conspiracy by the one part of the people against another and weaker," asserted that he promised to be present at Harpers Ferry. To begin with, stated Douglass, he had no personal acquaintance with Cook at all. The charge was false, ran Douglass' declaration, that he had pledged conditionally or otherwise that he would be present at the scene of action.[40]

As was usual in his remarks, Douglass did not spare the slaveholders. This denial of his, he pointed out, was motivated by a respectful consideration for the opinion of his fellow abolitionists rather than from the fear of being identified as an accomplice in the Brown movement. Any effort, no matter how misguided, was basically moral if it aimed at the overthrow of the slave system.

The letter continued with a statement of his reason for not joining Brown. To a pertinent quotation: "The tools to those who can use them," Douglass added that every man should work for the abolition of slavery in his own way. His (Douglass') sphere of activity for the cause did not extend to an armed attack on a government arsenal. No shame attached to him, he wrote, for keeping out of the way of United States marshals. Would a government that recognized the validity of the Dred Scott decision be likely to deal fairly with him? [41]

With this letter Douglass rested his case concerning his connection with Harpers Ferry. It did not, however, save him from further criticism. Fifty years after the event the surviving members of Brown's family — Henry Thompson, Salmon Brown, Annie Brown Adams and Sarah Brown — told Oswald Garrison Villard, Brown's biographer, that they felt that Douglass had failed "to live up to his obligations." [42] Yet at no time had Douglass ever

---

[40] New York *Herald*, Nov. 4, 1859. *Anglo-African Magazine*, VI, 383 (Dec. 1859).

[41] New York *Herald*, Nov. 4, 1859.

[42] Villard, *John Brown*, 323, and footnote, 627.

expressed any intention of joining Brown's band. Equally as definite was the fact that Douglass had planned to leave for Europe in November 1859, as he wrote a friend early in October of that year.[43] Douglass' intention to go abroad in November clearly indicates that he could not have planned to participate in Brown's raid.

Brown was doomed to disappointment in his expectation that all runaways were like Green. Most of those who had escaped from slavery were unwilling to risk the danger of a return to the house of bondage. "The black Douglass," wrote the *Herald* with heavy humor, "having some experiences in his early life of the pleasures of Southern society had no desire to trust himself again even on the borders of the Potomac." [44]

Douglass' flight, if unheroic, was not an isolated case. After Brown's arrest, most of the other men who had been informed about his plans were apprehensive. Sanborn started to leave for Quebec, getting as far as Portland, Maine. Dr. Howe asserted that the Harpers Ferry event was "unforeseen and unexpected by me; nor does all my previous knowledge of John Brown enable me to reconcile it with his characteristic prudence and his reluctance to shed blood or excite servile insurrection." [45] Howe and George Stearns remained in Canada until after Brown's execution on December 2. Theodore Parker was in Europe at the time of the outbreak. Gerrit Smith suffered a mental aberration. Thomas Wentworth Higginson alone refused to deny complicity in the abortive scheme.

On November 12, in line with his previously laid plans, Douglass took passage from Quebec. His heart was heavy — he felt that he might be going into a lifetime exile. For some days after his fourteen-day trip he stayed at the

---

[43] Douglass to Robert Kinnicut, Oct. 9, 1859. *MS.* in Schomburg Collection (New York City).

[44] *Herald*, Nov. 4, 1859.

[45] Villard, *John Brown*, 531.

home of the Rev. R. L. Carpenter of Halifax.[46] As in his earlier visit Douglass tried to impress upon the English people their responsibility for an active interest in the anti-slavery movement.[47] No longer a come-outer as he had been thirteen years ago on his first visit, Douglass spent much of his energies in emphasizing the anti-slavery nature of the Constitution.[48] Everywhere he went he was urged to explain his connection with the Brown affair.

Douglass' pleasant visits with friends of long standing were cut short by the news of his daughter's death. Douglass sailed for America with the intention of returning in a few months to tour Ireland and southern England.[49] Although the course of events impelled him to abandon this plan — he did not see England again until nearly thirty years later — his five months' visit in 1859 and 1860 was not without results. Douglass' anti-slavery speeches laid some of the groundwork for the support that the English masses were to demonstrate for the North during the Civil War.

Douglass returned to America in May 1860, to find that the hysteria over the Brown episode had largely subsided. Six months earlier a Senate committee, headed by James M. Mason of Virginia, had been appointed to investigate the affair. Shortly after Douglass reached Rochester, the committee, on June 14, made its report. Reluctant to call witnesses who might have used the hearings as a sounding board for abolitionism, and anxious to avoid creating any additional martyrs, the committee brought forth a report so restrained as to be almost completely ignored throughout the country.

---

[46] *British and Foreign Anti-Slavery Reporter*, VII, 1 (Jan. 2, 1860).

[47] *Ibid.*, 125 (June 1, 1860).

[48] *The Constitution of the United States: Is It Pro-Slavery or Anti-Slavery* (Halifax, 1860).

[49] Douglass to Smith, July 2, 1860. *Smith MSS.* Also *Douglass' Monthly*, June 1860.

But the anti-slavery cause needed no additional martyrs. Brown sufficed. The ensuing rapid current of events gave him a lasting fame. Less than a year after his execution, Lincoln was elected president. Within another eight months the song, "John Brown's Body," had been improvised by four soldiers from the Twelfth Massachusetts regiment. Emerson's peroration that Brown's death would make the gallows glorious like the cross, was prophetic. The fate of God's angry man became a rallying cry and with Northern success on the battlefield his memory took stature. Public speakers eulogized him. The resounding tones of Douglass must needs swell the chorus:

If John Brown did not end the war that ended slavery, he did at least begin the war that ended slavery. If we look over the dates, places and men for which this honor is claimed, we shall find that not Carolina, but Virginia, not Fort Sumter, but Harpers Ferry, and the United States Arsenal, not Major Anderson, but John Brown began the war that ended slavery and made this a free republic. Until this blow was struck, the prospect for Freedom was dim, shadowy and uncertain. The irrepressible conflict was one of words, votes and compromises. When John Brown stretched forth his arm the sky was cleared — the time for compromise was gone — the armed hosts stood face to face over the chasm of a broken Union and the clash of arms was at hand.[50]

---

[50] Commencement address at Storer College, Harpers Ferry, May 30, 1882. *Douglass MSS.*

CHAPTER XI

A Day for Poetry and Song

The very neutral ground of Compromise is that which is trampled at last by the contending Forces of the good and evil principle. Our legislators might as well try to stay Niagara with a drip-net, or pass acts against the law of gravitation, as endeavor to stunt the growth of avenging Conscience. Do they think that the Union can be stuck together with mouth-glue when the eternal forces are rendering it asunder.

LOWELL

On the first day of February 1859, Hinton Rowan Helper wrote to William Lloyd Garrison asking him to raise five one-hundred-dollar subscriptions to "aid in the publication of 100,000 copies of The Impending Crisis of the South." [1] This request was eloquently meaningful; the man who saw the clash between the sections as an economic issue was getting in touch with the great agitator who for thirty years had translated the sectional controversy in terms of moral and humanitarian imperatives. By 1860, economics had caught up with ethics and the two forces had fused to produce a composite Northern mind-set that created a Republican party and a section psychologically prepared for a resort to arms.

In turn, the South had become unified in its willingness to fight for its way of life. Over the quarter century that the abolitionists had developed a technique of denunciation, the South had developed a philosophy of defense. To the South the last straw was the election of a Republican president in November 1860. When, four months

---

[1] Helper to Garrison, Feb. 1, 1859. *Garrison MSS.*

later, Lincoln took office, he was confronted by the ominous fact that the states of the lower South had left the Union. Lincoln called for 75,000 volunteers "to maintain the honor, the integrity and the existence of our National Union." The "irrepressible conflict" had come.

The outbreak of the war had a bracing effect on Douglass. He was delighted at the turn of events. No longer would it be necessary for the Harriet Tubmans and the John Browns to strike single-handedly; now the full might of an aroused North was to be hurled against the slaveholders. If hostilities continued indefinitely, the Negro problem, in its various guises, would assume increasing proportions, and as the nation's most articulate colored man, he would shine in reflected importance. The prospect of position and preferment put him in high spirits and took the edge from the bitter memories of the preceding months. The death of Annie was still fresh in mind, but now he could regard philosophically such recent adverse experiences as his precipitous flight to England, the declining influence and circulation of his weekly, the failure to effect the removal of the property qualification for Negro voting in New York, and his futile membership in parties which existed on the outer margin of political reality.

Obviously Douglass' response to the war was an immediate assertion that it was a crusade for freedom. On the first page of the May issue of the *Monthly*, Douglass inserted drawings of an American eagle and the flag, accompanied by the caption, "Freedom for all, or chains for all." With a foresight mothered by wishful thinking, Douglass saw in the conflict the end of slavery. For the consummation of this aim he trusted — correctly appraising humanitarian sentiment — "less to the virtue of the North than to the villainy of the South." [2]

Some observers may have seen the war as another illus-

---

[2] Holland, *Frederick Douglass*, 285.

tration of the eternal class struggle; others may have seen it as a second American revolution with agrarianism fighting a losing battle. People below the Mason-Dixon line saw the war as a threat to the way of life of a conscious minority proud of its traditions. To Douglass the war was none of these things; in his thinking the war was a struggle for humanity, and its manifest destiny was to tear out the living vitals of the slave system.

Because he conceived it as a war of emancipation, Douglass was anxious that the Negro strike a blow. As Lincoln called for volunteers immediately after the firing on Fort Sumter, Douglass urged colored men to form militia companies. To Lincoln he proffered advice on "How to End the War." "Stop it on the soil upon which it originated, and among the traitors and rebels who started it. This can be done by 'carrying the war into Africa.' Let the slaves and free colored people be called into service and formed into a liberating army, to march into the South and raise the banner of Emancipation among the slaves." [3]

Negroes were readily accepted in the navy, "it being no departure from the established practice in the service." [4] But Lincoln was loath to enlist Negroes in the army. When Douglass learned of the President's hesitancy he valiantly asserted that the colored man could "wield a sword, fire a gun, march and countermarch." If he could have conversed with Lincoln, wrote Douglass to his public, he would have related the story of the Negroes with Andrew Jackson at New Orleans. [5] To Douglass the last straw was the contrast between the coolness toward the Negro and the rousing welcome given to foreign-born citizens — Poles, Italians, Irish, Cubans and Germans — who signed up as recruits.

---

[3] *Douglass' Monthly*, May 1861.

[4] Joseph T. Wilson, *The Black Phalanx* (Hartford, Conn., 1888), 103.

[5] *Douglass' Monthly*, Sept. 1861.

For Douglass had expected better of the President. During the last months of Buchanan's vacillating administration Douglass had been impressed by Lincoln's "stately silence," his unwillingness to commit himself to any of the compromise proposals, and his "refusal to have any concessions extorted from him under the terror instituted by thievish conspirators and traitors." [6] Late in May, Lincoln authorized General Butler to retain all fugitive slaves within his lines. Ten weeks later the President signed a confiscation measure which declared free those slaves who were being used for military or naval purposes by the Confederacy.[7] But, to the dismay of the abolitionists, it became increasingly evident that Lincoln could not be rushed into the use of drastic measures. In the early months of the war his desire to hold the fidgety border states made him wary of any premature move in the direction of altering the time-honored status of the Negro, North or South. As Douglass was to discover, the keynote of Lincoln's Negro policy could be summed up in the word "expediency."

Douglass' keen interest in the activities of the national government was, in part, a consequence of the virtual disappearance of the organized abolition movement. With the outbreak of hostilities and the public absorption in the news from the battle fronts, the abolitionists dropped their distinctive program and soon became indistinguishable from any other patriot group. The American Anti-Slavery Society continued to hold meetings, but it was simply a process of going through the motions. Logically, as disunionists, the members of the Society should have welcomed the secession of the Southern states as good riddance. Logically, the Society should have frowned on

---

[6] *Ibid.*, Mar. 1861.

[7] For the confiscation measure and similar legislation see Henry Wilson, *History of the Anti-Slavery Measures of the Thirty-Seventh and Thirty-Eighth United States Congresses, 1861–1864* (Boston, 1864).

compensated emancipation. But, driven by the force of events, the Society did neither. On the contrary, within six months after the bombardment of Fort Sumter the Executive Committee of the Society drew up a petition to Congress, requesting that body to lose no time in declaring slavery abolished throughout the land, "and while not recognizing the right of property in man, allowing for the emancipated slaves of such as are loyal to the Government, a fair pecuniary reward." [8] This petition, anti-Southern as it was, gave evidence of the ideological bankruptcy of Garrisonian abolitionism.

The ambiguous position of the parent organization was reflected in the curtailed programs of its auxiliaries. Gone, in the main, were the meetings with their never-ending debates. Fewer were the donations, collections, pledges and subscriptions. The women who had conducted the anti-slavery fairs and bazaars now had a wider scope for their energies. Gone, too, after the outbreak of the war were the violent reactions of audiences to the platform appearances of abolitionists. The catcalls, the shouting and the throwing of missiles gave way to a patter of polite applause which was perhaps less emotionally satisfying to a true abolitionist than a resounding chorus of boos.

Douglass' experience at Syracuse in November 1861 was an augury of the changed order of things. He was scheduled to lecture in that city on the fourteenth of the month at eight in the evening. Placards threatening him with violence had been put up throughout the city. To cope with the expected outbreak the mayor, Charles A. Andrews, appointed fifty special policemen and mustered out a military company.[9] Gerrit Smith, dropping by Samuel J. May's residence to take tea late that afternoon, informed his host that the soldiers and armed police were already

---

[8] Printed notice issued by the Executive Committee of the American Anti-Slavery Society, dated Oct. 30, 1861. *A. S. Let.*, XXXI.

[9] May to Garrison, Nov. 16, 1861. *A. S. Let.*, XXXI.

standing guard at the hall where Douglass was scheduled to speak.[10] But the demonstration never materialized. There was no sign of disturbance throughout Douglass' ninety-minute discourse. "Honor to your city," wrote Garrison to May.[11]

As Douglass focussed his attention on national affairs he became increasingly suspicious of the Chief Executive. Rumor whispered that it was only with great reluctance that the President, early in August 1861, had signed the confiscation bill. Ignoring the varied political considerations that inevitably condition a president's course of action, Douglass confessed his growing disappointment. "It now seems to me," he wrote to May late that month, "that our Government has resolved that no good shall come to the Negro from this war, and that it means to convince the slaveholders that slavery is safer in than out of the union." Douglass confided that his "anti-slavery confidence is blown to the winds," by the government's policy "that Negroes shall smell powder only in the character of cooks and body servants in the army." The national government would not do justice by ethical promptings: "Nothing short of dire necessity will bring it to act wisely." [12]

Douglass became even more bitter in mid-September when Lincoln over-ruled General Frémont's proclamation establishing martial law in Missouri and declaring free the slaves of those masters fighting against the North. When, in December 1861, Lincoln's first message to Congress recommended colonization for slaves and free Negroes, Douglass' language became unrestrained. He termed colonization "an old Whig and border state prepossession,"

---

[10] *Samuel J. May Diary*, Nov. 14, 1861. (Diary in keeping of W. F. Galpin, Syracuse, N. Y.)

[11] *Ibid.*, Dec. 6, 1861.

[12] Douglass to May, Aug. 30, 1861. *MS.* in possession of Arthur B. Spingarn.

and acknowledged himself "bewildered by the spectacle of moral blindness, infatuation and helpless imbecility which the government of Lincoln presents." [13]

Early in February 1862, Douglass was given an opportunity to sound his criticism at Boston in a public address under the auspices of the Emancipation League. This organization was formed late in 1861 by four men, three of whom — Howe, Sanborn and Stearns — had received public notice in connection with the financing of Brown's raid. By means of public addresses the League hoped to create a widespread sentiment favorable to freedom for the slave.[14] The selection of Douglass as the League's first speaker was routine.

The topic announced was, "The Black Man's Future in the South," but in his speeches Douglass never permitted himself to be imprisoned by the title of his subject or the hands of the clock. Douglass directed the most stinging of his many hits at "the doubting, hesitating and vacillating policy of the government in regard to the real difficulty — slavery." The "numerous assembly" cheered as he excoriated the administration's failure to adopt a program of immediate emancipation. The nation's highest duty, continued the aroused orator, was to free the Negro and then accord to him equal justice and "a chance to live." Any effort to sustain slavery was an attempt to "outwit Jehovah, and defy the laws of God's universe." [15]

At New York City six days later, Douglass delivered substantially the same address. Garnet presided and the Hutchinsons sang. The *Standard* reported that "more than one judge expressed the opinion that no more effective discourse had been delivered in the city." [16] The response to both addresses was revealing. Despite the

[13] Douglass to Smith, Dec. 22, 1861. *Smith MSS.*
[14] Ware, *op. cit.*, 93.
[15] Boston *Journal*, Feb. 6, 1862.
[16] *Standard*, Feb. 22, 1862.

severity of Douglass' tone, there had been no hissing or disorder at the meetings. The force of circumstances was impelling the country toward the goal of slave emancipation. Former abolitionists who had repeatedly insisted that slavery would go out in a sea of blood were being regarded as latter-day prophets as abolitionism slowly but definitely became the higher patriotism.

As the winter months wore on, Douglass and other Negro leaders were gratified to observe that "the slow coach at Washington" was beginning to pick up speed. Lincoln had refused to mitigate Captain Nathaniel P. Gordon's death sentence for commanding a slave ship. Gordon was hanged for piracy on February 21. Three weeks later the President signed a bill forbidding the army or navy to return fugitive slaves.

These two events proved accurate signposts. During the winter months visitors to the halls of Congress had listened to the debates on the expediency of compensated emancipation in the District of Columbia. Sixty years earlier, Congress had passed a law stipulating that the slave codes of Maryland and Virginia be enforced in the District. In 1850, as part of the great compromise enactment of that year, the slave pens at the national capital had been abolished. In the ten years preceding the war the number of slaves had decreased. This downward trend had been speeded by the withdrawal of the Southern Congressmen in 1861.[17] After the outbreak of the war the Massachusetts senators, Sumner and Wilson, were especially active in pushing the proposed measure. The former, in a lengthy address delivered on the last day of March 1862, urged immediate passage of the bill. "Nobody," ran one of his sustained sentences, "can read that slaves were once sold in the markets of Rome . . . without confessing the scandal to religion; and nobody can hear that slaves are now sold in

[17] For the complete story see Mary Tremain, *Slavery in the District of Columbia* (New York, 1892).

the markets of Washington, without confessing the scandal to liberal institutions." [18]

Douglass sent a letter of thanks to Sumner for his support of the bill. "Ahead of everybody," wrote he, "the slaveholder and the slave look to you as the best embodiment of the anti-slavery idea now in the counsels of the nation." [19]

The bill outlawing slavery or involuntary servitude in the District passed the Senate, received the final vote in the House on April 11, and five days later became a law by Lincoln's signature. Negroes assembled in their churches to rejoice. Douglass' enthusiasm was now as unrestrained as his recent denunciation. This measure, he informed his readers, was "the first great step toward the righteousness which exalts a nation." The occasion demanded highflown rhetoric. "Let high swelling anthems (such as tuned the voice and thrilled the heart of ancient Israel, when they shouted to heaven the glad tidings of their deliverance from Egyptian bondage) now roll along the earth and sky." [20]

But although emancipation in the District was an unmistakable straw in the wind, the progress of the cause went too slow for Douglass. He soon resumed his task as whip and spur of the administration. His impatience was aroused in May 1862 by Lincoln's disavowal of General Hunter's declaration that slaves in Georgia, Florida and South Carolina were forever free. Before a sympathetic Fourth of July audience at Himrod's Corners, New York, Douglass again assailed Lincoln for failure to adopt a decidedly anti-slavery policy. The crowd of 2,000 was stirred by the declaration that the administration was waging war with the olive branch rather than the sword. A listener's protest against the severity of his remarks deterred Douglass not

---

[18] Wilson, *Anti-Slavery Measures*, 56.
[19] Douglass to Sumner, Apr. 8, 1862. *Sumner Letterbooks.*
[20] *Douglass' Monthly*, May 1862.

at all. Rebellion and slavery, he shouted, "were twin monsters . . . and all attempts at upholding one, while pulling down the other" would be calamitous.[21]

Douglass' insistent criticism of Lincoln sprang from an entirely different source from that of the so-called Congressional Radicals. If a man could be identified with a group simply because both had a common enemy, Douglass would come as close to being a Copperhead as to being a Radical. Douglass' hostility to the President's policies sprang from racial and reformist roots. Douglass was a professional Negro reformer; agitation was his stock in trade. He was forced by his calling to be ever in advance of the program of the authorities in power. As soon as he got the half loaf for which he asked, he found it necessary to increase his ration. Douglass' whole concern in the conflict then in process was to turn it into a black man's war.

Douglass' censures of Lincoln sprang from no sympathy with or understanding of the aims of the Radicals. It is doubtful if he ever shook hands with Ben Wade or Thaddeus Stevens, Republicans most powerful in mapping the party's high strategy in Congress. Douglass' connection with the feeble Liberty party had given him no insight into the machinery of practical party politics. In answer to the question, "What makes politicians tick?" he could bring no first-hand information. The clash between the Radicals and Lincoln over the respective powers of the legislative and executive branches of the government was a political controversy foreign to Douglass' interests. He knew nothing of the politically-inspired activities of the Committee on the Conduct of the War.

He was unaware also of the economic aims of the Radicals. He felt no vital interest in problems relating to the tariff, internal improvements, a national banking system and free homesteads. Great was his interest in the Repub-

---

[21] Holland, *Frederick Douglass*, 288.

lican party after the Civil War, but during the years of the conflict Douglass never detected the fine hand of a small group of Republican politicians who were taking a new party and committing it to a program that spelled economic dominance for the rising industrialists of the North.

If Douglass remained unaware of the off-stage vendetta between the President and a group of his fellow-Republicans, his response was immediate to any issue involving the Negro. And the administration faced such questions. One of the most insistent of these problems related to the thousands of runaway slaves who were attaching themselves to the Union armies. Lincoln well knew that the presence of these fugitives in the slave-holding border states was proving embarrassing to the national government. In his debates with Stephen Douglas, Lincoln had advocated the deportation and colonization of the black population, and now as President he again considered this possibility. He was in a position, in 1862, to take action. The measure freeing slaves in the District had also provided $100,000 to aid in colonization. Congress subsequently added an appropriation of half a million, and the Confiscation Act of July 16, 1862 authorized the President to make provision for the transportation and colonization of those freed slaves who were willing to leave the country. In September, Lincoln submitted to his cabinet " the question of the propriety of seeking to make treaties with Latin America or European countries with colonies or tropics" for the purpose of providing "a refuge for colored people." [22] On the last day of the month, Secretary of State Seward addressed a circular letter to the governments of England, France, Holland and Denmark, informing them of Lincoln's colonization plans and asking their cooperation. Lincoln appealed to the Negro to accept this solution.

[22] *Bates' Diary*, Sept. 25, 1862. Howard K. Beale, ed., *Diary of Edward Bates* (Washington, 1933), 262.

The response of the colored people was negative. To Douglass the project was anathema. To the President's contention that the difference between the white and the black races rendered it impossible for them to live side by side without detriment to both, Douglass pointed an answering finger at the example of Latin America. "A horse thief pleading the existence of the horse as the apology for his theft or a highwayman contending that the money in the traveler's pocket is the sole first cause of his robbery are about as much entitled to respect as the President's reasoning at this point." [23] With an air of impatience Douglass dismissed Lincoln's assertion that the "ban of nature" prevented intermarriage. "Public opinion and prejudice may prevent intermarriage. . . ." But the existence of mulattoes and quadroons disproved the "ban of nature" theory. "If any such ban existed, artificial 'bans' such as legal enactments and popular prejudices would not be necessary to keep the races asunder. Nature would do her work." [24] In dejection over Lincoln's course, Douglass informed Smith that "the nation was never more completely in the hands of the slave power." [25]

Douglass' answer to the insistent question as to the future of the slave was markedly different from that of Lincoln's colonization scheme. Confronted by a gigantic social problem, Douglass did not hesitate. "What shall be done with the slaves, if they are emancipated?" Douglass' response was a magnificent evasion of the question. "Do nothing with them" he wrote, "mind your business and let them mind theirs." The Negro, Douglass informed his countrymen, had been undone by the doings of others. Had the Negro been free from interference originally he would not have been spirited from his homeland and sold in Christian slave-markets. As a rule, the Negro had

---

[23] *Douglass' Monthly*, Sept. 1862.

[24] *Ibid.*

[25] Douglass to Smith, Sept. 8, 1862. *Smith MSS.*

suffered from the attempts to do something for him. "Deal justly with him." [26] To Douglass the problem was as simple as that.

Late in September 1862, Douglass' mercurial temperament shot up. Lincoln's colonization projects and his answer to Greeley's "Prayer of Twenty Millions" ("What I do about slavery and the colored race, I do because I believe it helps to save the Union") had been depressing. But the President had made up his mind on the subject of emancipation as a military necessity. After the victory at Antietam, Lincoln issued a proclamation on September 22, declaring free all slaves within any state or district in rebellion on January 1, 1863.

Douglass' attitude toward the administration instantly assumed a more positive phase. An expression of his changing attitude was revealed in his "Slaves' Appeal to Great Britain," a pamphlet issued shortly after Lincoln's preliminary declaration. In this appeal Douglass strove to influence the British public to prevent England from recognizing the Confederacy as a sovereign state. On behalf of the slave Douglass besought England to "frown sternly" on the conspirators. "Oh! I pray you, by all the highest and holiest memories, blast not the budding hopes of these three millions by lending your countenance and extending your honored and potent hand to the blood-stained fingers of the impious slave-holding Confederate States of America." Slavery was the chief cause of the struggle; hence, ran Douglass' statement, the war was an anti-slavery war and as such "should command the ardent support of good men in all countries." From September 22, 1862 on, the war was "invested with sanctity," and England was morally bound to hold aloof from the Confederacy.[27]

---

[26] William Wells Brown, *The Black Man, His Antecedents, His Genius, His Achievements* (New York, 1863), 184–187.

[27] Holland, *Frederick Douglass*, 291.

The appeal was widely circulated in the British Isles. "I have no doubt," wrote Henry Richardson to Douglass, "that it has appeared in whole or in part in very many English newspapers."

Douglass' joy at the preliminary proclamation soon gave way to doubts. Signs of political reaction became evident; the people were becoming impatient with currency fluctuations, and there was a growing dissatisfaction with the uninspired tactics of the Union generals. Perhaps, ran the fear in abolitionist circles, emancipation would not be proclaimed. But Douglass and other friends of the slave went hopefully ahead with their plans of celebration. Rejoicing meetings were advertised throughout the North.

The passing of the old year found Douglass in Boston prepared to take part in the program arranged by the Union Progressive Association. Preparations had been made for three monster meetings at Tremont Temple on the first day of the new year. The exercises were conducted by Negroes. Douglass, speaking at the afternoon session, declared that he was thankful that he was living to witness the beginning of the end of slavery. The dark yesterdays were now to be followed by days made luminous "by the rosy dawning of the new truth of freedom." He praised His Maker that "we are here to rejoice in it." Douglass' closing sentences were punctuated by cries of "Amen," and "Bless the Lord." [28]

The afternoon gathering had been enthusiastic, but everyone looked forward to the meeting in the evening. By nightfall Lincoln would have shaken hands with the inevitable procession of New Year's well-wishers and then, free from routine duties, he could fulfill his promise.

As Douglass left his lodgings and progressed toward Tremont Temple he became aware that twilight had

[28] Boston *Journal*, Jan. 2, 1863.

merged into an evening of singular beauty. A fresh snow covered the earth. The night took on an unwonted brightness from the lanterns and giant candles [29] whose radiance seemed to presage good tidings. In high spirits Douglass entered the packed hall shortly before eight o'clock. A seat on the platform had been reserved for him.

The first hour of waiting was occupied by brief addresses. Among the speakers were a Negro clergyman, J. Sella Martin, and the woman's righter, Anna E. Dickinson, who had been discharged from the United States mint in 1861 as a consequence of her ultra-abolitionist sentiments. Nine o'clock came; a general restlessness pervaded the hall. William Wells Brown, and then Douglass, spoke in hopeful platitudes. But, as another hour passed without word from Washington the despondency mounted. Many in the audience reminded themselves that with Lincoln political considerations frequently over-rode all others.

But the prudent occupant of the White House had come to a decision. That very morning he had rewritten the document. It had been engrossed at the State Department during the mid-day hours and had been duly signed late in the afternoon.

Shortly after ten o'clock, as the intelligence was spreading throughout the land, a messenger bursting with the good news hastened into Tremont Temple, shouting, "It is coming! It is on the wires!" [30] A tumultuous chorus sounded to Boston Common. The promise of the future had become today's reality.

The excited audience could not restrain itself during the reading of the proclamation. Overcharged emotions demanded release. Cheers and shouting finally gave way to more formal group expression. All voices joined in as Douglass' rich baritone swelled the song, "Blow ye the

---

[29] Boston *Transcript*, Jan. 2, 1863.
[30] Douglass, *Life and Times*, 329.

trumpet, blow." [31] A Negro minister led in another stirring anthem,

> Sound the loud timbrel o'er Egypt's dark sea,
> Jehovah hath triumphed, his people are free.

For two hours the celebration continued. The Tremont Temple had been hired until twelve o'clock but enthusiasm was still at a high pitch when the hour of midnight struck. Douglass and the other more ardent spirits were in no mood to go to bed. A proposal that the meeting continue elsewhere was adopted by acclamation.

Within sixty minutes the crowd filled the Twelfth Baptist Church on Phillips Street. Its Negro pastor, Leonard Grimes, who had once been imprisoned in Virginia for attempting to aid fugitives to escape, led in public prayer. Spontaneous singing followed, filling the church.[32] Douglass had a hearty appetite for the refreshments that had been prepared in anticipation of the occasion. The rejoicing continued into the small hours, and not until the night was far spent did the celebrants leave.[33]

Douglass was unaware of any feeling of weariness as he walked out into the faint dawn. To him the day had been memorable. He had not yet perceived that the Emancipation Proclamation had its loopholes; at that transfigured hour he saw only "its anti-slavery side." [34] Gratifying to him was the conception which read into Lincoln's words a declaration of independence for nearly four million slaves. At that hour he shared the mood of elation described by Emerson in his "Boston Hymn," written on that very day:

> I break your bonds and masterships,
> And I unchain the slave:
> Free be his heart and hand henceforth
> As wind and wandering wave.

---

[31] Boston *Transcript*, Jan. 2, 1863.
[32] *Ibid.*
[33] Douglass, *Life and Times*, 430. [34] *Ibid.*, 431.

Boston Negroes were not alone in their demonstrations of joy.[35] For colored people throughout the North, January 1863, was a month of jubilee meetings. Naturally, the orator Douglass was in great demand; a red-letter occasion, such as one in celebration of emancipation, required the appearance of the most gifted public speaker in the Negro race.

In the thirty days following the issuing of the proclamation Douglass travelled over 2,000 miles in a zigzag line from Boston to Chicago.[36] Everywhere he was welcomed by large audiences, attentive to every word; everywhere the colored people responded as though they believed the New Jerusalem were at hand. It was, in Douglass' words, "a day for poetry and song." [37]

---

[35] For the joyous effect of the proclamation on Negroes see W. E. B. DuBois, *Black Reconstruction* (New York, 1935), 87.

[36] *Douglass' Monthly*, Feb. 1863.

[37] *Ibid.*, Jan. 1863.

CHAPTER XII

War Services of a Civilian

Ho, the car Emancipation
Rides majestic through our nation!
Abolitionist Song

As soon as the emancipation celebrations subsided and sobriety set in, Douglass again turned his attention to the question of colored troops. Fond of pillorying inconsistency, he told a Cooper Institute audience that it was "claimed in one breath that Negroes won't fight, and in the next that if you arm them they'll become dangerous." [1]

But in the early months of 1863 Douglass and other Negroes were agreeably surprised to find that the slowly changing sentiment in Washington had finally reached the point of approval, even though reluctantly. With the growing conviction that the war might be long drawn out, the administration had gradually shifted its position on the question of Negro soldiers. Heavy losses on the battlefield, plus increasing desertions, were placing a premium on manpower. Moreover, the point that "every black man who joins the army enables a white man to stay home," began to carry weight. A popular jingle expressed the opinion of the white soldier:

In battle's wild commotion
I shouldn't at all object
If Sambo's body should stop a ball
That was coming for me direct.[2]

---

[1] New York *Tribune*, Feb. 8, 1863.
[2] Charles G. Halpins in E. C. Stedman, ed., *An American Anthology* (Cambridge, 1900), 32.

Taking the hint, Congress passed a bill which gave the President authority to organize "persons of African descent" for military or naval service. Lincoln signed the bill on July 17, 1862, but there had been no follow-up. The final spur had been the Emancipation Proclamation which stipulated that freed slaves would be received into the armed forces of the United States "to garrison forts, positions, stations and other places, and to man vessels of all sorts in said service."

Capitalizing on the changed attitude, the advocates of Negro troops bestirred themselves. The movement was spearheaded by John A. Andrew, Massachusetts' zealous war governor, who requested permission to raise two regiments of Negro troops to serve for three years. On January 20, 1863, Secretary of War Stanton gave official authorization to Andrew's petition.

But Massachusetts had a very small colored population from which to recruit; within the first six weeks a scant 100 volunteers had signed up. Andrew anxiously summoned George L. Stearns and persuaded him to take full charge of recruiting.[3] In a short time Stearns' committee collected $5,000 — Gerrit Smith alone gave $500 — and advertised widely for enlistments. To speed up the work, Stearns got in touch with Negro leaders such as William Wells Brown, J. W. Loguen and J. Mercer Langston. Soon Stearns had organized a line of recruiting posts from Boston to St. Louis. To enroll Douglass as an agent Stearns left for Rochester on February 23.[4]

Douglass needed little persuasion. Eight months earlier, at a Philadelphia meeting, he and Anna Dickinson had made a strong plea to the people of Pennsylvania to permit the raising of a Negro regiment, but the appeals had been in advance of local thinking.

---

[3] Louis F. Emilio, *History of the Fifty-Fourth Regiment of the Massachusetts Volunteer Infantry, 1863–1865* (Boston, 1894), 11.
[4] *Ibid.*, 12.

Within three days after Stearns' visit, Douglass, through the columns of his monthly, issued a stirring call, "Men of Color, to Arms!" He urged his colored compatriots to "fly to arms, and smite with death the power that would bury the government and your liberty in the same hopeless grave." It was better, so ran Douglass' entreaty, to die free than to live slaves. "Liberty won only by white men will lose half its lustre." He charged young Negroes to remember Denmark Vesey and Shields Green. He closed with the information to prospective applicants that he would undertake to forward them to Boston if they would contact him within two weeks.[5] With his headquarters at Buffalo [6] Douglass undertook to raise at least one company for the regiment.[7] His son Charles was his first enrollee, as he proudly informed Smith.[8] Shortly afterward, Lewis also signed up.

During the month of March Douglass covered various towns in up-state New York.[9] At Albany he was aided by Stephen Myers who "turned over to him eighteen." [10] Going westward, Douglass stopped at Syracuse where he enlisted twenty-five, two of whom failed to pass the required physical examination.[11] At his one meeting in

---

[5] *Douglass' Monthly*, Mar. 1863.   [6] Emilio, *op. cit.*, 13.

[7] *Douglass' Monthly*, Apr. 1863.

[8] Douglass to Smith, May 6, 1863. *Smith MSS.*

[9] Among Smith's papers is a sheet containing an account of Douglass' receipts and disbursements for March 1863. Some sample entries read as follows:

March 24	Received from Stearns	$300
	For ration to men en route to camp	
	Subsidizing ten men in Rochester three days . .	20
27	Examination of men at Albany	
	Examination of men at Rochester	63
30	Round trip to Buffalo to consult with George Stearns	3

[10] Myers to Smith, Mar. 24, 1863. *Smith MSS.*

[11] S. J. May to *Standard*, Mar. 27, 1863. *Standard*, Apr. 4, 1863.

Buffalo he got seven recruits. Little Falls, Canajoharie, and Glen Falls contributed a total of twenty-three.[12] By the middle of April Douglass had despatched more than one hundred men to Boston, for service in the Fifty-Fourth regiment. His recruiting expenses had run to $700 which, Douglass ventured to say, was less than half as much as was expended for the raising of any other company.[13]

Although he had succeeded in raising his quota, Douglass was not satisfied with the relatively small number of Negroes who were signing up. He presented a long list of reasons in support of enlistment. A colored man should join the army because (1) manhood required him to take sides, (2) he was a citizen with a citizen's obligations, (3) all lovers of slavery regarded the arming of the Negro as a calamity, (4) the Negro should learn the use of arms in order to secure and defend his liberty, (5) battle encounter would give him a chance to demonstrate his courage, (6) enlistment would enable the Negro to recover his self-respect, (7) the war was being waged for the emancipation of Negroes, and (8) the enlistment of Negroes was a certain means of preventing the country from drifting back into the whirlpool of pro-slavery compromise.[14] Supplementing words by action, Douglass set about to recruit another company. In April and May he toured western New York, visiting Oswego, Syracuse, Ithaca, Troy and Auburn, urging young men to sign up.[15]

While Douglass was raising his second company, the work of training the earlier volunteers was progressing at the Readville, Massachusetts camp where one thousand Negroes from the four quarters of the country were learning the manual of arms. The regimental command was assigned to Robert Gould Shaw, a college-trained young

[12] *Douglass' Monthly*, Apr. 1863.
[13] Douglass to Smith, Apr. 14, 1863. *Smith MSS.*
[14] *Douglass' Monthly*, Mar. 1863.
[15] *Ibid.*, May 1863.

man from one of Massachusetts' oldest families. Toward the close of May the freshly-trained soldiers made ready to answer the summons of General David Hunter, commander of the Department of the South, requesting that the Fifty-Fourth be sent to South Carolina.

Thinking it unsafe to send Negro troops to the front by railroad, the officers in command decided to send the contingent by water, and thus forestall any demonstrations of hostility or prejudice en route. The regiment came to Boston to embark. On the morning of May 28, the city had an expectant air. The national colors flew everywhere. One hundred reserve policemen were on duty to clear the streets and keep order,[16] for it was not known how even liberty-loving Boston would respond to Negroes in military uniform.

The excitement grew as the Negroes marched through the downtown streets on their way to the Common. Observers noted the flags carried by the regiment: among them was a national flag presented by the young colored women of Boston; another, showing the state colors, was a gift of the Colored Ladies' Relief Society. Sure to catch the eye were the regimental banners, of superb white silk, adorned on one side by the coat-of-arms of Massachusetts, and on the other by "a golden cross and a golden star, with 'In hoc signo vinces' beneath." [17]

Thousands cheered the impressive spectacle. The poet Whittier forsook his pacifism for an hour to get a glimpse of the marching Negroes. It was the only regiment he viewed during the war, and he never forgot the scene.[18] Another great abolitionist beheld the parade. "Passing

---

[16] Marcha Nicolson McKay, *When the Tide Turned in the Civil War* (Indianapolis, 1929), 10.

[17] William Wells Brown, *The Negro in the American Rebellion* (Boston, 1867), 156.

[18] Lydia Maria Child to Sarah Shaw, Apr. 8, 1866. *Shaw Family Correspondence* (New York Public Library).

the house of Wendell Phillips, on Essex Street, William Lloyd Garrison was seen standing on the balcony, his head resting on a bust of John Brown," wrote Captain Emilio,[19] whose regard for historical detail outran his respect for the symmetrical sentence.

Of course, Douglass was present. He was proud to see two of his sons in this first Negro regiment from the North. Charles was an orderly, and Lewis was in the uniform of a sergeant-major.[20] The Negro orator followed the crowd to the jammed Common where the troops passed in review before Governor Andrew, the mayor of Boston, and Senator Wilson. The eyes of twenty thousand spectators followed the motions of the marching men, who made an excellent appearance. A newspaper reporter noted the "general precision attending their evolutions," and their "ease and uniformity in going through the manual." [21]

From the scene of the dress parade the regiment marched to Battery Wharf. En route the band played the John Brown song, "while passing over ground moistened by the blood of Crispus Attucks," a Negro who was the first patriot to shed his blood in the Revolutionary War. Shortly after one o'clock the soldiers boarded the *De Molay*, made ready for her maiden voyage. Three hours later the lines were cut and the steamer eased from her moorings, bound for Port Royal, South Carolina. A privileged character, Douglass remained on the ship until she was well down the harbor. He returned on a tug.[22] Well might he feel proud of his part in raising men for the Fifty-Fourth. The example of Massachusetts in recruiting Negro soldiers was soon followed by other Northern states.

Douglass had bent his effort to make the Negro a soldier; now he attacked the problem of the treatment of the Negro

---

[19] Emilio, *op. cit.*, 32.

[20] *Ibid.*, 34.

[21] Boston *Transcript*, May 28, 1863.

[22] Emilio, *op. cit.*, 32.

behind the gun. One of the sore spots was the matter of pay. The solicitor of the War Department, William Whiting, was of the opinion that the Negro should be paid as a laborer, not as a soldier. Negroes in the army received $10 a month, of which $3 was paid in clothing. White soldiers received $13, plus clothing.

Negroes resented this differential. After the citizens of Philadelphia, on June 17, received permission to raise colored troops, the recruiting agents had difficulty in getting signatures. Stearns, the supervisor of enlistments, arranged for Douglass to speak at National Hall on July 6.

Douglass urged Negroes to join the army regardless of salary. "Do you say you want the same pay that white men get. . . . Don't you work every day for less than white men get. . . ." Douglass touched on the matter of Negro officers for Negro soldiers. "Is it not ridiculous in us all at once refusing to be commanded by white men in time of war, when we are everywhere commanded by white men in time of peace." [23]

Douglass asserted that if the government offered the Negro a chance to serve even without any salary, it would be best to enlist. Douglass shrewdly divined in the Negro as soldier a foundation for the Negro as citizen and the Negro as voter. "Once let the black man get upon his person the brass letters, U. S.; let him get an eagle on his button and a musket on his shoulder and bullets in his pocket, and there is no power on the earth . . . which can deny that he has earned the right to citizenship in the United States." [24]

The Negro soldier had other grievances that could not be rationalized away. White soldiers received enlistment bounties; Negro soldiers received none. The colored man

---

[23] *Address by Frederick Douglass at National Hall, Philadelphia, July 6, 1863, for the Promotion of Colored Enlistments* (Phila., 1863), 3.

[24] *Ibid.* If the Negro could become a brave soldier there could be no justification for his subordination.

had no opportunity to advance to the rank of a commissioned officer. Greatest grievance of all was the dread of the fate that threatened the Negro who fell into the hands of the enemy. The Negro in a soldier's uniform "offended the Southern view of 'the eternal fitness of things.'" The South refused to exchange Negro soldiers as prisoners of war. On April 30, 1863, the Confederate Congress decreed that Negroes engaged in war against the South should if captured be dealt with according to the laws of the state in which they were seized. This punishment was equivalent to a death sentence.

Douglass did not attempt to answer these complaints. He had been instrumental in recruiting the Massachusetts Fifty-Fifth, which was declared ready for action within four weeks of the sailing of the Fifty-Fourth. During the summer months Douglass was engaged in securing volunteers for a Pennsylvania contingent. He had gone into the work with enthusiasm, but his efforts and his zeal were gradually abating as he heard rumors of the harsh treatment of Negro soldiers. He began to feel that the administration was not keeping faith with the colored man. Particularly was he disturbed by the news from South Carolina, where in mid-July, Colonel Shaw and hundreds of his men had been killed in an ill-starred assault on Fort Wagner. His own sons had come through unharmed, but he had heard that many of the captured Negroes had been sold into slavery.

Aroused by the reports from the South, and with his faith in the administration shaken, Douglass decided to seek an interview with the President. It was granted. Sometime late in July Douglass was ushered into Lincoln's presence.[25] "When I went in, the President

---

[25] This interview must have taken place between the disaster of Fort Wagner on July 18 and the presidential proclamation of July 30 ordering retaliation for every Union soldier enslaved or killed in violation of the laws of war. Lincoln's biographers, Nicolay and

was sitting in his usual position, I was told, with his feet in different parts of the room, taking it easy." [26] Lincoln put his visitor at ease by saying that he knew him by reputation and that he and Seward had conversed about him.

Douglass came to the point at once. He informed Lincoln that as a recruiting agent he wished to present the case of the Negro soldier. If the War Department proposed to continue to enlist colored men it must give them equal pay with whites and promotion for meritorious service. In addition, the national government should insist that the Confederacy treat captured Negro soldiers as prisoners of war and not as insurrectionist slaves. If captured Negro soldiers were brutally treated, the Union army should retaliate in kind.[27]

Lincoln listened "with patience and silence, was serious, even troubled." [28] His answers were direct. The employment of colored troops, he reminded Douglass, was an experiment; the enlistment of the Negro was "a serious offense to popular prejudice." Douglass could not refute Lincoln's telling point that if the administration went too fast on the Negro question, it would invite upon itself all the hatred which existed against the black man. The difference in pay, explained the President, was a concession to popular feeling. Lincoln admitted the justice of the request for the promotion of Negroes in the army. As an evidence of good faith he promised "to sign any commis-

Hay, do not mention Douglass' visit. For Douglass' account of the interview see *Thirtieth Anniversary of American Anti-Slavery Society, Philadelphia, Dec. 3 and 4, 1863* (New York, 1864), 110–118. Twenty years later Douglass remembered a much fuller account: see Allen Thorn Rice, ed., *Reminiscences of Abraham Lincoln by Distinguished Men of His Time* (New York, 1886), 185–188.

[26] *Thirtieth Ann. Rep. of Amer. A. S. S.*, 115.

[27] Rice, *op. cit.*, 187.

[28] Carl Sandburg, *Abraham Lincoln: The War Years* (3 vols., New York, 1939), II, 182.

sion to colored soldiers whom his Secretary of War commended." He differed with Douglass on the matter of retaliatory measures against captured Confederate troops. His sense of justice revolted at the "thought of hanging men for a crime perpetrated by others." [29] Douglass left the White House carrying with him the impression that the President "was an honest man." [30]

From the Executive Mansion Douglass went to the War Office. Cognizant of the growing efficiency and importance of the black soldier, Secretary of War Stanton consented to see him. Still fresh in Douglass' mind, as he talked with Stanton, was Lincoln's promise to sign a commission to a Negro. Pressing the issue, Douglass told Stanton that he was willing to accept a military commission. Somewhat cornered, Stanton promised that he would make him an assistant adjutant on the staff of General Lorenzo Thomas, Adjutant-General of the United States Army. Thomas was then in Mississippi where he had begun recruiting operations in the spring.

In high spirits Douglass hastened to Rochester to bring out the last issue of his monthly. His valedictory struck a note of triumph unmingled with regret. He made it clear to his readers that he was leaving the field of journalism not because his publication was no longer supported, not because its editor was motivated by a love of change or adventure, and not because he thought that writing and speaking were no longer necessary. But the fight for Negro right could spare the loss of his monthly inasmuch as there were other periodicals — the New York *Independent*, the New York *Tribune*, and the *Anglo-African* — in whose columns the colored man could voice his hopes and fears. In a simple sentence Douglass stated his final and most compelling reason for abandoning his monthly: "I am going South to assist Adjutant General Thomas in

[29] This is a summary of Rice's account, *op. cit.*, 187–188.
[30] *Thirtieth Ann. Rep. of Amer. A. S. S.*, 117.

the organization of colored troops." [31] With this explanation *Douglass' Monthly* signalled the withdrawal of its editor from a field in which for sixteen years he had labored to create an equalitarian socio-racial frame of public opinion.

But Douglass' withdrawal from journalism to accept a commission proved premature. A letter from the adjutant-general's office, dated August 13, ordered him to report to Thomas at Vicksburg, to assist in recruiting colored troops and to aid his superior "in any way his [Douglass'] influence with the colored race can be made available." [32] But no commission accompanied the letter. On the anxious seat, Douglass wrote to the War Office. Stearns, very likely at Stanton's request, informed Douglass that his salary would be $100 a month, subsistence added and, presumably, transportation.[33] But Douglass refused to budge without the commission.

It never came. The disappointment and chagrin embittered Douglass. Stanton had made the promise in good faith, but he (or Lincoln) had undoubtedly come to the conclusion that a commission to a Negro was too far in advance of Northern sentiment.

The failure to receive an army appointment divorced Douglass' attention permanently from military affairs. He turned again to the lecture platform. His speeches at the annual meeting of the American Anti-Slavery Society in December 1863 showed his re-absorption with problems relating to the civil status of the Negro.

The convention was held in Philadelphia in commemoration of the founding of the Society in that city thirty years previously. At the opening session a group of colored soldiers were seated on the platform. To add a further dramatic touch, a slave auction block, placed on the ros-

---

[31] *Douglass' Monthly*, Aug. 1863.
[32] *Douglass MSS.*
[33] Stearns to Douglass, Aug. 29, 1863. *Douglass MSS.*

trum, served as a stand for the speakers. Most of the old-line abolitionists were present — Garrison, Phillips, the two Fosters, and Henry C. Wright among others. Many of the sessions were attended by Senator Wilson and Henry Ward Beecher, brother of Harriet Beecher Stowe and eminent in his own right as a clergyman. The rejoicing over the progress of the slave took on a tone of reminiscence as Samuel J. May, Lucretia Mott, and the former underground railroad operator, J. Miller McKim, spoke of the convention of 1833.

When Douglass took the platform, in response to several calls, he expressed regret that the convention seemed to be in a reminiscent, self-congratulatory mood, as though nothing remained to be done. The freeing of the slave was simply the first step; it now became necessary to work for his elevation. The best way to advance the black man's interest, said Douglass, was to help him to get the ballot. The Negro was as well qualified to vote as many others who then participated in political life. "If he knows an honest man from a thief, he knows more than some of our white voters. If he knows as much when sober as an Irishman knows when drunk, he knows enough to vote." [34]

Douglass then commented on the Union, skillfully interweaving nationalism and Negro suffrage. Men who talked about saving the Union, he pointed out, and restoring it as it was, were victims of self-delusion. "We are fighting for something incomparably better than the old Union. We are fighting for unity; unity of idea, unity of sentiment, unity of object, unity of institutions, in which there shall be no North, no South, no East, no West, no black, no white but a solidarity of the nation, making every slave free, and every free man a voter." [35]

Many present did not agree with Douglass as to the new obligation he believed the Society should assume, but the

---

[34] *Thirtieth Ann. Rep. of Amer. A. S. S.*, 117.
[35] *Ibid.*, 118.

issue did not come to a head until two years later. The most important work of the convention was the drafting of a petition requesting Congress to submit a constitutional amendment abolishing slavery forever in the United States.

During the winter of 1863–64, Douglass travelled throughout the North delivering a series of lectures on the topic, "The Mission of the War." In Boston he was greeted "with long applause," [36] and at Cooper Institute he was the only speaker, aside from Phillips, to draw a full house that season.[37] His definition of the war's purpose was perhaps over-simplified. His lecture was a ninety-minute elaboration of his familiar dictum that the be-all and end-all of the current struggle was to achieve for the Negro a fuller participation in the life of the nation.

With the passing of the winter Douglass took stock of the Negro's gains. The inventory was not as rewarding as a year ago he would have expected it to be. Negro troops were proving their mettle, but the disabilities against them remained in force. Henry Wilson's measure, introduced in the Senate in early January, to equalize the pay of Negro soldiers, was making slow progress through the legislative mill. Douglass had grave doubts concerning the efficiency of the administration. His favorite papers, the *Tribune* and the *Independent* thought Lincoln irresolute, incompetent and unworthy of reelection.

Although discouraged by the slow course of events, Douglass had gradually withdrawn from the chorus of Lincoln critics. Undoubtedly his visit to the Executive Mansion had modified his thinking about its occupant. To Douglass, as to the mass of Negroes, Lincoln had become a legend prior to Booth's bullet. Lincoln captured the imagination of the colored people. They were attracted by his sense of drama as shown in the style of his dress and

---

[36] Boston *Transcript*, Feb. 11, 1864.
[37] *Independent*, Jan. 21, 1864.

his semi-Biblical phraseology. He was approachable, without "airs." To Negroes he was the Great Emancipator; he had "set my people free." He was Abraham, "father of the faithful." Thousands of freed slaves knew the name of only one man north of the Potomac, "Massa Linkum."

If Douglass did not completely share this hero-worship, he was unwilling to challenge it. His high regard for Lincoln was evidenced in the campaign of 1864. Douglass, although a professional reformer, held aloof from the Cleveland convention of Lincoln critics headed by Phillips and Mrs. Stanton. On the last day of May the four hundred self-appointed reformist delegates nominated John C. Frémont and John Cochrane, nephew of Gerrit Smith, as president and vice-president, respectively.

Late in August Douglass' feeling of friendliness for Lincoln was strengthened by a second audience. The acute despondency in the North during July and August led Lincoln to fear that he might have to conclude the war. The President pondered over the probable fate of the slaves should the Union be compelled to grant peace terms to the Confederacy. He decided to talk the question over with Douglass.

The latter, in company with Senator Pomeroy of Kansas, visited the White House on August 10.[38] Lincoln asked Douglass his opinion of establishing an unofficial agency which would urge slaves to escape prior to the completion of possible peace negotiations. For this government-sponsored underground railroad the President suggested the need for a general agent (presumably Douglass) with twenty-five assistants. These men would conduct squads of runaways into the Union lines.[39]

---

[38] Tyler Dennett, *Lincoln and the Civil War in the Diaries and Letters of John Hay* (New York, 1939), 79.

[39] For an account of this interview see document, apparently in Douglass' handwriting, dated Aug. 29, 1864, in *Douglass MSS.* See also F. B. Carpenter's account in the *Independent,* Apr. 5, 1866.

The plan, reminiscent of John Brown, could have appealed to Douglass but little. It was never put into effect. The fall of Atlanta on September 2 put an end to the peace-at-any-price sentiment. The success of Northern arms also strengthened Lincoln's chances of re-election. The Republicans had renominated Lincoln, sensing that "it is not best to swap horses while crossing the river," as he phrased it. Late in September Frémont retired from the race. The contest narrowed down to Lincoln and General George B. McClellan, the candidate of the Democrats. Negroes were quite prepared to make a choice between the two men.

Two days after Frémont's withdrawal, a National Convention of Colored Men, numbering 144 delegates from eighteen states, met at Syracuse. Garnet called the convention to order; Langston was temporary chairman. Douglass, on assuming the presidency, sounded a defiant note: "In what is to be done we shall give offense to none but the mean and sordid haters of our race." The delegates petitioned Congress to remove the remaining grievances of the Negro soldier. They thanked the national government for the abolition of slavery in the District of Columbia, the recognition of Liberia and Haiti, and the retaliatory military order of July 30, 1863.

The two aims of the colored people in the election of 1864, as stated in the convention's "Address to the People of the United States," were the complete abolition of slavery and the granting of impartial suffrage. The "Address" dealt at length with the latter request. The right to vote was the keystone of the arch of human liberty. "In a republican country where general suffrage is the rule, without the ballot personal liberty and the other foregoing rights become mere privileges held at the option of others. What gives the newly arrived immigrants special consequence; not their virtue, because they are often depraved; not their knowledge, because they are often ignorant; not their wealth, because they are often poor." They are important because they were "clothed with the franchise." The convention predicted that as soon as the South was defeated "a sullen hatred toward the National Government would be transmitted from father to son as 'a sacred animosity.'" In the Negro's hands the ballot would be the most effective counterpoise against Southern hostility.[40]

The "Address" passed judgment on the contending political parties. Despite the passage of a few ameliorative measures, the Republican party had shown "a contempt for the character and rights of the colored man." But to the Negro, the Republican party was sweetness and light compared to its rival. "In the ranks of the Democratic party all the worst elements of American society fraternize." From that quarter Negroes "need not expect a single voice for justice, mercy or even decency." [41] So ran the address — a forthright plea for Lincoln's re-election.

The Democrats, writing off the Negro vote as lost, attempted to "smear" Lincoln with the tar-brush. They issued a pamphlet, *Miscegenation Indorsed by Republican Party*, which quoted from Douglass' speech of the preceding December, describing his visit to the White House. Douglass' statement that "the President of the United States received a black man at the White House just as one gentleman received another," was broadcast in an effort to capitalize on Negrophobia, and to revive the associations connoted by the term "Black Republican," used effectively in the elections of 1856 and 1860.[42] Such tactics drove the Negroes en masse into the ranks of Republicanism. The election of 1864 marked the beginning of the staunch affiliation between the Republican party and the colored man.

---

[40] *Proceedings of the National Convention of Colored Men Held in Syracuse, New York, October 4–7, 1864* (New York, 1864), 50.

[41] *Ibid.*, 55. The Republicans won the Negroes and political abolitionists by treating the Constitution as an anti-slavery instrument.

[42] Sandburg, *op. cit.*, III, 255.

After Lincoln's re-election Douglass resumed his lecturing activities. His winter tour took him as far south as Baltimore, where he delivered six lectures.[43] Later in the season, at a Faneuil Hall meeting, Douglass was introduced by a chairman who, in his opening remarks, referred to Negroes as "fellow-citizens." Douglass observed, when he arose, that Negroes were always citizens in times of trouble. They were citizens in 1776. They were citizens in 1812 "when Jackson had a little for them to do at New Orleans." They were citizens two years ago when Massachusetts raised two regiments of black men. What Douglass wanted was "to have the black man a citizen in time of peace." [44]

Douglass saw Lincoln for the last time at the public reception in honor of his second inaugural. Douglass was one of the more than two thousand well-wishers who stampeded into the White House on the evening of March 4, 1865, to pay their respects. Douglass bolted past the detaining guards at the entrance, but once inside the reception room he was seized by two policemen. On the point of being unceremoniously put out, Douglass sent an appeal to the President. Ever gracious, Lincoln summoned Douglass to his presence and chatted with him while other handshakers waited.[45]

Douglass was in Rochester, just returned from a lecture circuit, when the news came from Washington that Lincoln had been assassinated by a half-crazed actor, John Wilkes Booth. On the evening following the tragic event Douglass attended a meeting at the Rochester city hall to pay homage to the memory of the martyred President. Douglass had not been scheduled to speak, but he came forward in response to the audience demand. He breathed vengeance.

[43] *Independent*, Mar. 2, 1865.
[44] *Ibid.*, Apr. 21, 1865.
[45] Margaret Leech, *Reveille in Washington, 1860–1865* (New York, 1941), 370.

"Let us not be in too much haste in the work of restoration. Let us not be in a hurry to clasp to our bosom the spirit that gave birth to Booth." Recurring to his constant theme, Douglass asked that when the North took back to its bosom its "Southern foes," "let us see to it that we take also our Southern friends." Justice to the Negro was safety to the nation.[46]

Douglass felt a sense of personal loss in Lincoln's death. His affectionate remembrance deepened when he discovered, shortly after the tragedy, that the late President had remembered his visits. Lincoln had spoken to his wife of his desire to present Douglass with some token of his regard. After her husband's death, Mrs. Lincoln sent his walking stick to Douglass.[47] Of all the numerous gifts he ever received — including objects from Daniel O'Connell, Elizabeth Cady Stanton, Lucretia Mott, Charles Sumner and Queen Victoria — Douglass prized Lincoln's cane above all others.

With Lincoln gone, the Negroes turned to their other great champion in politics. Late in April 1865, Douglass wrote Sumner. He spoke of the faith that the friends of freedom had placed "in you of all men in the Senate during the war." They looked to him all the more, wrote Douglass, now that peace had come, "and the final settlement of our national troubles is at hand." [48]

With the abolition of slavery by the ratification of the Thirteenth Amendment in December 1865, the Negro question entered upon a new phase. Douglass prepared to move with it. If he paused to review the recent course of events he must have felt a sense of satisfaction. For exactly a quarter of a century he had been pleading the cause of the slave. But, as he told a friend years later,

---

[46] Amy Hanmer-Croughton, "Anti-Slavery Days in Rochester," *Pub. Roch. Hist. Soc.*, XIV, 153 (1936).

[47] Rochester *Express*, in *Standard*, July 14, 1866.

[48] Douglass to Sumner, Apr. 29, 1865. *Letterbooks.*

even in his most hopeful moods he had never been sanguine of success in his lifetime.[49]   Three years after the war Douglass came to the conclusion that slavery was destroyed "not from principle, but from policy, and there was little to be grateful for except the emergency that created the necessity." [50]   But in the spring of 1865, as he learned the news that Lee had surrendered at Appomattox and the Confederacy had sued for peace, as he witnessed the death throes of chattel slavery, that "relic of barbarism," Douglass must have felt a sense of personal gratification toward the historic process for having been so considerate.

---

[49] Parker, *loc. cit.*, 553.
[50] New Orleans *Crescent*, Feb. 11, 1868.

CHAPTER XIII

The Negro's Hour

"Our last battle approaches.
Its countersign — Equality before the law."
Sumner to Garrison, May 29, 1865.

Douglass' attitude was different from that of most Negroes in the South and many Negroes in the North who believed that with the collapse of the Confederacy and the ratification of the Thirteenth Amendment the millennium had come. Ever realistic in his thinking, Douglass clearly foresaw the ordeal of Reconstruction as it related to the freed slave. Douglass rejoiced in emancipation, but he knew that there was a world of difference between the abolition of slavery and the attainment by the Negro of political and civil equality. Withal, Douglass hoped for these blessings as a logical consequence of the victory of the North.

His point of view was consistent. To him the war had been waged for the express benefit of the Negro. Because, therefore, it had been an abolitionist war, Douglass demanded an abolitionist peace. Further, he believed that the North had a heavy debt to pay to the nearly two hundred thousand Negro soldiers who had borne arms against the Confederacy. Douglass' position on the Negro question agreed in all details with that of the Radical Republicans. But his motivation was different.

The Republican party is perhaps guiltless of the charge of having started the Civil War in order to maintain its political supremacy, but in 1865 the Republicans were prepared to make a Carthaginian peace in order to assure to the victors the spoils of war. The designs of the Radicals were partly obscured, as their efforts were distinctly aided, by a bitter wrangle between the President and Congress. Even those Congressmen who were not Radicals questioned the constitutionality of Lincoln's ten-per-cent plan of bringing the seceded states back into the Union. Holding that the restoration of the Southern states was a function of Congress, the Radicals had attempted, in the Wade-Davis Bill of July 1864, to unite their fellow-legislators against any further expansion of the President's swollen war-time powers. Lincoln's death had served simply to transfer the quarrel to his successor, Andrew Johnson, who also held that restoration was a presidential function.

The Radicals had reason for alarm. If the Southern states were speedily re-admitted they would elect to Congress enough Democrats to insure that party's political dominance. This would never do, vowed the Radicals, as they readied themselves for a tooth-and-nail struggle. Johnson, never slow to accept the gage of battle, set about to complete the restoration of the seceded states before December 1865, when Congress was scheduled to convene.

Determined to give Johnson a lesson in politics, the Radicals, after perfecting their plans in caucus, opened the historic Thirty-Ninth Congress with a program that called for a postponement of the admission of the recently-elected representatives from the Southern states, and the establishment of a Joint Committee on Reconstruction which would inquire into conditions in those states. Friends of the Negro were highly pleased by the passage of these measures. Theodore Tilton, editor of *The Independent*, wrote an effusive letter to Stevens: "The way which you have opened Congress and thrown down the gauntlet to the President's policy has pleased our Radical friends hereabouts so thoroughly that we are hearty, merry and tumultuous with gratitude." [1] The quarrel between Johnson and the Radicals had entered the first phase.

The Radicals quickly came to the conclusion that it would be advisable to work for Negro suffrage. Douglass also believed in Negro enfranchisement, but his reasons differed from those of the Radicals. To Douglass the ballot was the open sesame to the advancement of the colored man. "I am just now deeply engaged in the advocacy of suffrage for the whole colored people of the South," he wrote in the summer of 1865. "I see little advantage in emancipation without this." [2] During January and February of 1866, Douglass travelled here and there in the North — in Massachusetts, New York, Pennsylvania and Washington. His announced subject was "The Assassination and Its Lessons," but his theme was the ballot. On February 6, he drew a large house, "every seat was occupied," at the Brooklyn Academy of Music, after the directors had at first refused the use of the hall. ("We understand," wrote Tilton who presided, "that the names of the five dissenting directors are to be written on shells and deposited in the Brooklyn Historical Society's collection of Long Island fossils." [3]) Two days later Douglass gave the same address at Philadelphia as first speaker in a series of lectures scheduled by a local Negro group headed by William Still. At Douglass' lecture in Washington Chief Justice Chase presided.

In these addresses Douglass expressed the conviction that the Negro had as much political intelligence as anyone else. Douglass believed that participation in political life was the normal condition of man. [4] On the other hand,

---

[1] Tilton to Thaddeus Stevens, Dec. 6, 1865. *Stevens MSS.* (Library of Congress.)

[2] Douglass to Lydia Maria Child, July 30, 1865. *MS.* in possession of Arthur B. Spingarn, New York City.

[3] *Independent*, Feb. 8, 1866.

[4] New York *Tribune*, Jan. 30, 1866.

the Radicals (aside from Sumner) were completely indifferent to the Negro's political capacity. They looked upon Negro suffrage as a means of punishing the South and as a guaranty that the control of the national government would remain in Republican hands.

The Radicals also differed from Douglass in their attitude toward white disfranchisement in the South. To insure Republican party supremacy the Radicals systematically attempted to exclude the mass of Southern whites from the polls. This policy was foreign to Negro sentiment. In the early days of Reconstruction, the Negroes, especially those in the South, were desirous that former Confederates be enfranchised.[5]

From a feeling devoid of vindictiveness and partisanship, Douglass' attitude and that of the mass of Negroes underwent a gradual change. One of the forces impelling Douglass' gravitation toward the extreme position of the Radicals was the conduct and personality of Lincoln's successor. In 1864 the patriotic Northern press had hailed the "Tailor of Tennessee" as the man "to sew the winding sheet of the Union." But after his unsuccessful attempt to readmit the Southern states on lenient terms Johnson had steadily lost influence in the North. Friends of the Negro became apprehensive. "My spirit is greatly tried with Andy Johnson," fumed Lydia Maria Child.[6] Douglass, with the prescience of a man writing his autobiography, remembered seeing Johnson on Inaugural Day, in March 1865. When Lincoln, riding in a carriage with Johnson, pointed Douglass out, the first expression which came over Johnson's face "was one of bitter contempt and aversion. Seeing I observed him," wrote Douglass, "he

---

[5] William A. Russ, "The Negro and White Disfranchisement During Radical Reconstruction," *Journal of Negro History*, XIX, 171 (Apr. 1934).

[6] Lydia Maria Child to Theodore Tilton, Feb. 14, 1866. *Tilton MSS.* (New York Historical Society.)

tried to assume a more friendly appearance, but it was too late." [7]

Vitally interested in such measures as the Freedmen's Bureau Bill, the Civil Rights Bill and the proposed Fourteenth Amendment, a convention of colored men appointed a committee to visit Johnson and ascertain his views. The delegation was comprised of William Whipper, George T. Downing, a successful Washington caterer, John Jones, a well-to-do, civic-minded Chicagoan with a large merchant tailoring establishment, Douglass and his son, Lewis. On February 7, 1866, they called at the White House.

They found Johnson slouched in a chair, "his hands in his pockets, and looking a trifle sour." [8] He shook hands with each of the visitors. Downing, the chairman of the delegation, opened with a few perfunctory words of respect to "your Excellency." The President, he said placatorily, was to understand that the delegation came "feeling that we are friends meeting a friend." Downing explained that the object of their visit was to call attention to the lax manner in which the Thirteenth Amendment was being enforced, and to express the hope of the Negro that he would be fully enfranchised throughout the land. In expansion of Downing's remarks, Douglass followed with a brief statement that the Negro was entitled to the ballot because he was subject to taxation and to military service and should "share in the privileges of this condition."

Johnson replied that he had "perilled" a great deal for Negroes and that he was opposed to adopting any policy which he believed would lead to the sacrifice of Negro lives. Johnson (who had "approached very near to Mr. Douglass") brought forth his familiar argument about a war of the races. He contended that the poor white and

---

[7] Douglass, *Life and Times*, 442.

[8] William Wells Brown, *The Negro in the American Rebellion* (Boston, 1867), 338. For a complete account of the interview see New York *Tribune*, Feb. 8, 1866.

the Negro were bitter enemies. If they were thrown together at the ballot box, "without preparation, without time for passion and excitement to be appeased," a race war would ensue. When Johnson stated that he was not in favor of forcing the majority to "receive a state of things they are opposed to," Downing asked him to apply his remarks to South Carolina where the Negroes outnumbered the whites.

Ignoring this interposition, Johnson asserted that it was the duty of the people of the state, not that of the national government, to determine the qualifications for voting. He was against forcing the people to accept Negro suffrage. In closing, he indicated that the problem was beyond human powers: "I would it were so that all you advocate could be done in the twinkling of an eye; but it is not in the nature of things, and I do not assume or pretend to be wiser than Providence, or stronger than the laws of nature."

Douglass thanked the President and in the same breath indicated a desire to controvert some of his statements. Johnson replied that he had expected simply to indicate his views. Douglass declared that the enfranchisement of the colored man would prevent, rather than stimulate, a race conflict. The Negro was still under the control of the master class. Johnson, expressing his long-held conviction, answered that the problem could best be solved by emigration.

As perhaps agreed on by the delegation, Douglass and Downing had been the only Negroes to speak. On leaving, Douglass remarked to his fellows, "The President sends us to the people, and we go to the people." "Yes, sir," said Johnson, closing the one hour discussion, "I have great faith in the people. I believe they will do what is right." [9] Upon leaving the White House, the Negroes were

[9] New York *Tribune*, Feb. 8, 1866.

invited to an anteroom in the House of Representatives where a group of Radicals quizzed them as to their visit.

The Negro delegation, not to be outdone by Johnson's refusal to listen to a criticism of his assumptions, immediately addressed a letter to the editor of the Washington *Chronicle*, requesting permission to use its columns to publish an open letter to the President. Johnson's views, ran the communication in a style unmistakably Douglass', were unsound and prejudicial to the best interests of the Negro race as well as inimical to the best interests of the country as a whole. The hatred between the poor whites and the slaves had been incited by the planter aristocracy, and now that those promoters of discord were toppled, Negro-white adjustment should present no insuperable barriers.

But even if the alleged hostility existed, ran the open letter, how could Johnson's professed desire to promote the welfare of the Negro square with a policy of depriving him of a means of defense while bestowing it upon his enemy? "Men are whipped oftenest who are whipped easiest" ran one sentence — a recurring line in Douglass' writings. Johnson's colonization theory, continued the communication, would be detrimental to the best interests of the country in view of the usefulness of Negro labor in time of peace and Negro arms in time of war. The letter concluded with an expression of impatience at the implication that the two races could not live side by side in peace and prosperity.[10]

Although the Radical Republicans welcomed his aid, Douglass' increasingly condemnatory attitude toward the White House was not part of a conspiracy between Johnson's political enemies and Douglass. The latter's advocacy of the ballot arose from no desire to embarrass the President; it sprang from a deep conviction that it was

---

[10] *Tribune*, Feb. 8, 1866. McPherson, *loc. cit.*, 55–56.

dangerous to deny to any class the right to vote. To Douglass, and to other Negro leaders, "Negro equality" was not intended as a bugbear to frighten conservative whites. Douglass believed that the hue and cry against Negro suffrage was based on a hypocritical self-interest that was more fearful of Negro ability than of Negro depravity.

Within ten days after the visit by the colored delegation the breach between Johnson and the Radicals became irremediable. Late in February 1866, Johnson vetoed the Freedmen's Bureau Bill. The Radicals were unable to muster a two-thirds over-riding vote in the Senate, but it was Johnson's last victory. Early in April Congress over-rode his veto of the Civil Rights Bill; similarly, in July Congress enacted a second Freedmen's Bureau Bill.

To meet the challenge of the Radicals, Johnson's friends urged him to rally the Democrats and the non-Radical Republicans. Late in June "The National Union Club" issued a call for a meeting of Johnson supporters throughout the country. Delegates from every state met at Philadelphia in mid-August and held a spirited convention. Profusely they praised Johnson and appealed to the country to elect men to Congress who would follow his leadership.

The Radicals, noting the success of the convention, decided to follow suit. Although it had been originally intended that the gathering should be comprised exclusively of Southern "loyalists," [11] its sponsors decided to have a heavy Northern representation in order to give the convention a national flavor. The Northern delegates were to be considered "honorary" members.[12] Late in August the Republican Convention of Rochester appointed Douglass as one of its delegates "to meet with the true

[11] New York *Herald*, Sept. 2, 1866.
[12] *Ibid.*

Southern Unionists about to convene in Philadelphia." Douglass accepted the "unexpected honor." [13]

The Radicals, not sure of the temper of public opinion, were dismayed by the selection of Douglass. One of Thaddeus Stevens' friends in New York wrote that it was the unanimous belief in that city that the selection of Douglass was unfortunate. The writer requested Stevens to use his influence to advise Douglass to remain in Rochester. "If he goes it will certainly injure our cause and we may lose some Congressmen in the doubtful districts." [14]

Before Douglass arrived in Philadelphia he was met by a committee who informed him that his presence at the convention would jeopardize Republican success at the polls, especially in the doubtful state of Indiana, and asked him to return to Rochester.[15] Believing that these fears were groundless, Douglass continued his trip, fortified en route by the enthusiastic reception he received at each station stop.[16] Amid cheers he arrived at Philadelphia on September 2, in company with Generals Butler and Burnside.

The next day the "two or three hundred delegates" gathered at Independence Hall to march to National Hall where the meetings were to be held. As the procession was forming, Douglass became aware that everyone except Butler shied away from him. Even Henry Wilson, whom he counted a personal friend, seemed reserved. Just when it appeared as if Douglass would have to walk without a companion, Theodore Tilton came up and locked arms with him. No two delegates in the entire line of parade aroused more cheers.[17]

---

[13] For his letter of acceptance see New York *Tribune*, Aug. 31, 1866.

[14] Samuel Shock to Stevens, Aug. 27, 1866. *Stevens MSS.*

[15] Theodore Stanton, "Frederick Douglass in Paris," *The Open Court*, I, 151–152 (Apr. 28, 1887).

[16] New York *Herald*, Sept. 3, 1866.

[17] Stanton, *loc. cit.*, 151.

Although many critics construed it as a sarcasm upon the arm-in-arm marching of the South Carolina and Massachusetts delegations at the Union Convention three weeks previously, Tilton's act was simply one of spontaneous friendliness. This practical exhibition of affection was disturbing to those who kept their ears close to the ground of politics. "It does not become radicals like us particularly to object," wrote Stevens, "but it was certainly unfortunate at this time. It loses us some votes." The aged leader of the House Radicals viewed the act as "a foolish bravado." The Massachusetts and South Carolina arm-in-arm episode had been "disgusting," but he feared that the Tilton-Douglass exhibition would "neutralize" it.[18]

The Southern loyalists met separately from the Northern delegates. Prominent among the latter were Ben Butler, Ben Wade, Horace Greeley, Simon Cameron, czar of the Republican political machine in Pennsylvania, James A. Garfield, a member of the House of Representatives, Carl Schurz, German-American political leader from Missouri, and ex-Governor Curtin of Pennsylvania, the chairman. The New York delegation, headed by Tilton, met separately and committed itself to Negro suffrage. The other Northern delegations wished to avoid any appearance of extremism. Fearing the ultra-radicalism of those Southern delegates whose only constituency was a purely Negro one, the eight governors and eleven ex-governors among the Northerners met in secret and urged caution and moderation on the suffrage issue.[19]

At a public meeting that evening Douglass was invited to speak. A note of thanksgiving and exultation ran through his address. "For two hundred and fifty years we have been subjected to all the exterminating forces of slavery — marriage abolished, organization unknown, if more than

[18] Stevens to William D. Kelley, Sept. 5, 1866. *Stevens MSS.*
[19] New York *Herald*, Sept. 5, 1866.

five met together, stripes; education denied, the right to learn to read the name of the God that made us denied, the family tie broken up — yet under it all, under all the exterminating forces of slavery here we are today." [20] The next morning, as if in dramatization of his assertion of the Negro's progress, Douglass met Lucretia Auld, daughter of his former master, in the street. It was "a touching incident to Douglass"; [21] she had been very kind to him in the slavery days.

Meanwhile the Southern delegates, meeting at National Hall, had completed their organizational meeting. The chairmanship fell to James Speed of Kentucky who earlier in the year had followed the advice of the Radicals in resigning as Attorney-General in Johnson's cabinet. For the first three days the work of the delegates consisted mainly in criticizing Johnson and his policies. On the evening of the third day the Southerners held a joint meeting with their Northern allies. The occasion was one of unsullied joy. Squads of soldiers with torches enlivened the demonstration in front of Union Hall. The noise of several bands split the ear, followed by a display of rockets and Roman candles which dazzled the eye.[22]

But this love feast was shattered on the fourth day when Douglass entered the meeting-hall of the Southern loyalists. The border state delegates — those from Missouri, Kentucky, West Virginia and Maryland — extremely cool toward Negro suffrage, intended to force an adjournment without taking any stand on the vexed question of the franchise. Sensing this intention and anxious to forestall it, Douglass, Tilton and Anna Dickinson presented themselves at the convention.

On Douglass' entry the speaker "was unable to proceed for some minutes in consequence of the excitement." In

[20] New York *Herald*, Sept. 5, 1866.
[21] *Ibid.*
[22] *Ibid.*, Sept. 6, 1866.

consternation, the border state delegates tried to force a motion to adjourn *sine die*. The delegates from the former Confederate states defeated the attempt and called on Miss Dickinson and Douglass for speeches. The former responded "after wiping her fingers with a dainty cambric handkerchief." She reproved the border state delegates and asked a rather forceful rhetorical question: "When you talk about deprecating discussion, opposition, argument, are you blind to the fact that there is no backward flow of ideas, more than of rivers? . . . Stepping onward is glory." Douglass followed with another eloquent suffrage appeal.[23]

The issue could no longer be dodged. Realizing the wide divergence of opinion on the question and anxious to provide a face-saving compromise, Governor Boreman of West Virginia suggested that the convention permit the delegates from the unreconstructed states to submit a report that would not be binding on the convention as a whole. This suggestion was adopted, but the next morning, as the convention opened, Chairman Speed withdrew, declaring that as far as he was concerned the work of the convention was done.

Thereupon the first vice-president, John Minor Botts of Virginia, seized the gavel and called for the report of the Committee on the Condition of the Unreconstructed States. Of the lengthy resolutions submitted the most important was a petition that the national government "confer on every citizen in the states we represent the American birthright of impartial suffrage and equality before the law." This resolution evoked great applause, but Botts immediately countered with a series of resolutions denying Congressional authority to legislate on the suffrage. Denied the right to enter his dissenting views in the "Journal of Proceedings," Botts left in a huff.

[23] New York *Herald*, Sept. 7, 1866.

The rump convention then adopted the report advocating Negro suffrage, expressed thanks to Douglass and Anna Dickinson, and after a closing prayer, "tumultuously adjourned *sine die*." "The city," wrote the *Herald's* reporter, "once more assumed its normal condition." [24]

It is unlikely that the convention would have approved Negro suffrage had it not been for the appearance of Miss Dickinson and Douglass. And with the official indorsement of Negro suffrage by the National Loyalist Convention, the history of the Fifteenth Amendment may logically be said to have originated.

Of course, Douglass took the stump during the elections for Congress in 1866. He was overjoyed when the counting of the ballots revealed that Johnson and the Democrats had been decisively defeated. The Republicans, now completely dominated by the Radical wing, obtained more than a two-thirds majority in both houses. Douglass did not see the campaign as a successful effort by Eastern industrialists to prevent an alliance between Southern and Western agrarianism. Douglass' personal views on the significance of the decisive Republican victory were expressed in an article in the *Atlantic Monthly* — a circumstance in itself an indication of the increasing respectability of the fight for Negro rights.

Douglass wrote that he viewed the outcome of the elections as a mandate to treat the ten-percent governments as shams and impositions. The people demanded a reconstruction policy that would protect loyal men of both races. The unfortunate blunder of permitting the Southern states to disfranchise their Negro citizens should be "retrieved." In short, the people had pronounced in favor of a root-and-branch policy. Douglass exhausted his vocabulary on the occupant of the White House. Johnson was "ambitious, unscrupulous, energetic, indefatigable,

[24] New York *Herald*, Sept. 8, 1866.

voluble, and plausible — a political gladiator, ready for a
'set-to' in any crowd — he is beaten in his own chosen
field, and stands today before the country as a convicted
usurper, a political criminal." [25]

Ignoring a thousand such fustian explosions, Johnson,
bloody but unbowed, vetoed a bill conferring suffrage on
the Negroes of the District of Columbia. The President's
action made sense inasmuch as a referendum in Washington
in 1865 had resulted in 6,521 votes against and only 31
votes for Negro enfranchisement. Within three days after
Johnson's action, however, Congress had passed the measure over his veto.

Douglass, completely losing his sense of balance, came
out with a sweeping proposal for the abolition of the vice-
presidency, the veto power and the pardoning power.[26]
The country had had bad luck with vice-presidents, said
Douglass, they did not follow in the footsteps of their
predecessors.[27] Douglass conveniently forgot that Johnson's troubles came because he had tried — perhaps too
faithfully — to carry out his predecessor's plans.

Douglass spent the first three months of 1867 in the
West on a lecture tour,[28] comforted by the reflection that
the Radicals were taking care of what Stevens called
"Andy Johnsonism." After a brief return to Rochester
Douglass packed up and went westward again, this time
on a two months tour of Indiana. At this period Douglass'
platform appearances brought him fees of from fifty to
one hundred dollars, but frequently he was asked to lecture
gratis for the benefit of some cause or of some individual.
Such an instance occurred in 1867 when he was approached
to conduct a series of lectures to raise money for
Mrs. Lincoln.

---

[25] Douglass, "Reconstruction," *Atlantic Monthly*, XVIII, 764
(Dec. 1866).
[26] New York *Herald*, Dec. 15, 1866.   [27] *Standard*, Jan. 12, 1867.
[28] Douglass to Smith, Mar. 31, 1867. *Smith MSS.*

The wife of the martyred President was in pressing need; she had been able to save little from his salary. Elizabeth Keckley, who had been Mrs. Lincoln's personal maid and confidante, took the initiative in trying to raise money for her former mistress. Mrs. Keckley, a colored woman, asked Douglass and Garnet to lecture in the interests of Mrs. Lincoln. Both acquiesced. Douglass wrote four letters of comment and advice to Mrs. Keckley.[29] He suggested that she try to secure the best speakers in the country. The money-raising testimonial should be more than a Negro enterprise, wrote Douglass, but the colored man should sense his especial obligation to the widow of his benefactor.[30] Mrs. Lincoln's husband would have been living and thus able to support her had his life not been sacrificed for freedom.[31]

Another of Mrs. Keckley's plans was to send circulars appealing to the generosity of the American public. She and Garnet visited Horace Greeley who gave the plan his tentative approval. The disposal of Mrs. Lincoln's wardrobe was another suggested expedient. However, none of these money-raising measures was successful.

Mrs. Lincoln's shawls, dresses, fine laces and furs were placed on sale but buyers were few. Many people criticized Mrs. Lincoln's course as undignified; others found fault with the quality and cut of her garments. The circular letter proposition fell through because Greeley had no confidence in Mrs. Lincoln's broker. The plan to have lecturers contribute their services gratis was so coolly received by Mrs. Lincoln that Douglass withdrew his efforts.[32]

Douglass' lecturing activities in 1867 left him little time for politics. In mid-April he had been nominated as a delegate to the convention to revise New York's constitution.[33] He had been defeated in the election; he seems

---

[29] Elizabeth Keckley, *Behind the Scenes* (New York, 1868), 316, 318, 320, 320–323.   [31] *Ibid.*, 321.

[30] *Ibid.* 318.   [32] *Ibid.*, 326.   [33] *Independent*, Apr. 25, 1867.

to have put forth little effort to win. His chief political interest during the year centered around an offer from the President.

Although Johnson opposed unrestricted Negro suffrage he considered himself a friend of the race. At the time of the visit of the Negro delegation he had offered to be the colored man's Moses, "to lead him from bondage to freedom." A few days after the visit he had given a thousand dollars to a Negro school.[34] In April 1866 he had reiterated his friendship in a speech to the Negroes of the District who were celebrating an emancipation anniversary.[35] However, his decision to offer Douglass a position was guided less by a feeling of friendliness to the Negro than by considerations of political expediency.

The circumstances were these. Johnson, unfortunately for himself, had retained Lincoln's cabinet. Resignations in the post-office, interior and justice departments had enabled him in 1866 to appoint men of his own views. However the War Office was still under Stanton whose role as a Radical partisan had become apparent by the summer of 1867. Johnson finally made up his mind to remove the meddlesome secretary. As a counterpoise to the storm of Radical disapproval such a step would arouse, Johnson hit upon a plan to appoint Douglass as Commissioner of the Freedmen's Bureau.

Johnson first sounded out a few of his friends. In the course of a conversation with O. H. Browning, his Secretary of the Interior, Johnson expressed the belief that "it would be a good thing" to appoint Douglass. Browning agreed, but added the precautionary suggestion that Douglass had better be contacted first to see if he would accept.[36] Two

---

[34] George Fort Milton, *Age of Hate* (New York, 1930), 287.

[35] McPherson, *op. cit.*, 63.

[36] James G. Randall, ed., *The Diary of Orville Hickman Browning* (2 vols., Springfield, Ill., 1925–33), II, 151.

weeks later Johnson asked the opinion of his Secretary of the Navy. Welles was against appointing a man to so responsible a position simply because he was a Negro.[37] Welles further confided to his diary that, unlike Sumner, he did not particularly care to see Negroes fill trusted public positions. But, as he informed the President, if a Negro were to be appointed to any office, Commissioner of the Freedmen's Bureau was appropriate. Besides, added Welles, while the incumbent, O. O. Howard, was a "very good sort of man," he was "loose in talking and appropriating public property," and was intensely Radical, to boot.[38]

Undeterred by Welles' negative attitude, Johnson dispatched intermediaries to obtain Douglass' reaction. On July 17, Carter Steward, a White House hanger-on, was sent to ascertain if Douglass would accept the position.[39] Douglass was out of town. Less than two weeks later William Slade, one of Johnson's personal friends, wrote a note to Douglass asking "if I secure the appointment, will you accept?" As if in justification for the step, Slade added that Howard was timid and lacked moral courage.[40]

In mid-August, after pondering the offer for two weeks, Douglass declined. "I could not accept office," he wrote, "with my present views of duty." [41] To Tilton he confided that his refusal was based on an unwillingness to "facilitate the removal of a man as just and good as General Howard and especially to place himself under any obligation to keep the peace with Andrew Johnson." [42]

But Slade did not give up, sensing that Douglass was undergoing a struggle. As if no correspondence had passed

[37] *Diary of Gideon Welles* (3 vols., Boston, 1911), III, 143. Entry dated July 25, 1867.

[38] *Ibid.*, 142.

[39] Charles R. Douglass to Douglass, July 18, 1867. *Douglass MSS.*

[40] William Slade to Douglass, July 29, 1867. *Ibid.*

[41] Douglass to Slade, Aug. 12, 1867. Carbon copy, *Ibid.*

[42] Douglass to Tilton, Sept. 2, 1867. *Tilton MSS.*

between them, he wrote to Douglass late in August that he had learned that the President would appoint a Negro to the Freedmen's Bureau if he could find one suitable for the position.[43] Douglass held to his refusal although his slowness in writing a letter of rejection and his failure to make the offer public indicate that he had undergone much mental wrestling. He had been sorely tempted. The position was important. In 1865 the Bureau handled nearly a million dollars and its Congressional appropriation for the fiscal year ending June 30, 1867 had been nearly seven times as large ($6,940,450).[44] As the three thousand dollar a year head of the Bureau, Douglass would have under his supervision over two thousand employees, including assistant commissioners such as Generals Clinton B. Fisk and Rufus Saxton.

But as one of Johnson's bitterest critics, Douglass could not have accepted a position from him without stultifying himself. As Schurz pointed out, a Republican who accepted appointment from Johnson to take the place of an official dismissed for fidelity to his principles could never be forgiven: "The so-called 'bread-and-butter brigade' was looked down upon with a contempt that could hardly be expressed in words."[45] Douglass did not dare place himself under obligation to keep peace with Johnson and at the same time facilitate the removal of a man so universally respected as General Howard.

Tilton, in extravagant phraseology, praised Douglass' action: "The greatest black man in the nation did not consent to become the tool of the meanest white."[46] Doug-

[43] Slade to Douglass, Aug. 18, 1867. *Douglass MSS.*

[44] *Autobiography of Oliver Otis Howard* (2 vols., New York, 1907), II, 331.

[45] *The Reminiscenses of Carl Schurz* (3 vols., New York, 1908), III, 239.

[46] *Standard*, Sept. 21, 1867.

lass dismissed the matter with a wry comment that barely concealed his disappointment. "Friend Tilton has made much of my declining the Freedmen's Bureau," he wrote Smith. "I told him that I had been applied to by parties near the President to know if I would accept the offer and I said no." [47]

It was well for Douglass that he refused; the Republican party, in power until his death save for the Cleveland interludes, would never have forgiven his acceptance. Furthermore, the Johnson administration had been thoroughly discredited by the summer of 1867 and was, except for its dwindling patronage, without influence. The former Confederate States had been divided into military districts under five generals who were making the South safe for Republicanism, temporarily at least. As if to furnish the *coup de grâce*, the House of Representatives started impeachment proceedings against the President. Johnson was acquitted, but the episode was enough to ruin his already slim hope of getting the Democratic nomination in the approaching election.

Douglass had favored Ulysses S. Grant even prior to the General's nomination by the Republicans.[48] Although his friend Gerrit Smith was anxious to see Salmon P. Chase become president, Douglass found objection. Chase, chief justice of the Supreme Court, had been stung by the presidential bee. When his chances for the Republican nomination grew dim, he let it be known to the Democrats that he was available. To Douglass this was the height of perfidy. Chase, wrote he in a letter to Smith, had abandoned the Negro in order to make himself acceptable to the Democrats.[49]

But the Democratic convention failed to select Chase; a "dark horse," Horatio Seymour of New York, received

[47] Douglass to Smith, Aug. 24, 1868. *Smith MSS.*

[48] *Independent*, Mar. 12, 1868.

[49] Douglass to Smith, Aug. 24, 1868. *Smith MSS.*

the nomination. Negroes in general were hostile to Seymour for his failure, as governor, to quell the draft riots in New York City in 1863. Beginning as a protest against compulsory military service the riots had quickly become an anti-Negro demonstration in which colored men were beaten and hanged and a colored orphanage burned.

The identity of the Democratic candidate meant little to Douglass. By 1868 it had become crystal clear to him that the Democrats were the party that had supported the rebellion and now opposed Negro suffrage. He proposed to do a little electioneering in the interests of his proved friends. As he expressed it, "I am not much of a stumper, but I shall do a little in this line during the canvass." [50]

Douglass' efforts consisted of name-calling and "waving the bloody shirt." In an oft-repeated speech, "The Work before Us," Douglass referred to Seymour as a "confessed trickster and falsifier who gained the nomination by a source of cunning, duplicity, lying, treachery and bribery unparalleled in the history of party politics." [51] Douglass reminded those with short memories that it was the Democrats who annexed Texas, prosecuted war against Mexico and repealed the Missouri Compromise. Worst of all, Seymour and his running mate, Francis P. Blair, Jr., represented the forces of secession and rebellion, whose one purpose, warned Douglass, was to deliver the black laborer of the South back to the slaveholding class. The terrorism in the South would continue as long as Johnson remained in the White House and the Democratic party continued to feed "the rebel imagination with the prospect of regaining through politics what they lost by the sword." [52]

Grant defeated Seymour, largely because of the Negro vote which Douglass helped deliver to the Republicans.

---

[50] Douglass to Smith, Sept. 1, 1868. *Smith MSS.*
[51] *Independent*, Aug. 27, 1868.
[52] *Ibid.*

But the Radicals preferred to construe the outcome of the election as a justification of their program of Reconstruction. The conservative Northern press might rail that the South was "tumbling and rolling about in this Black Sea of Negroism," [53] but below the Mason-Dixon line the carpetbaggers and scalawags and many of their pliable Negro associates and followers went ahead, cynically disregarding the decencies of good government. It was a heyday for adventurers, fortune-seekers and speculators. "The wine cup, the gaming table, and the parlors of strange women charmed many of these men to the neglect of important public duties," wrote a contemporary Negro historian.[54]

Douglass was shocked by the tales of corruption and graft reported by James Pike of the New York *Tribune* and other observers from the North. Looking backward fifteen years later Douglass expressed misgiving as to the wisdom of universal suffrage. "An abnormal condition born of war carried the colored voter to an altitude unsuited to his attainments," wrote Douglass in 1884.[55] But in the years immediately following the war Douglass saw nothing to condemn in the Radical political program.

But if Douglass kept silent when condemnation was in order, he also failed to praise the accomplishments of the carpetbag regimes. Those who expressed moral indignation over the tales of bribery and misappropriation of public monies ignored the constructive work of state legislatures under Republican-Negro control. Along with all that was fraudulent these Reconstruction governments brought to the South modern educational concepts, wrote equalitarian principles into Southern state constitutions and placed social legislation on the statute books. Douglass and other Negro leaders in the North remained uninformed of the

[53] New York *Herald*, Oct. 11, 1867.
[54] Williams, *History of the Negro Race*, II, 383.
[55] "The Future of the Negro," *North American Review*, CXXXIX, 85 (July 1884).

constructive work of these legislatures and hence failed to come to the defense of the Southern Negro in his first experiments in assuming political responsibility.

Douglass' own plan of reconstruction centered around a policy of helping the freedmen become landowners. He favored the establishment of a National Land and Labor Company with a capitalization of a million dollars, which would sell land, on easy terms, to colored men. Obviously Douglass misread the times and the manners. The industrial, protectionist and capitalist forces behind the Northern Radicals would not dream of furthering a program to make the Negro a small landholder and hence a potential ally of Southern and Western agrarianism.

In 1868 the Radicals had a rôle for the Negro but, as usual, it was in the realm of politics. Grant had won by an electoral vote of 214 to 80. His popular vote, however, was only 300,000 more than that of Seymour. Without the 450,000 Negro votes Grant would have been defeated. This lesson was not lost on the Radicals. With a fine show of righteousness, they discovered that the election was a mandate to enfranchise the Negro. Early in 1869 they launched a movement to protect and extend the Negro vote; they proposed a constitutional amendment that a citizen's right to vote should not be denied by a state or by the national government because of race or color.

That conservatives and Democrats would oppose Negro suffrage was expected. But immediately after the Civil War the movement for Negro suffrage was hampered by (of all people!) the woman's righters, led by Miss Anthony and Mrs. Stanton. It was another instance of reformers at odds. The large objectives were the same but the issue now at stake was the question of priority.

During the war the feminists had sidetracked the fight for woman's rights and had identified themselves with the mass of citizens pledged wholeheartedly to the support of the war effort. In common with other women in the

North, the champions of sex equality had expended their energies in the activities of the Sanitary Commission and the National Loyal League.

With the coming of peace the woman's righters renewed their agitation. But, as it at once became evident, the political program of Radical Reconstruction placed a severe strain on the amicable relations between those who placed first the interests of the Negro and those to whom woman's rights were paramount. The true reformers (as distinguished from those who were interested in Negro suffrage as a political expedient) were advocates of male and female suffrage, impartially. But since suffrage for the Negro and suffrage for women could not both be won simultaneously, an inescapable question intruded: Was it more important that Negroes should vote first, or that women should vote first? Seldom were the true reformers faced with so ticklish a business.

Mrs. Stanton and Miss Anthony, more concerned with the woman question than any other, sought to link the political enfranchisement of their sex to the movement for male Negro suffrage. In May 1866 these indefatigable feminists changed the Woman's Rights Convention into an Equal Rights Association, whose chief aim was universal suffrage. Douglass was chosen one of the three vice-presidents.[56]

This dodge deceived no one. Later in the year at an Albany meeting attended by Remond, William Wells Brown and the Negro poet, Frances E. W. Harper, Douglass warned the Equal Rights Association that it was in danger of becoming an organization devoted solely to woman's rights. To women, said Douglass, the ballot was desirable; to the Negro it was all-important. "With us disfranchisement means New Orleans, it means Memphis,[57] it means New York mobs." [58]

---

[56] New York *Tribune*, May 12, 1866.

[57] These cities were scenes of race riots earlier in the year.

[58] New York *Tribune*, Nov. 21, 22, 1866. Also New York *Herald*,

By the end of 1866 the difference in emphasis between the Stanton and Douglass view points was unmistakable, but their respective proponents had not yet reached the breaking point. One area of remaining cooperation centered in a state constitutional convention that was scheduled to begin its work in the summer of 1867. The voters of New York had, in 1866, authorized the legislature to call a convention. Negroes would be interested in the convention because the New York constitution still required that a colored man own $250 worth of property before he could vote. The Cady-Stanton group hoped that the convention would strike at the discriminations against women. Anxious that the convention be reform-minded, Miss Anthony and Mrs. Stanton both wrote to Douglass asking that he join them in petitioning the legislature to permit women and colored men to participate in the balloting for the selection of delegates.[59] When the legislature ignored this request, the Equal Rights League at its May meeting appointed Henry Ward Beecher, Mrs. Stanton and Douglass as lobbyists to the convention.[60]

The work of the convention went slowly — it was in session for nine months — and in the meantime the Cady-Stantonites were becoming more and more embittered that their cause seemed to be moving at a snail's pace, especially as contrasted with the rapid improvement of the lot of the Negro. In 1866, when Mrs. Stanton had run as an independent candidate for Congress from the eighth district in New York, she had received twenty-four votes. The feminists could not help contrasting Mrs. Stanton's

---

Nov. 21, 22, 1866. The sessions were held at Tweedle Hall. "Twaddle at Tweedle Hall," ran the *Herald's* headline (Nov. 21).

[59] Anthony to Douglass, Dec. 15, 1866. *Douglass MSS.* Stanton to Douglass, Jan. 8. *Ibid.* (The date of the year is omitted from the Stanton letter but that it is 1867 is obvious from the context.)

[60] *Standard*, June 1, 1867.

political career with that of the Negro. In the three years
since the Civil War a Negro had delivered a sermon in the
House of Representatives, the Civil Rights Bill had been
passed, Negroes in the District of Columbia had been enfranchised and in the former Confederate states Negroes
were sitting in state legislatures raising points of order and
questions of privilege. The Republican party was promoting the Negro's interest, but where, ran the plea of the
women, could they look for succor? Particularly were the
Stantonites vexed by the repeated pronouncement of
Tilton's phrase that it was "the Negro's hour."

The issue came to a head at the second anniversary
meeting of the Equal Rights Association in New York.
Douglass attempted to soothe the aroused feelings of the
Cady-Stanton group. After a reminder of his long advocacy of woman's rights, he begged them to hold their
claims in abeyance. To the Negro, he reiterated, the ballot
was "an urgent necessity." [61]

The identical controversy broke out later in the year
at the Boston Woman's Convention. This meeting was
attended by many names long prominent in reform. Garrison and Whittier were there. Conspicuous also were
Thomas W. Higginson, now a colonel, having commanded
a Negro regiment, Julia Ward Howe, now famous as the
author of "The Battle Hymn of the Republic," and Bronson Alcott, educator, mystic ("the most transcendental of
the Transcendentalists"), and lecturer. Douglass was one
of the speakers. His most telling point was that the question of woman suffrage depended upon the preliminary
success of Negro suffrage. Douglass' stand was supported
by Congressman Henry Wilson, but Lucy Stone (married
long since, but insistent on the use of her maiden name)
vigorously dissented. The reporter for the *Independent*
found her appeal for the priority of claims of women "not

---

[61] *The Revolution*, May 21, 1868.

more touching than those of Frederick Douglass and
Mrs. Harper for those of their race." [62]

The parting of the ways was reached in May 1869 at the
annual meeting of the Equal Rights Association. Because
the proposed Fifteenth Amendment contained no clause
exempting sex as a basis of political discrimination, the
more ardent feminists regarded the measure as a new
affront. At the meeting the leaders of the Association,
many of them personal friends of Douglass, listened with
impatience to his familiar argument. "When women because they are women, are dragged from their homes and
hung upon lampposts; when their children are torn from
their arms . . . then they will have an urgency to obtain
the ballot equal to the black man." Many ways were open
to women to redress their grievances; the Negro had but
one.[63] Loud applause greeted Douglass' rhetoric, but the
majority opinion did not favor his point of view. His
efforts to force through a resolution committing the Association to the support of the Fifteenth Amendment "as
the culmination of one half of our demands," were
unavailing.[64]

However, Douglass' attitude brought home to the Stantonites the realization that they could not tie their movement in with Negro suffrage — hence before the convention
adjourned the Equal Rights Association was transformed
into the National Woman's Suffrage Association. Later
in the year a rival group favorable to Negro suffrage prior
to woman suffrage was organized as the American Woman
Suffrage Association with Henry Ward Beecher as
president.[65]

---

[62] *Independent*, Nov. 26, 1868.
[63] *Revolution*, May 20, 1869.   [64] *Ibid.*, May 27, 1869.
[65] The breach between the two groups of women was caused also
by bitter personal animosities. For an explanation of this angle by
a pioneer in the movement see Paulina Wright Davis to Gerrit
Smith, Nov. 7, 1869. *Smith MSS.*

The Negroes' interest in the elective franchise led them, early in 1869, to hold one of the old-time conventions. Possibly as a subtle pressure on those members of Congress who might waver on the passage of the Fifteenth Amendment, the convention met in Washington. The delegates, among them Garnet, John Mercer Langston, George B. Vashon and William Whipper, elected Douglass president. The convention went on record as favoring the setting aside annually of January 1 — the day on which the Emancipation Proclamation was signed — "as the proper time to celebrate the practical carrying out of the great principles enunciated in the Declaration of Independence." In tribute to a champion of Negro suffrage the sentiment was expressed that green wreaths should be entwined around the memory of "the great commoner, Thaddeus Stevens." [66]

The convention congratulated Congress on its Reconstruction measures and praised the Grant administration. The delegates condemned the moribund colonization movement and petitioned the Senate to pass a pending bill which would throw open the public lands of Mississippi, Georgia and Alabama to homeless Negroes. The convention appointed a committee to interview the Senate Committee on Military Affairs, asking that slave soldiers be given whatever bonuses other veterans might receive. Congress was requested to appoint two Negro justices of the peace in the District. Henry Wilson delivered one of the closing addresses.[67]

The adjourning delegates exuded a confidence that subsequent events seemed to justify. The political advance of the Negro was underscored late in February 1870 when Hiram R. Revels from Mississippi came to take the Senate seat that Jefferson Davis had occupied ten years

---

[66] *Proceedings of the Colored Convention, Washington, D. C., Jan. 12 and 13* (Washington, 1870), 3–17.

[67] *Ibid.*, 18–30.

previously. This was a fillip. A month later, on March 30, 1870, the Fifteenth Amendment received the requisite number of state ratifications.

At the time of its passage the measure was conceived as an event of historic significance. Indicating that it was unusual to send a message to Congress on the adoption of an amendment, Grant wrote that he could not forbear to comment on "the greatest civil change," and "the most impõrtant event that has occurred since the nation came into life." [68] Negroes and their friends could scarcely contain themselves. There in the Constitution of the United States, on paper in black and white, it was written that no state could deny the right to vote on account of race or color. "We have washed color out of the Constitution," exulted Phillips.[69] Among the colored people there was much rejoicing and giving thanks to God. With not the dimmest perception of the political ingenuity of the Anglo-Saxon in legally circumventing the spirit of the law, the enraptured Negro believed that the ballot would be his pillar of cloud by day, his pillar of fire by night. "Our poor people," wrote "Pap" Singleton in retrospect, "thought they was goin' to have Canaan right off." [70]

Celebrations were numerous. Ten days after ratification the American Anti-Slavery Society held its last meeting. All the outstanding pioneers this side of the grave — Wendell Phillips, Mrs. Mott, and Stephen S. Foster among them — were present except Garrison who had withdrawn permanently after the stormy meeting of 1865, when his motion to disband had been rejected. These reformers, genuinely humanitarian, felt a sense of gratification in the accomplishment of the work for which they had organized thirty-seven years ago. Douglass circulated among them,

---

[68] McPherson, *loc. cit.*, 545.

[69] Sherwin, *op. cit.*, 430.

[70] Walter L. Fleming, "'Pap' Singleton, The Moses of the Colored Exodus," *American Journal of Sociology*, XV, 62 (July 1909).

exchanging reminiscences, happy to see the familiar faces and hear the familiar voices. Gone into the misty recesses of the subconscious were the memories of his breach with the Massachusetts abolitionists. He had no room for any lesser emotion than the satisfying sentiment of high achievement that comes to those who have fought against odds for a righteous cause and have triumphed after a long struggle.

The greatest of the ratification celebrations was held in Baltimore in mid-May. Weeks had been spent in preparation for the occasion and the weather man, as if cooperating unfolded a clear sky. Preceded by "twenty carriages containing distinguished guests," the line of march which paraded the streets comprised twenty thousand Negroes, representing clubs, regiments, drum corps, labor organizations and secret lodges.[71] Arriving at Monument Square, the paraders fell out of line and the formal part of the day's proceedings got under way, before an audience of six thousand.

The chairman, Isaac Myers, opened with the reading of letters from two great champions of the Negro. Sumner expressed regret that he could not attend; Garrison remembered that forty years ago he had lain in a jail in that city "for bearing an uncompromising testimony against certain Northern participants in the domestic slave trade." He dated his anti-slavery career from that episode.[72] The chairman then presented John Mercer Langston, professor of law at Howard University, who, as "the orator of the day," spoke at length and in a very flowery fashion. He closed with an exhortation: "Let the colored race ever go forward, with the motto 'Perpetua' inscribed on their banners." Langston was followed by the Postmaster-General of the United States, John A. J. Cresswell.

---

[71] Baltimore *American*, in Washington *New National Era*, May 26, 1870.
[72] *Ibid.*, May 26, 1870.

A selection from one of the bands set the stage for Douglass. His speech, applauded throughout, was reminiscent and rambling. Like Garrison, he recalled his previous experiences in Baltimore. After reciting a chapter of personal history, Douglass called attention to the progress of the colored man: "The Negro has now got the three belongings of American freedom. First, the cartridge box, for when he got the eagle on his button and the musket on his shoulder he was free. Next came the ballot-box; some of its most earnest advocates now hardly saw it three years ago, but we'll forgive them now. Next we want the jury box." Indulging in a technique that he rarely used, Douglass asked the audience questions that would elicit a verbal mass response: "Will you work as hard for yourselves as you did for your masters? . . . Will you be as sober and temperate as you were before?" In closing he admonished his colored fellows to get education and get money in their pockets. "We have a future; everything is possible to us." [73]

The concluding addresses were given by Judge Hugh L. Bond and Senator F. A. Sawyer of South Carolina. As the day-long celebration drew to its close, the secretary read a series of resolutions. The first three of these expressed the Negro's thanks respectively to the Almighty, the Republican party and the President of the United States. The last of the eight resolutions, and one adopted with "loud acclaim," was a personal tribute:

Resolved, That in recognizing in Frederick Douglass the foremost man of color in the times in which we live and proud to claim him as one "to the manner born," we do here most respectfully, yet earnestly, request him . . . by the power of his magnificent manhood help us to a higher, broader, and nobler manhood. [74]

---

[73] Baltimore *American*, in *New National Era*, May 26, 1870.
[74] *Ibid.*

CHAPTER XIV

Republican Wheelhorse

The Democratic Party has worn, when it has worn
anything tolerably decent, the old shoes and second-
hand clothing of the Republican Party.

DOUGLASS

The ratification of the Fifteenth Amendment did not
usher in the New Jerusalem. Southern whites, it became
quickly evident, found many ways to thwart the law. To
minimize the Negro vote they resorted to such devices as
stuffing the ballot box, holding elections at sites whose
whereabouts were kept secret from the Negro voter, and
falsely arresting the Negro the day before election, followed
by his release the day after election, with apologies for
the error. If a Negro persisted in pressing for his voting
privileges, he found that a terroristic organization, the
Ku Klux Klan, was prepared to employ some peculiarly
persuasive techniques. First it threatened the Negro,
then it burned his property, then if he were still undaunted
the Klan waylaid him and administered some form of
brutality — whipping, maiming, tar-and-feathering, lynch-
ing or burning at the stake.

The national government passed a series of measures
against the Klan but the North, in the early seventies,
began to grow weary of "the eternal nigger." The Republican party was not guiltless of this growing indifference.
Once the vital industrial-capitalist legislation of the Civil
War was safe, once it became certain the Western and
Southern agrarianism would not unite, the Republican
party was prepared to abandon the bewildered Negro to
the dubious mercies of local sentiment in the South. Now

252

that the country had been made safe for the masters of finance, increasingly it became bad form to dilate on the Negro question. In fact, it was best, reasoned Northern capitalists, to permit the South to handle its race question. By controlling the local situation and raising the bugbear of Negro equality, the rising class of Southern Bourbons could obscure their financial tie-up and their economic kinship with Northern businessmen and bankers. The injection of the race angle would convince the Southern poor white that the Negro was his social and economic competitor. Such an attitude would prevent the masses of people, white and black, from uniting to make common cause against the ruling oligarchy in an exploitative economy.

The conspiracy to play down the Negro, plus the absorption of the North with the problems of an emerging urban society, emphasized the continuing need for Negro reformers. Douglass, still enchanted by the ballot, saw politics as the Negro's chief salvation. He was not discouraged by the record of the Negro voter in the South. Douglass found extenuating circumstances. These included the failure of the former slaveholding class to give guidance to the Negro, the absence of a Negro middle class "of intelligence and patriotism," and the pressing necessity of working at top-speed.[1]

This emphasis on politics and political participation as the Negro's open sesame is the key to Douglass' behavior in the seventies. His own advancement and that of his people he linked inseparably with the fortunes of the Republican party. As an individual he had sound reasons for expecting a reward from the party. He was the most prominent living Negro — a fact which Washington could not ignore indefinitely. For his services in the campaign of 1868 Douglass had hoped to get the Rochester post-

---

[1] *New National Era*, Aug. 31, 1871.

mastership, but by 1871 he had given up hope of receiving a high appointive office during Grant's first administration. However, expecting the White House occupant to succeed himself, Douglass took pains to keep in official good graces even though it entailed the unpleasant necessity of taking a stand opposite Charles Sumner.

Douglass stood second to none in his admiration of Sumner. Whenever he was in Washington at a time when Sumner was scheduled to speak, whatever the subject, Douglass could be found in the Senate gallery. In July 1870, he wrote a letter in praise of Sumner's speech holding that the franking privilege was an educational force that preserved freedom of communication between the people and their representatives. He rejoiced also that Sumner, who favored striking the word "white" from a proposed naturalization bill, was "in the right place upon the Chinese question. As usual," he continued, "you are in the van — the country is in the rear." [2] Early in 1871 Douglass disagreed for the only time with the Senator from Massachusetts. It was over Santo Domingo.

In 1870 a combination of patriotic-economic motives led Grant to attempt to annex the revolution-racked island Republic.[3] A member of Grant's military staff, Orville E. Babcock, had negotiated a treaty of annexation with Buenaventura Baez, a scheming Dominican adventurer. Grant believed that he had Sumner's promise that he, as chairman of the Senate Committee on Foreign Affairs, would support the treaty. To Grant's surprise, Sumner made a vigorous attack on the bill, which was defeated on June 30, 1870. The next day Grant requested John Lathrop Motley, Sumner's personal friend, to relinquish his position as Minister to England. Douglass gave expression to what everybody knew when he wrote Sumner that he

---

[2] Douglass to Sumner, July 6, 1870. *Letterbooks.*

[3] For the question of Dominican annexation see Sumner Welles, *Naboth's Vineyard* (2 vols., New York, 1928), II, 359–408.

had heard that Motley "has received a blow really meant for you." [4]

Impatient of opposition, Grant reopened the question in his message to Congress on December 5. As a way out of the imbroglio, Grant's supporter, Senator Oliver P. Morton of Indiana, suggested the appointment of an investigative commission which would sound out Santo Dominican sentiment on annexation. Later in the month Douglass listened to Sumner's bitter Senate speech denouncing Morton's plan. Douglass wrote Sumner that while he objected to the severe criticism of Grant, "I heard every word and would go miles to hear a similar effort." [5] The commission proposal passed Congress. In January 1871, Grant announced his selection of commissioners: Ben Wade, formerly Senator from Ohio, Andrew D. White, president of Cornell University and Samuel G. Howe.

In view of his friendship with Sumner, Howe's appointment was unexpected. Even more surprising, on the surface, was the selection of Douglass as one of the commission secretaries. The move made political sense, however. Douglass was chosen in part because as a Negro his recommendations concerning a people thought to be colored would carry weight. But more important — the selection of Douglass was a counterpoise to Sumner who might influence thousands of Negroes to vote against the Grant administration.

Douglass enjoyed the ocean voyage. He felt honored to be a guest on an American man-of-war, taking his meals at the captain's table, in company with Wade, Howe and White. He mixed easily with the ten newspapermen and the corps of scientists who went along — the former to feel the pulse of Dominican public opinion and report it

[4] Douglass to Sumner, Oct. 4, 1870. *Letterbooks.*
[5] Edward L. Pierce, ed., *Memoirs and Letters of Charles Sumner* (4 vols., Boston, 1877–94), IV, 461.

in the American press, the latter to assess the mineral wealth and other natural resources of the country.

As the *Tennessee* neared Santo Domingo Douglass felt a thrill at the prospect of stepping on the shore where Columbus stood, breathing the air that first he breathed, and seeing the mountains and knowing that " these were the first lands to soothe the fevered eye of the great discoverer." [6] But once ashore Douglass was depressed by the backwardness of the island peoples — Dominicans and Haitians alike. He was dismayed by the evidence of cultural lag — the low standard of living, the absence of democratic political practices and the survivals of superstition. He confided his sentiments to White [7] and Howe: "If this is all my poor colored fellowmen have been able to do in seventy years, God help the race." [8]

Douglass had leisure to observe the way the people lived, as he had no official duties. His secretaryship turned out to be of an honorary nature; the letters of Grant and Secretary of State Hamilton Fish to the Dominican officials made no mention of him. But the work of the entire commission was cut and dried; it was sent out to find reasons favorable to annexation and after its five weeks' survey the commission recommended that step, reporting that the Dominicans themselves were anxious to establish close ties with the United States.

Douglass was genuinely convinced that annexation was desirable. A month before the junket he "saw no reason against the policy of receiving her . . . if that country wishes to come to us." [9] His trip strengthened that feeling. Shortly after his return he pointed out that annexation

---

[6] St. Louis *Times*, in New Orleans *Republican*, Jan. 19, 1873.

[7] *Autobiography of Andrew Dickson White* (2 vols., New York, 1905), I, 501.

[8] Laura E. Richards, ed., *Letters and Journals of Samuel Gridley Howe* (2 vols., Boston, 1909), II, 575.

[9] Douglass to Sumner, Dec. 12, 1870. *Letterbooks.*

would abolish the evils of slavery, absentee landlordism, political revolutions and religious superstition.[10] Subsequently he asserted that the Dominicans believed that by placing their country under the United States they would secure peace and prosperity. They wanted "Saxon and Protestant civilization." [11] To Douglass it was primarily a matter of lending a helping hand: "It might be important to know what San Domingo could do for us, but it is a vastly nobler inquiry to ask what we could do for San Domingo." [12] Douglass ridiculed Schurz' contention that an advanced civilization could not flourish in a tropical latitude. The United States, countered Douglass, could lift Santo Domingo up to its standard, despite the tropical heat. In turn, we could get sugar, fruits, mahogany, lignum vitae, and other resources of a country with rich products and a fertile soil.[13]

Despite his avowed disinterestedness, Douglass' support of annexation had political implications. Just as the Senate debates on the establishment of the commission had served as a testing-ground for party loyalty, so a favorable recommendation would be construed as holding up the President's hands.

But the political support Douglass wished to give Grant was jeopardized by two incidents relating to the return of the commission. On the return trip, Douglass was excluded from the dining-room of a mail packet to which the commission members had been transferred. To Douglass it was particularly humiliating that "Jim-Crow" had raised its head on a government-owned vessel on the Potomac, almost within sight of the White House. Douglass felt that Grant should have rebuked the offending steward. But the President ignored the incident.

[10] *New National Era*, Apr. 20, 1871.
[11] *Ibid.*
[12] St. Louis *Times*, in New Orleans *Republican*, Jan. 19, 1873.
[13] *New National Era*, Jan. 23, 1873.

The other sin of omission was much more serious. The commission reached Washington on March 27. Three days later, White, Howe and Wade dined at the White House. Although conspicuously in Washington at the time — he was presiding at a convention to name a delegate to Congress from the District — Douglass was not invited. He was deeply injured and at the time he made no effort to conceal his pique. "In my own house," wrote Summer, "he complained to me," about Grant's oversight.[14]

Douglass' political acumen and his fidelity to Republicanism soon overcame his sense of injury. By working for a party victory in 1872 he would increase his chances of getting a political plum and at the same time, so he thought, advance the cause of the "sable sons of America." Douglass' support of the Republican party in 1872 destined him for the rôle of unwittingly diverting a Negro labor-class movement into the channels of party regularity. For by 1872 the Negro worker had begun to organize.

This movement for unionism resulted from the segregation policies of white labor groups. The National Labor Union, which held its first meeting in 1866, took a stand for the full incorporation of the Negro, pointing out that capitalists would be quick to exploit any antagonism between white and black laborers. However, the following year the National Labor Union took no official stand on unqualified Negro admission into white locals, despite President W. H. Sylvis' warning that "if the workingmen of the white race do not conciliate the blacks, the black vote will be cast against them." [15]

Irked at the shilly-shallying of the National Labor Union, the Negro workers held a convention of colored laborers at Washington in January 1869. The 161 delegates discussed

[14] *The Works of Charles Sumner* (15 vols., Boston, 1875–83), XV, 207–208.

[15] Sterling D. Spero and Abram L. Harris, *The Black Worker* (New York, 1931), 25.

resolutions on political reform, equal citizenship rights and free land. The following year, the National Labor Union, still straddling, urged colored members to form locals of their own. But the Negro workers had now decided to organize separately; they abandoned the national union and concentrated on the formation of a union of Negro laborers.

Prior to the election of 1872 the Negro workers held two important conventions. One of these was held in Washington in January 1871, with Isaac Myers as president and Lewis Douglass as secretary. Douglass, *père*, was one of the featured speakers. He introduced Miss Anthony, telling of her support of suffrage for Negro men, and urging his listeners to assist her in obtaining the ballot for women, white and colored. He pledged his support to the labor movement, remembering as he did the discriminations he met thirty-six years ago in the Baltimore ship-yards. Douglass asked that the Negro be given educational opportunity and economic equality. The national government "should place a schoolhouse at every crossroad in the South and a bayonet between every ballot box." [16] The convention petitioned Congress to appoint a commission to investigate the condition of the freedmen, and itself appointed a committee of five to submit plans for their assistance. [17] The last business on the agenda was the selection of Douglass as president to succeed Myers.

Three months after this Washington meeting, the president of the Georgia State Convention, H. M. Turner, issued a call for a "Southern States Convention of Colored Men," to meet in October. This step was necessary, so ran the call, because "the peculiar condition of the colored people demanded a union of authorized effort and action." [18] At this meeting at Columbia, South Carolina, the Southern Negroes decided to sponsor the holding of a national con-

---

[16] *New National Era*, Jan. 12, 1871.
[17] *Ibid.*
[18] *Ibid.*, Oct. 12, 1871.

vention at New Orleans the following April. This call was signed by Alonzo J. Ransier, lieutenant-governor of South Carolina.

The New Orleans convention of 1872 was the last and the most important held by the colored "workers." With Douglass in the chair the assembly became a political rally rather than a laboring man's convention. The delegates pledged their unwavering support to the Republican party and whatever candidate it should name: "as all roads out of the Republican party lead into the Democratic camp, we pledge our unswerving devotion to support the nominee at Philadelphia." [19] The convention thanked Grant for the federal patronage he had turned the Negro's way, and prayed for its "stimulation." They indorsed Grant's administration "in maintaining our liberties, in protecting us in our privileges, and in punishing our enemies." "All the laws and all the amendments cannot protect the colored man if his enemies get control of the government," declared the convention. In a striking phrase, Douglass referred to the Republican party as the deck, "all else is the sea." As a condition of their support of the Republicans the convention insisted on the incorporation of a civil rights plank in the party platform.[20] And, finally, the "Negro Labor Convention" repudiated the National Labor Union which obviously was anti-Grant and anti-Republican.

The convention adjourned with the Negro laborer disadvantaged by leaders who proposed to deliver the Negro vote to a political party which represented big business and corporate wealth. Yet these leaders were following familiar compulsions. It was not simply that some of these leaders were political appointees with debts to discharge, and that others were petty bourgeois on the make. Their lack of vision in labor leadership was in part a reflection of their typically American philosophy of class mobility.

[19] *Harper's Weekly*, May 11, 1872.
[20] *Ibid.*

Americans of their day, they did not think in terms of a strong working class movement organized in full panoply for the inevitable class struggle. Their vision in labor relations was further blurred by a traditional hatred of the Democratic party — a hatred which the Civil War had more deeply intensified.

This animosity toward the Democrats is one of the clues to Douglass' political behavior in 1872. As a professional reformer he could have been expected to support the Missouri liberals in their crusade to stem the tide of political corruption in national life. Capitalizing upon public disgust with the low tone of political life under Grant's administration, the Missourians, Schurz and B. Gratz Brown, summoned the reformist elements in the party to a convention at Cincinnati. These "Liberal Republicans" selected Horace Greeley as their candidate for the presidency. The Democrats, sensing a chance to win, also nominated Greeley. Because of his consistent championship of the slave and the freedman, Greeley had a claim to Negro support. But after he wooed and won the Democratic nomination, he lost the colored man.

Never uncertain, Douglass' course became definite when the Republican National Committee hired him for three months of campaigning. On the stump Douglass was frequently asked, as a Grant supporter, to explain the President's failure to invite him to the dinner for the Santo Domingo commissioners. Several months prior to election time Douglass had come to the conclusion that the oversight had been unintended and hence was unimportant. He explained this to his interrogators. Congress had provided, ran his statement, for three commissioners. Having called at the White House as a group, the three men were invited informally to dine with Grant. Had he been present, said Douglass, he had no doubt that Grant would have asked him to sit down with the others. Furthermore, "other gentlemen accompanying the expedition equally with myself, though white, received no invitation." [21] Seeking to parry the awkward question, Douglass asked: "Where is a Democratic President who ever invited a colored man to his table?" [22]

Although his explanations were politically-inspired and unconvincing, Douglass had become philosophical about the slight. In private correspondence he expressed his changed view: "I cannot make the President a great sinner for that omission." [23] Eight weeks before election he apologized for Grant as not being "educated in the Gerrit Smith school." He wrote that he judged Grant by his opportunities: "in this light he is a good and able man." [24]

Having explained Grant's conduct in the commission affair, Douglass, throughout the campaign, gave reasons why the colored people should support him. On the battle-field, Grant, ran his standard address, had always been in advance, or never in the rear, of authority from Washington with reference to the treatment of refugees and Negro troops. As a general, Grant had given every aid to the proposals for improving the lot of the Negro soldier. He had commended the industry of the freedmen and rejoiced in the ratification of the Fifteenth Amendment. Douglass expressed regret at not being able to cite exact figures, but he pointed out that under Grant's administration colored men had become foreign ministers, collectors of customs, assessors of internal revenue and nominees to West Point. Grant had protected the Negro against the Ku Klux Klan. He was always gentlemanly and cordial, "after Lincoln and Sumner no man in his intercourse with me gave evidence of more freedom from vulgar prejudice. . . ." [25]

---

[21] Douglass, *Ulysses S. Grant and the Colored People* (Wash., July 17, 1872), 6. Campaign pamphlet.

[22] *New National Era*, Sept. 12, 1872.

[23] Douglass to Smith, May 15, 1872. *Smith MSS.*

[24] *Ibid.*, Sept. 11, 1872.   [25] *U. S. Grant and the Colored People*, 9.

Cognizant of the colored man's debt to Greeley, who, as editor of the New York *Tribune*, had fought unremittingly against slavery, Douglass had little to say of Grant's opponent. He seldom made a direct reference to the Democratic nominee; instead he spoke of the "Greeley movement," which he charged was pledged to overthrow Negro political equality.

While he was supporting Grant, Douglass was placed on a ticket for the vice-presidency of the United States. The circumstances resulted wholly from the effcrts of the unconventional Victoria Woodhull. An ardent spiritualist and an advocate of free love and a single standard of morality, the fascinating Mrs. Woodhull had had a chequered career before she came to New York in 1868 to open a brokerage office with her sister, Tennessee Claflin. Colonel Cornelius Vanderbilt, brought into Victoria's orbit by his interest in spiritualism, gave her valuable "tips" on the stock market. In 1870 the two sisters launched *Woodhull and Claflin's Weekly* and added woman's rights to their numerous enthusiasms.

In the spring of 1872 Victoria asked Mrs. Stanton's permission to use the National Woman's Suffrage Association as the sponsor of a "People's Convention" for the formation of a new political party. Momentarily carried away by the vivacious Mrs. Woodhull, Mrs. Stanton acquiesced. Subsequently Mrs. Stanton was severely criticized for identifying the national organization with Mrs. Woodhull, but the step had been taken.

On the day after the Woman's Suffrage Association convened, Mrs. Woodhull's nondescript followers, 668 strong, organized the National Radical Reformer's party. Pledged to "obtain the human rights of all mankind," the party drafted a Utopian program and by acclamation named Victoria as its candidate for President of the United States. A running mate was selected within an hour. After considering several possibilities, among them Ben Wade,

Robert Dale Owen, Tilton and Phillips, the choice of the convention finally settled on Douglass "who was eulogized by half a dozen speakers in succession." [26]

The convention was remarkable for its ebullition. At its close Mrs. Woodhull was in ecstasies. Ladies kissed her and embraced one another. A reporter from a Cincinnati sheet wrote that he had never seen so much hugging and kissing in public or private: "Men were not afraid to pass hands around women who were not their wives." [27] The contagious enthusiasm was not the only source of gratification. The sponsors of the convention were proud that although no spittoons had been provided, "not a stain of tobacco could be detected on the floor of the main hall." [28]

The officers of the convention went ahead with plans for an official notification meeting. *Woodhull and Claflin's Weekly* reported that Douglass would accept the nomination "since it is known that he has said that he 'will not decline it.'" [29] Early in June, Mrs. Woodhull was formally notified of her nomination. She accepted.

But similar action from Douglass was not forthcoming. He completely ignored the wholly impractical, hastily extemporized movement. Doubtless it was well that he declined the honor. Financial difficulties forced the sisters to suspend the publication of their weekly from the middle of June until early November; worse for their campaign, they spent election day in the Ludlow Street jail, having been charged with slander and libel against Henry Ward Beecher who, they alleged, had alienated the affections of Theodore Tilton's wife.

Uninterested in Mrs. Woodhull's ups and downs, Douglass spent the pre-election months in New York, Massa-

---

[26] *Woodhull and Claflin's Weekly*, June 1, 1872.

[27] Cincinnati *Commercial*, cited in *Woodhull and Claflin's Weekly*, June 1, 1872.

[28] *Woodhull and Claflin's Weekly*, May 25, 1872.

[29] *Ibid.*, June 1, 1872.

chusetts and Maine,[30] working for Grant's election. He stumped vigorously; after the war he had the satisfaction of campaigning for candidates whose chances for victory were excellent. His support of Grant was wholehearted despite a final complicating cloud — the attitude of Charles Sumner toward the election.

Early in July a group of twenty-four Washington Negroes addressed a letter to Sumner, as a proved friend of the race, asking which of the two candidates would best guard the civil and political rights of the colored man.[31] Having completely broken with the administration — he had been demoted from the chairmanship of the Committee on Foreign Relations and was not on speaking terms with Grant — Sumner in a lengthy reply to his colored admirers, roundly criticized the President's attitude toward the Negro. Raking up the Dominican controversy, Sumner alleged that Grant had struck a blow at the independence of the black republic of Haiti. He had caused Douglass to suffer indignities. Furthermore, during Grant's four-year administration the country had witnessed a period of corruption unparalleled in history. Rather than re-election, wrote Sumner, Grant deserved impeachment for high crimes and misdemeanors.[32]

In contrast to Grant, ran Sumner's letter of advice, Greeley had always been an abolitionist. He had worked valiantly for the black man; he was "your truest friend." According to Sumner, Negroes did not become Democrats if they turned their backs on Grant. A vote for Greeley and vice-presidential nominee B. Gratz Brown, was a vote for two "unchanged Republicans." [33]

To minimize the effect of the Sumner letter, the Republican party issued a pamphlet, "Grant or Greeley—Which?

[30] Douglass to Smith, Sept. 11, 1872. *Smith MSS.*
[31] For letter see *Works of Sumner*, XV, 174.
[32] *Ibid.*, 180.
[33] *Ibid.*, 184.

Facts and Arguments for the Consideration of the Colored
Citizens of the United States." This piece of campaign
literature quoted the opinions of former abolitionists such
as Garrison and Phillips, prominent political figures such
as James G. Blaine, men in the public eye such as Judge
E. R. Hoar and the author, Richard Henry Dana, and
Negro men of mark such as Douglass, Langston and
William H. Day.

United in urging the Negro voter to support Grant,
these advocates advanced varying reasons. Garrison dwelt
at length on the thirty-six-year services of vice-presidential
nominee Henry Wilson in championing the cause of the
slave. Phillips found that Grant had inaugurated a "truly
original statesmanlike and Christian policy toward the
Indians," in addition to doing justice to the workingman
"relative to the execution of the eight-hour day." Langston asserted that Grant had given the Negro political
power, that he had "sustained" a Negro in the United
States Senate in the seat formerly occupied by Jefferson
Davis, and that he had bestowed upon the Negro his
"full share of clerkships" in Washington. Douglass added
his note to the song of praise; it was Grant "whose
sword cleft the hydra-head of treason, and by whose
true heart and good right arm you the Negro gained the
ballot." [34]

The counter-blast was effective. The Negro vote went
solidly to Grant, who, aided also by the patronage and by
heavy war-chest contributions from party "fat cats,"
swept to an easy victory, carrying every state in the North.
Greeley died within a month after the election, heartbroken
over his poor showing. Particularly did he feel keenly the
lack of support among the colored voters. Wrote he, "I
was an Abolitionist for years when to be one was as much

---

[34] *Grant or Greeley — Which? Facts and Arguments for the Consideration of the Colored Citizens of the United States* (Washington, 1872),
passim.

as one's life was worth even here in New York, and the Negroes have all voted against me." [35]

To Douglass the election afforded another satisfaction in addition to having supported the successful candidate. At Utica, late in August 1872, the Republican State Committee assembled to select New York's presidential electors. The delegates chose Gerrit Smith as one of the electors-at-large. The selection of the other posed no problem. Thurlow Weed, an influential figure in state politics, informed the committee that "in his judgment the best name to be associated with G. Smith as elector-at-large, was that of Frederick Douglass." [36] Weed's suggestion was received "with great satisfaction"; Douglass was nominated by acclamation. Upon meeting, the electors chose Douglass to make the trip to Washington to deliver the certified statement of the vote. Toward the close of the year Douglass, as official messenger, conveyed the result of the balloting to the President of the Senate.[37] The entire procedure was a formality, but Douglass was proud of the honor to present the thirty-five electoral votes of the most populous state in the Union.

The appointment to the Electoral College, while a source of gratification, was disquieting in one respect. Douglass had been an elector-at-large; no particular district selected him. It was evident that from a Northern white constituency Douglass could never hope to receive election to any office of consequence. Knowing this, Douglass had focussed his attention on national politics and now, as a two-time supporter of Grant, he might reasonably expect a federal appointment. More and more he thought of the nation's Capitol as the future scene of his labors. He knew

---

[35] George W. Julian, *Political Recollections* (Chicago, 1884), 348.

[36] Thurlow Weed Barnes, ed., *Memoir of Thurlow Weed* (2 vols., Boston, 1883–84), II, 486–487. (Vol. I is edited by Harriet A. Weed.)

[37] *Proceedings of the New York Electoral College* (Albany, N. Y., 1873), 11.

something of the city, having, in 1871, served for two months on the Legislative Council of the District of Columbia.

His decision to move to Washington crystallized in the summer of 1872 when his Rochester home burned to the ground. Rochesterians, now proud of their two nationally-known reformers, Miss Anthony and Douglass, urged him to rebuild. But Douglass had no roots in Rochester; he quit the city with no indication of heartbreak. His stated reason for moving southward was that in Washington, with its large Negro population, his wife would be in "her element."[38]

But Douglass was disappointed in his expectation that his residence in Washington would serve as a prelude to political preferment. Months passed and no federal appointment came his way. Later in life Douglass protested that he neither sought nor expected an appointive position from Grant.[39] But as the General's second administration wore on without proferring him any reward for services rendered, Douglass belatedly discovered that the national government was in the hands of dishonest men. "The moral atmosphere is tainted, rotten," he wrote Smith late in 1874. "Avarice, duplicity, corruption, servility, fawning and trickery of all kinds confront us at every turn."[40]

Douglass' conclusions about the low level of national honesty had been reinforced by his connection with the Freedmen's Bank. This establishment had run the gamut from prosperity to bankruptcy in less than ten years. As "The Freedman's Savings and Trust Company," it had been chartered by Congress, with fifty prominent men, among them O. O. Howard, Gerrit Smith and George L. Stearns, as trustees and incorporators.[41] The object of

---

[38] Wyman and Wyman, *op. cit.*, II, 110.

[39] Douglass, *Life and Times*, 509.

[40] Douglass to Smith, Sept. 24, 1874. *Smith MSS.*

[41] For an extended treatment of the bank see Walter L. Fleming, "The Freedman's Savings Bank," *Yale Review*, XV, 40–77 (May 1906), and XV, 134–146 (Aug. 1906).

the bank was to receive monies from Negroes and thus to foster the habits of thrift and sobriety. With branches in the leading cities of the South, the bank welcomed deposits of five cents upward. In advertisements in the Negro press, the colored people were urged to "Cut off your vices — don't smoke — don't drink — don't buy lottery tickets. Put the money you save into the Freedman's Savings Bank." [42] Told that Lincoln had favored the establishing of the bank, the colored people responded enthusiastically. To have a bank account became fashionable. At one time the bank had deposits of $57,000,000.

But after the initial flourish of great prosperity the bank began to experience reverses. The reasons were numerous. There was no careful oversight of the manipulations of the corrupt and inefficient officials who gradually replaced the first trustees. Bad loans — the speculator Jay Cooke borrowed half a million — and shrinkage of securities held in real estate also sped the downfall. White Southerners opposed the bank as a carpetbag innovation. Many of the clerks were inexperienced. Douglass spoke of the "elegantly dressed colored clerks with pens behind their ears and button bouquets in their coat fronts." He expressed his amazement at the facility with which they made change: "they threw off the thousands with the dexterity, if not the accuracy, of old and experienced clerks." [43]

In the spring of 1874, with a deficit of over $200,000, and having undergone three runs in the space of eighteen months, the bank was threatened with collapse. In an effort to forestall disaster, the trustees hit upon the idea of making Douglass president. John M. Langston opposed the step as ill-advised,[44] but he was out-voted. Douglass knew nothing about banking, but his influence among Negroes was expected to effect a restoration of confidence.

[42] *New National Era*, Oct. 1, 1871.
[43] Douglass, *Life and Times*, 488.
[44] John Mercer Langston, *From the Plantation to the Capitol* (Hartford, Conn., 1894), 343.

Ignorant of the real financial status of the bank, Douglass accepted the presidency. Immediately he sent a quieting telegram to all the branch banks, assuring the depositors that if they exercised a reasonable degree of patience they would be paid dollar for dollar.[45] To the Senate Committee on Finance, Douglass sent word that the bank could go on if the confidence of depositors could be restored and if non-paying branches could be closed and current expenses reduced. He expected success in three months.[46]

Many Negroes took heart. Douglass' name was synonymous with integrity. With him at the prow, the bank would ride the storm.

But they who believed that the presence of Douglass at a glass top desk was superior to the workings of economic law were soon disillusioned. Shortly after assuming the presidency, Douglass learned that many of the trustees had withdrawn their personal deposits and placed them elsewhere. His suspicions aroused, he forced the trustees to reveal the full extent of the bank's insolvency. Surprised and dismayed, Douglass recommended to John Sherman, chairman of the Senate Committee on Finance, that the bank be closed. There was nothing else to do. Late in June the trustees placed the bank's accounts in the hands of a liquidating commission.

The salaries of three commissioners at $3,000 each a year, plus other fees, cost the defunct bank $135,000 in three years. This sum was nearly equal to that paid to the depositors during the same period. All told, the bank paid less than fifty cents on the dollar. Its failure had a detrimental effect. Many Negroes lost the incentive to work or save. A contemporary observed that they spent money as fast as they got their hands on it. "No more Banks for me, I'll use my money as I get it, and then I'll know where it has gone to," said one of them.[47]

[45] *New National Era*, May 7, 1874.   [46] *Ibid.*
[47] William Wells Brown, *My Southern Home* (Boston, 1880), 211.

Douglass' hands were clean in the business. His son, Frederick junior, had borrowed from the bank,[48] but during Douglass' presidency no loans were made. His statement that he was ignorant of the real condition of the bank until after his election to the presidency is unquestioned.[49] His own summary was that the bank had been "the black man's cow but the white man's milk." [50]

Douglass' own pecuniary loss in the failure of the bank was less than $1,000. Over a four-year period the burning of his house and his investment in the *New National Era* cost him $16,000 more. That these losses did not prove embarrassing attested his drawing power on the lecture platform. In the winter of 1872–73, for example, he lectured "from Bangor to Omaha, and from St. Louis to St. Paul." [51] Anxious to get their ten per cent fee, managers of Lyceum Bureaus booked him to the maximum of his physical powers. It was the heyday of lecturing and the work paid well. But the wear and tear of travel — failure of trains to run on schedule, rapid weather changes, badly ventilated and poorly lighted halls — was inescapable. "In the West, women with babies uniformly occupied the front seats so that the little ones, not understanding what you said, might be amused with your gestures and your changing facial expressions." After thirty years of it, finding its fascination gone, Douglass longed for a stationary existence.

In proportion as a future on the lecture platform lost its lure, Douglass began to live more and more in the past. He rejoiced to see old friends and attend the innumerable anniversaries of the various reformist groups. As his emotionalized memory played tricks on his sense of per-

---

[48] New Orleans *Weekly Times*, May 29, 1875.
[49] Douglass to Smith, July 3, 1874. *Smith MSS.*
[50] *Ibid.*
[51] Douglass to John Greenleaf Whittier, Mar. 15, 1873. *MS.* in New York Historical Society.

spective, the harsh features and unpleasant episodes of by-gone days receded from view. His outlook took on a flavor reminiscent of faded clover leaves in the family Bible. "I sometimes," he observed in 1874, "try my old violin; but after all, the music of the past is sweeter than any my unpracticed and unskilled bow can produce. So I lay my dear, old fiddle aside, and listen to the soft, silent, distant music of other days. . . ." [52]

Typical also of a dissatisfied man, smarting under his failure to receive an expected reward, was his increasingly critical attitude. He was nettled that nothing came of his suggestion that Gerrit Smith succeed O. O. Howard as President of Howard University.[53] The appointment of a white missionary led him to remark that a Negro should have been elected to the post.

In the mid-seventies the cause of the Negro seemed to Douglass to have reached a stalemate. He was bitter at the Supreme Court's ingenious promulgation of dual citizenship in the Slaughter House Cases. A state, ran the opinion of the court, could not abridge rights springing from national citizenship, but the Constitution of the United States did not apply if a state abridged the rights that came from state citizenship. Douglass caustically remarked that "dual citizenship means no citizenship." One defeated the other.[54]

He was indignant that the Klan outrages continued. Despite the passage of the Force Acts, violence against the Negro persisted in the South. Douglass urged that "some formal and impressive notice be taken of the murderous warfare going on against the newly emancipated citizens. . . ." He proposed a "National Convention of the friends of equal civil and political rights." [55] Five months later,

[52] Holland, *Frederick Douglass*, 367.
[53] Douglass to Smith, Sept. 23, 1873. *Smith MSS.*
[54] *Ibid.*, July 3, 1874.
[55] *Ibid.*, Oct. 7, 1874.

at the centennial anniversary of the Pennsylvania Society for Promoting the Abolition of Slavery, he called attention to the necessity for statesmanship that would give the Southern Negro protection in the exercise of his "sacred" rights. "Today in Tennessee," ran his urgent plea, "Lucy Haydon is called from an inner-room at midnight and shot down because she teaches colored children to read. Today in New Orleans . . . and in parts of Alabama, the black man scarcely dares to deposit the votes which you gave him for fear of his life." [56]

As if in ironic commentary to Douglass' call for a renewed effort, the colored people, in the mid-seventies, lost two of their greatest champions in public life. In the spring of 1874 Charles Sumner died. Appropriately enough, two of the three persons at his bedside — raising him and changing his position to the last breath — were Negroes. On the news of Sumner's critical condition Douglass hastened to the house, but the sick man was too far gone to recognize him. In company with James G. Blaine and Senator Morrill of Vermont, Douglass remained in the study until the end. He immediately made arrangements to participate in the funeral procession. The services were held in the Senate chamber. On a bleak March day, hundreds of colored citizens followed the hearse from Sumner's residence to the Capitol. Douglass marched at the head of this Negro guard of honor. Negroes everywhere were saddened. In Haiti the flags on all public buildings were hung at half-mast for three days. [57]

Sumner merited a tribute from colored people. Except for a short period during the Dominican imbroglio he had never seized the popular imagination. But no race-conscious Negro could fail to show gratitude for the long public

[56] *Centennial Anniversary of the Pennsylvania Society for Promoting the Abolition of Slavery, April 14, 1875* (Philadelphia, 1876), 25.

[57] J. N. Léger, *Haiti; Her History and Her Detractors* (New York, 1907), 221.

service of an advocate who espoused equal rights for the Negro passionately, as an article of faith — who would demand the floor in Congress if a single Negro were ejected from the street cars in the District of Columbia, and to whom the career of Douglass was an obvious demonstration of the potentialities of every colored man. Negroes whose sense of honoring their benefactors exceeded their knowledge of history might name their sons after Lincoln, but Douglass, with a truer appreciation, knew that if Negroes wished to honor the greatest friend they ever had in public life they should place wreaths on the tomb of Charles Sumner.

The colored people suffered another loss in November 1875, in the death of Vice-President Henry Wilson. Douglass had known Wilson since 1848 when they met at the Free-Soil convention. He knew of Wilson's efforts to persuade Lincoln to issue the Emancipation Proclamation, and of the flood of anti-slavery measures he had introduced in the Senate. Douglass acted as one of the pallbearers at the Washington obsequies. The Senate selected him, along with Purvis and another Negro, James Wormley, to accompany the body to Wilson's home in Natick, Massachusetts.

The full meaning of the loss of such champions as Wilson and Sumner was brought home to the Negro by the Pinchback case. P. B. S. Pinchback, a mulatto, had entered Louisiana politics shortly after the end of the Civil War and by dint of shrewdness and ability had been elected to the state legislature in 1868. Subsequently he became lieutenant-governor and, upon the impeachment of Governor Warmoth in 1872, he served a few months as acting governor of the state.

By the time of the elections of 1872, Louisiana Negroes felt that Pinchback should be elected to the United States Senate. William G. Brown, able Negro state superintendent of schools, urged Douglass to use the columns of the

New National Era in support of Pinchback's candidacy. Brown furnished Douglass with a mailing list.[58] Pinchback was also supported by the New Orleans *Republican,* a Radical newspaper devoted to the promotion of Negro advancement through participation in politics.

Pinchback's candidacy became entangled in the irregularities of Louisiana politics. For in the elections of 1872 both Republicans and Democrats claimed victory. The returning boards — there were four instead of one — returned two different sets of state officials. The Republican group seized control and a Republican legislature elected Pinchback as United States Senator. The Democrats countered with a nominee of their own. Pinchback's credentials were presented to the Senate in March 1873. Nine months later the Senate referred the case to its Committee on Privileges and Elections.

Negroes throughout the country felt that a vital point in the interests of the race turned upon the admission of Pinchback. Pending the outcome of his case, the Louisiana politician took residence in Washington where he often dined with Douglass.[59] In Congress and out, Negroes and their supporters urged the validity of Pinchback's election. But, although Grant's attorney-general had recognized as legal the Republican regime in Louisiana, the Senate acted slowly, cognizant of fraud and corruption on each side. Finally, on March 8, 1876, three years after Pinchback presented his credentials, the Senate voted 32–29 against his admission. Four months later, as a sop, the Senate voted Pinchback a senator's pay for the period during which his case had been in abeyance.

Negroes were indignant at the rejection of Pinchback, especially in view of the rumor that the action of the senators had been influenced by their wives who let it be known that they did not propose to associate with Mrs.

[58] Brown to Douglass, Dec. 19, 1872. *Douglass MSS.*
[59] New Orleans *Telegram,* Jan. 22, 1875.

Pinchback. Particularly were Negroes pained that seven Republicans had voted against the seating of Pinchback. Douglass himself could but half-heartedly apologize for the Republican party's lukewarm support of Pinchback, finding cold comfort in the reflection that "the logic that would make us quit a roof with small holes in it in exchange for the open field and the pitiless storm is not for me."

Douglass' sense of disappointment and despair was lessened whenever he was asked to be orator of the day at an imposing celebration. Such an occasion arose early in 1876 at the unveiling of the freedmen's memorial monument to Abraham Lincoln. The monument had an interesting origin. Charlotte Scott, an ex-slave, on hearing of Lincoln's assassination, ran with tear-filled eyes to her employer and exclaimed that she would give $5 of her wages towards the erection of a monument to his memory. The idea of a monument took hold. Negroes raised $16,242, three-quarters of which came from colored soldiers. Thomas Ball, an eminent sculptor, was commissioned to design a bronze group. He received $17,000, and the national government appropriated an additional $3,000 for the monument's foundation and pedestal.

The date set for the unveiling was April 14, the anniversary of Lincoln's assassination and of the emancipation of the slaves in the District of Columbia. By a joint resolution Congress declared the day a general holiday in order that "all persons desiring to do so should be given the opportunity of attending" the exercises. The flags on all public buildings were hung at halfmast. At noon the procession moved from Seventh and K streets through the grounds of the Executive Mansion to the park. Taking seats on the platform were Grant and his cabinet, Supreme Court justices and numerous senators.

The chairman of the committee on arrangements, John Mercer Langston, called for prayer which was followed by a reading of the Emancipation Proclamation. Then the monument was presented by the President of the Western Sanitary Commission, under whose auspices the money had been raised. Langston was scheduled to receive the monument, but with a happy inspiration he turned to Grant who advanced to the front of the stand and pulled the cord.

The unveiling revealed Lincoln in a standing position, holding in his right hand the Emancipation Proclamation, while his left was poised above a slave whom he gazed upon. The slave was represented in a rising position with one knee still on the ground. The shackles on his wrists were broken. At the base of the monument the word "EMAN-CIPATION" was carved. The monument aroused "noisy manifestations of admiration" whose volume was deepened by the booming of cannon.[60]

Douglass subsequently confessed that he did not like the statue: "it showed the Negro on his knees when a more manly attitude would have been indicative of freedom." [61] However, his fault-finding did not affect the tenor or delivery of his address, which followed the unveiling. Langston's introduction of Douglass as "orator of the occasion" was followed by loud applause.

Douglass spoke impressively and with dignity. "We stand at the national center to perform something like a national act," he began. Disclaiming arrogance and assumption, Douglass briefly reviewed the Negro's contributions to American civilization. Then followed a lengthy and penetrating analysis of Lincoln. After describing his vacillation, his procrastination and his slowness in pushing anti-slavery measures, Douglass entered into a sustained eulogy of the Lincoln of the closing war years. "Though the Union was more dear to him than our free-

---

[60] *Inaugural Ceremonies of the Freedmen's Memorial Monument to Abraham Lincoln* (St. Louis, 1876), 10.

[61] Freeman H. M. Murray, *Emancipation and the Freed in American Sculpture* (Washington, 1916), 199.

dom or our future, under his wise and beneficient rule we saw ourselves gradually lifted from the depths of slavery to the heights of liberty and manhood." By honoring Lincoln's memory the Negro honored himself: "we have been fastening to ourselves a name and fame imperishable and immortal." Furthermore, the Negro was defending himself from "a blighting slander." No one could now accuse the Negro of having no appreciation of his bene-factors: "when the foul reproach of ingratitude is hurled at us, and it is attempted to scourge us beyond the range of human brotherhood, we may calmly point to the monu-ment we have this day erected to the memory of Abraham Lincoln." [62]

From the standpoint of the character of the audience, the address, although distinctly not one of his best, marked the highest point in Douglass' career as a platform speaker. He remembered it; felt honored by the presence of the notables.

Less than a year later another reward came his way — this time something more tangible, something calculated to wipe out all disappointments. It was an offer of a federal position, resulting, oddly enough, from the disputed elec-tion of 1876. The election between Hayes, the Republican, and Tilden, the Democrat, was extremely close. A dispute arose as a result of the unusual procedure of three states — Louisiana, Florida and South Carolina — each of which sent in two different sets of election returns. In each of these states both Republicans and Democrats claimed victory. It was necessary, therefore, to create an electoral commission to examine the validity of the election returns from the competing returning boards in the three states.

The Electoral Commission was made up of seven Demo-crats and eight Republicans, and its decisions reflected the political affiliation of its members rather than the accuracy

[62] *Inaugural Ceremonies of the Freedmen's Memorial Monument,* *passim.*

of their investigations. By votes of eight to seven, along strictly party lines, the commission declared that Hayes had carried each of the states in dispute. Hayes' campaign managers were elated but they realized the necessity of placating the Democrats. As part of a bargain made by his managers with Southern Democrats, Hayes, shortly after his inauguration, withdrew the Federal troops from Columbia, South Carolina, and New Orleans.

Because the carpetbag regimes and Negro suffrage in the South were both dependent upon the presence of Federal troops for protection, their withdrawal inevitably spelled the collapse of the carpetbag regimes and the sharp curtailment of Negro voting. The Hayes administration had now to placate the Negro. To forestall criticism from Negro Republicans and "as a sort of vicarious atonement for the abandonment of the Fifteenth Amendment," Hayes appointed Douglass as Marshal of the District of Columbia. The editors of *The Nation* regarded the nomination as "picturesque but not reformatory." It was little more than "a pleasing event for those who are fond of poetic justice and dramatic denouement." [63]

Douglass accepted without delay. Ignoring the Negro "appeasement" implications, he professed to regard the appointment as a typical event in his life. To him it was "an innovation upon long established usage," and it ran counter to local public opinion. [64]

*　　*　　*

Now that his political appointment had come through, Douglass proceeded to make long range plans for sojourning in Washington. In 1878 he abandoned the small brick dwelling of five years' residence and purchased a suburban home just across the bridge that spanned the Anacostia branch of the Potomac. The fifteen-acre estate was topped

---

[63] *The Nation*, Mar. 22, 1877.
[64] Douglass, *Life and Times*, 512.

by a twenty-room house, commanding a sweeping view of the city and the adjacent country. The house followed the cottage style of architecture, a portico running across the front, and the main door in the center. It was surrounded by cedars, oaks and hickories; "Cedar Hill," Douglass named it, after the profusion of trees. The original owner had stipulated that the plot should never be owned by a Negro or an Irishman.

In the downstairs parlors of the two-story house Douglass hung portraits of Benjamin Lundy, Gerrit Smith, Garrison, Phillips and Lincoln. Large-size portraits of Susan B. Anthony and Elizabeth Cady Stanton flanked the hall at the entrance. One tinted print depicted Othello making his passionate appeal to Desdemona. Upstairs and down were busts in marble and plaster. In the book-lined study of two thousand volumes were a table and a large desk purchased from the effects of Charles Sumner.

Cedar Hill was good for Douglass' health. It gave him elbow room, it provided a setting for romps with his grandchildren — there were twelve in 1878 — and its quiet environs acted as a balm. He found moderate exercise invigorating: "I walk every morning from Cedar Hill to City Hall," [65] a distance of five miles, he wrote in 1882. Then over sixty, he was still a fine specimen. His eyes had lost none of their brilliancy, and his skin was a rich olive yellow. His hair and his beard were completely white; this, according to Mrs. Stanton, "adds greatly to the dignity and purity of his countenance." [66] He took good care of himself. In 1880 he gave up cigars; four years later he wrote, "I neither drink, smoke, chew nor take snuff." [67]

The spaciousness of Cedar Hill permitted Douglass to

[65] Douglass to S. M. Loguen, Oct. 27, 1882. *MS.* in Moorland Foundation.

[66] *Revolution*, March 25, 1869.

[67] New York *Tribune*, Sept. 3, 1884.

ANNA MURRAY DOUGLASS

HELEN PITTS DOUGLASS

keep open house for guests and relatives. His children knew they needed no invitation; they knew also that they could stay as long as they chose. Their families too were welcome, with the possible exception of Nathan Sprague, Rosetta's husband.

Sprague had not turned out well. Douglass had never approved the marriage but, as he wryly wrote, "Our children marry in this country without much deference to the wisdom and advice of their parents." [68] In the late 'sixties Douglass had secured Sprague a clerkship in the Rochester postoffice, but Sprague had been unable to resist the impulse to open letters addressed to others. In his business transactions he was something less than straightforward; he embarrassed his father-in-law by the exposures that inevitably followed his sharp practices. He constantly besought Douglass' aid in support of his family. Rosetta's white-washings of her husband did not blind Douglass to his faults; nevertheless, for his daughter's sake, Douglass invariably came to the rescue. Furthermore, he loved the seven Sprague children — Hattie (Harriette) was an especial favorite.

The Lewis Douglasses were frequent visitors at Cedar Hill. Lewis' wife, Amelia, was the daughter of a former abolitionist co-worker of Douglass, Bishop J. W. Loguen. Although devoted, the couple had no children. After his honorable discharge from the Union army, Lewis had entered the printing trade as a typographer. When color prejudice denied him admission to the Washington local of the typographers' union, Lewis, with his father's backing, published the *New National Era* for three years. Late in the 'seventies, after a fling at real estate, Lewis took a job as deputy-marshal under his father.

Douglass' other sons also lived within the orbit of Cedar Hill. Fred, junior, had married Virginia Hewlett of Cam-

[68] Douglass to Louisa Sprague, May 12, 1882. *MS.* in New York Historical Society.

bridge, Massachusetts. Until 1887 he held small-paying clerical jobs in government service. Charles, the youngest of the Douglass sons, after three years with the Freedman's Bureau, had obtained a clerkship in the third auditor's office of the treasury department. In 1875 Charles went to Santo Domingo as consul at Puerto Plata. He returned to Washington in 1878 on the news of his wife's illness, which turned out to be fatal. Charles' second wife was Laura A. Haley of Canandaigua, New York. Like Rosetta and Fred, Charles had a total of seven children, six of them by his first wife. These Douglass loved too. His favorite grandson was Charles' son Joe, who played the violin. Douglass was proud of his musical promise.

CHAPTER XV

Elder Statesman

To the white people I say, Measure not the colored
man from the heights you have attained, but rather the
depths from which he has come — those depths into
which you plunged him and held him for two centuries.

DOUGLASS

Douglass' duties as Marshal of the United States for the
District of Columbia were not exhaustive. Upon his incumbency the office was shorn of the functions of attending
presidential receptions and introducing guests at the
White House on state occasions. Although marshals under
Lincoln and Grant had performed these duties, Douglass
convinced himself that President Hayes was bound neither
by law nor custom to continue their exercise by his
marshal.

Happily for him, Douglass' position as a government
official meant no silencing of his views in the interests of
political expediency. All during his tenure on the public
payroll he continued to press the claims of his colored
fellows. "They still need the help of all who can say a
word in their behalf," he wrote in answer to an invitation
to attend a jubilee celebration at Oberlin. "If I come to
you in July, I shall bring the colored man with me." [1]

Ever spokesman for his people, as he grew older he took
on the toga of an elder statesman, guiding, counselling,
warning. He became mentor, advocate and sage rolled into
one. As America's most prominent Negro and as a recog-

---

[1] Douglass to William G. Frost, April 3, 1883. *MS.* in Oberlin
College Library.

nized race leader, he was "pelted with all sorts of knotty questions, some of which might be difficult even for Humboldt, Cuvier or Darwin, were they alive. . . ." [2] Some of these inquiries, wrote Douglass, descended to the depths of impertinent and vulgar curiosity. To be able to answer "the higher range of these questions" required a Baconian learning; as Douglass put it, he would have to "be profoundly versed in psychology, anthropology, ethnology, sociology, theology, biology, and all the other ologies, philosophies and sciences." [3]

The American people, so Douglass found, were concerned about the problem of race. From him they expected light on such questions as: "How stands the case with the recently emancipated Negro people? What is their condition today? What is their relation to the people who formerly held them as slaves?" [4] Willy-nilly, Douglass found the rôle of elder statesman thrust upon him by both white and colored; the inquiries of the whites must be answered, and the needs of the Negro required the sounding-board of his stentorian tones. He had no choice but to assume such responsibilities as commending Clara Barton for opening an establishment in Washington to give employment to destitute Negro women,[5] of explaining the causes for the mounting number of lynchings, and of urging Negroes not to take too literally the Biblical injunction to refrain from laying up treasures on earth.

One of the movements in the 'seventies which Douglass urged Negroes to support was Cuban independence. Chafing under the semi-feudal rule of Spain, the Cubans in 1868 had struck the standard of revolt. In the United States, humanitarians and champions of the underdog insisted that the State Department grant to the gallant

---

[2] *Life and Times*, 532.

[3] *Ibid.*

[4] *Ibid.*, 666.

[5] Douglass to Clara Barton, April 10, 1869. *Douglass MSS.*

patriots the status of belligerents. To Negro leaders the securing of Cuban independence meant the emancipation of 400,000 slaves. Langston added a broader reason: "Especially let the colored American realize that wherever battle is made against despotism and oppression, wherever humanity struggles for National existence and recognition, there his sympathies should be felt, and his word and succor inspiring, encouraging and supporting." [6]

Douglass shared these sentiments. Editorially he pointed out that the support of the American Negro would cause the Cuban Negro to take heart and all Cuban insurgents to gain courage. He urged the raising of money to publish the Constitution of the Republic of Cuba, which declared slavery abolished. Ignoring the official neutrality of the United States, Douglass besought young Negro Americans voluntarily to surrender their citizenship "to join their fortunes with those of their suffering brethren in this hour." Finally, he urged the calling of a national colored convention for the cause of Cuba. [7] In follow-up of the convention idea, Douglass met with Pinchback and Downing, both of whom apparently approved the proposal. But no convention was held, due doubtless to the inability of the majority of Negro leaders to cooperate.

For Garnet had proceeded, early in 1873, to organize a "Cuban Anti-Slavery Committee," of which he became secretary. This group solicited funds from Gerrit Smith who sent $200. [8] Then the Committee drew up a petition for presentation to President Grant. Armed with 5,000 signatures, a delegation headed by Garnet called at the White House. Grant graciously received them, in the presence of Secretary of State Fish and other officials. Grant "made a short and neat speech," commending the petitioners for their interest in Cuban independence, ex-

---

[6] New Orleans *Republican*, June 18, 1874.
[7] *New National Era*, Feb. 13, 1873.
[8] Garnet to Smith, Feb. 20, 1873. *Smith MSS.*

pressing his sympathy for the Cubans, and assuring the delegation that the Cabinet had taken the whole matter under consideration.[9] Garnet and his followers filed out of the President's Room in high hopes.

However, when weeks passed and the State Department showed no disposition to act, Negro leaders felt betrayed. Douglass, in a letter to Samuel Scottern, chairman of the Cuban Anti-Slavery Committee, asserted that Washington's failure to grant belligerent status to the Cubans would have brought his reproaches except for his high confidence in America's good intentions. "I have deemed our Government, with the facts of the situation before it, a safer guide than my feelings." [10]

Douglass' faith in the State Department was not misplaced. The United States thought seriously of intervening but the other major powers, on being sounded out, indicated their reluctance to bring pressure on Spain. Unwilling to intervene without the moral support of other nations, the United States made itself content with securing Spain's promise to establish a more liberal government in Cuba, to emancipate the slaves there and to remove trade restrictions on American commerce.

Inevitably in the 'seventies Douglass was called upon to declare his attitude on another movement of interest to his Negro constituency — the colored migration to Kansas. Within ten years after the Civil War the Southern Negro had become restless as his lot had steadily worsened. Acts of violence against the Negro went unpunished. The price of cotton was low. The coming of the vicious crop-lien system with its perpetual tenant indebtedness and the growing legal insecurity of the Negro following his elimination from the political sphere had put many Southern Negroes in a mood to "leave a summer land behind."

---

[9] Garnet to Smith, Feb. 20, 1873. *Smith, MSS.*
[10] Douglass to Scottern, March 9, 1873. *Douglass MSS.*

In contrast to the sombre outlook below the Mason-Dixon line, Benjamin "Pap" Singleton, an illiterate, Tennessee-born ex-slave, vividly described the opportunities in "Sunny Kansas." Self-styled "Moses of the Colored Exodus," Singleton loaded with circulars itinerant preachers, train porters, steamboat employees and others who could scatter his pamphlets in outlying regions. In person and in print he urged Southern Negroes to come to Kansas and get free land or a job in railroad construction.

Singleton's advice was vigorously seconded by Langston and Richard T. Greener, who in 1870 had become the first Negro graduate of Harvard and who, at the time of the migration, was dean of the Howard law school. The logic of Langston and Greener and the colloquial persuasiveness of Singleton spurred many of the hesitant, and the late 'seventies witnessed hundreds of footloose "exodusters" "from the uttermost regions of the South," heading north and northwest with their possessions tied in bags, bundles and red bandanas.

Negro leaders were divided as to the wisdom of migration. Negro politicians like Pinchback and Blanche K. Bruce, former Senator from Mississippi, took a stand against the movement. The most powerful voice in opposition was that of Douglass. He found "something sinister in this so-called exodus, for it transpired that some of the agents most active in promoting it had an understanding with certain railroad companies, by which they were to receive one dollar per head upon all such passengers." [11]

In a public debate with Greener, national secretary of the Emigration Aid Society, Douglass condemned migration by bell, book and candle. He listed his objections. The "noisy advocacy of a general stampede of the colored people from the South to the North" was a tacit admission that " on the soil of the South, the United States Consti-

[11] *Life and Times,* 472.

tution cannot be enforced, and that the National Government is either unwilling or powerless to protect the lives and liberties of loyal citizens." [12] Emigration was a solution by flight rather than by right, and was "a confession of the impracticability of equal rights upon the soil of the South." [13] Further, warned he, Negroes should know that a wandering, nomadic life was a wasteful expenditure of time and energy. Hope still existed in the South, and the Negro "may yet rise there to power and manhood." [14]

True, tyranny and oppression characterized the Southern scene. But migration would simply substitute one evil for another and make "the last state of our people worse than the first." In the South, continued Douglass, the Negro had a ready market for his labor; the climate there made physical exertion uninviting to the white man, whereas "the Negro walks, labors and sleeps in the sunlight unharmed." In sections other than the South the Negro had no monopoly on the demand for labor. Migration was also a mistake politically because it took the colored people from a section where they were potentially capable of electing Negroes to office and placed them in a section where they would have no such power. To move to this "new Canaan of Kansas" would not advantage the Republican party since the Republicans were already strong in that state. [15]

Douglass' blast was widely circulated. His critics rather pointedly asked why he had not remained in the South as a living example of his preachment. But the controversy waned as the volume of migration slowed down to a trickle. Despite the fanfare and the publicity that surrounded his efforts, Singleton's influence by 1880 had brought fewer than 7,500 Negroes to Kansas. [16] Word had travelled back

---

[12] *On the Impolicy of the Exodus* (n. d., n. p.), 3.
[13] *Ibid.*, 3.   [14] *Ibid.*, 6.   [15] *Ibid.*, 7.
[16] Fleming, "'Pap' Singleton, the Moses of the Colored Exodus," *loc. cit.*, 69.

to the southern regions that Kansas was no bed of roses — the weather was cold and public opinion was hostile to the newcomers. In St. Louis the mayor issued a proclamation advising Negroes without funds to steer clear of that city.[17] White workers made no secret of their fears that unorganized Negro labor would bring about a lowering of wages. Those migrants who were agriculturally inclined had no money to buy land.

Many of them faced a Kansas winter unhoused and clad in summer attire. "Many were sick and dying from exposure, and many were suffering for food, clothing and medical assistance." [18] Their plight aroused national concern. Moved by their destitute condition, Douglass appealed to philanthropic friends, among them Mrs. Eliza Thompson of New York. Famed for her benefactions, she sent $250. Aid was also forthcoming from Negro churches and from sympathizers abroad. These donations served further to publicize the hardships of "these poor deluded people," as Douglass termed them. Recruitments slowed down; by 1880, as hundreds of weary migrants returned south or struck out in new directions, the migration was no longer front-page news in the Negro press.

The failure of the movement would seem to have supported Douglass' criticisms. But the controversy had left in Douglass' mind a sense of doubt concerning the wisdom of his advice. Six years after the movement had spent its course, he came to the conclusion that "men, like trees, may be too thickly planted to survive," and that therefore "diffusion is the true policy of the colored people of the South." Of course, it was not expedient or desirable for all to leave, "but some can, and the condition of those who remain will be better because of those who go." [19] His

---

[17] *Appleton's Annual Cyclopedia for 1879* (New York, 1880), 358.
[18] *Ibid.*, 537.
[19] Douglass, *Three Addresses on the Relations Subsisting between the White and Colored People of the United States* (Washington, 1886), 64.

advice took on a personal note after a visit through South Carolina and Georgia in 1888. In those two states he "learned and saw enough to give my hearty 'God-speed' to emigration." [20]

As tribune of his people, Douglass strongly condemned the Supreme Court for declaring unconstitutional the Civil Rights Act. Passed in 1875, this measure sought to secure equal rights for all citizens at hotels, theatres and other places of public amusement. It also stipulated that no person should be disqualified to sit on juries because of race. When, seven years after the measure had been on the statute books, the Supreme Court handed down an adverse ruling, Negroes were up in arms. Douglass and Robert G. Ingersoll were the chief speakers at an indignation meeting at Lincoln Hall in Washington. Douglass' address was a good illustration of his forceful language and close reasoning.

After his opening assertion that the Court's decision was a "further illustration of the reactionary tendencies of public opinion against the black man," Douglass took up the cudgels. When a measure, said he, had been discussed for weeks and months and calmly debated by the most learned lawyers in the land, the reasons for voiding it should be irresistible and conclusive. Furthermore, "inasmuch as the law in question is a law in favor of liberty and justice, it ought to have the benefit of any doubt which could arise from its strict constitutionality." [21]

In the Civil Rights case, went on Douglass, the judges plainly ignored the intention and purpose of Congress. This was an unpermissible omission, and contrary to the rules of interpretation laid down by the court in every one of its decisions with reference to slavery and the slave trade. In those cases, the court always referred to the intention of the framers of the Constitution rather than

[20] Holland, *Frederick Douglass*, 368.
[21] *Life and Times*, 567.

to its letter. Douglass then ridiculed the court's ruling that the unconstitutionality of an act depended upon the party committing the act, and that hence the people of a state may violate a national law which is binding upon the state itself. "What is a State," questioned he, "in the absence of the people who compose it?" [22]

That the Civil Rights Law had been a dead letter and could not be enforced, continued Douglass, was no reason for giving it the *coup de grâce*. "That bill, like all advanced legislation, was a banner on the outer wall of American liberty; a noble moral standard uplifted for the education of the American people." Douglass made a final point. Opponents of the measure, said he, had attempted to call it a "Social Rights Act." This was a familiar distortion, used to inflame popular prejudice. "Social equality and civil equality rest upon an entirely different basis, and well enough the American people know it." If the Civil Rights Act were an act for social equality, then so was the Declaration of Independence, the Sermon on the Mount, the Golden Rule and "the teaching of the Apostle that of one blood God has made all nations to dwell on the face of the earth." [23]

In delivery, no less than in content, this speech was typical of Douglass' post-war addresses. He had completely abandoned mimicry and his use of humor was sparing. He held his audiences by the most striking feature of his oratory — a steady and intense earnestness, an incandescent quality which the clergyman Alexander Crummell termed his "over-soul." Douglass also retained the same rich flow of language, his long sentences fashioned to lead up to a point of striking emphasis or a climax in contrast.

As vigorous as was his oratory in behalf of Negroes, Douglass did not stop there. As elder statesman he set

[22] *Ibid.*, 575.
[23] *Ibid.*, 576.

an example by his efficiency in the discharge of his duties. True, he placed his children in minor governmental posts. But he insisted on an honest day's work of all who took orders from him. He never politicalized his office; on the contrary, he conducted it blamelessly. It was necessary to turn down innumerable job-seekers of questionable competence. A typically considerate rejection was his letter to the elderly Reverend Thomas James: "You must take the will for the deed." [24]

He was not unhappy in his job as marshal. Invariably he was treated with the respect due his office and his personal bearing. His most dramatic duty as marshal was the honor, at inauguration ceremonies, of escorting the President and the President-elect from the Senate Chamber to the east front of the Capitol. At the inauguration of James A. Garfield, in March 1881, Douglass led the solemn column that marched through the long corridors and grand rotunda of the Capitol. Here he witnessed the Chief Justice deliver the oath of office. The inaugural address followed. Then the new President turned and kissed his mother. Not given to cynicism, Douglass felt that the kissing was not done for effect but was "a beautiful and touching act," springing from a spontaneous impulse.[25]

Garfield had promised that Douglass would be continued as marshal. The commitment was made to Senator Roscoe Conkling, Douglass' closest acquaintance in Congress after Sumner's death. However, Garfield came to the conclusion that he would prefer a personal friend as marshal. Furthermore, his indebtedness to Douglass was a party rather than a personal obligation. Garfield, doubtless, did not forget that in the Republican national convention of 1880, Douglass' first choice had been Grant.

Whatever the reason, Garfield did not renew the appointment. Instead, however, Douglass received the job of

[24] Douglass to James, April 6, 1877. *MS.* in Spingarn Collection.
[25] *Life and Times,* 540.

Recorder of Deeds for the District of Columbia. Douglass confessed no disappointment. On the contrary, he felt that his new job would be more to his liking, since it did not involve the responsibility of over-all surveillance of criminals — a task which he found distasteful. The recorder's job, moreover, involved no social duties. Douglass also found satisfaction in that he was the first Negro to hold the new position.

* * *

As elder statesman Douglass' great hold on the Negro people remained firm to the end. So strong was his sway over Negroes that his leadership remained substantially unimpaired even though he was guilty of two of the most serious unorthodoxies in Negro life: a detachment toward organized religion and marriage to a white woman.

The overwhelming mass of nineteenth-century Negroes were churchgoers, fundamentalist in doctrine, sectarian in affiliation, religious if not pious, and completely untouched by the Higher Criticism of the intellectuals or the opiate-of-the-people concept of the Marxists. Douglass, on the other hand, held such liberal views as to open him to charges of atheism. Partly due to his early association with Garrison, partly due to the inability of church groups to transcend color prejudice, and partly due to his disapproval of the poorly-trained Negro clergymen who pandered to credulity and superstition, Douglass remained outside the fold of organized religion. He was constantly contrasting the practices of churchgoers with their public avowals of brotherhood and love.

One of his most lasting impressions was the occasion of his first acquaintance with the militant atheist, Robert G. Ingersoll. At the close of an evening lecture in Elmwood, Illinois, Douglass found it necessary to leave immediately for Peoria, twenty miles distant. The night was cold; it was, writes Douglass, "one of those black and flinty nights when prairie winds pierce like needles, and a step on the snow sounds like a file on the steel teeth of a saw." [26] Douglass feared, remembering a previous experience, that no hotel in Peoria would accommodate him, and he knew no one in that city. On the point of leaving Elmwood, he told a friend of his predicament. The friend informed him that in Peoria there was a man, Robert G. Ingersoll, who would gladly receive him at any hour of the night and in any weather. Upon arriving in Peoria, Douglass found that he could get a hotel room.

Impressed, however, by the warmth of his friend's recommendation of Ingersoll, Douglass resolved to make him an early morning call. The Ingersolls cordially received their unexpected visitor. Douglass found Ingersoll "a man with real living human sunshine in his face, and honest, manly kindness in his voice." The heartfelt welcome by the Ingersolls touched Douglass. "Incidents of this character," he writes, "have greatly tended to liberalize my views as to the value of creeds in estimating the character of men." [27] Inevitably Douglass contrasted Ingersoll with many professing Christians; "many pious souls hate the Negro while they think they love the Lord." [28]

All emotional outcroppings in religion, so common to many Negro groups, met with Douglass' condemnation. When, in 1887 at Gizeh in Egypt, he saw the howling dervishes at worship, it reminded him of a colored Methodist camp meeting in the South. It saddened him to think that "rational beings could be made to believe that such physical distortions could be pleasing to God." [29]

He was equally critical of those in high place whom he counted superstitious. "Queen Victoria," he wrote, "gets water from the Jordan to christen her children, as if the

[26] *Life and Times*, 507.
[27] *Ibid.*, 508.
[28] *Ibid.*, 590.
[29] *Douglass' Diary*, Feb. 25, 1887 (Anacostia Heights).

water of that river were better than the water of any other river. Many go thousands of miles in this age of light to see an old seamless coat supposed to have some divine virtue. Christians at Rome kiss the great toe of a black image called St. Peter, and go upstairs on their knees, to gain divine favor." [30] Attending some of the "religious shows" in Rome at the time of his trip abroad, Douglass' reaction was similar to that of Ben Wade who, when he heard the howling and shouting at a Negro camp-meeting, said, "This is nothing to me, but it must surely be something to them." [31]

Douglass' coolness to organized religion sprang in part from the "otherworldliness" of much that went on in the Negro church. Himself a militant, ever braced to "take arms against a sea of troubles," Douglass held that too many Negro clergymen preached a gospel of resignation, of passiveness, of being so pre-occupied with the city called heaven that they did not rebel against the *status quo* here below. To Douglass religion should have been an instrument for social reconstruction; instead it was largely, he felt, the chief stock in trade of a theologically-untrained and "folksy" clergy who used it as a device for making the underprivileged Negro forget social reality by fixing his eyes on a distant land of milk and honey to be reached by prayerfully waiting for the chariot to swing low.

Douglass was not a praying man. During his early years as a slave, he went down on his knees regularly. But it was not, he writes, until he "prayed with his heels" that he became free. "All the prayers of Christendom cannot stop the force of a single bullet, divert arsenic of its poison, or suspend any law of nature." [32] Small wonder, then, that Douglass' religious outlook was suspect among the mass of

---

[30] Douglass, *Lecture on Haiti* (Chicago, 1893), 29.
[31] *Life and Times*, 603.
[32] *Ibid.*, 529.

Negroes. As he put it, his views received "but limited endorsement among my people." [33]

But although not a praying man, Douglass, unlike Ingersoll, did not attack organized religion. Never did he deny any of the attributes of Deity. He was shocked by irreverence; if he did not come to church to pray, likewise he did not come to scoff. While he subscribed to no particular creed, he contributed financially to individual churches. He held that the church was in a position to promote honorable character and conduct. He believed that on the whole churches contributed "to the improvement and moral elevation of those who come within the reach of their influence." Furthermore, "a large, commodious and well-appointed church in pulpit, choir and architecture is attractive to the people who assemble and commands respect from the outside world." [34]

Although not a regular churchgoer, Douglass did not sit with the ungodly. Indeed, he numbered several prominent clergymen among his closest acquaintances. The numerous letters he received from the Congregational pastor, Jeremiah E. Rankin, president of Howard University, testify to a high personal regard. Douglass was also on good terms with Bishop Daniel A. Payne of the African Methodist Episcopal church. "Age had made their friendship as mellow as the morning light," wrote Douglass.[35] Francis J. Grimké, and another promising young minister, Walter H. Brooks, pastor of the Nineteenth Street Baptist church in Washington, knew Douglass personally and admired him.

Douglass, in essence, was a free religionist, with trust in God. Even as he labored for his people, he walked by

---

[33] *Life and Times*, 529.

[34] Douglass to the Reverend Theophilus G. Steward, July 27, 1886. Carbon copy, *Douglass MSS*.

[35] *Ceremonies Attending the Unveiling of the Monument to Bishop Daniel A. Payne* (Balto., 1894), 8.

faith and not by sight, as he was quick to avow, leaving to Divine Providence the time and manner, the honor and glory, of bringing about a better America. Douglass' speeches are studded with Scriptural references and quotations. "No man," wrote a close acquaintance "read the Bible more." [36]

Always he considered himself within the shadow of the Everlasting Arm, and as he grew older he became possessed by a conviction of salvation. "I have no uneasiness about the hereafter," he was heard to say in later years, "I am in the tradewinds of God. My bark was launched by him, and he is taking it into port." [37] The Reverend J. T. Jenifer related that "several times within a few months" before his death, Douglass expressed to him the joy he experienced in God and in spiritual life.[38]

In his later years Douglass occasionally attended Jenifer's church, the Metropolitan African Methodist Episcopal church. Douglass seems to have found this denomination not uncongenial although he was critical of its long name. His attendance at A.M.E. service, however, did not signify that he felt that in the theology of this sect he had found the complete insight into revealed religion. To the last he approvingly quoted Theodore Parker's dictum: "All the space between man's mind and God's mind is crowded with truths that wait to be discovered and organized into law for the better government of mankind."

If the majority of Negroes were puzzled by Douglass' religious latitudinarianism, they were downright shocked by his second marriage. Anna, nearing seventy and long infirm from rheumatism, took a turn for the worse in the

---

[36] Theodore Tilton, *Sonnets to the Memory of Frederick Douglass* (Paris, 1895), 7.

[37] Jane Marsh Parker, "Reminiscences of Frederick Douglass," *Outlook*, LI, 553 (Apr. 6, 1895).

[38] *In Memoriam: Frederick Douglass*, 26.

summer of 1882. Despite "faithful constant care and nursing " [39] she died after an illness of four weeks. Seventeen months after her death, Douglass married Helen Pitts, a white woman of forty-six.

Born in Rochester of a family old in the history of western New York — one of her ancestors, Captain Peter Pitts, was the first settler in the township of Richmond — Helen had Colonial and Revolutionary ancestry, and was thereby entitled to membership in the Colonial Dames of America and the Daughters of the American Revolution. She had been graduated in 1859 from Mt. Holyoke Female Seminary. Late in the 'seventies she had met Douglass through her uncle who owned the estate adjoining Cedar Hill. She had worked in the recorder's office as Douglass' secretary. To the outward eye her most striking qualities were dignity and respectability. She gave one "the idea of a woman who had been matron or superintendent of some philanthropic institution in which charity plays the principal part."

Although the marriage came as a universal surprise, undoubtedly the principals had discussed it at length since neither was in the habit of acting on impulse. "Love came to me," said Helen, "and I was not afraid to marry the man I loved because of his color." [40] They took the step on an evening late in January 1884. In company with Blanche K. Bruce and his wife, the couple drove to the residence of the Presbyterian Reverend Mr. Grimké, who performed the ceremony. Upon leaving the house, the "contracting parties," reported Grimké, "were all radiant and happy." [41] Within two hours after the marriage the news leaked out.

---

[39] Douglass to S. M. Loguen, Aug. 12, 1882. *MS.* in Moorland Foundation.

[40] Washington *Post*, May 30, 1897.

[41] Francis J. Grimké, "The Second Marriage of Frederick Douglass," *Journal of Negro History*, XIX, 325 (July 1934).

Douglass' second marriage was a risky step for a race spokesman. To the overwhelming mass of Negroes, acutely race-conscious, intermarriage was highly questionable. Amos G. Beman, a Negro leader in ante-bellum New Haven, lost his church and his community pre-eminence when he dared marry across the color line.

The grounds on which Negroes condemned Douglass' second marriage were various. Helen was charged with marrying him for his money. Douglass, said some, was foolish to marry at his age. Further, he was roundly censured on the grounds of showing contempt for his race; by his choice he had implied that no Negro woman was good enough for him. Greener said that he could account for the marriage only by the axiom that "reason ceases where love begins." Impressed by the weight of this adverse comment, one Negro young woman, subsequently destined to become prominent, vowed that under no circumstances would she marry a white man.[42]

The unpopularity of the marriage extended to Douglass' own children. Apparently he had not confided in them. "It was an unhappy time," wrote a daughter of Rosetta, "for all the senior members of the family at the time of the marriage." [43] Rosetta and her husband were particularly resentful. Sprague's sister, Louisa, Douglass' housekeeper for more than ten years, took umbrage and left Cedar Hill. Douglass, in explanation of the family response to the marriage, ruefully remarked that he had no children who were not more or less dependent upon him for support for themselves and their families.

The marriage angered many whites. Douglass kept a scrapbook containing their outraged letters. The most irate comment came from a Virginia newspaper which

---

[42] Mary Church Terrell, *A Colored Woman in a White World* (Washington, 1940), 93.

[43] *MS.* from Fredericka Douglass Sprague Perry to author, Nov. 4, 1940.

dubbed him "a lecherous old African Solomon." [44] An apoplectic Atlantan wrote Grimké that a "Little Tar and Fetters would be good for you," for performing the ceremony. [45]

Douglass could ignore the hostility of choleric whites. If he chose he could also view without alarm the critical attitude of the mass of Negroes. For with his many long-standing friends and acquaintances in both races, Douglass was beyond the reach of social ostracism; indeed, because his list of congenial acquaintances was so extensive, Douglass never felt the need to join Negro social and fraternal organizations. Furthermore, his removal from economic dependence on Negroes gave security that a loss in prestige would not entail a loss in pocket.

Despite his social and financial independence, Douglass wished to avoid the appearance of flouting Negro sensibilities. He felt that he was misunderstood, that Negroes were in error in thinking he had deserted them. He conceived his mission as that of breaking down social barriers and scaling the high wall of race. Douglass believed that colored people themselves shortsightedly drew the color line. The American people as a whole, he said, do not object to a mixture of the races, but rather, honorable marriage between them. Unwilling to brand himself a moral coward by shunning adverse criticism, Douglass preferred to follow his convictions. He had not abandoned the Negro; on the contrary, he held that his marriage to a white woman was in itself a burning protest against color prejudice. Elder statesman that he was, though his people reprove him, yet would he deliver them!

---

[44] Franklin, Virginia, *Gazette*, Feb. 1, 1884.

[45] Carter G. Woodson, ed., *The Works of Francis J. Grimké* (4 vols., Washington, 1942), IV, 1.

CHAPTER XVI

Indian Summer with Helen

We have spent a very happy year together.
DOUGLASS *to Helen*

Although Douglass found a certain satisfaction in stirring up a hornet's nest among conservatives, his second marriage was more than a gesture of social defiance. It was a mutually rewarding emotional experience. To Richard Allen in Ireland, Douglass wrote that his marriage had "brought strong criticism, but there is peace and happiness within." [1] That it was a happy marriage cannot be doubted. It was a step neither ever regretted — a union of harmonized personalities. Their mutual understanding was deep. They had common interests — more exactly, perhaps, Helen made Douglass' interests hers. No over-demonstration of affection pained the sensitive guest at Cedar Hill, who, however, could not escape the impression that a quiet rapture attended the couple.

To Helen the only shadow was the obstinacy of her father and her uncle. Her mother and her sister quickly became reconciled to the marriage, spending the winter of 1888–89 at Cedar Hill. But her father remained unforgiving. He would not obligate himself to Douglass even to the extent of accepting a copy of his autobiography, preferring to buy the book commercially. Her uncle was also adamant; although residing nearby, he never visited the couple.

---

[1] Hannah Maria Wigham, *Memoir of Richard Allen* (London, 1886), 229.

With a touch of the martyrdom common to the righteous, Helen's love for her husband was perhaps strengthened by the very coolness of her male relatives. At least no criticism of their marriage ever weakened her affection for Douglass; she was, in the words she used in closing her letters to him, " ever in love." She came to Cedar Hill immediately after their marriage, and, as she played croquet with him, the very ground they trod became enchanted. But when he was absent, it was a different story: "Cedar Hill," she wrote, "is almost gone when you are gone." [2] Such enkindling devotion animated Douglass; with Helen he seemed young for the first time.

Douglass' new zest for living led to a fancy to travel abroad. His decision was facilitated by his freedom from office-holding. His removal from the public payroll resulted from a Republican defeat — the first in twenty-four years — in the presidential election of 1884. Grover Cleveland defeated James G. Blaine in a mud-slinging campaign. Upon taking office, Cleveland, to the dismay of party regulars, had been in no hurry to make a clean sweep of governmental employees. He did not ask for Douglass' resignation until January 1886, permitting him to retain it for ten months under a Democratic administration. Criticized for holding office under his arch-enemies, the Democrats, Douglass found a ready answer: Cleveland had been elected by Republican votes as well as by those of his own party; an enemy of the spoils system, he could not afford to remove government employees for political reasons; the District of Columbia was non-political since its citizens did not vote, hence the Recorder of Deeds for the District was an officer whose position should be unaffected by national politics.[3]

Upon his removal Douglass was a trifle sour. Cleveland, he asserted, had shrewdly permitted him and a number of

[2] Helen to Douglass, Aug. 14, 1890. *Douglass MSS.*
[3] *Life and Times*, 554–556.

other Republicans to retain their positions for a few months. By so doing, Cleveland had won the approval of the civil service reformers. When he began to remove Republicans from office, the civil service reformers, having previously praised him to the skies, found it difficult publicly to reverse their opinions.

But Douglass personally had little actually to complain of in Cleveland. As he himself somewhat wryly pointed out, under Cleveland colored men suffered no more from dismissals "than one-armed soldiers and other loyal white men whose places were wanted by deserving Democrats." Moreover, Cleveland proved himself a pioneer in presidential social graciousness. Under no president were Douglass and his wife ever invited to a State dinner. Unlike Hayes, Garfield and Arthur, however, Cleveland invited Douglass "and the ladies of his family" to his receptions to Congress, to the diplomatic corps, and to the army and navy. At these affairs the Douglasses suffered no embarrassment.

Following his resignation Douglass made ready for a tour of Europe. To Lewis he entrusted his business affairs, giving him power of attorney. With Francis J. Garrison, son of the great abolitionist, he checked on the correct addresses of mutual friends in the British Isles. Then, late in August, he obtained his passport. It gave a thumb-nail physical description: age—69; stature—6 ft.; forehead—medium; eyes—dark; nose—prominent; mouth—medium; chin—beard; hair—gray; complexion—dark; face—oval.

Everything in order, Douglass and Helen went to New York and there boarded the *City of Rome*. They came aboard a day before sailing time, so eager was Helen to see their cabin. In company with her sister, Eva Pitts, she made a brief inspection. The cabin met with her approval; it was "a nice, cozy little place." [4] The Douglasses re-

---

[4] *Helen's Diary*, Sept. 15, 1886. (Anacostia Heights.)

mained on the ship overnight. The next morning, September 15, the *City of Rome* pulled away from the dock, gliding into a smooth sea, Liverpool-bound.

Douglass was recognized shortly after he and Helen went on deck and stretched in their easy chairs. To Douglass this was not unexpected; he had surmised that "the voyage would not be one of solitude." [5] Douglass was approached by the Reverend Henry Wayland who introduced himself and then discussed politics. Douglass found him "free from pretense, but a little biased in his politics by Mugwumpism." [6] Wayland informed the other passengers of Douglass' identity, and soon he gained Douglass' consent to make an address later in the trip. Captain Munro presided on the occasion of Douglass' brief speech.

The Douglasses had no complaint on the attitude of the other sixty-nine passengers; husband and wife were treated with cordial good-will by all. Helen appreciated this friendliness although she did not find her fellow-passengers very stimulating. "I do not think we have on board a very brilliant company," she wrote.[7] Possibly she was biased; on the second day out, while strolling throughout the ship, she had been shocked on catching a glimpse of a card-room "where 4 men sat around a table gaming — the first time, I believe, that I ever saw it." [8]

The Douglasses enjoyed the trip during the first three days. "We have missed no meals," crowed Douglass on their third day out. But Helen took seasick thereafter. She found the long, plunging motion of the vessel "most unpleasant," and expressed a fervent wish that she could step ashore.[9] Her husband proved a better sailor. He was

---

[5] *Douglass' Diary*, Sept. 15, 1886.
[6] *Ibid.*
[7] *Helen's Diary*, Sept. 19, 1886.
[8] *Ibid.*, Sept. 16, 1886.
[9] *Ibid.*, Sept. 18.

exhilarated that in the rough sea the *City of Rome* "comported herself in a manner to commend her to all who go down to the sea in ships and do business in the deep." [10] With Helen confined to the cabin, Douglass spent many hours in the library, reading *English Traits*. He was gratified to find that Emerson's views on the characteristics of the English people were the same as his.[11]

After a week's sailing they came in sight of the Irish coast. "Poor barefoot Ireland," murmured Douglass in Helen's hearing, "Rich in wit, but poor in wisdom." [12] The *City of Rome* stopped one hour at Queenstown and then went on to Liverpool. Douglass found "everything about the docks the same as forty years ago except forty years older." [13]

The couple stayed in Liverpool a week, putting up at a private rooming house. They visited the art galleries and the public library and they spent a day at the Great Easton piers. One day they went to the International Exhibition, where Douglass showed great interest in the mechanical displays, concluding, however, that the fair was not equal to the Centennial Exposition held at Philadelphia in 1876.[14] During the evenings the Douglasses generally went for a walk. A social worker at heart, Helen was struck by the "begrimed and tattered" appearance of the children they saw on the streets. Doubtless reflecting her husband's thinking, she attributed the cause to strong drink: "Liverpool was second only to Glasgow in the amount of drunkenness among women." [15] Helen also noted that the Liverpudlians turned around to get a second look at Douglass, "but they wear no unpleasant expression," she added.[16]

---

[10] *Douglass' Diary*, Sept. 21, 1886.
[11] *Ibid.*, Sept. 20
[12] *Helen's Diary*, Sept. 24, 1886.
[13] *Douglass' Diary*, Sept. 23, 1886.
[14] *Ibid.*, Sept. 24, 1886.
[15] *Helen's Diary*, Sept. 25, 1886.   [16] *Ibid.*, Sept. 27, 1886.

On the first day of October Douglass and Helen left for St. Neots, a town of 4,000. Here Julia Crofts met them "with open arms" and the three of them had tea. Douglass had not seen Julia for thirty-two years. Her husband had been dead for nearly ten years; she supported herself by running a school for girls.

The morning after the arrival of her guests, Julia walked them to the church and through the cemetery with its "lovely lanes." In the afternoon they took a jaunt to the village of Buchden, Douglass driving. On Sunday Julia and Douglass attended a Wesleyan meeting. The following day the trio went to Cambridge, some fifteen miles away, where they attended services at King's Chapel. On one of the afternoons Douglass addressed the children at Julia's school.

The Douglasses enjoyed their five-day stay at St. Neots. Julia and Douglass had many memories in common and Julia's powers of recall were exceptional. Did Frederick remember, she asked, a soiree for him in March 1847, "when Eliza Wigham pinned a white camelia in your coat."

From St. Neots the Douglasses went southward to London, fifty-one miles away. Here they followed their Baedeker; they "did" St. Paul's, the National Gallery, the British Museum, the Tower, Madame Tussaud's and Westminster Abbey. They also took in the Colonial Exposition. A highlight to Douglass was his visit to Parliament where he heard the seventy-seven year old Gladstone deliver an address on home rule for Ireland. Douglass and Helen made London their headquarters for two weeks. During that fortnight they made a trip to Newcastle where Douglass saw Anna and Ellen Richardson, the women who forty years previously had raised the money for his freedom.

The couple left for Paris on October 20. So anxious was Douglass to get there that he chafed as the customs officials at Calais methodically examined his luggage. "Happily for me," he wrote, "nothing of dynamite, contraband, incendiary or suspicious character was found." [17]

Their eleven-weeks stay in Paris proved interesting largely because of the efforts of two of Douglass' friends. Theodore Stanton, son of Elizabeth Cady Stanton, took the Douglasses to many points of interest. Another valuable friend was Theodore Tilton. A lecturer and newspaper editor of great promise in the 'sixties, Tilton had left America in 1883 after a long and unsuccessful front-page court battle with Henry Ward Beecher. Tilton was overjoyed to see Douglass:

> He came to Paris; and we paced the streets
> As if we twain were truants out of school! [18]

Tilton proved an excellent guide. He took the couple to see the tomb of Lafayette, which Douglass termed "doubly sacred ground" since "this patriot has two countries for his own." [19] They visited the Bibliothèque Nationale, where Douglass was a bit puffed up to find his *Narrative* in circulation.[20] With Tilton they stood before the statue of the poet-politician Lamartine, who, in 1848, signed the decree that freed the slaves in the French colonies.

With young Stanton the couple went to see Doré's statue of the elder Dumas. Despite its artistic qualities, Douglass was unmoved, remembering "how this son of a negress had never spoken a word or written a line in defense of his mother's people." [21] Stanton procured Douglass tickets of admission to the French Senate. Here Douglass was impressed by the "gentlemanly bearing" of the sena-

---

[17] Douglass, *Travels Abroad* (undated manuscript, Anacostia Heights), 18.

[18] Tilton, *op. cit.*, 9.

[19] *Ibid.*

[20] *Travels Abroad*, 16.

[21] Theodore Stanton, "Frederick Douglass in Paris," *Open Court*, I, 151 (Apr. 28, 1887).

tors in their formal dress, but to him a session of the French Senate presented "a scene as wild and tempestuous as that in our House of Representatives when James G. Blaine debated with Hill of Georgia the question of the exclusion of Jefferson Davis from amnesty." [22]

Stanton introduced Douglass to one of the senators, eighty-two-year-old Victor Schoelcher, who had framed the measure of emancipation that Lamartine had signed. Schoelcher was then writing a biography of Toussaint Louverture. The aged senator and Douglass exchanged remembrances of anti-slavery activities in their respective countries. On a visit to Schoelcher's home, Douglass found the library ornamented with broken chains, fetters and iron-pronged collars formerly worn by slaves in the French colonies. These relics had been sent to Schoelcher in gratitude by former slaves.[23]

Aside from the Continental Sabbath, which seemed to them like a secular holiday, the Douglasses liked Paris. Douglass was pleased to discover that his modest acquaintance with the French language was serviceable enough, after a fashion. As he wrote Lewis, he was able to make known his wants "by speaking as much bad French as I can and filling out with English and action." [24] Helen's French, if less muscular, was no less effective.

Douglass liked Paris for its absence of color prejudice. There were no minstrel shows in the city; the Negro was not made the butt of ridicule. Douglass reflected that the Negro had never been in Paris as a slave but he had often been there as a scholar. Douglass credited the absence of color prejudice to the Catholic Church which "welcomes to its altars and communion men of all races and colors." [25]

---

[22] *Travels Abroad*, 13.

[23] *Ibid.*, 27.

[24] Douglass to Lewis Douglass, Nov. 29, 1886. *MS.* in possession of Mrs. Joseph H. Douglass.

[25] *Travels Abroad*, 27.

Douglass and Helen left Paris early in January, bound for Rome. The trip took nearly two weeks, the couple travelling in easy stages. On the way they visited Avignon, "the quaintest and queerest city I ever saw," wrote Douglass. Still standing was the ancient Palace of the Popes. As Douglass viewed its room where once sat a Court of Inquisition, he was moved to philosophic speculation on freedom and tyranny. Avignon also gave him a sense of the panorama of history; one of the city's feudal castles caused him "to see, hear and feel the past." [26]

At Arles, where they paused on their way southward, Douglass confessed a disappointment. Informed by a guide-book that the town was noted for its beautiful women, Douglass remarked that "they must have been in their homes." [27] An hour's ride from "quaint and sinuous" Arles brought them to Marseilles, "by the blue and tideless waters of the Mediterranean." Here, on a sunshiny morning, they hired a boat and were rowed out to Château d'If, "the old prison anchored in the sea and around which the genius of Alexander Dumas has woven such a network of enchantment. . . ." [28]

Leaving Marseilles they passed through Nice, "the most expensive place we found abroad." At Genoa they viewed "the old masters in painting and sculpture." At the Museum of Genoa, Douglass had difficulty tearing himself away from the violin of Paganini. At Pisa they saw the leaning tower and the cathedral where Galileo conducted his experiment on falling bodies.

Douglass and Helen arrived in Rome late in the evening of January 19. They came to the Eternal City with great expectations, and they were not disappointed. The day after their arrival they went to St. Peter's. They were impressed by its gorgeousness, "it awes us into silent,

[26] *Douglass' Diary*, Jan. 11, 1887.
[27] *Ibid.*, Jan. 12, 1887.
[28] *Life and Times*, 592.

speechless admiration," but Douglass felt that it was a contradiction to the simplicity of Jesus.[29] Douglass related that he "had some curiosity in seeing devout people going up to the black statue of St. Peter — I was glad to find him black; I have no prejudice against his color — and kissing the old fellow's big toe. . . ."[30]

Later in their eight-day stay in Rome they were privileged to see the interior treasures of St. Peter's, the costly vestments and precious stones worn by the priests on grand occasions. They were shown, too, many sacred relics, among them the shin bone of Lazarus and two of the thorns which pierced the brow of Jesus on the day of Crucifixion. Their guide, a gowned priest, "seemed to believe what he said," commented Douglass.[31]

The couple saw the other places of historic interest. They visited the Vatican, they "walked on the same Appian way where Paul walked," they viewed the ruins of the Coliseum and the Forum, and they waxed philosophical over the stupendous baths of Titus and Diocletian. One day while strolling on Pincian Hill overlooking the city, they met Edmonia Lewis, the first Negro sculptor of note. She had been living in Rome for twenty years, "speaking Italian constantly has somewhat impaired her English," wrote Douglass.[32] She was delighted to see them and lent Helen some books. While in Rome Douglass renewed his acquaintance with Sarah Remond, sister of his early friend Charles, and one who herself had served as an abolition lecturer.

Leaving Rome late in January, Douglass and Helen moved southward. They found the winter ride from Rome to Naples "delightful," and Mt. Vesuvius "a grand spectacle." They spent three days in Naples, visiting the

[29] *Douglass' Diary*, Jan. 20, 1887.
[30] *Life and Times*, 602.
[31] *Douglass' Diary*, Jan. 24, 1887.
[32] *Ibid.*

Bourbon palace, the tomb of Virgil, the former palace of the Capuchins and, in company with Miss Lewis, the museum. From Naples they visited the ancient city of Pompeii, buried 79 A.D. The Pompeians, reflected Douglass, were slaveholders.[33]

Now that they were in southern Italy, the Douglasses could not resist the desire to go to Egypt and Greece, places not originally in their itinerary. They took ship for Port Saïd on February 13. The following day, his birthday, Douglass confided to his diary that he was seventy years old "if I am right in the estimate of the length of time I have been in the world." [34] Two days later they passed Port Saïd and were sailing down the canal to Ismalia. The country they passed through was barren and hushed. Douglass, commenting on the pin-drop quiet, wrote that he now understood how men became religious in places where silence makes the soul "hear quicker." From Ismalia they took the six hour trip through the Land of Goshen to Cairo.

During their eleven-day stay in Cairo they visited, among other places, numerous mosques, the tomb of the Mamelukes and the Mohammedan Bible House where 12,000 of the faithful were studying the Koran. They saw the Khedive in a holiday procession. A few days later they witnessed a parade of British troops — "the people were not pleased with the sight," observed Douglass.[35]

One day they made the twelve mile trip to the site of ancient Memphis. On another memorable occasion they visited Gizeh, where Douglass went to the top of the great pyramid of Cheops. He made the 470 foot climb with the help of four Arabs — two before pulling him and two behind pushing. Despite this aid, it took Douglass two

---

[33] *Douglass' Diary*, Feb. 4.
[34] *Ibid.*, Feb. 14. Douglass selected February 14 as his birthday because his mother had called him her "Valentine."
[35] *Ibid.*, March 2, 1887.

weeks to recover fully from his exertions, although he counted the aches and pains well worth while when he remembered the breath-taking view of the Sphinx, the Nile and the desert.

Douglass had long been interested in the color classification of the Egyptian people. He concluded that most of them would be classified with mulattoes and Negroes. This, he hastened to add, would not be a scientific description but an American description. As in Paris, he was pleased at the absence of color prejudice. He understood, he wrote, why Mohammedanism, which "did not make color a criterion of fellowship," commended itself to dark-skinned people.[36]

Not all that he saw in Egypt pleased him. The status of the women, hooded and veiled, distressed him. They were degraded and kept ignorant, a plaything or a beast of burden, he remarked. Another of his reproofs was levelled at the country's primitive methods of agriculture: "Egypt may have invented the plow, but it has not improved on the invention." [37]

In early March the couple left Cairo and took a five-day trip up the Nile to Alexandria. Here they booked passage for Athens, where they spent twelve exciting days. Douglass counted it an unforgettable experience "to stand upon Mars Hill, where Paul preached; to ascend Lycabettus and overlook the plains of Marathon, the gardens of Plato, and the rock where Demosthenes declaimed against the breezes of the sea; to gaze upon the Parthenon, the Temple of Theseus, the Temple of Wingless Victory, and the Theatre of Dionysius." [38]

Leaving Athens, Helen and Douglass spent two weeks at Naples and then returned to Rome. Here they witnessed the impressive Easter services at St. Peter's. They were among those present at the unveiling of a monument to

[36] *Douglass' Diary*, Feb. 18.
[37] *Life and Times*, 611.   [38] *Ibid.*

Galileo. Another highlight was their attendance at a reception given by the American Minister, Judge Gallo. "Many wanted to be presented to Frederick," wrote Helen of the occasion.[39] While at Rome Douglass received a call from a woman who introduced herself as Mrs. John Biddulph Martin. It was some moments before the groping Douglass discovered that his visitor was the former Victoria Woodhull.[40]

Arriving at Florence, after a month at Rome, the "first thing" Helen and Douglass did was to make their way to the Protestant Cemetery. Here they reverentially stood before the little mound that covered the remains of the Unitarian clergyman, Theodore Parker, who, as Douglass phrased it, "had a voice for the slave when nearly all the pulpits of the land were dumb." [41] The couple then sought the tombstone of Elizabeth Barrett Browning, whose soul, like Parker's, was "devoted to liberty." They stood silent, too, before the grave of Richard Hildreth whose book, *Despotism in America*, had made a harsh attack on slaveholders.

During their five-day sojourn, Helen and Douglass visited the Uffizi Palace, the mausoleum of the Medici and the tombs built by Michelangelo. They loved Florence with its life and color — its beautiful Arno and its "charming environs." In mid-May they left for Venice. Douglass enjoyed the scenery en route "with the ardor of a boy to whom all the world is new." [42] From Venice, where they found "climate, sea and sky, beautiful," [43] they went to Milan, "not remarkable aside from its splendid cathedral," [44] and then to Lucerne, "most beautifully situated." [45]

---

[39] Helen to Jennie Pitts, Apr. 25, 1887. *Douglass MSS.*
[40] *Douglass' Diary*, Apr. 15, 1887.
[41] *Life and Times*, 615.
[42] *Ibid.*, 616.   [43] *Douglass' Diary*, May 15, 1887.
[44] *Ibid.*, May 19.   [45] *Ibid.*, May 21.

They arrived in Paris late in May. Here they arranged passage to America for Helen, whose mother, they learned, was seriously ill. They saw the Stantons, but Tilton was out of town. They stayed only five days; "Senator Schoelcher kissed me on both cheeks in parting," wrote Douglass.[46]

After seeing Helen off, Douglass remained in the British Isles for two months. He would have accompanied his wife on her homeward journey but he had made promises to many of his British friends to be their guest. As it was, he cut his trip short. He avoided London, not wishing to be jostled by the crowds making merry over Queen Victoria's jubilee. He visited friends in Newcastle, Edinburgh and Glasgow. At Carlisle he found Eliza Barlow's cottage "a place of rest and sweet repose." [47]

In July he fulfilled several additional promises. He spent nearly a week at St. Neots, the guest of Julia. At Bridgeport he saw three other dear friends of long standing, Mary Carpenter and her brother and his wife, the Russell Lant Carpenters. At Bridgeport he also visited Helen P. B. Clark, eldest daughter of John Bright. Bright had written the preface to the English edition of Douglass' *Life and Times*. In Dublin Douglass saw the Webbs, Wilhelmina and Susanna.

Early in August Douglass decided to return to America. He missed his wife and he had a growing anxiety about his business affairs. Helen had written him that she was ready to leave Honeoye for Cedar Hill, her mother having weathered the crisis.

To Douglass the trip had been memorable both in the viewing of so many historic and artistic shrines and in the seeing again of dear friends whom he had "loved long since but lost awhile." It had been stimulating also to get away from the color line, to "walk the world unquestioned, a

---

[46] *Douglass' Diary*, May 29.
[47] Douglass to Helen, June 28, 1887. *Douglass MSS.*

man among men." [48] But, as in his previous trips abroad,
he was glad to set sail for his native land. As Tilton somewhat extravagantly put it:

> He said that every famous land he saw
> Taught him the more to love his own the best! [49]

Shortly after his arrival in Washington, his Negro
admirers gave him a public reception at the Metropolitan
A.M.E church. The Reverend R. E. Stewart presided and
the Reverend Walter Brooks recited an original poem.

---

[48] *Life and Times,* 617.
[49] Tilton, *op. cit.,* 10.

CHAPTER XVII

Minister to Haiti

Speaking for the Negro, I can say, we owe much to Walker for his Appeal, to John Brown for the blow struck at Harpers Ferry, to Lundy and Garrison for their advocacy, and to the abolitionists in all the countries of the world. But we owe incomparably more to Haiti than to them all. I regard her as the original pioneer emancipator of the nineteenth century.

DOUGLASS

As Douglass settled into the routine at Cedar Hill, following his tour abroad, he found that the politicians were already laying plans for the election of 1888. As the campaign approached he was like an old war horse detecting the smoke of battle. As usual he stood four-square for Republicanism. Four months before the party selected its candidates, Douglass suggested a nation-wide convention of colored men to declare against any departure from fealty to Republican principles. He scouted the idea that the Negro should unite with the Democrats: "we have heard of people marrying to get rid of each other, but whoever heard of a people uniting with a political party to get rid of its hatred and persecution." When, in May 1888, the Colored Young Men's National Republican Club elected him to honorary membership, he replied that while he was "almost too old to be enrolled with young men," he would stop in at their headquarters at his earliest convenience.[1]

---

[1] Douglass to J. E. Bruce, May 13, 1888. *MS.* in Schomburg Collection.

At the Republican National Convention, at Chicago in June, Douglass, although not a delegate, was much in evidence. At the opening meeting a spontaneous call for him from 10,000 Republicans could not be ignored; accordingly Douglass responded with a brief speech which urged the delegates, in drafting the party platform, to remember the Negro's services to America, particularly those of the brave black soldier whom Lincoln called "to reach forth with his iron arm and catch with his steel fingers your faltering flag, and he came, he came full two hundred thousand strong." [2] Douglass supported Senator John Sherman of Ohio for the presidential nomination, but after the balloting was over he expressed the belief that in Benjamin Harrison the party had made a good selection.

In the campaign the Republican National Convention assigned Douglass to cover Connecticut, New York, New Jersey and Michigan. Happy that Douglass' stumping would bring him to the Empire State, one admiring New Yorker wrote, "A Presidential Campaign in this state in which your eloquent voice was not heard would resemble the play of Hamlet, without Hamlet." [3] In company with Charles S. Morris, young but already a public speaker of great persuasiveness, Douglass made electioneering speeches "in-doors and out-of-doors, in skating-rinks and public halls, day and night." [4]

Against Cleveland, again the Democratic candidate for President, Douglass could say little. He pointed out, however, that Cleveland was just one man. His running mate, Allen G. Thurman, had, charged Douglass, attacked the Civil Rights Bill in the halls of Congress and had ridiculed the idea that the Negro was entitled to equal citizenship. To Douglass this was a serious accusation for to him the paramount issue of the campaign was the treat-

[2] *Life and Times*, 620.
[3] J. N. Knapp to Douglass, Aug. 20, 1888. *Douglass MSS.*
[4] *Life and Times*, 621.

ment of the Negro. "What to me," he wrote, "are questions of silver and gold, of tariffs and currency, while my people are torn from their little cabins, snatched from jails by furious mobs with no chance to prove their innocence of the crime imputed to them, shot down, hanged and burned to death?"

Staunch as was his advocacy of the Negro, in the campaign of 1888, Douglass was in the anomalous position of supporting a white candidate for Congress over a Negro opponent. In the fourth congressional district of Virginia, John M. Langston aspired to the Republican nomination. The chairman of the state Republican committee, William Mahone, had a candidate of his own, Judge R. W. Arnold.

At the convention that met at Farmville to nominate the party candidate, an open breach developed. After a hectic session, Langston claimed that he had been nominated. The Mahone faction insisted that their candidate had won. Mahone, strong in the party's councils, appealed to the Republican National Committee to settle the dispute. The committee was willing, but Langston refused. He constantly reminded the colored voters that the Mahone faction contested his nomination solely because he was a Negro. This was shrewd politics on Langston's part in a district where the Republican vote was overwhelmingly Negro.

Chagrined, Mahone struck back. He called Langston a bolter and accused him of making his canvass on the race issue, a move injurious to the party and to the Negro. Taking further steps to undermine Langston's appeal to race pride, Mahone, with the blessing of the national committee, persuaded Douglass to enter the lists. It was common knowledge that there was no love lost between the two Negro leaders. Langston had criticized Douglass' appointment to the presidency of the Freedmen's Bank; he had opposed Douglass on the Negro migration movement, and he had charged Douglass with commending

Cleveland's inaugural address from a desire to retain office.

Doubtless at Mahone's instigation, Douglass wrote a lengthy letter to a group of Negro voters in the fourth district who ostensibly had asked his opinion about Langston. Printed and widely circulated by Mahone, this letter handled Langston somewhat severely. Douglass charged that Langston had served on the finance committee of the Freedmen's Bank when the bad loans were made, and that he had insisted on keeping it open at a time when he knew it was insolvent. Langston had gone to Howard University, said Douglass, plotting to become its president. He had coquetted with the Democratic party. He was also guilty of duplicity, ran Douglass' bill of indictment, in keeping the name of Blaine at the head of his newspaper while shouting for Sherman at the Republican convention at Chicago.

Langston dismissed the charges with a sharp denial. Douglass' testimony, he wrote, was "cunning, false and base," a masterpiece of "poor logic, irrelevant philosophy and malicious assertions." [5]

Despite Douglass' harsh criticism, the Negro voters supported Langston almost to a man. Langston, therefore, ran far ahead of Arnold, the Mahone nominee. However, in the close vote between Langston and the Democratic candidate, E. C. Venable, the latter was declared elected. Charging that the large number of votes awarded to Venable were "unlawfully cast, received, counted and returned; and that a large number of votes cast for him were refused, rejected and destroyed," [6] Langston contested the election and thereby threw the decision into the House of Representatives. The Republican majority in the House could

---

[5] John Mercer Langston, *From the Virginia Plantation to the National Capitol* (Hartford, 1894), 466.

[6] *Notice of Contest: John M. Langston, Contestant, vs. E. C. Venable, Contestee* (Petersburg, 1888), 1.

be depended upon to support Langston as over against a Democrat, but in order to punish him for running independently of the party, the House Republicans delayed a decision until the first session of Congress was nearly over. Finally, in September 1890, they declared in favor of Langston who thus became the first (and only) Negro to represent Virginia in the halls of Congress.

The campaign was fruitful to Douglass also. President Harrison showed his gratitude for Douglass' political stumping. Douglass attended the inaugural reception in company with white-haired John Hutchinson. Harrison made it a point to shake hands with Douglass, and he listened gravely while Douglass informed him that forty-eight years previously Hutchinson had sung "Tippecanoe and Tyler too" songs in political support of the President's grandfather.[7]

Harrison had something more tangible for Douglass than recognition at a public reception. During the campaign Douglass had asked Harrison, if he won, to consider him for recorder of deeds. Two weeks after the election, R. R. Wright, a prominent young Negro educator, publicly suggested that Douglass be made a member of Harrison's cabinet. Douglass thanked him but, with a more realistic view of political probabilities, renewed his application for the recorder's job. Harrison, however, had something else in store. On July 1, 1889, he announced Douglass' appointment as Minister-Resident and Consul-General to the Republic of Haiti. "President Harrison," wrote Douglass, "has done more and better for me than I asked — and has done it without my asking." [8] As if to do even more for him, Harrison, in late September, added the post of Chargé d'Affaires for Santo Domingo.

As Douglass had written, the Haitian appointment had

---

[7] Hutchinson, *op. cit.*, II, 154.

[8] Douglass to unknown correspondent, July 20, 1889. *MS.* in Schomburg Collection.

come unsought. But he had been fully aware that there was precedent for the step. Twenty years previously, after Grant's first election, Douglass had been mentioned for the Haitian appointment. But he had been lukewarm toward the post,[9] preferring to throw his influence to another Negro, Ebenezer Bassett, a Connecticut-born high school principal who had studied at Yale. The latter had held the position during Grant's two terms, thereby becoming the first Negro minister appointed to a foreign government. Bassett had been succeeded by Langston who had also been minister-resident and consul-general for some eight years (1877-85).

Appointment to the diplomatic service had occupied Douglass' thoughts during the short presidency of Garfield. Shortly after Garfield's inauguration Douglass called on him at the Executive Mansion. Garfield expressed his intention of sending Negro representatives to nations other than Haiti and Liberia. Douglass informed the President of his hearty approval. Garfield then asked Douglass if he would care to be considered for such an appointment. But Garfield's death, six months after taking office, wrote *finis* to any follow-up of the proposal.

If appointment of a Negro to a foreign post was not, in Douglass' thinking, revolutionary, his selection by Harrison evoked apprehension in other quarters. The mercantile class, particularly the merchants in New York City, believed that a white minister could obtain better commercial concessions than could a Negro.[10] Many businessmen feared that a Negro minister would not approve of transactions that favored American interests at the expense of Haitian interests. Other critics, ignoring the precedents established by Bassett and Langston, asserted that the Haitian people did not wish a Negro representa-

---

[9] *Independent*, April 29, 1869.

[10] For the attitude of the New York merchants see Bassett to Douglass, July 11, 1889, Sept. 2, 1889. *Douglass MSS.*

tive. Douglass dismissed much of this cricitism with the assertion that there was always a demand made for a white man when there was $5,000 attached to the office. But among those who had misgivings were well-wishers and friends. Their reasons sprang from solicitude over his personal welfare. From England Mrs. Crofts communicated her fears that life was unsafe in an insurrectionary country like Haiti.[11] In another letter she pointed out his language handicap: "You will be bothered about French and that's a pity. I wish I could give you a part of my French conversational ability."[12] One correspondent, a Haitian residing in the United States, warned him against walking in the noon-day sun: "One of the first things you will have to do is to purchase a saddle horse."[13] Other admirers feared that Douglass' tendency to speak his mind freely unfitted him for diplomacy, that he would leak like a sieve. As Douglass himself observed in a letter to a congratulating friend, he could not say, as did a great Russian diplomat, "I have learned to hold my tongue in six languages."[14]

There were other sour notes. Many Negroes thought that the position was not big enough. Some gloomily asserted that he could ill be spared when there was still so much to do in the United States for the cause of Negro advancement. The suffragist Lucy Stone wrote that the woman's rights movement would miss him: "I am not sure we are glad to have you go. We need you here."[15]

Case-hardened to criticism from foe and friend, and determined to succeed, Douglass made preparations to leave Washington. He found that he could not get first-class accommodations on a steamboat or train going south.

---

[11] Crofts to Douglass, July 17, 1889. *Douglass MSS.*
[12] *Ibid.*, Aug. 3, 1889. *Ibid.*
[13] Arthur Bird to Douglass, July 5, 1889. *Ibid.*
[14] Douglass to Lucy Stone, July 25, 1889. Carbon copy, *Ibid.*
[15] Lucy Stone to Douglass, July 21, 1889. *Ibid.*

He finally sailed on a naval vessel, the *Kearsarge*, late in September. He was accompanied by his wife and by Ebenezer Bassett whom he took as his secretary. Bassett knew the country well and spoke French fluently. Bassett had originally hoped that Harrison would give him the ministership and had solicited the intercession of Douglass on his behalf.[16] When Douglass received the appointment, Bassett asked him for the job of secretary, reflecting that "even $850 is better than nothing." [17]

On the slow eleven-day trip Douglass was seasick much of the time. Arrived at Port-au-Prince on October 8, his spirits revived when the ever-courteous Haitians told him that he bore a striking resemblance to Victor Hugo.[18] Generous, too, in his reception to Douglass was the new President of Haiti, Louis Mondestin Florvil Hyppolite, to whom he presented his credentials. At the presentation ceremonies Douglass spoke of the growing intercommunication of nations, a beneficent tendency which enlarged human sympathies and developed " opportunities for the exercise of a generous spirit of forbearance and concession, favorable to peace and fraternal relations between them." [19] Hyppolite graciously replied that Douglass was the incarnation of Haiti's ideal, "the moral and intellectual development of the men of the African race by personal effort and mental culture." [20]

Hyppolite's characterization of Douglass was not a perfunctory gesture to the dean of the American diplomatic corps; it was an earnest of the attitude of all Haitians toward him. For more than a quarter of a century they had followed the course of his career. "Frederick Douglass

---

[16] Bassett to Douglass, March 6, 1889. *Ibid.*

[17] *Ibid.*, June 27, 1889.

[18] Parker, "Reminiscences," *loc. cit.*, 553.

[19] Louis Martin Sears, "Frederick Douglass and the Mission to Haiti," *Hispanic American Historical Review*, XXI, 226 (May 1941).

[20] *Ibid.*

is well known here," Bassett had written in 1869.[21] Neither the government nor the people ever withheld from Douglass any respect or courtesy due him as a person or a diplomat.

In turn, Douglass found much to praise about the Haitians. They were, he thought, "a fine looking people." There was about them a sort of majesty. They carried themselves proudly erect "as if conscious of their freedom and independence."[22] Particularly did he admire the women; they were "elastic, vigorous and comely." The country's wealth and prosperity owed much to them.[23]

Douglass had been appointed and had assumed office during a recess of Congress. His confirmation by the Senate was taken for granted. Harrison's letter of nomination was presented on December 5.[24] Four days later Douglass' name was referred to the Committee of Foreign Relations, which reported favorably. On December 17 the Senate voted acceptance of the committee's recommendation.[25]

Aware of the high esteem of the Haitians and of the many eyes upon him, Douglass strove to make good. Only after a full day at his desk, from eight to five, did he rejoin Helen at the pleasant home of the American minister, three miles out of Port-au-Prince. He found long work hours necessary if he was to give full attention to details. Much of his time went, he discovered, in handling requests. A father who hadn't heard from his son in five months solicited Douglass' aid;[26] a philatelist wished Douglass to send him some Haitian stamps;[27] another correspondent

[21] Bassett to Douglass, Aug. 15, 1869. *Douglass MSS.*
[22] Douglass, *Lecture on Haiti*, 13.
[23] *Ibid.*
[24] *United States Senate Executive Journal*, XXVII, 73.
[25] *Ibid.*, 162.
[26] James B. Dry to Douglass, Aug. 26, 1889. *Douglass MSS.*
[27] R. B. Anderson to Douglass, Nov. 6, 1889. *Ibid.*

urged him to use his influence to persuade the Haitian government to permit an American firm — the St. Louis Bank Note Company — to supply Haiti's postage stamps.[28] He was asked to "procure information relative to the malt and beer trade." Wrote an antiquarian in Kansas, "Tell me where can be found relics of Columbus or the early Spanish explorers in Haiti." [29] Captains of sailing vessels asked him to register protest with the Haitian government on the delays they met with in discharging their cargoes and obtaining clearance.[30] To his office came the requests of Americans who had claims against the Haitian government or Haitian citizens for injuries to person and property. Douglass settled five such claims.[31]

The most important request handled by Douglass came from the Clyde steamship lines. William P. Clyde, head of the company, had been interested in a West India line since 1878. He had sent Douglass a "bon voyage" letter [32] which was handed to the Haiti-bound minister just as he boarded the *Kearsarge*. Two weeks after his arrival, Douglass received from Secretary of State James G. Blaine a letter introducing Clyde's son, Thomas. Guardedly, Blaine wrote, "I bespeak for him your cordial official assistance in whatever manner you properly can." [33] The Clydes sought to persuade the Haitian government to permit the establishment of a steamboat service between New York and seven Haitian ports, and also to reduce the tonnage and port duties on American vessels. Douglass' negotiations with Anténor Firmin, the Haitian Secretary of State for Exterior Relations, aided in obtaining execu-

[28] F. J. Pope to Douglass, Nov. 1, 1889. *Ibid.*
[29] Walter Scott to Douglass, Feb. 20, 1891. *Ibid.*
[30] *Douglass' Notebook*, Jan. 7, 1890.
[31] Ludwell L. Montague, *Haiti and the United States, 1741–1938* (Durham, N. C., 1940), 91.
[32] Clyde to Douglass, Sept. 30, 1889. *Douglass MSS.*
[33] Blaine to Douglass, Oct. 19, 1889. *Ibid.*

tive approval of both of these requests. The elder Clyde thanked him heartily for "his good offices." [34]

As consul-general, working to promote the commercial interests of the United States, Douglass found much of his work routine. More stimulating were his ceremonial duties as minister-resident. These embraced such activities as speaking at a New Year's celebration, which was observed with pomp and fanfare, and attending the opening of the nineteenth session of the Haitian legislature. As a figure of consequence, his attendance was respectfully requested, in letters with large, black-bordered envelopes, at funerals of Haitian notables. On an official visit to Santo Domingo he was gratified by the cordial reception he received.

Another honor attending his office was the transmitting of the first cable message from Haiti. Addressed to Blaine, the message read: "Progress Cable completed to Port-au-Prince, 30 December 1890." In reply Blaine cabled Douglass, "Congratulate President Hyppolite that the two Republics are nearer today than they have been." [35]

Blaine's message that the two Republics were "nearer" must be interpreted in a purely physical sense only. For at the time of Douglass' mission the relations between the United States and Haiti were strained. The tension grew out of the attempt by the United States to secure Môle St. Nicolas, a port at Haiti's northwest tip, as a naval base and a coaling station. Blaine had his heart set on making the United States the world's foremost political power. Most Americans approved Blaine's design. Anxious to expand in the Caribbean, which was becoming important in view of the prospect of building a canal connecting the Atlantic and the Pacific, the United States made no concealment of its ambitions. The desire to lease Môle St. Nicolas was alike in motivation to the aspiration, in the 'seventies,

---

[34] Clyde to Douglass, Feb. 3, 1890. *Douglass MSS.*
[35] Sears, *loc. cit.*, 231.

to annex Santo Domingo. As he had favored Dominican annexation, so Douglass favored the lease of the Môle, and for much the same reasons.

But the Haitian lease presented complications. Foremost of these was the unwillingness of the Haitians to negotiate. With the acute sensitivity of a small nation in a predatory world, Haiti feared that even a toe hold on her territory by a foreign power would mark the beginning of her loss of sovereignty. The Haitians knew of the camel who was permitted to put his head in the tent, and they fancied that the fable pointed a present danger.

Another difficulty in obtaining the lease stemmed from the unstable nature of Haitian politics. Hyppolite had come into power as President by a violent overthrow of the government of his predecessor, François Légitime. The latter's brief presidency of eight months terminated largely because the United States withheld its recognition. Hyppolite's success in seizing control was due to a concentration of American naval vessels which anchored in Haitian waters at the time of the overthrow. Hyppolite was, therefore, greatly indebted to the United States. But this indebtedness was a liability in such a delicate matter as arranging the lease of a port. For the anti-Hyppolite faction in Haiti would be quick to make political capital by charging the administration with sacrificing Haitian interests in a "deal" with the United States.

That the United States sensed these difficulties was evident, in part, by the selection of Douglass as minister. While primarily political in intent, Douglass' appointment was expected to facilitate the transaction. Surely, reasoned the State Department, the Haitians could trust a man of Douglass' integrity and pigmentation. Officially, the Secretary of State did not press Douglass with the lease in the months immediately following his arrival at Port-au-Prince. It was thought best to give him time to win the friendship of the Haitians. It was not, therefore, until

January 1891, nearly fifteen months after his arrival, that Douglass received any official correspondence on negotiations for the lease.

On the first day of January 1891, Blaine wrote Douglass that a lease of Môle St. Nicolas would promote the welfare of both countries, and that President Harrison wished him (Douglass) to cooperate "in bringing about the end to which the Admiral will give all his energies." [36] The admiral was Bancroft Gherardi, nephew of the historian-diplomat, George Bancroft. In command of the North Atlantic fleet, Gherardi had been a staunch advocate of the lease. Over the previous period of Douglass' ministership, the relationship between him and Gherardi had been amicable, and Blaine hoped that they would work well as co-negotiators.

Gherardi arrived at Port-au-Prince in late January. He thereupon sent one of his officers to the United States legation to invite Douglass to his flagship, the *Philadelphia*. Douglass went, although he knew that in accordance with strict protocol, Gherardi should have called on him. On board ship Douglass sat attentively as Gherardi delivered his message briefly. Douglass was informed that it was the wish of the State Department that he participate in the negotiations for the lease.

Douglass was chagrined as he left the flagship. He had been prepared to overlook Gherardi's lack of diplomatic courtesy. But the appointment of the Admiral to assume leadership in the negotiations was a pill not easily swallowed. Though never inordinately sensitive, Douglass had an impulse to resign. He concluded, however, that as a good soldier he must obey the will of his government.

Two days after their brief discussion the two American negotiators held a conference with Hyppolite and Firmin. Gherardi did most of the talking. He stated that the lease

---

[36] Blaine to Douglass, Jan. 1, 1891. *Douglass MSS.*

would be a source of strength, rather than of weakness, to Haiti. Furthermore, he went on, the United States expected Hyppolite's support because of services rendered in his behalf during the Légitime disturbance. The Hyppolite revolution had been successful because of American aid during the course of the strife. Gherardi concluded by asserting that Hyppolite's agents in Washington had promised that the new government would support the lease.

Gherardi stated his case well although Douglass did not fancy his blunt statement of naked *quid pro quo* diplomacy. The three hour conference — slowed by the necessity for an interpreter — closed amicably, with the American negotiators sanguine.

Five days after the interview the United States made formal request for a lease on the Môle. The application bore Gherardi's signature, but not that of Douglass. Firmin, playing for time, then asked Gherardi for an official written statement of his full powers. "An able man and well skilled in the technicalities of diplomacy," as Douglass characterized him,[37] Firmin pointed out that the Haitian government would be unwise to negotiate with any person unless his responsibility was officially attested by the country he purported to represent. Pending the arrival of the credentials, said Firmin, he would see to it that Hyppolite presented the lease proposal to his cabinet (six officials collectively called the Council of the Secretaries of State).

Gherardi had not deemed it necessary to bring credentials. Vexed, he intimated to Douglass that Firmin was seizing a pretext for delay. Douglass informed the Admiral that in his opinion it would be advisable to comply with Firmin's request. Gherardi thereupon wired for a letter of credence. Two days afterward he received word from Washington that such a letter would be sent immediately.

---

[37] *Life and Times*, 635.

However, it was not until mid-April, nearly two months later, that the credentials arrived.

This letter, signed by Harrison and Blaine, granted full powers of negotiation to Gherardi and Douglass jointly. In making application for a naval base and a coaling station, this official dispatch, unlike Gherardi's request to Hyppolite, did not stipulate that Haiti be prohibited from selling or leasing territory to any nation other than the United States. Thereupon the two American negotiators were faced with the question: should these new instructions, imposing no restrictions on Haiti's right to sell or lease to other nations, supersede the previous ones? Here arose a difference of opinion. Douglass favored confining the lease to a simple contract without limiting conditions; Gherardi favored a lease on the terms he had originally stated to the Haitian officials.

This division of opinion between Douglass and Gherardi was not the only factor jeopardizing success. Unfortunately too for the lease, Admiral John G. Walker, bearer of Harrison's letter, was accompanied by four warships. The sight of two American squadrons comprising 100 cannon and 2,000 men, instead of overawing the Haitians, provoked loud public protest. Amid such overwhelming Haitian disapproval, no lease could be negotiated without inevitably bringing on a popular uprising.

Nevertheless, it was necessary, in accordance with protocol, to go through the motions. Douglass and Gherardi called on Firmin on April 21. He promised an immediate reply. The next day it came; Haiti declined to grant the lease. In support of the refusal Firmin advanced the point that if, as the lease terms stated, Haiti could not lease or sell her territory to any nation except the United States, she would be renouncing her sovereign right to dispose of her domain as she saw fit.

Douglass telegraphed the unpleasant news to Blaine. Then, in a joint dispatch to Firmin, the two American negotiators expressed their regret over the unsuccessful attempt to lease the Môle. Douglass asked Firmin whether the matter might be re-opened after the sailing of the warships. Firmin gave an evasive reply, confident that under no circumstances would Harrison seize the Môle by force. Firmin's intuition was sound; the ships withdrew shortly after the rejection — Walker's fleet leaving Port-au-Prince on April 24, and Gherardi following three days after.

In retrospect, the negotiations for the lease could have had no other outcome. However much Hyppolite and Firmin might have been charged with bad faith, they had no alternative other than the rejection of the proposal. Opposition in Haiti was strong against any such step. The Haitian Constitution forbade the sale or cession of any territory; Haitian public opinion would have construed a lease as equally unconstitutional.

There are other reasons for the Haitian refusal. Latin in temperament, the Haitians were quick to take offense. While not openly hostile to the United States, they had historic grievances toward their powerful neighbors to the north. Although an independent nation since 1803, Haiti was not diplomatically recognized by the United States until 1864. Congressmen from slave-holding states had blocked recognition for sixty years. The proposal to annex Santo Domingo in the 'seventies had aroused so much Haitian opposition that Secretary of State Fish had officially warned Haiti that her interference would be resented. Haitians, furthermore, were traditionally bitter at the uncomplimentary manner in which American journalists and travellers dealt with Haitian politics and customs. This gratuitous chorus of condemnation from Americans ran from charges of political venality and incessant civil war to allegations of cannibalism and voodoo. Haitians, moreover, were keenly aware of the deep-seated color prejudice that existed in the United States.

In view of these factors the lease of the Môle was foredoomed no matter who represented the United States. Nevertheless, Douglass took the failure personally. His relations with Gherardi had steadily worsened during the period of negotiation, especially after the Admiral had quoted him to Blaine as advising that the Môle be seized outright, thus presenting the Hyppolite administration with a *fait accompli*. On April 27, a few hours before he sailed, Gherardi bade Douglass good-bye, emphasizing their pleasant relations. Douglass, pondering the criticism against him in the New York press, that was attributed to Gherardi, was puzzled by Gherardi's departing show of cordiality. Unbosoming himself in the privacy of a notebook, Douglass wondered whether "the brave Admiral is a man of duplicity, one who can smile to your face and stab you in the back." [38]

Douglass was bitter also over the editorial comment in American newspapers stating that his color identity with the Haitians prevented him from putting forth his best efforts to obtain the lease. Much of this press vilification Douglass attributed to the Clyde people. As their commercial contract with Firmin languished in the Haitian legislature, the Clyde company made Douglass the scapegoat — their attitude toward him becoming cool, then condemnatory, then abusive.

All this doubtless was in Douglass' mind when, two weeks after the Haitian note of rejection, he requested the State Department to grant him a leave of absence. Upon the granting of the request late in May, Douglass returned to Washington. He sent in his resignation on the last day of June. Undoubtedly, Harrison and Blaine were relieved by Douglass' decision to bow out. Harrison had perhaps originally offered Douglass the post in the belief that he would decline it. But after Douglass' acceptance, the administration dared not force his resignation. Harrison

---

[38] *Douglass' Notebook*, undated entry.

could not forget that in the close election of 1888 the Negro vote had spelled Republican success. Douglass' uncoerced resignation cleared the air. The State Department accepted it on August 11.[39]

Never one to quit under fire, Douglass' resignation was perhaps due less to the failure of the lease than to considerations of personal well-being. Then over seventy, his health required constant watching. The climate in Haiti had not agreed with him. Mid-way during the period of his ministry he had written Hannah Pease that a year in Haiti aged him more than two in America.[40] "I think," he told a reporter two months after his resignation, "I aged more during the two years I spent in Haiti than I would have done in five years in the states." [41] Helen too had been adversely affected by the tropical climate. Never enthusiastic about the Haitian appointment, she had carried a fever during her last months at Port-au-Prince.

In Haiti the news that Douglass would not return was received with universal regret. The national feeling was echoed in a letter sent to Douglass over the signatures of twenty-three members of the Haitian college. He was, they declared, Haitian by heart and by sentiment. To them he represented "one of the greatest champions of liberty, justice and equality." [42] Such was the common appraisal in Haiti. The descendants of the great liberator, Toussaint Louverture, never remembered Douglass as a foreigner. He remained in their national memory as the visiting ambassador of millions of American Negroes, pressing forward in the wake of his pioneering, stronger to stand because of his strength.

---

[39] Wm. F. Wharton, Acting Sec. of State to Douglass, Aug. 11, 1891. *Douglass MSS.*

[40] Douglass to Hannah Pease, Oct. 4, 1890. *Ibid.*

[41] Baltimore *Sun*, Sept. 7, 1891.

[42] Faculty of the Haitian College to Douglass, Dec. 12, 1891. *Douglass MSS.*

CHAPTER XVIII

Valedictory

Truth is patient and will finally prevail.
DOUGLASS *to Charles H. Moore*

President Harrison had permitted Douglass to resign at leisure and had, throughout Douglass' ministership, tried to save him from embarrassment. In handling Douglass carefully, Harrison had an eye on the Negro vote in the presidential election of 1892. In this contest Harrison and Cleveland were again the opposing candidates. Douglass supported the Republican cause but with less enthusiasm than of yore. He felt that the Republican party had come to take the Negroes for granted — his appointment to Haiti had been one of the few political plums to come their way.

Cleveland's triumph at the polls prompted Douglass to remark drily that the victory of the Democrats was not brought about by the prominence of Republican zeal to advance the Negro's cause. Going further, he assured Negroes that Cleveland was an honest man. Douglass' critics attributed his praise of Cleveland to a desire for office. Douglass retorted that he wished to allay the apprehension Negroes felt as a consequence of a Democratic victory.

Douglass' explanation may be taken at face value. He never deserted the "grand old party." Three days before his death he advised a correspondent, in reference to the election of 1896, that although the Republican party had become increasingly indifferent toward protecting the rights of the Negro, "still we have a chance of getting a better man from the Republicans than from the Democrats or Populists." [1]

Despite Douglass' stalwart devotion to the party of Lincoln and Grant, Cleveland's fearless honesty caused many Negroes to question the wisdom of delivering the colored man's vote blindly and solidly to the Republicans, thus voting for party rather than for principles. Those who favored political independence pointed out further that the Democrats would have less opposition to the Negro in politics if there were a large number of Negro Democrats. So weighty were these arguments that Douglass felt impelled to reply. Dividing the Negro vote, he contended, would neutralize the Negro's political power because if both parties got an equal share of the Negro vote, "we shall be neither felt nor feared." [2] Furthermore, dividing the Negro between the two parties was based on the assumption that they were equally worthy of Negro support. As for himself, wrote Douglass, "I had just as soon think of dividing our vote between light and darkness, truth and error, Heaven and Hell, as to divide that vote with the Republican and Democratic parties." [3]

Cleveland's victory in 1892 meant that Douglass could not hope for political appointment; as a matter of fact, his ministership to Haiti proved to be his last public office. But Douglass' absence from the public payroll did not spell personal want or insecurity. His financial independence was another illustration of his preachments squaring with his practices. For Douglass advocated the gospel of wealth, holding that "Negroes would never be respected until they respect themselves, and that they would never respect themselves until they had the means to live respectably." [4]

---

[1] Douglass to E. D. Passmore, Feb. 17, 1895. *MS.* in Schomburg Collection.

[2] Handwritten address, untitled, undated. *Douglass MSS.*

[3] *Ibid.*

[4] *Life and Times,* 670.

Douglass did not count himself a worshipper of the Almighty Dollar; rather it was that he believed that "the destruction of the poor is their poverty." He admonished his fellow-Negroes that "it requires industry, economy, and good sense to acquire property. Any fool can spend it." [5] The things of the mind and of the spirit are fine, but render unto Mammon the things that are Mammon's: "Aristotle and Pericles are all right; get all that, too; but get money besides, and plenty of it." [6]

Douglass' income came from divers sources. His fee for lecturing was $125 until 1888, and $150 thereafter, local expenses added. After 1876 the number of lectures never exceeded twenty a year. This figure went down, perhaps to eight a year, during the periods he held Federal office. Over the span of eleven years he received a salary from the national government. Another portion of his income was supplied from property investment. In Rochester and Baltimore he owned houses; in Washington he had title to real estate other than Cedar Hill. He was in the private loan business — a list of his assets in 1889 revealing $48,993 in outstanding debts.

Douglass had a finger in banking and insurance. He was the first president of the Industrial Building and Savings Company, one of the heaviest depositors in the Capital Savings Bank, and a large stockholder in the Alpha Life Insurance Company — all managed and controlled by Negroes. Douglass also tried to turn an honest dollar into manufacturing. He was director and president of the Freedom Manufacturing Company, established in 1892, and capitalized at $300,000. According to its prospectus, the company proposed to manufacture cotton goods out of raw material furnished by small farmers. The project quickly petered out. Douglass sent in his resignation

---

[5] Rochester *Democrat and Chronicle*, Aug. 7, 1883.

[6] Holland, "Frederick Douglass," *Open Court*, IX, 4414 (Mar. 7, 1895).

within a year after the organization of the company. He probably lost something in the venture.

Another source of revenue that proved disappointing was his third autobiography, *Life and Times of Frederick Douglass.* The Park Publishing Company of Boston, which brought the book out in 1881, contracted to give Douglass a generous royalty. He was to receive 25¢ on each copy until 20,000 were sold; thereafter he was to receive 20¢ a copy. Settlement was to be made every four months. Two hundred thousand were run off, priced at $2.50 for a copy with "sprinkled edges," and $3.00 with "gilt edges." The Park Publishing Company soon discovered that "interest in the days of slavery was not as great as we expected." [7] They "pushed and repushed" the book, but to no avail. Over a period of seven years they sold a total of 463 copies. In July 1889, they sent Douglass a check for $69.45 — they had cut his royalty to 15¢ a copy — his total receipts from the book.

The unhappy experience of a rival publishing house should have served as a warning to De Wolfe, Fiske and Company of Boston. Believing, in 1890, that Douglass' appointment as Minister to Haiti had aroused unusual interest in his career, they purchased the plates of *Life and Times.* Published in 1892, the new edition met with the same public indifference. Over a two-year period 399 copies were sold, on which the author got 15¢ royalty. The sale of the revised edition "was a great disappointment to us," wrote its publishers. [8] Douglass also received ten percent of the retail price of Frederic May Holland's *Frederick Douglass,* published in 1891. This netted him a few hundred dollars.

Another minor source of income was derived from the

[7] Park Publishing Company to Douglass, July 19, 1889. *Douglass MSS.*

[8] De Wolfe, Fiske and Company to Helen Douglass, Mar. 9, 1896. *Ibid.*

will of Ottilia Assing, a Prussian-born linguist and music teacher whom Douglass had known since 1868. Their friendship had been close, as her letters denote. Miss Assing took an overdose of laudanum in 1884. She bequeathed to Douglass her gold pens, those of her books "which please him," and the interest on $13,000 as long as he lived. Upon his death the principal was to go to the American Society for the Prevention of Cruelty to Animals. From the terms of this will, Douglass received about $600 annually.

The popular rumors of his great wealth made Douglass a target for numerous requests. One correspondent asked him "for the modest sum of four thousand dollars" to buy " a house that would exactly suit herself and daughter for a home." Another — an esthetically inclined person — besought the price of a piano, "assuring me that she had never before troubled me for money." [9] Not all supplicants were as direct as the journalist-author, I. Garland Penn, who wrote, "To be brief and to the point I am in financial straits just now." [10]

Another type of request was that of travelling and lecturing "at my own expense for this or that good cause." One such petition to speak came from a church secretary: "Will not he who has reached transcendent eminence remember the rock from which he was hewn, and the pit from which he was digged, and reflect back the empyreal effulgence in which he now basks." [11] Douglass responded to many of these appeals. Among other acts of benevolence, he contributed $20 to an annuity fund for the great abolitionist, Theodore D. Weld; he spoke in the interests of Storer College at Harpers Ferry; he lectured gratis for the Washington YMCA, and his uncompensated public

---

[9] *Life and Times*, 551.

[10] Penn to Douglass, May 15, 1894. *Douglass MSS.*

[11] Thomas Hall, Secretary, Board of Trustees, Waugh M. E. church, Balto., Jan. 12, 1894. *Douglass MSS.*

address at the Metropolitan A.M.E. church netted $220.25 for the church.

Douglass could permit himself modest charities; he was a man of means. He waxed indignant over reports in the Negro press that he was worth half a million; he was, he wrote in 1892, never "worth one-fifth of that sum and never expect to be." [12] But by Negro standards, Douglass was a wealthy man. During the last fifteen years of his life, his total resources probably amounted to $100,000. His will, drawn up in 1886, reveals assets of $85,000, exclusive of Cedar Hill. [13] This accumulation resulted in part from a careful budgeting. Douglass kept a record of all household expenditures — the purchase of a three-cent lamp wick was duly entered into an account book. All receipted bills were filed.

To give close supervision to the running of Cedar Hill lay within Douglass' reach. Aside from his trip abroad and his sojourn in Haiti, there was little to prevent him from spending practically all his time under his own roof. This was to his liking for Cedar Hill had grown on him over the years. A nature lover, he customarily rose at five in the morning and walked over the grounds. " How often have I heard him speak," wrote Grimké, "as I have sat with him on the front porch of his beautiful home, or under trees on the hillside, with the lovely landscape stretching out on all sides around us, of the pleasure it gave him to commune with nature." [14]

The pattern of his days at Cedar Hill varied little. After breakfasting and walking, he went to his library where he spent some five hours daily. Here he answered his correspondence and wrote his speeches and articles. He confined his writings to prose. "I once wrote verses," he confided

---

[12] *Life and Times,* 550.

[13] *In the Supreme Court of the United States, October Term, 1899. Helen Douglass, Appellant, vs. Lewis H. Douglass et. al., Appellees,* 6.

[14] Grimké, *op. cit.,* I, 52.

to the Rev. Mr. Brooks. "Unhappily none of them got into print. I have never ceased to regret it, and my only consolation is that my friends were kind enough and brave enough to tell me to stick to prose." [15]

His library was well stocked and he put its contents to good use. His wide and extensive range of reading included Shakespeare, Byron, Burns, Whittier and Longfellow. He showed an interest in Paul Laurence Dunbar, the Negro poet. To Mary Church Terrell, visiting Cedar Hill, he read Dunbar's "The Drowsy Day," adding: "He is very young but there is no doubt he is a poet." [16] Douglass' favorite novelists were Victor Hugo, Walter Scott, the elder Dumas and Nathaniel Hawthorne. Constantly bent on widening his cultural horizon, he began the study of German after he had passed seventy.

Leaving the library in mid-afternoon, Douglass generally went for a drive. In the evening he chatted with guests or played the violin. He had a passionate love for string music. "No man," he used to say, "can be an enemy of mine who loves the violin." [17] He loved to play Scottish airs, his wife accompanying him on the piano.

After her mother's death in 1892, Helen grew even closer to her husband. It is unlikely that the couple ever exchanged a cross or petulant word. But Helen never succeeded in winning over Douglass' children. Their aloofness toward her went even beyond a not un-natural resentment toward the second wife of an elderly parent. Time did not bring healing in its wings. On the contrary, the silent-treatment attitude of Douglass' children toward Helen was in turn transmitted to their offspring. The numerous letters addressed to "Dear Grandfather Douglass" almost never made even a conventional reference to his second wife.

---

[15] Douglass to Walter H. Brooks, Dec. 15, 1894. *MS.* in Moorland Foundation.
[16] Terrell, *op. cit.*, 110.   [17] Grimké, *op. cit.*, I, 52.

The disaffected attitude of the Douglass offspring toward his spouse never resulted in any estrangement between father and children. To the end they showed him a filial respect and he loved them with a parental affection. He was always urging his grandchildren to write him an account of their activities. It pleased him to receive a letter from Joe, off on a violin tour, writing, "I shall look forward to having a game of croquet with you this summer." [18]

Doubtless Douglass' interest in his family took deeper root as the friends of former years passed away one by one. Men of three score and ten, he remarked, are apt to live in the past. During the last fifteen years of his life Douglass made no close friendships. This same period witnessed the passing of many co-workers of abolitionist days. Gerrit Smith died in 1874; from the British Isles in the middle 'eighties, Douglass received similar sad news about James Haughton, Richard Webb and Henry Richardson.

Happily time erased the bitterness between Douglass and the Garrisonians. He and Garrison were never again on speaking terms after the breach in the early 'fifties. But at the memorial exercises for Garrison at Boston in 1879, Douglass was one of the encomiasts. His tribute came from the heart: "To every anti-slavery man and woman in the land, to every friend of impartial liberty, at home or abroad, and especially to every colored man, this is a sad and mournful hour." [19] Shortly after their marriage, he took Helen to see "Rockledge," Garrison's old home in Roxbury.

The death of Garrison served as a bridge of reconciliation between his former associates and Douglass. The latter visited Whittier in 1882; they talked of the humanitarian advances that had been effected since the formation of the

---

[18] Joseph H. Douglass to Douglass, Jan. 15, 1894. *Douglass MSS.*
[19] Douglass, *Speech on the Death of William Lloyd Garrison* (printed pamphlet, n. p. n. d.), 2.

American Anti-Slavery Society in 1833. From other Garrisonians who were willing to let bygones be bygones, Douglass received cordial letters: Abby Kelley Foster, Oliver Johnson, James Buffum and Parker Pillsbury among others. Elizabeth Buffum Chase, a Quaker acquaintance of earlier years, invited him to Valley Falls for her eighty-fifth birthday.[20] A letter from Charles K. Whipple, after extending the olive branch, raised a point of information which bore testimony that time had not muted his intransigent abolitionism: "During the predominance of the slave power, who was it that said, 'The most profitable product of Virginia is her virginital crop?'"[21]

To Douglass one of the most welcome of peace-offerings came from Robert Purvis, destined to be the last of the surviving abolitionists who organized the parent anti-slavery society. It was through his son, Dr. Charles B. Purvis, that he composed his ancient quarrel with Douglass. In 1886 Dr. Purvis wrote Douglass that his father had authorized him to deliver this message: "You may say to Mr. Douglass, I will meet him cordially and rub out from memory all of the unpleasantness of the past."[22]

Douglass' spirit of hatchet-burying embraced his former master, Captain Thomas Auld. The two met without formal pre-arrangement during the time that Douglass was Marshal of the District. Douglass happened to be in the vicinity of St. Michaels on a nostalgic visit to the scenes of his childhood. Auld, on learning that Douglass was in the neighborhood, sent word that "he would be very glad to see me. . . ." The meeting, held in the sick man's bed-room, was affecting; Auld shed tears, Douglass' voice choked. He was moved by the sight of the palsy-stricken, dying man, "his tremulous hands constantly in motion."

[20] E. B. Chace to Douglass, Nov. 29, 1891. *Douglass MSS.*

[21] Charles K. Whipple to Douglass, Oct. 11, 1893. *Ibid.*

[22] Charles B. Purvis to Douglass, July 1, 1886. *Ibid.*

FREDERICK DOUGLASS MONUMENT IN ROCHESTER, NEW YORK

The Home of Frederick Douglass, Anacostia, Washington, D.C.

Douglass stayed only twenty minutes — "seeing his extreme weakness I did not protract my visit." [23]

The passing of most of the friends and acquaintances of his abolitionist days almost made Douglass "the last leaf." But he never became morbid about his advancing years. Psychologically he was fortified against old age by the continuing multiplicity of his interests and by the sustaining belief that he had spent his life in trying to make the world better than he found it. That others shared this opinion was reflected in the numerous honors bestowed upon him. One of these marks of esteem came from the citizens of Rochester. Raising over $1,000, they commissioned a resident sculptor, Johnson Munday, to do a bust of Douglass. The unveiling exercises were held at Sibley Hall, at the University of Rochester, which was chosen as the location for the marble portrait. The committee in charge made the formal presentation; the mayor, on behalf of the city, responded in a brief speech of acceptance. [24]

Another evidence of public approbation was the many letters seeking his services as chief speaker at historical or memorial exercises. Typical of these was the invitation extended by Oliver Ames, governor of Massachusetts, asking him to deliver an oration at the dedication of a bronze plaque in memory of Crispus Attucks. [25] Among the universities honoring Douglass were Wilberforce and Berea: Wilberforce conferred on him the doctor of laws degree in 1893; Berea, the following year, invited him to deliver the commencement address. [26] Douglass' prominence led a descendant of John Calhoun, greatest champion of Southern interests during the ante-bellum period, to trace down a rumor that he was related to that family. After genealogical inquiry and research, Charlotte Calhoun

---

[23] *Life and Times*, 487   [24] Rochester *Democrat*, June 17, 1878.
[25] Oliver Ames to Douglass, Sept. 29, 1888. *Douglass MSS.*
[26] J. G. Fee and Daisy H. Carlock to Douglass, Jan. 23, 1894. *Ibid.*

Childs wrote that she regretted to learn that the rumor was false; she had given it credence because "brains are never an accident, but, rather, the result of generation after generation of mental culture." [27]

Perhaps no less indicative of Douglass' influence than the honors that came his way were the numerous requests from office- and job-seekers. George T. Downing, the Negro caterer, wrote that "I am trying for the Senate restaurant," and asked Douglass to promote his bid for the contract by "seeing" Senators Allison, Cameron, Conkling and Sherman. [28] When, in the spring of 1891, it became known that Douglass was thinking of resigning his ministership to Haiti, T. Thomas Fortune and Mifflin W. Gibbs each solicited his aid in securing the post. [29] Another letter of request came from Paul Laurence Dunbar, asking Douglass to "use your influence" in getting him a job as teacher of English literature in the Washington public schools. "I have been somewhat successful," added Dunbar, "in practical literary work." [30]

Douglass' influence extended into the camp of the enemy. C. H. Taylor, a Democrat seeking the recorder of deeds post in 1894, asked Douglass to put in a good word for him. Douglass did so and Taylor was named for the position. Taylor then required bond, but George F. Hoar, longtime Senator from Massachusetts, cautioned Douglass to call a halt: "I should advise you as a friend never to go the bond, for $10,000, of a colored man who supports the Democratic party. If he does it to get office, he is not to be trusted morally. If he does it from honest conviction, he hasn't enough sense to be trusted with $10,000." [31]

---

[27] C. C. Childs to Douglass, Nov. 15, 1885. *Douglass MSS.*

[28] Downing to Douglass, Feb. 26, 1877. *Ibid.*

[29] Fortune to Douglass, May 22, 1891. *Ibid.* Gibbs to Douglass, June 2, 1891. *Ibid.*

[30] Dunbar to Douglass, Sept. 7, 1894. *Ibid.*

[31] Hoar to Douglass, May 16, 1894. *Ibid.*

Probably the greatest honor conferred on Douglass in his declining years was the appointment as Haitian Commissioner at the World's Columbian Exposition — the first world's fair — at Chicago in 1893. The post was offered to him in February, 1892, in recognition of his warm friendship for Haiti. Accepting the position as a gesture of esteem from the Haitian people and as a token of appreciation from Hyppolite, Douglass let it be understood that his rôle would be primarily advisory, and that the correspondence and active work of the Commission would be done by someone else. Thereupon Hyppolite appointed Charles A. Preston, formerly secretary of the Haitian legation at Washington, as co-commissioner.

Under the joint supervision and direction of Douglass and Preston, the erection of the Haitian Pavilion was completed. The building was formally dedicated on January 2, 1893, with Douglass as speaker. His opening phrases expressed high tribute to Haiti and Hyppolite. He then thanked the officials of the fair for giving "us one of the very best sites which could have been selected. . . . We are situated upon one of the finest avenues of these grounds; standing upon our verandah we may view one of the largest of our inland seas, we may inhale its fine and refreshing breezes, we can contemplate its tranquil beauty in its calm and its awful sublimity and power when its crested billows are swept by the storm." [32] Douglass then invited the general public to visit the Haitian pavilion "as long as the gates of the World's Columbian Exposition shall be open." Haiti's emblems of welcome would be neither brandy nor wine, said he, "but we shall give all comers a generous taste of our Haitian coffee, made in the best manner by Haitian hands." [33]

Douglass enjoyed the eight months, on and off, that he spent in Chicago. Entering into the festive mood of the

[32] *Lecture on Haiti*, 49.
[33] *Ibid.*, 50.

exposition, he played the violin at the opening of the New England log cabin.[34] Many who came to the fair-grounds had heard of him; he was continually approached by admirers who wished to shake hands. Numerous persons introduced themselves as offspring of his former co-workers in the abolition crusade. One of his new acquaintances was Paul Laurence Dunbar, who excitedly wrote his mother that Douglass "had me read to him my Ode to Ethiopia." Douglass, continued Dunbar, invited him to Cedar Hill — "it would do me good to have you in my study working away at your poetry." [35]

Although American Negroes were proud of Haiti's exhibit and of her chief commissioner, they had several grievances against the managers of the exposition. Not a solitary Negro, ran their complaint, sat on the two-hundred-eight-member National Board of Commissioners. Furthermore, a similar omission of the Negro was revealed in the personnel of the National Board of Lady Managers. In reply, the latter group explained that the composition of the national board was determined by the state boards. But, as Negroes were quick to point out, when the matter had been referred to the state boards none took remedial action except New York. To Negroes another sore spot was the non-employment of colored at the fair. There were no Negro guards and only three Negroes held clerical jobs, all of minor importance.

The chief grievance of many Negroes was the failure of the fair's managers to arrange an exhibit depicting the contributions of the Negro to American life. "All classes and conditions are represented," ran their protest, "except the American Negro." A petition was sent to Congress, requesting an appropriation "for a statistical exhibit showing the advance of the Negro since Emancipa-

---

[34] Holland, "Frederick Douglass," loc. cit., 4416.
[35] Dunbar to Matilda Dunbar, June 6, 1893. Dunbar MSS. (Ohio State Archeological and Historical Society.)

tion." [36] At Washington the petition lost its way in the legislative mill.

As a sort of a compromise, the managers of the exposition set aside a date, August 25, 1893, on which to celebrate the progress of the Negro. To advocates of a separate exhibit, the designation of a "Colored American Day" was a sop to be spurned. They proposed a boycott. Douglass was not prepared for so radical a step, although he questioned the reasoning advanced in support of the proposal for the one-day observance. Despite all objections, plans for the celebration went forward, spurred by the contagious enthusiasm of Will Marion Cook, the composer. In charge of the program planning, Cook succeeded in breaking down Douglass' resistance, persuading him to deliver the principal address. "Colored American Day" went off well; the large crowd that turned out was richly rewarded. Speech-making by Douglass was supplemented by esthetic features. Joe played the violin, Dunbar read several of his poems and Harry T. Burleigh sang in his rich baritone, the audience applauding for encore after encore.

A few weeks after his participation in the "Colored American Day" program, Douglass relinquished his post as Commissioner for Haiti. For his eight-months services he received a check for $2012.50 from the Haitian government. The Haitians were well pleased with his work. Hyppolite sent him a large-size photograph of himself, be-starred and be-ribboned in presidential attire. From another prominent figure in Haiti, Bishop Theodore J. Holly, Douglass received high praise: "The services in conducting Haiti's part in the Columbian Exposition you have rendered to the cause of spurned and downtrodden

<hr />

[36] For an account of the Negro's grievance and his efforts to obtain a separate exhibit see the eighty-one page pamphlet, *The Reason Why the Colored Man Is Not Represented in the World's Columbian Exposition* (Chicago, 1893).

humanity reflects the beautiful halo of a golden sun-set over your long, brilliant and glorious career." [37]

Holly's tribute was in tone a benediction, as though Douglass' Haitian honors were his last. Douglass himself had some such premonition. Wrote Bassett, a few months after Douglass resigned as Haitian Commissioner, "I am saddened by your remark that the end cannot be far off." [38] Later in the same year (1894), in response to a request to write an introduction to *The Story of the Hutchinsons*, Douglass penned word to its author, "Send me a copy of the book if I am living when it is published." [39] No copy of the published work was ever sent.

The end came suddenly, on February 20, 1895. In the early afternoon Douglass left Cedar Hill to attend a meeting of the Women's Council at Metzerott Hall. A long-time exponent of woman's rights, he was warmly received. As he entered the hall, the presiding officer, Mary Wright Sewall, suspended business while Susan B. Anthony and the Reverend Anna H. Shaw escorted him to the platform, "each member rising to her feet and waving her handkerchief."

Douglass returned to Cedar Hill a few minutes after five o'clock. After eating dinner he had a few minutes to spare before going out to fulfill a seven o'clock speaking engagement at a local church. While describing the events of the day to Helen, he fell to his knees. Helen, for a moment thinking that he was in process of dramatizing his description, as was his wont, became suddenly dumb with consternation as he sank lower and lower. He never regained consciousness, passing quickly and without pain just as the carriage rolled up to take him to his speaking engagement.

---

[37] Holly to Douglass, Oct. 23, 1893. *Douglass MSS.*

[38] Bassett to Douglass, Jan. 18, 1894. *Ibid.*

[39] Douglass to John Hutchinson, Dec. 6, 1894. *MS.* in New York Historical Society.

News of his death was flashed throughout the United States. An extended account of his life was carried in all newspapers "of any pretensions in the country." Upon receiving the news, the North Carolina legislature voted to adjourn for the day out of respect to his memory. The legislatures of Indiana, Illinois, Massachusetts and New York adopted resolutions of regret.

The body remained at Cedar Hill for three days. On the morning of February 25, the immediate family assembled in one of the front parlors where a Baptist clergyman, the Reverend Hugh Stevenson, conducted brief services — a Scripture reading and a prayer. The body was then removed to the Metropolitan A.M.E. church where it lay in state for four hours. Thousands walked down the aisle to take a last look. Negro parents lifted their youngsters — the colored public schools were officially closed for the day — to see the great champion of the race. "Here and there in the long, persistent stream of humanity, came one bearing a flower, a fern leaf or a bouquet which was silently laid upon the casket." Sorrow-stricken Negroes sensed their loss: "Howl, fir-tree, for the cedar of Lebanon is fallen."

The church doors were closed at 1 : 30 o'clock. Then followed the long and impressive services. The faculty of Howard University attended in a body — Douglass had been a trustee for twenty-five years. Senators Hoar and Sherman and Justice Harlan of the Supreme Court were seated in the packed church. Among those on the rostrum who eulogized or prayed were Alexander Crummell, Susan B. Anthony, J. E. Rankin, Bishops J. W. Hood and A. W. Wayman and the Reverends Stevenson and Jenifer. "Lay him low," ran the burden of John Hutchinson's requiem solo, his voice firm despite his years and his agitated emotions. Two hours after the services were over, the body was put on an early evening train for Rochester. Accompanying it were Helen and the three surviving

Douglass offspring — Rosetta, Lewis and Charles — the dead man's children and his second wife composing their differences in a short-lived truce.

At Rochester the following morning the flags floated at half-mast as the city put on mourning garb. The body lay in state at the City Hall, where a constant throng filed in and out. Hundreds of children, dismissed from the public schools and in the custody of their teachers, passed the dais. At three o'clock in the afternoon the body was removed to Central Church where the mayor and the board of aldermen headed the list of local notables who came to pay final respects to "one of Rochester's most honored and representative men," one whose memory "will remain a bright one on the gilded scroll of history." Those assembled at the services gave ear to "sincerest eulogiums by the best known citizens." [40]

Leaving Central Church, the funeral procession followed the hearse through the crowd-lined streets. The bands played dirges. With measured pace, the slowly moving column reached Mt. Hope, a lovely spot commanding a view of the Genesee River. A brief service at the cemetery's chapel and then the lowering. . . .

---

[40] Rochester *Union and Advertiser*, Mar. 2, 1895.

BIBLIOGRAPHY

I   *Manuscript Collections*

Anti-Slavery Letters Written to William Lloyd Garrison and Others, Boston Public Library, 30 volumes.

Douglass MSS., Anacostia Heights, Washington, D. C., 305 folders.

Douglass MSS., Possession of Mrs. Joseph H. Douglass, 6 letters.

Douglass MSS., Moorland Foundation, Washington D. C., 5 letters.

Douglass MSS., New York Historical Society, 3 letters.

Douglass MSS., Oberlin College Library, 3 letters.

Douglass MSS., Rochester Public Library, 4 letters.

Douglass MSS., Schomburg Collection, New York City, 6 letters.

Douglass MSS., Spingarn Collection, New York City, 5 letters.

Dunbar MSS., Ohio State Archeological and Historical Society, 3 folders.

Garrison MSS., Boston Public Library, 15 volumes.

Shaw Family Correspondence, New York Historical Society, 1 folder.

Smith MSS., Syracuse University Library, 50 boxes.

Stanton MSS., Library of Congress, 7 volumes.

Sumner Letterbooks, Harvard University, 11 volumes.

Tilton MSS., New York Historical Society, 1 folder.

Douglass, *Diary*, Anacostia Heights.

Douglass, *Travels Abroad*, undated manuscript, Anacostia Heights.

Douglass, Helen, *Diary*, Anacostia Heights.

Ledger Book of Douglass and Delany, Anacostia Heights.

Goodell, *Scrapbooks Relating to Slavery, 1855–57*, Oberlin University Library.

May, Samuel J., *Diary*, possession of W. Freeman Galpin, Syracuse University, Syracuse, N. Y.

Minute Book of Western Anti-Slavery Society, Library of Congress.

II   *Newspapers and Other Contemporary Periodicals*
(Dates indicate year or years for which periodical was consulted.)

The Abolitionist (Boston), 1833.

African Episcopal Church Magazine (Philadelphia), 1842.

African Repository (Washington, D. C.), 1850–53.

American Jubilee (New York), 1855.

Anglo-African Magazine (New York), 1859–61.

Anti-Slavery Standard (New York), 1840–70.

Baltimore *Sun*, 1891.

Boston *Atlas*, 1850.

Boston *Herald*, 1850.

Boston *Journal*, 1862–63.

Boston *Transcript*, 1860–64.

British and Foreign Anti-Slavery Reporter (London), 1845–60.

Bugle (Salem, O.), 1847–53.

Douglass' Monthly (Rochester), 1859–63.

Franklin, Virginia, *Gazette*, 1884.

Frederick Douglass' Paper (Rochester), 1851–60.

Gerrit Smith Banner (New York), 1858.

Harper's Weekly (New York), 1872.

Herald of Freedom (Concord, N. H.), 1842–44.

The Liberator (Boston), 1839–65.

The Lily (Seneca Falls, N. Y.), 1852.

Lynn *Pioneer* (Mass.), 1845.

Lynn *Pioneer and Herald of Freedom*, 1847.

The Nation (New York), 1877.

New National Era (Washington, D. C.), 1870–74.

New Orleans *Republican*, 1874.

New York *Independent*, 1865–74.

New York *Herald*, 1852–66.

New York *Tribune*, 1854–66.

Niles' Weekly Register (Baltimore), 1837.

The North Star (Rochester), 1847–51.
Ohio *Statesman* (Columbus), 1846–47.
Pennsylvania *Freeman*, 1845.
The Radical Abolitionist (New York), 1855–58.
The Revolution (New York), 1868–69.
Rochester *Chronicle and Democrat*, 1878, 1883.
Rochester *Union and Advertiser*, 1895.
Syracuse *Daily Standard*, 1850–56.
Syracuse *Daily Star*, 1847.
The Una (Providence, R. I.), 1853.
Washington *Post*, 1897.
Washington *Star*, 1895.
Woodhull and Claflin's Weekly (New York), 1872.
Worcester *Spy*, 1851.

III *Contemporary Broadsides and Pamphlets*

American Anti-Slavery Society, *Anniversary Proceedings*, 1840–70.
Blackwell, Henry B., *What the South Can Do*, New York, 1867.
Centennial Anniversary of the Pennsylvania Society for Promoting the Abolition of Slavery, Phila., 1876.
Commemoration of the Fiftieth Anniversary of the American Anti-Slavery Society, Phila., 1884.
Douglass, Frederick, *Abolition Fanaticism in New York, Speech by a Runaway Slave from Baltimore, at an Abolition Meeting in New York, on May 11, 1847*, Baltimore, 1847.

Address at the Annual Meeting of the American Missionary Association in Lowell, Mass., 1894, New York, n. d.

Addresses of the Hon. W. D. Kelley, Miss Anna E. Dickinson, and Mr. Frederick Douglass, at a Mass Meeting, Held at National Hall, Philadelphia, July 6, 1863, for the Promotion of Colored Enlistments, Phila., 1863.

The Anti-Slavery Movement, A Lecture Before the Rochester Ladies' Anti-Slavery Society, Rochester, 1855.

Claims of the Negro Ethnologically Considered, An Address Before the Literary Societies of Western Reserve College, July 12, 1852, Rochester, 1854.

The Constitution of the United States: Is It Pro-Slavery or Anti-Slavery? Halifax, Nova Scotia, n. d. (1860?).

The Equality of All Men Before the Law, Claimed and Defended by William D. Kelley, Wendell Phillips, and Frederick Douglass, Boston, 1865.

Eulogy of the Late Hon. William Jay, Delivered on the Invitation of the Colored Citizens of New York City, in Shiloh Presbyterian Church, New York, May 12, 1859, Rochester, 1859.

Lecture on Haiti, Chicago, 1893.

Men of Color, to Arms! Rochester, 1863.

On the Impolicy of the Exodus, n. p., n. d.

Oration, Delivered in Corinthian Hall, Rochester, July 5, 1852, Rochester, 1852.

Speech on the Death of William Lloyd Garrison, n. p., n. d.

Three Addresses on the Relations Subsisting Between the White and Colored People of the United States, Washington, 1886.

Two Speeches: One on West India Emancipation, Delivered at Canandaigua, August 4th, 1857, and the Other on the Dred Scott Decision, Delivered in New York on the Occasion of the Anniversary of the American Anti-Slavery Society, May, 1857, Rochester, n. d. (1857?).

U. S. Grant and the Colored People, Washington, 1872.

Inauguration Ceremonies of the Freedmen's Memorial Monument to Abraham Lincoln, Washington City, April 14, 1876, St. Louis, 1876.

Massachusetts Abolition Society, *Second Annual Report*, Boston, 1841.

Massachusetts Anti-Slavery Society, *Reports*, 1840–56.

Memorial Discourse of Henry Highland Garnet, Washington, 1865.

New York Committee of Vigilance, *First Annual Report, 1837*, New York, 1837.

Poem on the Embarkation at Liverpool of Mr. Frederick Douglass upon His Return to America, Manchester, 1847.

Proceedings of the Colored National Convention, Washington, D. C., Jan. 12, 13, 1870, Washington, 1870.

Proceedings of the Colored National Convention Held in Rochester, July 6, 7, 8, 1853, Rochester, 1853.

Proceedings of the National Convention of Colored Men, Held in Syracuse, N. Y., Oct. 4–7, 1864, New York, 1864.

Proceedings of New York Electoral College, Albany, 1873.

Proceedings of the Radical Abolitionist Convention, June 26, 27, 28, 1855, New York, 1855.

The Reason Why the Colored Man Is Not Represented at the World's Columbian Exposition, Chicago, 1893.

Report of a Public Meeting Held at Finsbury Chapel, Moorfields, to Receive Frederick Douglass, the American Slave, London, 1846.

Sprague, Rosetta Douglass, *Anna Murray Douglass: My Mother as I Recall Her,* Washington, D. C., 1900.

Suffrage Question in Relation to Colored Voters in the State of New York, New York, 1860.

Wright, Henry C., *Letter to Frederick Douglass and His Reply,* Manchester, 1847.

IV *Printed Primary Sources*
   (Memoirs, Reminiscences, Diaries, Letters, Autobiographies)

Abel, Annie H., and Klingberg, Frank J., *A Sidelight on Anglo-American Relations, 1839–1858.* Washington, 1927.

Bancroft, F., and Dunning, W. H., eds., *Reminiscences of Carl Schurz.* 3 vols., New York, 1908.

Barnes, Gilbert and Dumond, Dwight L., eds., *Weld-Grimké Letters.* 2 vols., New York, 1934.

Beale, Howard K., ed., *Diary of Edward Bates.* Washington, 1933.

Bremer, Fredrika, *The Homes of the New World.* 2 vols., New York, 1853.

Narrative of William Wells Brown. Boston, 1847.

Douglass, Frederick, *Narrative of the Life of Frederick Douglass*. Boston, 1845.

My Bondage and My Freedom. New York, 1855.

Life and Times of Frederick Douglass. Hartford, 1884.

Dumond, Dwight L., ed., *Letters of James Gillespie Birney.* 2 vols., New York, 1938.

Garrison, W. P., and Garrison, F. J., *Life of William Lloyd Garrison.* 3 vols., New York, 1885–89.

Hallowell, Anne D., ed., *James and Lucretia Mott: Life and Letters.* Boston, 1894.

Howard, Oliver Otis, *Autobiography.* 2 vols., New York, 1907.

Hutchinson, John Wallace, *Story of the Hutchinsons.* 2 vols., Boston, 1896.

In Memoriam: Frederick Douglass. Philadelphia, 1897.

James, Thomas, *Wonderful Eventful Life of Thomas James.* Rochester, 1887.

Keckley, Elizabeth, *Behind the Scenes.* New York, 1868.

Langston, John Mercer, *From the Virginia Plantation to the National Capitol.* Hartford, 1894.

Loguen, Jermain Wesley, *The Reverend Jermain Wesley Loguen as a Slave and as a Freeman.* New York, 1859.

Marsh, John, *Temperance Recollections.* New York, 1866.

May, Samuel J., *Some Recollections of Our Anti-Slavery Conflict.* Boston, 1869.

Payne, Daniel A., *Recollections of Seventy Years.* Nashville, 1888.

Pennington, J. W. C., *The Fugitive Blacksmith.* London, 1849.

Pierce, Edward L., ed., *Memoirs and Letters of Charles Sumner.* 4 vols., Boston, 1877–94.

Pillsbury, Parker, *Acts of the Anti-Slavery Apostles.* Boston, 1884.

Powell, Aaron M., *Personal Reminiscences.* New York, 1889.

Richards, Laura E., ed., *Letters and Journals of Samuel Gridley Howe.* 2 vols., Boston, 1909.

Sanborn, Franklin B., *Life and Letters of John Brown*. Boston, 1885.

Recollections of Seventy Years. Boston, 1909.

Stanton, Henry B., *Random Recollections*. New York, 1886.

Still, William, *Underground Railroad*. Philadelphia, 1872.

Terrell, Mary Church, *A Colored Woman in a White World*. Washington, 1940.

Ward, Samuel Ringgold, *The Autobiography of a Fugitive Negro: His Anti-Slavery Labours in the United States, Canada, and England*. London, 1855.

Woodson, Carter G., *The Mind of the Negro as Reflected by Letters Written During the Crisis, 1800–1860*. Washington, 1926.

Woodson, Carter G., ed., *The Works of Francis J. Grimké*. 4 vols., Washington, 1942.

Wortley, Lady Emmeline Stuart, *Travels in the United States During 1849 and 1850*. New York, 1851.

V   *Articles and Essays*

Anonymous, "John Brown and His Friends," *Atlantic Monthly*, 30:50–61 (July, 1872).

Atherton, Lewis, "Daniel Howell Hise: Abolitionist and Reformer," *Mississippi Valley Historical Review*, 26:350–68 (Dec., 1939).

Douglass, Frederick, "The Condition of the Freedmen," *Harper's Weekly*, 27:782–83 (Dec. 8, 1883).

"My Escape from Slavery," *The Century Magazine*, 1:124–31 (Nov., 1881).

"Future of the Colored Race," *North American Review*, 142:437–40 (May, 1866).

"Reminiscences," *Cosmopolitan*, 7:376–82 (Aug., 1889).

"Reconstruction," *Atlantic Monthly*, 18:761–65 (Dec., 1866).

Fleming, Walter G., "The Freedmen's Savings Bank," *Yale Review*, 15:40–67 (May, 1906); 15:134–46 (Aug., 1906).

Grimké, Francis J., "The Second Marriage of Frederick Douglass," *Journal of Negro History*, 19:324–29 (July, 1934).

Hamner-Croughton, Amy, "Anti-Slavery Days in Rochester," Rochester Historical Society *Publications*, 15:152–59 (1936).

Holland, Frederic May, "Frederick Douglass," *Open Court*, 9:1414–17 (March, 1895).

McQuire, Horace, "Two Episodes of Anti-Slavery Days," Rochester Historical Society *Publications*, 4:219–26 (1925).

Parker, Jane Marsh, "Reminiscences of Frederick Douglass," *Outlook*, 51:552–55 (April 6, 1895).

Porter, Dorothy, "David Ruggles, an Apostle of Human Rights," *Journal of Negro History*, 28:23–50 (Jan., 1943).

Quarles, Benjamin, "The Breach Between Douglass and Garrison," *Journal of Negro History*, 23:144–54 (April, 1938).

　　"Frederick Douglass and John Brown," Rochester Historical Society *Publications*, 17:291–99 (1939).

　　"Frederick Douglass and the Woman's Rights Movement," *Journal of Negro History*, 25:35–44 (Jan., 1940).

　　"Sources of Abolitionist Income," *Mississippi Valley Historical Review*, 32:63–76 (June, 1945).

Rayback, Joseph G., "The American Workingman and the Anti-Slavery Crusade," *Journal of Economic History*, 3:152–63 (Nov., 1943).

Russ, William A., "The Negro and Disfranchisement During Radical Reconstruction," *Journal of Negro History*, 19:171–91 (April, 1934).

Sears, Louis Martin, "Frederick Douglass and the Mission to Haiti," *Hispanic American Historical Review*, 21:222–38 (May, 1941).

Stanton, Theodore, "Frederick Douglass in Paris," *Open Court*, 1:151–52 (April 28, 1887).

Stearns, Bertha Monica, "Reform Periodicals and Female Reformers," *American Historical Review*, 38:690–99 (July, 1932).

Van Deusen, John G., "The Exodus of 1879," *Journal of Negro History*, 21:111–29 (Jan., 1936).

Warner, Robert A., "Amos Gerry Beman," *Journal of Negro History*, 22:200–21 (April, 1937).

VI *Biographies and General Works*

Andrews, E. A., *Slavery and the Slave Trade in the United States.* Boston, 1836.

Barnes, Gilbert, *The Anti-Slavery Impulse, 1830–1844.* New York, 1933.

Birney, William, *James G. Birney and His Times.* New York, 1890.

Bontemps, Arna and Conroy, Jack, *They Seek a City.* New York, 1945.

Brackett, Jeffrey R., *The Negro in Maryland.* Baltimore, 1889.

Bradford, Sarah, *Scenes in the Life of Harriet Tubman.* Auburn, N. Y., 1869.

Brown, William Wells, *The Black Man: His Antecedents, His Genius and His Achievements.* New York, 1863. *The Rising Son.* Boston, 1874.

Buckmaster, Henrietta, *Let My People Go.* New York, 1941.

Carey, John L., *Slavery in Maryland.* Baltimore, 1845.

Chesnutt, Charles W., *Frederick Douglass.* Boston, 1899.

Cromwell, John, *The Negro in American History.* Washington, 1914.

DuBois, W. E. B., *Black Reconstruction.* New York, 1935.

Dumond, Dwight L., *Anti-Slavery Origins of the Civil War.* Ann Arbor, Mich., 1939.

Emilio, Luis, *History of the Fifty-Fourth Regiment of the Massachusetts Volunteer Infantry, 1863–1865.* Boston, 1894.

Fletcher, Robert S., *History of Oberlin College.* 2 vols., Oberlin, 1943.

Foner, Philip, *Business and Slavery.* Chapel Hill, 1941.

Footner, Hulburt, *Rivers of the Eastern Shore.* New York, 1944.

Frothingham, Octavius, *Life of Gerrit Smith*. New York, 1878.

Goodell, William, *Slavery and Anti-Slavery*. New York, 1853.

Griffiths, Julia, ed., *Autographs for Freedom*. Boston, 1853.

    Autographs for Freedom. Auburn, 1854.

Harlow, Ralph V., *Gerrit Smith*. New York, 1939.

Higginson, Thomas Wentworth, *Contemporaries*. Boston, 1889.

Hinton, Richard J., *John Brown and His Men*. New York, 1894.

Holland, Frederic May, *Frederick Douglass*. New York, 1891.

Hume, John F., *The Abolitionists*. New York, 1905.

Johnson, Oliver, *William Lloyd Garrison and His Times*. Boston, 1885.

Leech, Margaret, *Reveille in Washington, 1860–1865*. New York, 1941.

Léger, J. H., *Haiti: Her History and Her Detractors*. New York, 1907.

Lloyd, Arthur, *The Slavery Controversy, 1831–1860*. Chapel Hill, 1939.

Logan, Rayford, *Diplomatic Relations of the United States with Haiti, 1776–1891*. Chapel Hill, 1941.

Lutz, Alma, *Created Equal: A Biography of Elizabeth Cady Stanton*. New York, 1940.

MacDougall, Marion Gleason, *Fugitive Slaves*. Boston, 1891.

McPherson, Edward, *The Political History of the United States of America During the Period of Reconstruction*. Washington, 1880.

Montague, Ludwell Lee, *Haiti and the United States, 1741–1928*. Durham, N. C., 1940.

Parker, Jane Marsh, *Rochester*. Rochester, 1887.

Penn, I. Garland, *The Afro-American Press and Its Editors*. Springfield, Mass., 1891.

Sketch of the Life of Charles B. Ray. New York, 1887.

Reilly, E. C., *The Early Slavery Controversy in the Western Reserve.* Unpublished Ph.D. dissertation, Western Reserve University, 1939.

Rollin, Frank A., *Life and Public Services of Martin R. Delany.* Boston, 1883.

Sherwin, Oscar, *Prophet of Liberty: A Biography of Wendell Phillips.* Unpublished Ph.D. dissertation, New York University, 1940.

Short, Harriette R., *Negro Conventions Prior to 1860.* Unpublished M. A. thesis, Howard University, 1936.

Siebert, William, *The Underground Railroad.* New York, 1898.

Smith, Theodore Clarke, *The Liberty and Free Soil Parties in the Northwest.* Cambridge, Mass., 1897.

Stanton, Elizabeth Cady, Anthony, Susan B., and Gage, Matilda Joslyn, eds., *History of Woman Suffrage.* 3 vols., New York, 1881–86.

Tappan, Lewis, *Life of Arthur Tappan.* New York, 1870.

Tilton, Theodore, *Sonnets to the Memory of Frederick Douglass.* Paris, 1895.

Tremain, Mary, *Slavery in the District of Columbia.* New York, 1892.

Tuckerman, Bayard, *William Jay.* New York, 1893.

Villard, Oswald Garrison, *John Brown.* Boston, 1911.

Vital Records of Lynn, Mass., to 1850. Salem, Mass., 1903.

Vital Records of New Bedford, Mass., to the year 1850. Boston, 1932.

Ware, Edith, *Political Opinion in Massachusetts During the Civil War and Reconstruction.* New York, 1917.

Warner, Robert A., *New Haven Negroes.* New Haven, 1940

Welles, Sumner, *Naboth's Vineyard.* 2 vols., New York, 1928.

Wigham, Eliza, *The Anti-Slavery Cause in America and Its Martyrs.* London, 1863.

Williams, George W., *History of the Negro Race in America from 1619 to 1860.* 2 vols., New York, 1883.

Wilson, Henry, *History of Anti-Slavery Measures of the Thirty-Seventh and Thirty-Eighth United States Congresses, 1861–64.* Boston, 1864.
    History of the Rise and Fall of the Slave Power in America. 3 vols., Boston, 1872–77.

Wilson, Joseph T., *The Black Phalanx.* Hartford, 1888.

Wright, James M., *The Free Negro in Maryland, 1634–1860.* New York, 1921.

Wyman, Lillie Buffum Chace, and Wyman, Arthur Crawford, *Elizabeth Buffum Chace and Her Environment.* 2 vols., Boston, 1911.

APPENDIX

Douglass' slaveholder's sermon had great popularity in abolitionist circles. Unfortunately, no complete copy of this famous piece of mimicry exists. Douglass left no copy since he always spoke without notes during his early years as an anti-slavery lecturer. A report of a Faneuil Hall meeting of the Massachusetts abolitionists in January 1842 contains an excerpt that gives the general nature of the sermon. The excerpt runs as follows:

The ministers would take a text — say this: — "Do unto others as you would have others do unto you." And this is how they would apply it. They would explain it to mean, "slaveholders, do unto *slaveholders* what you would have them do unto you"; and then looking impudently up to the slave's gallery, looking high up to the poor colored drivers and the rest, and spreading his hands gracefully abroad, he says (mimicking), "And you too, my friends, have souls of infinite value — souls that will live through endless happiness or misery in eternity. Oh, *labor diligently* to make your calling and election sure. Oh, receive into your souls these words of the holy apostle — 'Servants, be obedient unto your masters.'" (Shouts of laughter and applause.) "Oh, consider the wonderful goodness of God! Look at your hard, horny hands, your strong muscular frames, and see how mercifully he has adapted you to the duties you are to fulfill!" (continued laughter and applause) "while to your masters, who have slender frames and long, delicate fingers, he has given brilliant intellects, that they may do the thinking while you do the working." (Shouts of applause.) *Tenth Annual Report of the Massachusetts Anti-Slavery Society* (Boston, 1842), Appendix, p. 19.

INDEX

Other titles of interest

THE JEWEL OF LIBERTY
Abraham Lincoln's Re-election
and the End of Slavery
David E. Long
410 pp., 40 illus.
80788-2 $15.95

**THE BETRAYAL OF
THE NEGRO**
from Rutherford B. Hayes to
Woodrow Wilson
Rayford W. Logan
New introd. by Eric Foner
459 pp.
80758-0 $15.95

BLACK ABOLITIONISTS
Benjamin Quarles
310 pp.
80425-5 $13.95

THE BLACK PHALANX
African American Soldiers
in the War of Independence,
the War of 1812, and the
Civil War
Joseph T. Wilson
New introd. by Dudley Taylor Cornish
534 pp., 64 illus.
80550-2 $16.95

**THE BOOKS OF AMERICAN
NEGRO SPIRITUALS**
Two volumes in one
J. W. and J. R. Johnson
384 pp.
80074-8 $14.95

A BRAVE BLACK REGIMENT
The History of the 54th
Massachusetts, 1863–1865
Captain Luis F. Emilio
New introduction by
Gregory J. W. Urwin
532 pp., 89 photos, 9 maps
80623-1 $15.95

THE COTTON KINGDOM
A Traveller's Observations on
Cotton and Slavery in the
American Slave States
Frederick Law Olmsted
Edited with an introd.
by Arthur M. Schlesinger
704 pp.
80723-8 $18.95

**ENCYCLOPEDIA OF
BLACK AMERICA**
Edited by W. Augustus Low
and Virgil A. Clift
941 pp., 400 illus.
80221-X $37.50

**FREDERICK DOUGLASS ON
WOMEN'S RIGHTS**
Edited by Philip S. Foner
200 pp.
80489-1 $13.95

LINCOLN AND THE NEGRO
Benjamin Quarles
275 pp., 8 illus.
80447-6 $13.95

**THE MAKING OF AN
AFRO-AMERICAN**
Martin Robison Delany
Dorothy Sterling
368 pp., 3 illus.
80721-1 $14.95

**THE NEGRO IN THE
CIVIL WAR**
Benjamin Quarles
New introd. by William S. McFeely
402 pp., 4 illus.
80350-X $13.95

RICHARD WRIGHT READER
Edited by Ellen Wright and
Michel Fabre
910 pp., 66 photos
80774-2 $22.50

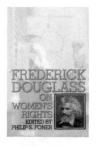

SLAVERY
A World History
Updated Edition
Milton Meltzer
584 pp., 251 illus. 3 maps
80536-7 $22.50

**THOMAS MORRIS CHESTER,
BLACK CIVIL WAR
CORRESPONDENT: His**
Dispatches from the Virginia Front
Edited by R.J.M. Blackett
375 pp., 3 photos, 1 map
80453-0 $13.95

THE TROUBLE THEY SEEN
The Story of Reconstruction in the
Words of African Americans
Edited by Dorothy Sterling
512 pp., 152 illus.
80548-0 $15.95

THE UNKNOWN SOLDIERS
African-American Troops in
World War I
Arthur E. Barbeau and
Florette Henri
New introd. by Bernard C. Nalty
320 pp., 20 photos
80694-0 $14.95

Available at your bookstore

OR ORDER DIRECTLY FROM

DA CAPO PRESS

1-800-321-0050